BEETHOVEN IN RUSSIA

BEETHOVEN IN RUSSIA

Music and Politics

Frederick W. Skinner

INDIANA UNIVERSITY PRESS

This book is a publication of

Indiana University Press
Office of Scholarly Publishing
Herman B Wells Library 350
1320 East 10th Street
Bloomington, Indiana 47405 USA

iupress.org

Manufactured in the United States of America

First printing 2022

Library of Congress Cataloging-in-Publication Data

Names: Skinner, Frederick W., author.
Title: Beethoven in Russia : music and politics / Frederick W. Skinner.
Description: Bloomington, Indiana : Indiana University Press, 2022. |
Includes bibliographical references and index.
Identifiers: LCCN 2022011615 (print) | LCCN 2022011616 (ebook) | ISBN 9780253063045 (hardback) | ISBN 9780253063052 (paperback) | ISBN 9780253063069 (ebook)
Subjects: LCSH: Beethoven, Ludwig van, 1770-1827—Appreciation—Russia—History. | Music—Political aspects—Russia—History.
Classification: LCC ML410.B42 S596 2022 (print) | LCC ML410.B42 (ebook) | DDC 780.947—dc23/eng/20220310
LC record available at https://lccn.loc.gov/2022011615
LC ebook record available at https://lccn.loc.gov/2022011616

For Lynda

CONTENTS

YouTube Playlist *ix*

Preface *xi*

Acknowledgments *xv*

Prelude: Music in the Tsar's Gulag *1*

PART I. RUSSIA BEFORE 1917

1 Encountering Beethoven: Salon and Concert Hall *11*

2 Engaging Beethoven: Writer and Critic *52*

3 Evaluating Beethoven: From *Freude* to *Freiheit* *93*

4 Embracing Beethoven: Concert Hall and Riverbank *125*

PART II. RUSSIA AFTER 1917

5 Beethoven as Revolutionary: Red Star Rising *147*

6 Beethoven as Icon: Cult and Canon *179*

7 Beethoven as Beethoven: The End of Ideology *216*

Postlude: Project Gulag 2010 *246*

Appendix: Tables *251*

Bibliography *267*

Index *311*

YOUTUBE PLAYLIST

NOTE: TO ACCESS A VIDEO, ENTER ITALICIZED REFERENCE line exactly as written. This will take you directly to the video that, in the opinion of the author, is the best performance currently available on YouTube. Note: Dates refer to posting of the video, not the performance.

1. Beethoven, String Quartet No. 12, Op. 127, Warner Classics, December 18, 2020, https://www.youtube.com/watch?v=IZfR3JzCV8I. To access: *beethoven quartet 12 mvt 2/ebene quartet* [08:00–24:05]. Note: Advance cursor to correct start time.
2. Beethoven, Grosse Fuge, Op. 133, Lincoln Center, May 3, 2016, https://www.youtube.com/watch?v=JmIr-7z3XdY. To access: *beethoven quartet 13 grosse fuge/danish quartet* [16:19].
3. Beethoven, Missa Solemnis (Benedictus), Op. 123, October 6, 2013, Liviu Prunaru, https://www.youtube.com/watch?v=yPNMYBfsqTY. To access: *beethoven missa solemnis benedictus/harnoncourt* [11:31].
4. Beethoven, Piano Concerto No. 5, Op. 73, April 16, 2018, Hochschule für Musik FRANZ LISZT, https://www.youtube.com/watch?v=3TiYGxOQDYw. To access: *beethoven piano concerto 5 mvt 1/bercu* [02:03].
5. Beethoven, Symphony No. 6, Op. 68, DW Classical Music, June 23, 2020, https://www.youtube.com/watch?v=jHFjeosKhr4. To access: *beethoven symphony 6 mvt 4/jarvi* [03:35].
6. Beethoven, Piano Sonata No. 23, Op. 57, Anastasia Huppmann, May 7, 2017, https://www.youtube.com./watch?v=yt9_QLamBBo. To access: *beethoven piano sonata 23 mvt 1/huppmann* [10:48].
7. Beethoven, Violin Sonata No. 9, Op. 47, Fazil Say, August 15, 2013, https://www.youtube.com/watch?v=OF9fneQ5oUs. To access: *beethoven violin sonata 9 mvt 1/kopatchinskaja/say* [13:01].
8. Beethoven, Piano Sonata No. 1, Op. 2/No. 1, truecrypt, July 22, 2009, https://www.youtube.com/watch?v=2jivu8n5KRM. To access: *beethoven piano sonata 1 mvt 4/richter* [06:18].
9. Beethoven, Leonore Overture No. 3, Op. 72b, Berliner Philharmoniker, July 20, 2018, https://www.youtube.com/watch?v=enIM1v9GBUE. To access: *beethoven leonore overture 3/jarvi* [02:27].
10. Beethoven, Egmont Overture, Op. 84, EuroArtsChannel, May 17, 2015, https://www.youtube.com/watch?v=ChcrZX2rZ1M. To access: *beethoven egmont overture/masur* [11:18].

11. Beethoven, Symphony No. 9, "Ode to Freedom," Op. 125, EuroArtsChannel, September 17, 2019, https://www.youtube.com/watch?v=cF9q922AJMw. To access: *beethoven symphony 9 ode to freedom blu-ray/bernstein* [02:26].
12. Beethoven, Fidelio, "O Gott! Welch Ein Augenblick!," Op. 72, OnlyGreatMusic, December 13, 2015, https://www.youtube.com/watch?v=rLRMTD3eY5w. To access: *beethoven fidelio o gott welch ein augenblick/bernstein* [06:55].
13. Beethoven, Piano Sonata No. 8, Op. 13, Anastasia Huppmann, December 12, 2019, https://www.youtube.com/watch?v=XuldgIRo2dY. To access: *beethoven piano sonata 8 mvt 1/huppmann* [09:14].
14. Beethoven, "Ich bitt'dich, schreib mir die Es-Scala auf," WoO 172, canon a 3 voces, El músico de Bonn por jcalvodiaz, February 9, 2014, https://www.youtube.com/watch?v=akTYEHeZpLM. To access: *beethoven ich bitt'dich, canon a 3 voces* [01:03].
15. Beethoven, String Quartet No. 14, Op. 131, uchukyoku1, July 14, 2016, https://www.youtube.com/watch?v=4BYIixIBaTk. To access: *capet quartet beethoven quartet 14 mvts 5-7* [13:31].
16. Beethoven, Piano Sonata No. 14, Op. 27/No. 2, Sony Classical, October 25, 2019, https://www.youtube.com/watch?v=9EGdL_P2iXE. To access: *beethoven piano sonata 14 mvt 1/levit* [05:17].
17. Beethoven, Piano Sonata No. 31, Op. 110, wocomoMUSIC, September 17, 2020, https://www.youtube.com/watch?v=8duMwTZ8yUg. To access: *beethoven piano sonata 31 mvt 3/grimaud* [08:45–12:25]. Note: Advance cursor to correct start time.
18. Beethoven, Piano Sonata No. 7, Op. 10/No. 3, Boris Giltburg, April 9, 2020, https://www.youtube.com/watch?v=iA_cMYACmgY. To access: *beethoven piano sonata 7 mvt 2/giltburg* [06:55–10:10]. Note: Advance cursor to correct start time.

PREFACE

MUSIC IS A DIFFICULT MEDIUM TO MEASURE. No other art form proves as elusive in content yet so immediately apparent in impact. Its effects cannot be controlled or described with any degree of accuracy. Its appeal, however, is universal. Music has enlightened elites and energized masses. It has been the preserve of the aristocratic salon and the shared experience of the underground. It has been dismissed as an effete form of snobbery and embraced by those who would move millions. Yet music works in peculiar ways. Some theorists argue that its effects are primarily physiological in nature. Others consider it a separate language that does not require normal cognition for understanding. Still others view it as a spiritual medium that operates on a different plane of perception altogether. How music interfaces with the soul is one of the great mysteries of life—and history.

Music moves subliminally through the web of human consciousness to conjure up fantastic imagery and forbidden dreams. There are those who have feared it for these reasons. Conservative regimes have done everything in their power to curb its influence, from jailing performers and composers to prohibiting performances considered subversive to restricting the length of applause at concerts. But because its tones penetrate instantly into the deepest recesses of the psyche, where they are deciphered and assimilated simultaneously, the effects of music, once unleashed, cannot be controlled. At once the most abstract and immediately accessible of all art forms, music exhibits a force that defies human understanding. Its influence extends far beyond the concert hall, though no one can say precisely why or how.

Yet there is an important distinction to be made between music as muse and music as text. If the former can be considered an absolute art form in the manner just described, the latter represents a cultural and performance artifact embedded in the matrix of reception history, and as such, it can be accessed and analyzed. Since it involves the investigation of the listening experience in a historical context, reception history establishes not only *what* is heard but most importantly, *how* it is heard. This in turn can inform an understanding of broader trends in a society's social, cultural, and political development. This is the methodological approach adopted in the present study, which explores the interaction between music and politics in modern Russia by examining the changing course and character of Russian Beethoven reception from the late eighteenth century to the present. The approach is topical within a broad chronological framework and based on a voluminous amount of hitherto untapped primary and secondary material.

Reception history is a well-established field in Beethoven studies. England, France, Germany, and America are all well represented in the literature. For Russia, on the other hand—aside from Boris Schwarz's 1960s groundbreaking articles in the *Musical Quarterly* and his *Music and Musical Life in Soviet Russia* (1972)—the scholar will search in vain for any substantial discussion of Beethoven reception history in the English language. To be sure, several articles in the *Beethoven Newsletter* and its successor, the *Beethoven Journal*, and some scattered commentary in the standard monographic literature on Russian and Soviet cultural history do offer commentary on Beethoven. In addition, several studies focusing on early Soviet history have appeared in recent years that touch on aspects of the reception history examined in this book. These include Pauline Fairclough, *Classics for the Masses: Shaping Soviet Musical Identity under Lenin and Stalin* (New Haven, CT: Yale University Press, 2016), a nuanced analysis of concert life from 1917 to 1953; Marina Frolova-Walker, *Stalin's Music Prize: Soviet Culture and Politics* (New Haven, CT: Yale University Press, 2016), a fascinating insider view of music and politics from 1940 to 1954; Marina Frolova-Walker and Jonathan Walker, *Music and Soviet Power, 1917–1932* (Woodbridge, UK: Boydell, 2012), an annotated anthology of Soviet writing on music up to 1932; and Amy Nelson, *Music for the Revolution: Musicians and Power in Early Soviet Russia* (University Park: Pennsylvania University Press, 2004), a comprehensive discussion of musical life in the 1920s. But there is as yet no systematic analysis of the entire course of Russian Beethoven reception in the English language. The present study seeks to fill this void.

The book is divided into two parts separated by the year 1917. Part 1 highlights the role Beethoven's music played in the revolutionary struggle culminating in the collapse of the tsarist regime in February 1917. The establishment in the late imperial period of the Russian Musical Society and its network of over fifty branches throughout the empire, together with the founding of a number of conservatories and music schools, resulted in more frequent performances of Beethoven's music and consequently substantially larger audiences. It is striking that the composer's more dramatic compositions—the Third, Fifth, and Ninth Symphonies; the *Coriolan*, *Egmont*, *Fidelio*, and *Leonore* Overtures; and the opera *Fidelio*—proved the most popular works performed in this period. In addition, leading music critics consistently argued that the word *freedom* should be substituted for *joy* in the choral movement of the

Ninth Symphony. These developments served to reinforce a growing awareness that outstanding problems of state and society could only be resolved through violence. In this subtle yet telling way, Beethoven became an actor in the twilight years of the old regime.

In the Soviet period, examined in part 2, the task was to harness the force of Beethoven's music to promote another kind of revolution—Stalin's "revolution from above," which was designed to transform the socioeconomic infrastructure of Russia through a rapid industrialization campaign and the forced collectivization of agriculture. Anatolii Lunacharskii, culture tsar in the early Stalinist period, emerged as a key player. In this context, Beethoven's noble art was transformed into a propaganda weapon to be deployed in the great struggle against backwardness. As the Russian Beethoven scholar Marina Raku observes, "Until the beginning of the 1920s, the Russian public still had a choice as to how to hear Beethoven but, beginning with the speeches of Lunacharskii, the possibility of such a choice narrowed conspicuously." The appropriation of Beethoven and his music to serve the interests of the state remained the hallmark of Soviet Beethoven reception until the end of communist rule, though political bias gradually gave way to more dispassionate analysis after the death of Stalin in 1953. In the post-Soviet era, Beethoven regained his integrity as a free artist and his works have been restored to their proper place in the canon.

Except for the rendition of certain common surnames (for example, Tchaikovsky rather than Chaikovskii), all citations in Russian conform to the Library of Congress transliteration system. This includes first names—thus Petr rather than Peter Tchaikovsky. Dates adhere to the Julian calendar for the nineteenth and twentieth centuries until February 1918, at which point the Soviet government adopted the Western Gregorian calendar (New Style). Dates thus lag twelve days behind the Western calendar for the nineteenth century and thirteen days for the twentieth until February 1918. Except where noted, all translations are my own.

FWS
The Academy Village
Tucson, Arizona
2022

ACKNOWLEDGMENTS

THIS STUDY ORIGINATED AS A RESEARCH PROJECT CARRIED out at Arizona State University in conjunction with an NEH Summer Institute grant, "Beethoven: The Age of Revolution and Restoration." I am indebted above all to William Meredith, director emeritus of the Beethoven Center at San José State University, who oversaw the original research project, published two of my articles, and has cheered me on ever since. I would also like to thank the late Richard Stites for his expertise and bonhomie; Andrei Nekrasov of the Yaroslavl Demidov State University in Yaroslavl, Russia, for his abiding friendship and assistance in tracking down obscure source material; Rudi Dietrich for his infectious love of music and interest in all things Beethoven; Dan Flores for his steady support and encouragement throughout the writing process; and Ted Hullar of the Arizona Senior Academy for his tireless enthusiasm and critical reading of the entire manuscript. For research assistance, I am indebted to the staffs of the University of Arizona and University of Montana interlibrary loan departments; Irina Lukka of the Slavonic Division of the Helsinki University Library; Elena Zhabko of the Russian National Library and Archive; Galina Retrovskaia, Nadezhda Stepanova, and Tatiana Znamenskaia of the St. Petersburg Philharmonic Archive; Nataliia Gareeva and Irina Dashkevich of the St. Petersburg Conservatory Archive; and Elena Koniukhova of the Galitzine Memorial Library. I also gratefully acknowledge support from the University of Montana faculty grant program and the history department's Ambrose and Boone endowments, which helped fund research at the University of Illinois and Helsinki University Library during early stages of the project. I also appreciate permission granted by Carol Stevens, editor of *Canadian American Slavic Studies*, and Erica Buurman, editor of the *Beethoven Journal*, to incorporate revised versions of articles that originally appeared in their publications. I owe a special debt of gratitude to the two anonymous readers who reviewed this book in manuscript form and offered valuable suggestions for revision that I believe have enhanced the overall quality of the study. Finally, the staff at Indiana University Press, especially my editor, Jennika Baines, and her assistant, Sophia Hebert, have been a joy to work with as this project has moved from the initial proposal to finished product.

BEETHOVEN IN RUSSIA

PRELUDE

Music in the Tsar's Gulag

On December 26, 1826, on the eve of her departure from Moscow to join her husband in Siberian exile, Princess Mariia Volkonskaia attended a party in her honor and was overheard whispering to a singer, "Again, again! Think that I shall never hear any more music."[1] Great hardships awaited the princess, but the absence of music would not be one of them. Many of those who participated in the revolt of December 14, 1825, had listened to and made music in the company of their aristocratic peers. It is therefore not surprising that this form of cultural activity continued after 1825. To be sure, instruments were few and sheet music was in even shorter supply. But to the extent conditions permitted, music making in the main prison complexes at Chita and Petrovskii Zavod and in the resettlement communities following incarceration provided solace to those who found themselves shorn of dignity, deprived of liberty, and subjected to the police powers of His Majesty's Own Chancellery.[2]

The transportation of fragile harpsichords and pianofortes across the vast expanses of Siberia, the formation of chamber groups, and the creation of vocal ensembles not only shed light on the cultural world of the exile communities but also provide a key to understanding the *mentalité* of those who organized the first revolutionary movement against the tsarist regime. In an authoritarian environment, music making by itself can be considered a seditious act. It enhances one's sense of autonomy while it forges bonds of solidarity with like-minded spirits, sharpens the critical faculty, and promotes self-awareness. Of greater importance, it ennobles feelings and opens up the mind to the incandescent power of inspiration, revelation, and prophecy. Listening to music has virtually the same effect.[3] In that these psychological traits are similar to those found in the complex personalities of many individuals encountered in this study, the role music played in the Decembrist exile experience is more than a passing interest.

If there is little evidence in the documentary material that Beethoven's compositions formed a core component of the music performed in the Decembrist prisons—and subsequently in the homes of the exile communities—the composer's unique sound world was certainly not foreign to those who attended such affairs. The following conversation demonstrates the extent to which the Beethovenian muse had penetrated the consciousness of the Decembrists before the events of 1825. In 1816, a young Frenchman named Hippolyte Auger engaged Mikhail Lunin in a discussion about music. Lunin recounted a soirée he had attended during which Matvei Viel'gorskii performed on the cello. "What a pity you weren't there," Lunin said to Auger. "That was true music. We didn't know whether we were on earth or in heaven. We forgot about everything." Lunin identified the composer as Beethoven and continued, "His music reminds one of Mozart, but it is far more serious. And what inexhaustible inspiration! What richness of conception, what amazing variety despite the repetition! He produces such a powerful impression upon you that you even cease to be amazed by him. Such is the power of genius, but in order to understand him you must study him. In France you have not yet learned to appreciate serious music. We, however, who live in the north, love everything that moves the soul and compels us to think."[4]

"Everything that moves the soul and compels us to think." Here, in a phrase, is testimony to the power of Beethoven's voice and a recognition of the interface between music and politics, which would shape an important aspect of Russian history in the years ahead.

Of the 116 "state criminals" sentenced to various terms of hard labor in Siberia, the largest group, eighty-two, was dispatched in 1827 to the salt mines of Chita and then transferred in 1830 to the ironworks of Petrovskii Zavod near Nerchinsk. Eventually fourteen of the wives journeyed east to join the exiles. In 1827 the population of Chita, a primitive trading post on the Ingoda River, numbered only some three hundred persons and mostly consisted of non-Russians. Inside the prison, conditions were brutal. The inmates were shackled at all times, crowded together in squalid living quarters, and permitted only rare visits with family members. Food was poor, the weather inhumane, and the work regimen arduous and unrelenting.[5]

Circumstances such as these would hardly seem conducive to music making, yet the prison complex and dwellings of the Decembrist wives boasted eight pianos, a harpsichord, a flute, several guitars, and a variety of stringed instruments. Some of the Decembrists were also accomplished singers. Out of these forces a choral ensemble and string quartet formed. Petr Svistunov led the choral group, which included Dmitrii Shchepin-Rostovskii and Aleksei Tiutchev as tenors and the brothers Aleksandr and Nikolai Kriukov as basses. The quartet, which was established by Svistunov and debuted on August 30, 1828, in a program that unfortunately has not been preserved, consisted of

Fedor Vadkovskii on first violin, Nikolai Kriukov on second violin, Aleksei Iushnevskii on viola, and Svistunov on cello. Others gave solo performances with either Vasilii Ivashev (a student of John Field) or Iushnevskii (an expert pianist as well as violist) accompanying on the piano. Andrei Rozen played the violin, Konstantin Igel'shtrom the flute, and Mikhail Lunin, Mikhail Naryshkin, and Ivan Shimkov the guitar. Aleksandr Odoevskii was an excellent pianist and Nikolai Bestuzhev and Kondratii Ryleev were proficient clarinetists, although it is unclear whether they had brought their instruments with them. Evidence is also sketchy regarding the repertoire that was performed at these concerts. Mariia Iushnevskaia remarked in a letter that on one occasion excerpts from Carl Maria von Weber's opera *Der Freischütz* and his "Russian Song with Variations" were played. Dmitrii Zavalishin observed that Italian arias were often performed, "but, above all, revolutionary songs resounded" throughout the prison complex. Romances by Russian composers and ensemble pieces for the instruments available to the musicians were undoubtedly performed as well.[6]

This music making helped alleviate the harsh conditions the Decembrists were forced to endure during the nearly four years they were incarcerated at Chita. Aleksandr Beliaev wrote in his memoirs: "Music in general and especially the music of the string quartet, which played compositions by the best and most notable composers, provided real enjoyment and immeasurably brightened our prison life."[7] The villagers also benefitted. Zavalishin noted that, in the summer, "all the residents of Chita gathered near the prison to listen to music and singing."[8] The gathering of native peoples in the open air to hear performances of European art songs and classical music is a startling juxtaposition of the traditional and modern. It also provides a vivid portrait of men, though shackled in leg irons and imprisoned behind ten-foot walls, demonstrating their individual self-worth through the power of music and song.

In August through September 1830, the prisoners were transported 634.5 versts (420.6 miles) to Petrovskii Zavod, where a new facility had been constructed to accommodate them. Along the way they learned of the July Revolution in Paris and saluted it by singing "La Marseillaise." Volkonskaia wrote in her memoirs: "At the last station before Petrovskii . . . we learned of the July Revolution; all night long songs and cries of Hurrah! resounded among the Decembrists. The guards could not understand how such people could entertain themselves with song when a prison awaited them."[9] The new facility was indeed a genuine prison, unlike the makeshift jail at Chita. It consisted of twelve identical sections with long corridors and rows of solitary

Figure 0.1. Sergei and Mariia Volkonskii in their cell at Petrovskii Zavod, 1832. Sketch by Nikolai Bestuzhev. Public Domain.

cells. The isolation resulting from this type of arrangement tended to break down the sense of community that had prevailed at the former camp, causing the prisoners to lead more independent lives. On the other hand, married inmates were occasionally allowed to spend the night in their wives' homes and wives without children were given permission to move into their husbands' cells, which they proceeded to domesticate. The quarters "came to look like cramped hotel rooms, with soft furniture and rugs, paintings, and porcelain dinner sets."[10]

Conditions for music making improved as well. There was a large meeting room in the prison complex where inmates could gather for lectures and concerts and, as a result of successful petitioning on the part of family members, they could now purchase books and journals, instruments, and music scores. The choral ensemble and string quartet continued to perform, and an orchestra of sorts was established. The repertoire expanded to include concertos by John Field and Johann Nepomuk Hummel, caprices by Henri Jérôme Bertini, mazurkas by Frédéric Chopin, the *Songs without Words* by Felix Mendelssohn, and excerpts from Italian operas, especially those of Gioacchino Rossini. Words by Odoevskii and other Decembrist poets were set to music composed by Vadkovskii, creating songs that were sung at musical gatherings. This vocal music was surreptitiously distributed to the local population and sung each year on December 14 to mark the anniversary of the Decembrist uprising.[11]

Beginning in 1835, their terms of imprisonment having come to an end, the Decembrists started leaving the Petrovskii prison and moving into resettlement communities scattered across Siberia. By the summer of 1839, the prison had been emptied of all remaining inmates. Vadkovskii wrote to his sister on August 20, "I have the honor to announce the happy delivery of Mme. Petrovskii prison. . . . She has brought twenty-three children into the world at once, after a somewhat difficult pregnancy of thirteen years! May the good Lord bless the mother! As for the little ones, they look pretty likely to live, though all are more or less asthmatic, or rickety, or valetudinary, or greying."[12]

Altogether, twenty-one Decembrists relocated in or near Irkutsk. Nine settled in Minusinsk, eight in Kurgan, and four or more each in Tobol'sk, Turinsk, and Ialutorovsk. Others led lonely lives in isolated villages and died in obscurity.

Among their many other activities, the Decembrists continued to make and promote music during the extended period of exile (1835–56). There were balls and dancing in Kurgan with a cellist, two violinists, and a clarinetist providing the music. In Irkutsk, Volkonskaia assisted the choir in the local girls school and Vadkovskii organized instrumental concerts. In Minusinsk, Svistunov established a children's choir and directed an adult one made up of former Decembrists; following his move to Tobol'sk, he formed a church choir and founded a piano trio, string quartet, and orchestra. Others engaged in private music making and participated in the activities of various salons. Svistunov held weekly Monday soirées at his home in Tobol'sk. Aleksandr von der Briggen wrote that the Naryshkin household in Kurgan was particularly noted for its musical evenings; during one of these (March 5, 1837), he heard Naryshkin's wife sing portions of a Beethoven mass, arias from Rossini's operas, and a number of Italian songs. Rozen also described a soirée at the Naryshkins (date unrecorded), where he heard portions of Beethoven's symphonies, presumably in piano four-hand arrangements. Yet others assisted traveling concertizers, pursued a variety of music-education projects, and established in Tobol'sk Siberia's first shop for the repair and construction of musical instruments. In 1840 Vasilii Davydov brought the first harpsichord to Krasnoiarsk, while the harpsichords of Ivashev, Svistunov, and Sergei Trubetskoi remained for many years in Petrovskii, Tobol'sk, and Irkutsk respectively. Others bequeathed their stringed instruments to local residents; incredibly these included three Stradivarii and a Guarneri.[13]

The endgame for all Decembrists was of course death. The fate of Iushnevskii, the pianist and violist, and Vadkovskii, the violinist, was particularly poignant. They had made music together during their thirteen years of confinement and had contributed in their separate ways to the cultural progress of Siberia in the period of resettlement. Music had sustained them and had given hope and spiritual sustenance to countless others as well. But life was hard, and both were aging. Iushnevskii wrote in March 1842, "Whether from lack of access to scores or my unsettled mind or age, I have become indifferent to music, which before was my greatest delight." In October he bemoaned the fact that "we live in such extreme circumstances that I do not know how we can last much longer."[14] But it was Vadkovskii who preceded him in death. The Decembrist died on January 8, 1844, and was buried on January 10 in the little cemetery at Razvodnaia near Irkutsk. Iushnevskii attended the funeral, helped carry his friend's coffin into the church, placed it on the catafalque, stepped away during the singing of the service—and all of a sudden clutched his chest and fell dead himself. He was laid to rest next to his beloved friend.

> And music resounded now and then
> Like an abandoned lyre from the sky.[15]

By the time the general amnesty of August 26, 1856, was promulgated, many other Decembrists had died as well. Of those remaining, some elected to stay in Siberia, while others, frequently broken men, migrated back to European Russia. But the sentences they had endured for having participated in the events of December 14 did not go unnoticed. As a living reproach to the police state tactics of the old regime, the Decembrist survivors provided a powerful model for those who succeeded them in the ongoing struggle against tsarist rule. Odoevskii famously proclaimed:

> Our grievous toil will not be lost,
> The spark will quicken into flame;
> Our people, blindfolded no more,
> A new allegiance will proclaim.[16]

Indeed, though far in the distance, the Decembrist Revolt proved the opening shot of the Russian Revolution.

Notes

1. Henri Troyat, *Pushkin*, trans. Nancy Amphoux (New York: Doubleday, 1970), 324. On Volkonskaia, see A. G. Mazour, *Women in Exile: Wives of the Decembrists* (Tallahassee, FL: Diplomatic, 1975), 57–77; Sophy Roberts, *The Lost Pianos of Siberia* (New York: Grove, 2020), 82–87; P. E. Shchegolev, "Podvig kniagini M. N. Volkonskoi," in *Zapiski kniagini Marii Nikolaevny Volkonskoi*, trans. A. N. Kudriavtseva (St. Petersburg: Prometei, 1914), 11–49. Volkonskaia's original pianoforte, depicted in figure prelude.1, traveled by sleigh with her from Moscow but later disappeared to unknown parts for unknown reasons. For a color photo of the unusually shaped "pyramid" piano, which she later acquired, and now on display at the Museum of the Decembrists in Irkutsk, see Tat'iana Kupert, *Muzykal'noe proshloe Tomska* (Tomsk: n.p., 2006), 19.

2. Aleksandr Bestuzhev had attended "almost all concerts of interest" while staying in St. Petersburg and enjoyed a "close friendship" with the composer Aleksandr Aliab'ev; Pavel Pestel' had "dedicated his free time to music making [and] composed songs and piano pieces"; Petr Svistunov had been "captivated by music, including composition [and] expertly played the cello; Vil'gel'm Kiukhel'beker "from his youth had a liking for music and the theater, played the violin . . . and was a student of M. I. Glinka." N. Khotuntsov, *Dekabristy i muzyka* (Leningrad: Muzyka, 1975), 42–44. Svistunov, Aleksei Iuzhnevskii, Fedor Vadkovskii, and Matvei Murav'ev-Apostol, among others, were professionally trained musicians, while Aleksei Tiutchev, Evgenii Obolenskii, and Petr Falenberg, among others, were passionate music lovers and talented performers. In regard to the other Decembrists, a modern-day scholar remarks, "If one takes into account the normal system of education for children of the nobility in the 19th century, one can conclude that the remaining 'state criminals' were not strangers to the art of music." T. A. Romenskaia, *Istoriia muzykal'noi kul'tury Sibirii ot pokhodov Ermaka do krest'ianskoi reformy 1861 goda* (Tomsk, Russia: Avtoreferat dissertatsii, 1992), 271.

3. Nikolai Ogarev (1813–77), a key figure in the intelligentsia movement of the 1840s, commented on this phenomenon: "When you know that you are not listening to or playing [music] alone, that others besides yourself are doing the same thing and they wink at you during those passages when the sounds swell up in heavenly harmony, when your mutual feelings are one, then you experience complete happiness." N. I. Voronina, *Ogarev i muzyka* (Saransk, Russia: Mordovskoe knizhnoe izdatel'stvo, 1981), 28.

4. N. Eidelman, *Conspiracy against the Tsar*, trans. Cynthia Carlile (Moscow: Progress, 1985), 14. See also L. Ginzburg, *Istoriia violonchel'nogo iskusstva*, II (Moscow: Muzgiz, 1957), 311. It is noteworthy that Beethoven's name, along with those of other Western and Russian composers, is written on the back of a notebook owned by Svistunov. The notebook is presently located in the Tobol'sk Regional Museum. Ginzburg, *Istoriia violonchel'nogo iskusstva*, II, 346–47n4.

5. Anatole Mazour, *The First Russian Revolution, 1825* (Stanford, CA: Stanford University Press, 1964), 213, 227; Glynn Barratt, *Voices in Exile: The Decembrist Memoirs* (Montreal: McGill-Queens University Press, 1974), 242. A reputable Soviet source on the Decembrist uprising lists a total of only ninety-nine men who were sentenced to various terms of exile in Siberia. See A. Chernovskii and M. Gavrilov, eds., *Chetyrnadtsatoe dekabriia: sbornik k stoletiiu vosstaniia dekabristov* (Leningrad: Gosudarstvennoe izdatel'stvo, 1925), 211–13. Concerning the Decembrist wives, not all settled in Chita. Of those who did, the following can be identified: Praskov'ia Annenkova, Aleksandra Davydova, Aleksandra Ental'tseva, Natal'ia Fonvizina, Mariia Iushnevskaia, Aleksandra Muravieva, Elizaveta Naryshkina, Anna Rozena, Ekaterina Trubetskaia, and Mariia Volkonskaia. Mazour, *Women in Exile*, 88–129. On Trubetskaia and Volkonskaia in exile, see N. Nekrasov, "Russkie zhenshchini," in *Izbrannye stikhotvorenii*, ed.

K. I. Chukovskii, II (Leningrad: Sovetskii pisatel', 1967), 309–72 and Orlando Figes, *Natasha's Dance: A Cultural History of Russia* (New York: Metropolitan Books, 2002), 87–101.

6. Barratt, *Voices in Exile*, 300; Ginzburg, *Istoriia violonchel'nogo iskusstva*, II, 336; V. Girchenko, "Muzyka v kazemate dekabristov v gody sibirskoi katorgi," *Sovetskaia muzyka*, XIV, 3 (March 1950): 62–64; Khotuntsov, *Dekabristy i muzyka*, 31, 55; P. Sizov, *Muzykal'naia Orlovshchina* (Tula, Russia: Priokskoe knizhnoe izdatel'stvo, 1980), 45; D. Zavalishin, *Vospominaniia* (Moscow: Zakharov, 2003), 340, 348. Rozen noted that, in addition to the pianoforte, the Decembrists had access to a grand piano on which Iushnevskii in particular loved to show off his technical prowess. A. E. Rozen, *Zapiski dekabrista* (Irkutsk, Russia: Vostochno-Sibirskoe knizhnoe izdatel'stvo, 1984), 236n247. On Ivashev and his singer-wife Kamilla, see Eidelman, *Conspiracy against the Tsar*, 97; on Svistunov, see Ginzburg, *Violonchel'nogo iskusstva*, II, 331–50.

7. Girchenko, "Muzyka v kazemate dekabristov," 64.

8. Zavalishin, *Vospominaniia*, 349.

9. Girchenko, "Muzyka v kazemate dekabristov," 65. The precise distance to Petrovskii Zavod is noted in Eidelman, *Conspiracy against the Tsar*, 97. The first group of prisoners left Chita on August 4, the second on August 5. The transfer took forty-seven days. Rozen, *Zapiski dekabrista*, 242–43.

10. Barratt, *Voices in Exile*, 273; Rozen, *Zapiski dekabrista*, 256, 261. The number of wives had increased due to the marriage of some of the Decembrists to local Siberian women.

11. Girchenko, "Muzyka v kazemate dekabristov," 65–66; Khotuntsov, *Dekabristy i muzyka*, 55; Romenskaia, *Istoriia muzykal'noi kul'tury Sibiri*, 272; A. N. Sirotin, "Kniaz A. F. Odoevskii: biograficheskii ocherk," *Istoricheskii vestnik*, XIV, 5 (May 1883): 405; Sizov, *Muzykal'naia Orlovshchina*, 47–48.

12. Barratt, *Voices in Exile*, 275. Vadkovskii was obviously including the four years spent at Chita.

13. On activities during resettlement, see Mazour, *The First Russian Revolution*, 243–56 and M. V. Nechkina, *Dekabristy* (Moscow: Mysl', 1975), 159–69. See also S. N. Brailovskii, "Iz zhizni odnogo dekabrista," *Russkaia starina*, XXXIV, 3 (March 1903): 552; Ginzburg, *Istoriia violonchhel'nogo iskusstva*, II, 341–45; Iu. Kharkeevich, *Muzykal'naia kul'tura Irkutska* (Irkutsk, Russia: Izdatel'stvo Irkutskogo universiteta, 1987), 24–27; B. G. Krivosheia, ed., *Muzykal'naia zhizn' Krasnoiarska* (Krasnoiarsk, Russia: Krasnoiarskoe knizhnoe izdatel'stvo, 1983), 171; Romenskaia, *Istoriia muzykal'noi kul'tury sibiri*, 276–87; Rozen, *Zapiski dekabrista*, 297, 319.

14. Girchenko, "Muzyka v kazemate dekabristov," 67.

15. N. P. Ogarev, "K dekabristam" (1838), as cited in Voronina, *Ogarev i muzyka*, 49.

16. Third stanza of A. I. Odoevskii's poem, "Reply to Pushkin's Message" (1827), as translated in Marc Raeff, *The Decembrist Movement* (Englewood Cliffs, NJ: Prentice-Hall, 1960), 179. On Odoevskii, see Sirotinin, "Kniaz A. F. Odoevskii," 398–414.

PART I

RUSSIA BEFORE 1917

1

ENCOUNTERING BEETHOVEN

Salon and Concert Hall

Russians first encountered Beethoven's music in Vienna in the late eighteenth century. Diplomats and military attachés posted by St. Petersburg to the Habsburg court formed part of the Viennese aristocratic elite of music lovers and concertgoers and took an interest early on in Beethoven and his art. This support proved significant in the success of the composer's early career and established at the outset a nexus between Beethoven's music and the Russian musical (and political) establishment. By the early nineteenth century, in conjunction with increasing diplomatic, commercial, and personal contacts between Russia and Vienna, the aristocratic communities in St. Petersburg and Moscow began taking an interest in the composer as well. Among early connoisseurs, Prince Nikolai Golitsyn (1794–1866) and Count Mikhail Viel'gorskii (1788–1856) played important roles in the initial reception of Beethoven's music in the Russian homeland.

First Impressions

Of those Russians living in Vienna who befriended Beethoven following his arrival from Bonn in 1792, Prince Andrei Razumovskii (1752–1836) proved the most influential. Razumovskii came from a distinguished line of courtiers attached to the Russian court and served as Russia's ambassador to Austria from 1792 to 1799 and from 1801 to 1807. In 1788 he married Countess Maria Elisabeth von Thun-Hohenstein, the elder sister of the wife of Prince Karl Lichnovsky, and in this capacity attained access to the highest echelons of Viennese society. Befitting his elevated station, Razumovskii built a grand palace in the city's Landstrasse District near the Donau Canal to serve as both his personal residence and the premises of the Russian embassy. A vast English-style pleasure garden also extended from the palace's main terrace to the banks of the canal. As an accomplished violinist and friend of Haydn and

Figure 1.1. Prince Andrei Razumovskii. Portrait by I. B. Lampa. Public Domain.

Mozart, Razumovskii played an important role in the musical life of Vienna, most notably in his 1808–16 patronage of the Schuppanzigh Quartet, which premiered many of Beethoven's string quartets. An amphitheater nestled in an arbor of the pleasure garden and a music room in the palace (later called Beethoven Hall) served as the venues for a rich concert life.[1]

Razumovskii retired from his ambassadorial position in 1807 but temporarily resumed service in 1814–15 to act as Russia's main representative to the Congress of Vienna; at the conclusion of the proceedings, he was rewarded with the title of prince for his services to the crown. A blow to his fortunes occurred during the New Year's Eve festivities of 1814, however, when a large portion of his magnificent palace burned to the ground—a ferocious "Vesuvius in full blast," according to one observer, starting in a wooden annex attached to the main structure. Virtually everything of value was destroyed, including a library of some seven thousand rare volumes and engravings; a priceless collection of paintings by Raphael, Rembrandt, Rubens, Van Dyck, and others; and masterpieces by the Italian sculptor Antonio Canova, which were crushed when the ceiling of the gallery fell through to the floor below. Though the palace was partially rebuilt in later years, Razumovskii never recovered. For a while he traveled Europe, returning to Vienna in 1826 "without money," as Beethoven's nephew Karl laconically reported in a Conversation Book entry of that year. He lived out his remaining years in the Austrian capital, dying an impoverished and largely forgotten old man on September 23, 1836.[2]

Razumovskii recognized Beethoven's genius early on and became an important patron of his art. "The world is too small for him," he once declared.[3] According to the composer Ignaz Seyfried, "Beethoven was as much at home in the Razumovskii establishment as a hen in her coop. Everything he wrote was taken warm from the nest and tried out in the frying pan."[4] In 1795 Razumovskii became one of the subscribers to Beethoven's first publication, the Opus 1 Piano Trios, and in 1803 his name appeared on the list of persons attending George Bridgetower's premiere of the Violin Sonata no. 9 in A (*Kreutzer*), op. 47. Razumovskii is best remembered for his 1805 commission of the three Opus 59 quartets, which have since been called the Razumovsky Quartets. Very little is known about this commission except for the dedicator's request that some Russian folk song themes be included in the compositions—thus the thematic material in the finale of no. 1, the scherzo trio of no. 2, and some music in the slow movement of no. 3, which expresses a "restless brooding" the composer may have associated with certain aspects of the Russian national idiom.[5] Johann Gottfried Pratsch had published a collection of Russian folk songs in St. Petersburg in 1790 (reissued in 1806 and later) that came into Razumovskii's possession around that time, and Beethoven probably drew the melodies from this collection. Razumovskii was also the codedicatee (with Austrian prince Joseph Lobkowitz) of Symphonies no. 5 in C minor, op. 67, and no. 6 in F (*Pastoral*), op. 68.

Beethoven's dedication in 1802 of the three Violin Sonatas, op. 30, to Emperor Alexander I underscored the fact Beethoven valued his connections with the Russian court. In the autumn of 1814, Razumovskii and Archduke Rudolph presented Beethoven to the assembled heads of state, including Alexander I, who had gathered in Vienna for the congressional proceedings. This led to a private audience between the composer and Empress Elizaveta Alekseevna of Russia. The empress paid Beethoven fifty ducats for the Opus 89 Polonaise for Piano in C, which he had dedicated to her, and on learning that her husband had not remunerated him for the Opus 30 inscription, she presented him with an additional bequest of one hundred ducats.[6] Beethoven also planned to dedicate his Ninth Symphony to Alexander I until the emperor's death in November 1825 prompted him to inscribe the work to Kaiser Friedrich Wilhelm III of Prussia. Interestingly, a Russian folk song theme is embedded in the scherzo of the symphony.[7] Another curious detail: until the end of his life, Beethoven kept an ink blotter on his worktable depicting a Russian Cossack astride a rearing steed as a reminder of the role the Russian army had played in European warfare during the Napoleonic era.[8] Was this perhaps a gift from Razumovskii? While the provenance is unknown, Beethoven's associations with the Russian Maecenas, and through him far-off St. Petersburg, clearly advanced his own career and inaugurated what would become one of the most significant and storied chapters in the reception history of his work.

Among the other prominent Russians associated with Beethoven's early career in Vienna, Count Johann Georg von Browne-Camus (1767–1827) was probably the most important. A brigadier general in the Keksgol'mskii Horse Regiment quartered in Vienna, Browne passionately adored Beethoven's music and provided the composer with financial support from 1798 to 1803. Beethoven frequently visited the count's home, and for a time, his student Ferdinand Ries (1783–1838) served as a piano instructor there. At one point, Browne presented Beethoven with the gift of a riding horse; either out of disinterest or forgetfulness, Beethoven neglected the animal, and it was eventually farmed out to others. But the main point was music. Browne was one of the subscribers to the Opus 1 Piano Trios. Beethoven in turn dubbed the general "the foremost Maecenas of my muse" and dedicated the following compositions to him: Three String Trios, op. 9; Piano Sonata no. 11 in B-flat, op. 22; Seven Variations for Piano and Cello on "Bei Mannern, welche Liebe fűhlen" from Mozart's *The Magic Flute*, WoO 46; and the Six Gellert Lieder, op. 48. Browne also commissioned the song "Der Wachtelschlag," WoO 129 and the Three Marches for Piano Four-Hands, op. 45, the latter subsequently dedicated to Princess Maria Josepha Esterházy of Hungary. Browne's wife, Countess Anna Margaret (1769–1803), was herself the recipient of three additional inscriptions: Piano Sonatas nos. 5–7, op. 10; Twelve Variations for Piano on a Russian Dance from Pavel Wranitzky's *Das Waldmädchen*, WoO 71; and Six Variations for Piano on "Tandeln und Scherzen" from Sűssmayr's *Soliman II*, WoO 76. In a touching gesture, Beethoven dedicated the Six Gellert Lieder to Browne on the occasion of the countess's death in May 1803.[9]

Yet another Russian who befriended Beethoven at this time was Baron Filipp von Klűpfeld (Klűpfell) (1756–1823), secretary at the Russian embassy in Vienna. Klűpfeld was particularly fond of chamber music and often invited Beethoven to perform in his home. According to the reminiscences of a certain Frau Bernhard, who lived in the Klűpfeld household from 1796 to 1800 and took lessons from Beethoven, the master performed "without notes" to the amazement of those in attendance. She also observed that "many handsome Russian officers" frequented the soirées.[10]

Of the Russian subscribers to the Opus 1 Piano Trios, besides Browne and Razumovskii, one encounters the names of M. M. Viel'gorskii, G. A. Stroganov, and V. S. Trubetskoi. Viel'gorskii is of particular interest in that he was the uncle of Mikhail Viel'gorskii, who would play such an important role in the promotion of Beethoven's music in Russia in the first half of the nineteenth century. Indeed, the younger Viel'gorskii appears in the historical record of this time. In 1808, on his way to Paris from Russia, he stayed in Vienna for a number of months. There he met Beethoven and often listened to him improvising on the piano at the home of Countess Maria Elenora Fuchs. In December he and seven others attended a rehearsal of the *Pastoral* Symphony, during which he applauded so vigorously between movements that Beethoven finally walked over and extended him a friendly if somewhat sardonic bow. In light of all that Viel'gorskii would do on the composer's behalf in the years ahead, this gesture had powerful symbolic meaning.[11]

Beethoven's music became a regular feature of concert life in Russia beginning in the second decade of the nineteenth century. At the outset, Moscow and St. Petersburg served equally as venues for the exploration of this new music. In Moscow, the main hall of the university served as a stage for concert performances, while the salons of Princess Zinaida Volkonskaia (late 1820s) and Mikhail Viel'gorskii (1823–26) and various homes of the nobility provided a setting for private music making. Sheet music became available as early as 1805, making it possible to perform works by such composers as Haydn, Mozart, Beethoven, Clementi, Pleyel, and Rode. In an extravaganza of sorts, two back-to-back concerts in the winter of 1828 treated concertgoers to a symphony, two overtures, and three piano concertos by Beethoven. But St. Petersburg—with its larger halls, greater constellation of performing forces, broader network of salons, and proximity to a court with its own traditions, personnel, and patronage systems—emerged over time as the main center for the performance of Beethoven's music. As early as 1799, a performance edition of the Clarinet Trio in B-flat, op. 11, went on sale in the Russian capital, just one year after it had been published in Vienna. Broader distribution of sheet music in the years ahead facilitated exploration of small and large genres alike. The Imperial Court Chapel Choir (Kapella) and, from 1802, the St. Petersburg Philharmonic Society (Philharmonia) offered a high level of professional expertise and stood at the center of musical activities in the city, as did the Viel'gorskii salon in the 1830s through the 1850s.[12]

In Moscow, the earliest known concert featuring works by Beethoven occurred on March 11, 1803, when a recital of songs by the composer and Mozart was staged. The second known performance took place on April 14, 1812—five months to the day (New Style) before Napoleon's forces entered the city—when a "grand symphony" was presented. Muscovites seemed remarkably unconcerned about their safety at the time. Sergei Aksakov attested to the almost carefree attitude of theatergoers, and Leo Tolstoy observed that it had been long since city dwellers had been so gay. Reality intervened, however, following the burning of Moscow in early September and the destruction of all of the city's theaters.[13] The next concert featuring a Beethoven work did not occur until March 11, 1814, at which time another unidentified symphony was performed at an undisclosed location. In the post-Napoleonic era until 1825, nine additional concerts were staged that featured symphonies (all unidentified); overtures (one to *Fidelio*, the remainder unidentified); the Septet in E-flat, op. 20; and *Wellingtons Sieg* (*Battle Symphony*), op. 91.[14] In St. Petersburg, a private performance of the Opus 59 quartets took place at Count Grigorii Saltykov's residence at the beginning of 1812. Two public performances one week apart in March 1813 followed: the Fantasia for Piano, Chorus, and Orchestra in C minor (*Choral Fantasy*), op. 80, and the oratorio, *Christus am Ölberge* (*Christ on the Mount of Olives*), op. 85. Both concerts were performed by the combined forces of the Philharmonia and Kapella. The oratorio was presented five more times in the years 1814–23, while the *Choral Fantasy* received an additional airing and *Wellingtons Sieg* and an unidentified symphony had single performances each. The opera *Fidelio*, op. 72, premiered in August 1818, with repeat performances in September and June 1819. Most significantly, the world premiere of the *Missa solemnis* in D, op. 123, occurred on March 26, 1824.[15]

The Kapella had been founded in Moscow in 1479 by Ivan III to serve as the choir for the court and Uspensky Cathedral. Peter the Great moved it to St. Petersburg in 1703, and in 1763 Catherine the Great designated it an imperial institution. From 1802 to 1850, the Kapella participated in all concerts of the Philharmonia requiring vocal forces. With the establishment in March 1850 of a concert society within the Kapella, the choir began restricting its Philharmonia performances and in 1853 discontinued them altogether. The concert society then joined the orchestra of the Imperial Opera to become a major new force in the concert life of the capital. Under the direction of Aleksei L'vov (1798–1870), the Kapella's director from 1837 to 1861 and a strong advocate of German music, the society performed many works by Beethoven. According to all accounts, the quality of the Kapella's singing was nothing short of miraculous. Adolph Adam was overwhelmed by a performance he attended during his stay in St. Petersburg in 1839–40: "The first time I heard this splendid chapel choir I was stirred with such emotion as I have never felt before. From the very first bars of the piece I began to shed tears; then, when the music quickened up and the thundering voices launched the whole artillery of their lungs, I found myself trembling and covered with a cold sweat. The most tremendous orchestra in the world could never give rise to this curious sensation, which was entirely different from any that I had supposed it possible for music to convey."[16]

Robert Schumann heard the choir in 1844 and was awestruck by the basses, which he likened to the drone of a deep-throated organ. And Hector Berlioz famously wrote of the Kapella in 1847, "To compare the singing of the Sistine Chapel choir in Rome with these glorious singers is like comparing a miserable little bunch of scratchers from a third-rate Italian theater with the orchestra of the Paris Conservatory."[17] Its venue on the Moika River near the Hermitage picture gallery, today the home of the State Academic Kapella of St. Petersburg, houses a lovely concert hall with pitch-perfect acoustics that is the envy of choral societies everywhere.[18]

The Philharmonia was founded in March 1802 for the specific purpose of combining forces with the Kapella to perform the Russian premiere of Haydn's *Die Schöpfung* (*The Creation*) held on March 24 and 31. Its charter, published in 1807, stipulated that the society's dual tasks were to stimulate public interest in "old and new" classical music and provide financial assistance to widows and orphans of former members. In the first hundred years of its existence, the Philharmonia performed 204 concerts and, through a percentage of ticket receipts, members' dues, and prudent investment in interest-bearing notes, was able to expend 641,329 rubles on assistance to almost two hundred widows and orphans. Iurii Arnol'd (1811–98), a noted music theorist, critic, and composer, attested to the fact that the public in the early years of the society's existence "was not yet adequately prepared to fully understand and 'digest' serious music. . . . The greater part of St. Petersburg salon habitués listened to compositions by Vanhal, Pleyel, Steibelt, Gyrowetz, and the like."[19] This of course changed over time. In 1839 writer and critic Vladimir Odoevskii (1804–69) observed that musicians and ordinary citizens alike awaited the Philharmonia concerts "with impatience" and returned home "with their souls truly refreshed by music."[20]

Over the years the Philharmonia introduced the public to many of the compositions of key European and Russian composers, including Beethoven, and became in the process an integral part of the St. Petersburg music scene. From 1802 to 1846, its main venue was the second-floor concert hall of the Engel'gardt House, located at 30 Nevskii Prospect. Designed by Bartolomeo Rastrelli, the architect of the Winter Palace, the building later became a department store and then a bank. Beginning in 1949, it has served as the Maly Zal (Small Hall) of the Philharmonia. Since 1846 the orchestra's main hall has been located in the old Gentry Club (Noble Assembly) building just off Arts Square across from the Grand Hotel Europe. Its colonnaded interior and marvelous acoustics continue to enrapture music lovers the world over.[21]

Golitsyn's Monomania

Among concertizers of Beethoven's music in the first half of the nineteenth century, the name Nikolai Golitsyn looms large. Yet Western cultural historians have paid little attention to the Russian prince, and even Beethoven scholars—the quartet commission and premiere of the *Missa solemnis* aside—have shown scant interest. This is surprising because Golitsyn did more than any other individual to promote the initial reception of Beethoven's music in Russia. As an accomplished cellist who performed in over three hundred solo, ensemble, and orchestral concerts, he introduced many of Beethoven's works to audiences in St. Petersburg and as far away as Tambov, Voronezh, Kursk, Khar'kov, Odessa, Kerch, and Simferopol'. He was also a respected music critic in the mold of his younger contemporaries, Vladimir Odoevskii and Aleksandr Serov, and had an understanding of Beethoven's music that placed him well ahead of most of his contemporaries, in Russia and abroad. He wrote and translated poetry, composed and arranged music, and counted among his friends the poets Aleksandr Pushkin and Vasilii Zhukovskii and the composers Mikhail Glinka and Aleksandr Dargomyzhskii. He knew Chopin and other Polish luminaries, such as the composer Michal Ogiński, the pianist Maria Szymanowska-Wolowska, and the cellist Antoni Radziwiłł.

Figure 1.2. Prince Nikolai Golitsyn. Alamy Stock Photo E8FB3X.

Additionally, he acquitted himself with distinction in the Napoleonic campaigns of 1812–14, the Persian War of 1827–28, and the Crimean War of 1854–56. Altogether, Golitsyn was a remarkable individual who deserves much fuller recognition in the historical literature.

Nikolai Borisovich Golitsyn (alternately transcribed Galitsyn) was born in Moscow on December 8, 1794. He came from the aristocratic elite—his father traced his princely lineage to the fourteenth century and his mother descended from the last tsar of Georgia—and thus enjoyed a privileged upbringing in the rarified atmosphere of Russian high society. He spent most of his childhood on his father's country estate and in St. Petersburg, where he obtained a solid education and developed an early interest in music. He studied the violin with Pierre Rode and the cello with Adolph Maingardt and Bernhard Romberg; in time he acquired a facility on the latter instrument that enabled him to hold his own in the company of such virtuosos as Romberg, Adrien-François Servais, and Matvei Viel'gorskii. Matriculating from military school in 1810, Golitsyn joined a dragoon regiment on September 2 with the intention of pursuing a military career. He served under General Petr Bagration in the Battle of Borodino on August 26, 1812, receiving a severe concussion during the engagement. He recovered from his injury in time to participate in the 1813–14 campaign against the retreating forces of Napoleon's Grand Army, which culminated in the taking of Paris on March 17–18, 1814. Among other decorations, he was awarded a golden saber with the inscription "For Bravery" in recognition of his heroic exploits during these campaigns. While not formally discharged from the army until March 25, 1832, he effectively discontinued his service in 1821 on receiving a medical leave of absence. From this point forward and notwithstanding his nominal position as an official of the Finance Ministry (1832–55), he devoted the remainder of his life to his musical endeavors and other cultural pursuits. He did return to active military service during the Persian War of 1827–28, and in 1854 he formed a private militia that fought in Sevastopol' during the Crimean War of 1854–56. But these were only interludes in a life devoted to music. Golitsyn spent his last years on his estate near the village of Bogorodsko in Kursk Province. He died from complications stemming from acute rhinitis on October 22, 1866, and was buried in the family vault at the nearby Sviatogorsk Uspenskii monastery.[22]

Golitsyn's lifelong love affair with Beethoven's music began at an early age. "As a child I was occupied with instrumental music and educated in the school of Haydn and Mozart," he wrote in 1845, "but I was always captivated by the divine harmonies that Beethoven generously scattered throughout his first quartets and quintets."[23] He undoubtedly came in contact with Beethoven's music while living in Vienna with his father in 1804–06. There is no record of his having met Beethoven himself, a circumstance he indirectly affirmed in an 1823 letter to the composer: "Too young to have known the celebrated Mozart, and having been present only in the last years of Haydn, of whom I caught only a glimpse during my childhood in Vienna, I rejoice in being the contemporary of the third hero of music, who can find his equal only in the first two, and whom one might properly proclaim the god of melody and harmony."[24] Had there been a personal meeting between composer and future patron, Golitsyn surely would have made some reference to it in this passage. But during his sojourn, he certainly had ample opportunity to hear Beethoven's music performed. The premiere of the Third Symphony, the first and second versions of *Fidelio* (*Leonore*), and the Violin Concerto occurred at this time, and ensembles in the city performed the early violin and cello sonatas, string trios, quartets, and other chamber music on a regular basis. Any of this would have made a lasting mark on an impressionable youth who was already well versed in the language of music.

Golitsyn continued to pursue his musical interests while enrolled in military school and, as circumstances allowed, during his tenure in the army. But only after his release from active military service in 1821 was he able to dedicate his life fully to music. His palace in St. Petersburg became one of the fashionable centers of salon life in the 1820s. Together with his first wife, Elena

Aleksandrovna (née Saltykova), an outstanding pianist, Golitsyn performed on the cello for a host of invited guests, and such regular habitués as his friend Aleksandr Pushkin. Beethoven's music quickly assumed a prominent place in these evening soirées, which expanded to include trio, quartet, and quintet playing, as well as performances of Golitsyn's arrangements for string quartet of some of Beethoven's piano sonatas. Golitsyn also took an active interest in the affairs of the Philharmonic Society and was elected an honorary member in 1823, joining the ranks of such personages as Joseph Haydn, John Field, and Dmitrii Bortnianskii. In 1828 he helped found the short-lived Society of Music Lovers (disbanded 1832), whose opening concert on February 12 in the home of A. L. Naryshkin included a "large symphony" by Beethoven. But it was the commissioning of three quartets from Beethoven in 1822 and the world premiere of the *Missa solemnis* in 1824 that brought Golitsyn international fame.

Golitsyn's letter to Beethoven on November 9, 1822, requesting that he write "one, two, or three quartets" at a price to be set by the composer is of course well-known, as is Beethoven's response of January 25, 1823, accepting the commission.[25] The German composer, pianist, violist, and friend of Beethoven, Karl Zeuner (1775–1841), who was living in St. Petersburg at the time and performing in the Golitsyn Quartet, is said to have recommended the commission and suggested that a request for up to three quartets might find favor with Beethoven in light of the three violin sonatas he had dedicated to Alexander I in 1802 and the trio of quartets he had written for Prince Razumovskii in 1805–6. And indeed three quartets were forthcoming: no. 12 in E-flat, op. 127; no. 13 in B-flat, op. 130; and no. 15 in A minor, op. 132. Beethoven's final two quartets—no. 14 in C-sharp minor, op. 131, and no. 16 in F, op. 135—followed swiftly in the wake of the burst of creative energy unleashed by the Golitsyn commission. Beethoven had begun sketching what would become the Opus 127 quartet in May 1822, but pressing work on the *Missa solemnis* and Ninth Symphony prevented him from completing the composition until February 1825. The Schuppanzigh Quartet gave the Vienna premiere on March 6, and the following St. Petersburg premiere occurred on June 20 with a performance by the Golitsyn Quartet (Lipiński, Bohm, Zeuner, and Romberg on this occasion). The Opp. 130 and 132 quartets were composed from February to November 1825 and reached Golitsyn in the summer of 1826.[26]

Golitsyn was well versed in the Beethoven quartet literature, having listened to the Opus 18 set since childhood and studied the middle quartets as an adult. "Prince Radziwiłł has been with us the past several months," Golitsyn wrote Beethoven in 1824, "and we only play your quartets, especially the last five [Opp. 59/1–3, 74, and 95]."[27] He had also given considerable thought to the overall character of Beethoven's music, as summarized in a letter published in the French newspaper, *La presse*, in 1845: "Beethoven's compositions fall into two distinct styles. The first—clear, melodic, and accessible to all—belongs to the purely classical school, burnished by creative genius. The second takes a completely new path that has more somber and melancholic colors and exhibits a higher degree of originality—a spark of genius akin to the crash of thunder. . . . In order to evaluate these two styles, one must listen to them repeatedly and perform them to perfection."[28]

That Golitsyn had a good understanding of Beethoven's music (if not yet of the three-style periodization set forth by François-Joseph Fétis in 1837) is underscored as well by the following anecdote. In 1849 the distinguished Russian journal *Otechestvennye zapiski* (*Notes of the Fatherland*) observed that Hector Berlioz had written an article describing the original score of Beethoven's ballet *Die Geschöpfe des Prometheus* (*The Creatures of Prometheus*), op. 43, which he had seen in Leipzig. The editor of the journal exclaimed: "Beethoven composed a ballet! Who could have imagined this?" Bemoaning the fact systematic catalogues of the works of eminent composers did not exist, the editor consulted studies by Anton Schindler and Ignaz Seyfried but could find no reference to such a work. Golitsyn thus felt called on to enlighten the readers of the journal concerning Beethoven's Opus 43. In a letter submitted to *Otechestvennye zapiski* later in the same year, he wrote that, yes, Beethoven had indeed composed a ballet. He summarized the libretto, commented on the staging of the work in Vienna and Milan, and observed that the overture had even been performed by the St. Petersburg Philharmonia. He noted as well that Beethoven had placed such high value on the composition that he later used the main theme of the finale as the motif for a piano work and the main theme of the fourth movement of Symphony no. 3 in E-flat (*Eroica*), op. 55. (The references are to the Fifteen Variations and a Fugue on an Original Theme in E-flat [*Eroica* Variations], op. 35, and the 2/4 Allegro molto melody, which begins in earnest at bar 76 of the fourth movement of Symphony no. 3.) He could have cited as well the Contredanse no. 7 in E-flat, WoO 14, but this would be asking too much given the obscurity of the piece. All in all, for both time and place, Golitsyn's familiarity with Beethoven's oeuvre and understanding of a significant element in the thematic structure of the Third Symphony testify to his skills as an early interpreter of the composer's music.[29]

Golitsyn always maintained that by their craftsmanship and depth of feeling, Beethoven's late compositions surpassed all of his earlier works. Thus he awaited the arrival of the first of "his" quartets with enormous anticipation.

When Opus 127 finally made it to St. Petersburg in the early spring of 1825, he wrote Beethoven on April 29:

> I have many thanks to give you . . . for the precious parcel with the sublime Quartet that I have just received. I have already had it played several times, and I find in it all the genius of the master, and when the playing of it has become more perfect, the pleasure will be all the greater. . . . For a few days we shall play your new Quartet with Bernhard Romberg, who has been here for a month. Do not delay, I ask you, in having it printed; such a beautiful masterpiece ought not to remain hidden for a single moment.[30]

Golitsyn later described Opus 127 as "possibly the most beautiful quartet Beethoven composed" and singled out the Adagio and Finale for their power to "penetrate the soul."[31] [YOUTUBE VIDEO 1] As for Opp. 130 and 132, we only have Golitsyn's last letter to Beethoven of November 22, 1826, acknowledging receipt of the quartets, which he described as "two new masterpieces of your immortal and inexhaustible genius."[32] He wrote this letter from Khar'kov on his way to Persia to participate in the war of 1827–28 and thus was unable to share his thoughts on these latest works with Beethoven before the composer's death on March 26, 1827. Coincidentally Beethoven's last letter to Golitsyn was dated February 26, 1827. "Apollo and the Muses have not yet let me starve," he wrote, "for there is still much I owe them that must be accomplished before I depart this life. Altogether I feel that I have only managed to write a few notes. Noble Prince! I wish you every success in your passion for art. . . . It is science and art that allow us to hope for a more elevated life."[33]

Following his return to St. Petersburg from the Persian War, Golitsyn sought to familiarize the concertgoing public with the quartets he had commissioned. The response was anything but favorable. In his 1845 *La presse* letter, he wrote that the quartets, "which were awaited with such impatience, greatly disappointed the virtuosos and connoisseurs of Petersburg. They were expecting music in the spirit and style of Beethoven's first quartets but what they got instead was something altogether different." He went on to note that only through perfection of performance could the "treasures" of the quartets, "hidden in rugged phrases," be properly revealed. To promote a fuller understanding, Golitsyn performed "nothing but Beethoven" in the years ahead, having to endure "not a little mockery, sarcasm, and censure" for what his detractors called his "Beethoven monomania." Yet he persisted and "within less than ten years, Beethoven's [late] music, previously considered absurd and clumsy, resounded through the salons and concert halls of our capital."[34]

But to what effect? Since Golitsyn does not indicate whether the quartets were received with any more favor than before, it is difficult to judge how, if at all, reception had changed as a result of his efforts. Probably not as much as this account would suggest. Certainly by the late 1830s and early 1840s some listeners had been won over, but most undoubtedly remained just as perplexed as those critics who had attended the first performances in Vienna. An "incomprehensible, incoherent, vague, over-extended series of fantasias," complained one commentator in 1825 in assessing Opus 127. "Chaos, from which flashes of genius emerged from time to time like lightning bolts from a black thunder cloud," he concluded. Another in 1826 dismissed the Opus 130 quartet as a work that "only the Moroccans might enjoy," particularly in light of the *Grosse Fuge* finale, which proved "incomprehensible, like Chinese," a "confusion of babel."[35] None of this is surprising when one considers that the quartets Golitsyn commissioned are some of the most complex and at times abstruse in the repertoire. This is especially true of Opus 130. The quartet's suite-like construction of six contrasting movements offers up such a wide range of musical ideas and states of human emotion that, despite the best work of musicologists, it is extremely difficult to gain a coherent view of the work as a whole, while the astonishing fugue finale with its harsh sounds, violent attacks, and furious scale work blazes a trail that can still stun the listener. Little wonder that Arnold Schoenberg considered the *Grosse Fuge* the foundation of modern musical expression and Igor Stravinsky characterized it as an "absolutely contemporary piece of music that will be contemporary forever."[36] [YOUTUBE VIDEO 2] But none of this should detract from Golitsyn's efforts to render the quartets accessible to his fellow listeners. And all who love the medium will forever be indebted to the Russian Maecenas for providing the impetus that brought this magnificent music into the world in the first place.[37]

The St. Petersburg premiere of the *Missa solemnis* in D, op. 123, represents the other key feature of Russian Beethoven reception in the first quarter of the nineteenth century. The premiere took place in the hall of Engel'gardt House on March 26, 1824, and marked the only time the mass was heard in its entirety during Beethoven's lifetime. The Philharmonia and Kapella once again combined forces to perform the work, while Golitsyn served as the main organizer of this historic concert. In recognition of his efforts, Beethoven dedicated the overture, *Die Weihe des Hauses* (*The Consecration of the House*) in C, op. 124, to the Russian prince when it was published in 1825.

Beethoven began writing his mass in early April 1819 in anticipation of having it performed on March 9, 1820, at the installation of the Archduke Rudolph as Cardinal Archbishop of Olműtz. But this was not to be. No other work, with the possible exception of *Fidelio*, caused Beethoven as much difficulty as the *Missa solemnis*. A wide variety of missal music needed to be studied, health issues intruded, the lengthy legal proceedings over the guardianship of nephew Karl lingered, and composition of the last three piano sonatas, Opp. 109–11, and the *Diabelli Variations*, op. 120, consumed inordinate amounts of time. By Rudolph's enthronement only the Kyrie and Gloria had been composed. Beethoven completed the remainder of the work in sketchbook form in 1822 but revisions and copying delayed presentation of the bound autograph copy of the score to Rudolph until March 19, 1823. At the head of the Kyrie, Beethoven wrote the following deeply felt dedicatory message to his longtime friend and pupil: "*Von Herzen—möge es weider—zu Herzen gehen*!" ("From the heart—may it return—to the heart"). Altogether, it had taken the composer nearly four years to complete this colossal work, which he characterized in a June 5, 1822, letter to his friend Carl Peters as "the *greatest* work which I have composed so far."[38] The British musicologist Barry Cooper compares the *Missa solemnis* to Bach's B-minor Mass as "one of the two towering pinnacles in the whole history of the genre."[39]

The original objective now moot and money, as usual, an issue, Beethoven postponed publication of the mass in an effort to sell autograph copies of the score to European monarchs, dignitaries, and musical societies at a price of fifty ducats each. Invitations were sent out in early 1823, but the solicitations engendered a less than enthusiastic response—all told only ten subscriptions were sold. Nevertheless, in addition to the kings of Denmark, Prussia, and France, the elector of Saxony, the grand dukes of Hesse-Darmstadt and Tuscany, Prince Radziwiłł of Poland, and the Caecilia Society of Frankfurt, both Alexander I of Russia and Prince Golitsyn purchased copies. In this way the score made it to St. Petersburg, laying the groundwork for the March 26, 1824, premiere. Beethoven's academy of May 7, 1824, in turn showcased the Kyrie, Credo, and Agnus Dei portions of the mass, along with the *Consecration of the House* overture and the Symphony no. 9 in D minor (*Choral*), op. 125. The poorly attended repeat performance of May 23, this time with only the Kyrie on the program, proved Beethoven's last public concert. After a protracted delay brought about by the subscription process and some rather unsavory dealings with a variety of publishers, Beethoven finally signed a contract with B. Schott's Sons of Mainz to issue the *Missa solemnis* as his Opus 123. The manuscript was published posthumously in 1827 with a dedication to the Archduke Rudolph.[40]

Golitsyn ordered his autograph copy of the mass on August 3, 1823, with the intention of having the work performed at Christmastime, but the score did not arrive until early November, necessitating moving the premiere to the 1824 Lenten concert season. In his letter to Beethoven on November 29, 1823, acknowledging receipt of the score, Golitsyn wrote that he found in it "that grandeur that distinguishes all your compositions and makes your works inimitable." He announced that he was "occupied in having this beautiful work performed in a manner worthy of him who composed it" and ensured the composer that "the singers of the court who will perform the choruses and the solo parts are very numerous and certainly the best that one can hear, as much for the beauty of their voices as for their ensemble."[41] At considerable expense to himself, Golitsyn obtained copies of the score for the orchestra players, choristers, and soloists and scheduled the first rehearsal for January 7, 1824.[42] On March 11 he informed Beethoven that "the time will soon be upon us when we shall hear your masterpiece" and noted that ten or more rehearsals were scheduled "so that this work will be performed with all the perfection that its sublimity merits."[43] With the preparatory work nearing completion, the *St.-Peterburgskie vedomosti* (*St. Petersburg Gazette*) carried the following announcement in its March 18 and 24 editions: "The directors of the St. Petersburg Philharmonic Society are privileged to notify the honorable public that on Wednesday, March 26, the Society will present for the benefit of widows and orphans of musicians a new Oratorio for four voices, chorus, and large orchestra composed by L. van Beethoven. . . . The directors hope that the public, which appreciates so many of the works of the immortal Beethoven, will honor this concert with its presence and will derive pleasure from this moving composition."[44]

One hundred and twenty-eight singers from the Kapella and leading soloists from the German Opera joined with the Philharmonia to present the mass. There is no record as to who directed this historic concert, which was attended by 450 persons.[45]

Two days after the premiere, Golitsyn wrote enthusiastically to Beethoven.

> For several months I have been extremely impatient to hear this music performed, all the qualities of which I foresaw in the score. The effect that this music made on the public is indescribable, and I doubt that I exaggerate when I say that, for my part, I have never heard anything so sublime; I do not except even the masterpieces of Mozart, which, with their eternal beauties, have not produced for me the same sensations that you have given me . . . by the Kyrie and Gloria of your Mass. The masterly harmony and the touching melody of the Benedictus transport the spirit to a truly blissful state. In short, this entire work is a treasury of beauties; one may say that your genius has anticipated the ages.[46][YOUTUBE VIDEO 3]

A short review in the St. Petersburg veterans newspaper, *Russkii invalid* (*The Russian Invalid*), noted the difficulty of the music and described the performance as "generally adequate."[47] The St. Petersburg correspondent of the Leipzig journal *Allgemeine musikalische Zeitung*, on the other hand, responded much more favorably: "Of the music performed during Easter, the high point was a mass by Beethoven. . . . The impression left by this original and inspired work on those Beethoven worshipers in attendance was enormous. Our thanks go out to this remarkable composer and to the noble prince, an energetic advocate of classical music, who made it possible for us to partake of this delectable feast."[48]

In all probability, the *Missa solemnis* would not have been heard in its entirety during Beethoven's lifetime had it not been for Nikolai Golitsyn. The Gesellschaft der Musikfreunde in Vienna certainly showed no interest in staging a premiere, citing "too high costs and too uncertain profits" when Beethoven sought a performance.[49] Golitsyn's great wealth, high social standing, love of music, and "monomania" for Beethoven made him uniquely suited to carry out this historic task. His passion for music was extraordinary. "During the time when Beethoven was composing the quartets for me," he wrote a friend, "I abandoned myself to classical music with such fervor that my musical evenings and concert tickets cost me annually 2,000 or more ducats [22,000 or more silver rubles]."[50] He spent an untold amount of money acquiring as many compositions by Beethoven as he could find. "I possess all that you have composed up to now for the piano as well as for all other instruments," he informed the composer on November 29, 1823. A month later he wrote that he had just purchased the *Diabelli Variations*, op. 120, at a music shop in St. Petersburg and was curious to know "the works that are found between the Sonata [in C minor], op. 111 and the aforesaid Opus 120. I have not been able to obtain them and I address myself to you to ask what are the works that I lack, so that I may acquire them."[51] His proselytizing efforts in the countryside bore witness to his unbounded enthusiasm for Beethoven's music. On one occasion, as he prepared to leave Tambov for the capital, a friend ruefully reflected in verse, "After your departure—who but you / Can welcome Beethoven and Mozart in the evening?"[52] Lev Ginzburg argued that Golitsyn's most important undertaking lay in "publicizing Beethoven's creative work at a time when it was far from being appreciated in other countries."[53] Indeed Golitsyn spent a lifetime seeking to broaden the appeal and deepen the understanding of Beethoven's music among his fellow countrymen. In this regard he played a role second to none and remains to this day one of the most remarkable proponents of Beethoven's art to be found anywhere in the reception literature.

An Evening at the Viel'gorskii Salon

The visitor rang the private entrance at 6/4 Ital'ianskaia Street and was welcomed by a smiling maidservant who escorted him to the salon upstairs. Twenty

Figure 1.3. Viel’gorskii residence, Mikhailovskaia Square, nineteenth century. P. Stolpianskii, *Muzyka i muzitsirovanie v starom Peterburge* (Leningrad: Muzyka, 1989), 129.

Figure 1.4. Viel’gorskii salon, nineteenth century. Sketch by A. Utkin. D. Zhitomirskii, *Robert i Klara Shuman v Rossii* (Moscow: Gosudarstvennoe muzykal’noe izdatel’stvo, 1962), 17.

or so fashionably dressed members of the cultural elite were conversing in small groups while the host circulated casually among them, enjoying the ripostes to his clever bons mots. A finely chiseled crystal chandelier cast a warm glow over the room. Sconces in equal measure shed halos of light on the salon's golden walls. A chorus of voices speaking Russian, German, French, and a smattering of English softly hummed in the air. Gradually the guests began taking their seats as the host motioned for the performers to assemble near the piano at the far end of the hall. This was to be an evening of chamber music and song with, to the delight of all, some dance included in the program. The conversation subsided as the first notes of the piano, once played by Franz Liszt, signaled the start of the soirée. And thus began another memorable evening at the Viel'gorskii salon in the heart of old St. Petersburg. It was July 2, 2004.

Of the scores of salons operating at one time or another in prerevolutionary St. Petersburg, the one maintained by the brothers Mikhail and Matvei Viel'gorskii was without a doubt the most prestigious and influential. Located on the corner of Mikhailovskaia Square (now Arts Square) and Ital'ianskaia Street at the hub of the city's artistic life, the salon served as a kind of unofficial concert hall for the capital and became a gathering ground for the cognoscenti. On any given evening one could expect to encounter such leading lights of the arts world as the painter Karl Briullov; the musicians Aleksandr Dargomyzhskii, Mikhail Glinka, and Anton and Nikolai Rubinshtein; and the writers Nikolai Gogol, Mikhail Lermontov, Nikolai Nekrasov, Aleksei Pisemskii, Aleksandr Pushkin, Fedor Tiutchev, and Vasilii Zhukovskii. The salon paid court as well to a host of renowned musicians from abroad, including Hector Berlioz, Ole Bull, Franz Liszt, Giovanni-Battista Rubini, Clara and Robert Schumann, Adrien-François Servais, Henriette Sontag, Sigismond Thalberg, and Pauline García-Viardot, all of whom performed in either the intimate small hall or the large three-hundred-seat auditorium. Berlioz styled the establishment as a "small ministry of fine arts" for the high quality of the music making and the close relations both brothers enjoyed with the imperial court. The last recorded visits to the salon were those of Giuseppi Verdi in 1862 (in conjunction with his oversight of the premiere of *La forza del destino* at the Bol'shoi Kamennyi Theater on November 10) and Richard Wagner in 1863 (in connection with his February–March concert tour of St. Petersburg and Moscow). Interestingly, the cellar off the second courtyard of the Viel'gorskii residence served as the venue for a very different kind of performance art in 1912–15: the famous Stray Dog (*Brodiachaia sobaka*) cabaret frequented by poets, artists, and musicians of the Silver Age (1890–1917). Following the 1917 Bolshevik Revolution, the property was nationalized and converted into communal

Figure 1.5. Mikhail Viel'gorskii. Portrait by Franz Kriuger. Public Domain.

Figure 1.6. Matvei Viel'gorskii. Portrait by Petr Sokolov. Alamy Stock Photo B9CWNG.

apartments; a kindergarten and gymnasium were also established and remain in existence today, the three-hundred-seat concert hall serving as the school auditorium. After the collapse of the Soviet Union in 1991, the street-facing portion of the structure was first acquired by a bank and then purchased in bankruptcy court by the present owner, who has restored the small salon to its original splendor in order to host invitation-only soirées similar to the one this writer attended, described in the *souvenir* penned above.[54]

Mikhail and Matvei Viel'gorskii were born in St. Petersburg on October 31, 1788, and April 15, 1794, respectively. Their father, Iurii Mikhailovich Viel'gorskii (Wielhorski) (1753–1808), came from a highly cultivated and politically powerful aristocratic family that originated in the Volhnyia region of Poland. He entered Russian service in 1786 and held a number of important positions in the tsarist administrative apparatus. He also wrote dramas, composed music, played the violin in a family ensemble he established, wrote a celebrated treatise on the education of children of the nobility, and in 1802 helped found the St. Petersburg Philharmonic Society. His sons in their turn received a solid grounding in music theory and performance and at an early age showed great promise as musicians—Mikhail performing on the violin and Matvei on the cello.[55] All members of the family participated in domestic music making that ranged from staging Italian and French opera to performing a wide variety of chamber music to singing popular songs and salon pieces. Certainly there was no lack of sheet music to support such undertakings. In 1804, as he was preparing to take his family on an extended trip to Paris, Iurii Viel'gorskii offered for sale performance editions of six hundred quartets, two hundred quintets and sextets, a variety of symphonies, more than four hundred arias, duets, and trios, forty French operas, and more than five hundred sonatas, concertos, and other music for piano. The collection included the "newest works" of such composers as Beethoven, Clementi, Dusek, Haessler, Haydn, Mozart, Paisiello, Sarti, Wranitsky, and Zhitovetskii.[56]

Iurii Viel'gorskii embarked on the 1804 journey to secure a publisher for his compositions and further the education of his sons. The family set out in December but mounting hostilities between Russia and France, which culminated in the War of the Third Coalition in 1805, forced them to secure lodgings in Riga, the capital of Latvia, where they remained for the following three years. During this time Mikhail studied the music of Bach and his Italian and German predecessors under the tutelage of the Riga organist Wilhelm Taubert and played in the family quartet as violist. Among other works, the chamber ensemble performed the music of Haydn and Mozart and for the first time explored Beethoven's as yet little-known Opus 18 quartets, which had been published in Vienna only in 1801. It was as if Beethoven had "glanced in through the window," to quote the Russian critic Wilhelm von Lenz. Mikhail became transfixed for life.[57]

Following the conclusion of peace between Russia and France in 1807, the family resumed their journey in 1808. However, tragedy struck at Kőnigsberg when Iurii Viel'gorskii died suddenly, forcing the family to return to St. Petersburg. It is unclear whether Mikhail returned to the capital at this time and then resumed his journey or continued on from Kőnigsberg by himself. We know that later in 1808 he was in Vienna, where he met Beethoven and attended the December rehearsal of the Sixth Symphony, noted previously. He then journeyed to Paris, where he studied composition with Luigi Cherubini and engaged in other unspecified activities before returning to St. Petersburg sometime in 1810. At this point he was appointed an official in the Ministry of Education, joined the Masonic lodge Palestine, and began amassing a large library of hermetic literature, which in the 1860s became part of the holdings of the Moscow Public Library. Meanwhile younger brother Matvei continued his study of the cello under the tutelage of Adolph Meingardt and Bernhard Romberg; in time he would become one of the great cello virtuosos of the nineteenth century.

Unlike Matvei, who remained single, Mikhail married twice. He wed his first wife, Ekaterina Karlovna Biron-Kurliandskaia (1793–1813), on February 18, 1812, in a ceremony held in the main church of the Winter Palace in St. Petersburg. Both Ekaterina and her older sister, Luiza, were wards and maids of honor of the Dowager Empress Mariia Fedorovna, and it is highly likely that the empress was instrumental in arranging the marriage. In June the couple traveled to Moscow to attend the wedding of Mikhail's sister Dar'ia (Doroteia) but hurriedly left the city in August for Tambov due to the fast approach of Napoleon's forces. Ekaterina, pregnant with her first child, hoped to return to St. Petersburg for her confinement, but circumstances forced the couple to circle back to Moscow, now lying in ruins, where Ekaterina tragically died in childbirth on January 31, 1813. Both mother and stillborn baby were buried in an undisclosed location.[58] Then on April 23, 1816, Mikhail secretly married his sister-in-law, Luiza Karlovna Biron-Kurliandskaia (1791–1853), an action that, once it became public knowledge, resulted in his loss of favor at court and dismissal from his government positions due to the Orthodox Church's prohibition against such marriages. The couple was exiled to Luiza's estate at Fateevka (Luizino) in Kursk province, where they remained until the end of 1823. At that time, they received permission to relocate in Moscow and in 1826, following Nicholas I's ascension to the throne and his subsequent pardon of Viel'gorskii, they had their favor restored and were allowed to return to St.

Petersburg. Mikhail quickly assumed important positions of authority in the tsarist and municipal administrations, and it was not long before, together with Matvei, he opened the famous salon that was to play such a large role in St. Petersburg's cultural life over the following three decades.[59]

While at Fateevka, Mikhail Viel'gorskii composed what critics consider his better music—a septet, overture, some romances, two symphonies, and a large choral work to the words of Vasilii Zhukovskii. He also established what an authoritative source calls "Russia's first purely musical salon."[60] Mikhail performed on the violin and piano in chamber repertoire and also sang romances and opera arias, while Matvei, who had rejoined the family following his participation in the Napoleonic campaigns, played the cello. There were also orchestral performances that drew on the combined forces of family members and both free and serf musicians from adjoining estates (the Chernyshev, Teplov, and Bariatinskii holdings). The staging of a mammoth concert series from December 1822 to April 1823 represented the high watermark of these affairs. In all, thirty-three concerts were held twice weekly and featured the orchestral and vocal music of Beethoven, Boccherini, Boieldieu, Cherubini, Haydn, Méhul, Mozart, Romberg, Rossini, Viel'gorskii, and others. Much of this was new music that had not yet been heard in the capitals, an amazing feat given the general paucity of sheet music for orchestra performances, the deplorable condition of European and Russian postal services at the time, and the isolated location of the Fateevka estate. Not surprisingly, Beethoven's music figured prominently in these concerts: the Second, Third, Fourth, Fifth, Sixth, and Seventh Symphonies were all performed—with the possible exception of the Second, these represented first performances in Russia—together with various overtures, concertos, excerpts from the *Mount of Olives* oratorio, and such incidental pieces as the *Battle Symphony*, op. 91. Luiza Karlovna, an obvious connoisseur of fine music, kept a journal of these concerts and wrote glowingly of the Beethoven performances and of her emotional responses to them. Overall she viewed Beethoven's music as a spiritual nepenthe, shielding the family from the "cold world of petty self-interest."[61]

Music making served as a mainstay of family activities during the 1824–26 sojourn in Moscow as well. As was the case at Luizino, these were private affairs that drew together family members and invited guests in a congenial and socially comfortable setting. Only those with the proper credentials were welcome. The writer Vladimir Odoevskii snobbishly observed in 1825 that musical soirées at the Viel'gorskii salon were "most remarkable because those who attend them have more right than others to listen to good music." Noting that such musical affairs had "little in common with the so-called *concerts d'amateurs,*” the critic asserted that “it is hardly possible to encounter in Russia anything similar to these concerts where the selection of music, the quality of the performers, and the precision of the playing are as one . . . and where there is no bias towards any one kind of music or the idle talk of self-styled connoisseurs or ignorant dilettantes, as is so often the case, but only a refined discrimination acquired through deep study and genuine passion for art.” Later, in 18[illegible], Odoevskii penned another review of a “musical morning” in which he helpfully included a program: a symphony by Bernhard Romberg conducted by the composer himself, a concerto by Méhul with John Field at the piano, a Mozart fugue, a concerto by Spohr played by the serf violinist I. I. Semenov, the overtures to Weber's *Der Freischűtz* and *Euryanthe* “played back to back for comparison purposes,” one of Mikhail Viel'gorskii's symphonies, and other unidentified pieces. “Nowhere have we heard such music,” Odoevskii enthused. The “richness and variety” of the concert created a “musical splendor” that was beyond the power of words to describe.[62]

Following the coronation of Nicholas I on August 22, 1826, Mikhail Viel'gorskii, as noted, regained favor with the court and shortly embarked for St. Petersburg. On September 9 he was appointed an official in the Ministry of Public Education and in January 1827 became a member of the Main Administration of the St. Petersburg Schools and the Committee of the Main Theater Directory. The family lived first on Herzen Street and in 1833 moved to Mikhailovskaia Square (no. 3 from 1833 to 1837, no. 5 from 1837 to 1844, and no. 4 from 1844 to 1856).[63] In a pattern by now well established, an average of two chamber recitals and/or large orchestral concerts were held on the premises each week. Beethoven's music continued to occupy a prominent place in these performances. While no complete catalogue of concerts at the Viel'gorskii salon is available, some of the Beethoven performances can be gleaned from scattered references in the secondary literature. For example, Symphony no. 7 in A, op. 92, was performed in the large three-hundred-seat auditorium in 1835, some five years before its first performance by the Philharmonia on March 6, 1840. In 1838 both Symphony no. 4 in B-flat, op. 60, and Symphony no. 9 in D minor (*Choral*), op. 125, received hearings (the first Philharmonia performance of the Fourth Symphony occurred six years later on March 27, 18[illegible]6, while the Russian premiere of the Ninth Symphony had taken place two years before on March 7, 1836).[64] The Quartet no. 8 in E minor, op. 59, no. 2 was performed on January 13, 1838, in the small recital hall, followed by the Quartet no. 10 in E-flat (*Harp*), op. 74, on March 26, and the Septet in E-flat, op. 20, on April 16. The violinists Henri Vieuxtemps from Belgium and

Figure 1.7. L'vov Quartet. Lithograph by P. Rorbach. Clockwise around table: Aleksei L'vov (first violin), Matvei Viel'gorskii (cello), Gustav Vil'de (second violin), Vsevolod Maurer (viola). Mikhail Viel'gorskii is seated behind his brother. Alamy Stock Photo RCP2T4.

Karol Lipiński from Poland participated in the March 26 and April 16 recitals respectively. During his visits to Russia in 1842 and 1843, Franz Liszt played the Piano Trio in B-flat (*Archduke*), op. 97, with Gen. Alexei L'vov and Matvei Viel'gorskii and gave a bravura performance of the Piano Concerto no. 5 in E-flat (*Emperor*), op. 73. On May 16, 1842, and February 9, 1844, the *Leonore 1* Overture in C, op. 72 was performed in the large concert hall. And in 1850 the *Archduke* Trio received another hearing, played this time by Adolf von Henselt, Henri Vieuxtemps, and Matvei Viel'gorskii in the small recital hall.[65]

Matvei Viel'gorskii also regularly performed the Beethoven cello sonatas and played in the quartet maintained by Aleksei L'vov, which concertized at both the Viel'gorskii residence and L'vov's home on Karavannaia Street off Nevskii Prospect. The personnel of the quartet changed over time but at its core in the 1840s consisted of L'vov on first violin, Vsevolod Maurer on second violin, Gustav Vil'de on viola, and Viel'gorskii on cello. L'vov is best known as the composer of the Russian national anthem *Bozhe, tsaria khrani* ("God Save the Tsar" 1833). He was director of the Kapella from 1837 to 1861 and a very fine violinist. Iurii Arnol'd knew him well and described the tone he elicited from his Guarneri instrument as "powerful, clean, and warm." Arnol'd also considered the L'vov quartet the best of the many he had heard in Russia and abroad. The group remained in existence from 1835 to 1855 and was particularly well-known for its performances of the Mozart quartets and the early and middle Beethoven quartets. As for Beethoven's late quartets, both the violinist Nikolai Afanas'ev and the critic Vladimir Stasov maintained that L'vov did not understand these works and even had difficulty interpreting the transitional Quartet no. 11 in F minor (*Serioso*), op. 95. Thus Matvei Viel'gorskii, who not only understood the late quartets but also held them in the highest regard, had to join forces with others to perform these works. Von Lenz noted, for example, that Viel'gorskii teamed up with Vieuxtemps, Sergei Volkov, and Vil'de to play the Quartet no. 12 in E-flat, op. 127, the first of the Golitsyn quartets.[66]

Mikhail Viel'gorskii's artistic credentials, proven networking skills, high office in the theater administration, and connections at court made him ideally suited to become Russia's first great impresario. Indeed, Afanas'ev claimed that no performing artist could secure a position in St. Petersburg, and by extension the rest of the country, without first having passed through the Viel'gorskii salon. While this claim is overstated, it signifies the large role Viel'gorskii played in bringing a variety of international stars to the St. Petersburg stage, above all Franz Liszt, Clara and Robert Schumann, and Hector Berlioz.

Viel'gorskii had met Liszt in Rome in 1839 while attending to his son Iosif, who was suffering from tuberculosis. Despite the ministrations of Iosif's friend, the writer Nikolai Gogol, he died on June 2 at twenty-three.[67] One can imagine Viel'gorskii's deep grief over the loss of his eldest son and the solace he must have found in listening to Liszt play Beethoven's late piano sonatas. That summer he wrote his children from Rome: "Liszt is here now and I have been getting to know him musically. He is the tsar of pianists. Until now no one on this instrument has produced such an effect on me. I never thought it possible to play Beethoven's music, for example the late sonatas, in such a way. They become transformed under his fingers, although he doesn't change anything except to double the chords in *forte* passages. Liszt is the only one of his kind for me."[68] In a similar vein, Wilhem von Lenz had written Iosif on March 1[illegible] urging him to invite Liszt to play some of Beethoven's sonatas for him, observing that Liszt performed them "fantastically." He specifically recommended Sonatas no. 12 in A-flat ("Funeral March"), op. 26; no. 14 in C-sharp minor (*Moonlight*), op. 27, no. 2; no. 23 in F minor (*Appassionata*), op. 57; and no. 29 in B-flat (*Hammerklavier*), op. 106. Lenz characterized these

Figure 1.8. Caricature of Franz Liszt performing at the Viel'gorskii salon. Mikhail Viel'gorskii applauds from the side. Unknown artist. Alamy Stock Photo K2YC96.

compositions as Beethoven's *Iliad*, a metaphor every bit as striking as Liszt's own: "For us musicians Beethoven's work is like the pillar of clouds and fire that guided the Israelites through the desert."[69]

Liszt arrived in St. Petersburg on April 3, 1842, for the first of his concert tours and over the next two months performed six times at the Engel'gardt House and Gentry Club, staged two private concerts at the Viel'gorskii salon, and gave a number of recitals for the Empress Aleksandra Fedorovna, Grand Duchess Elena Pavlovna, and select members of the aristocracy. Press coverage preceding his arrival had whipped the concertgoing public into a frenzy of expectation, and certainly those who managed to obtain tickets to the sold-out events were not disappointed. Never before had a Russian audience witnessed the spectacle of a single artist performing an entire concert without orchestral accompaniment. Most of the programs consisted of bravura pieces designed to show off Liszt's keyboard wizardry. But the virtuoso also made room for some Beethoven to lend a more dignified air to the concerts, playing his own transcriptions of the song *Adelaide*, op. 46 (two performances), the last three movements of Symphony no. 6, and the *Moonlight* Sonata. Interestingly the critics Vladimir Stasov (1824–1906) and Aleksandr Serov (1820–71), at the time law school students who avidly attended all of Liszt's public concerts, had not heard either the *Pastoral* Symphony or the *Moonlight* Sonata, though the Philharmonia had premiered the former on March 1, 1833. The concerts made an indelible impression on both young men and served as a kind of initiation rite into their musical manhoods.[70]

Liszt returned to Russia in April through June of 1843, performing two concerts in St. Petersburg at the Engel'gardt House, six more in Moscow at the city theater, and an encore engagement of sorts at the Viel'gorskii salon back in St. Petersburg. Iurii Arnol'd offers an entertaining account of this final performance in June. The Grand Duchesses Mariia Nikolaevna and Elena Pavlovna had expressed an interest to Mikhail Viel'gorskii in having Liszt perform Beethoven's *Emperor* Concerto for them. Viel'gorskii complied and arranged a late-morning concert in the three-hundred-seat performing hall. On the day of the concert, as the guests were arriving, Liszt was observed engaged in animated but *sotto voce* conversation with a young Russian princess, one Gagarina-Menshikova by name. Following the entrance of the Grand Duchesses, the guests were seated, and the concert began. Ludwig Maurer led the orchestra in the overture to Mozart's *Die Zauberflőte*, at which point Liszt was to play the concerto. But Liszt was nowhere to be found. Viel'gorskii thus asked the singer Polina Barteneva to sing her aria, which was scheduled as the third number on the program. Afterward, there was still no Liszt. So the violinist Aleksei L'vov was prompted to perform his scheduled piece, a sonata by Spohr, while Viel'gorskii, now perspiring profusely, frantically searched the adjoining rooms and grand staircase for his elusive soloist. But again no Liszt! At this point the host was forced to explain to the Grand Duchesses why there had been a change in the program and ask for their patience and indulgence as he called on L'vov to perform one of his own compositions, a violin solo entitled *The Duel*, while he continued his search. This time, to his enormous relief, he spotted Liszt ascending the staircase with the chattering young princess on his arm. "My God, Mr. Liszt, what happened to you," Viel'gorskii berated his guest. "All of this has been most insulting to the Grand Duchesses!"

"I ask your forgiveness a thousand times," Liszt blurted out. "I am guilty, I am guilty. But it was impossible to resist the princess's very kind invitation to accompany her on a short spring outing in her carriage." (Arnol'd learned later that the couple had actually driven to the far end of Elagin Island, a distance of some twenty kilometers there and back.) And with that Liszt bounded into the hall, bowed low to the Grand Duchesses, sat down at the piano, signaled to Maurer to launch the opening orchestral tutti, and commenced playing the cadenza-like flourish that ushers in the *Emperor* Concerto. [YOUTUBE VIDEO 4] Initially, the countenances of the royalty—and indeed of all the aristocrats in the hall—were of "icy indifference," but soon Liszt's "fiery playing" inflamed the hearts of one and all. At the end of the performance, the audience broke out in boisterous applause. In 1885, Arnol'd reminisced with Leonid L'vov, brother of the violinist Aleksei L'vov, about this concert. "I have heard that concerto performed a hundred times or more by a whole host of pianists," L'vov remarked, "but never to such perfection as played by Liszt on that occasion." As for what may have transpired, besides polite conversation, during that long carriage ride to Elagin Island and back, presumably died with Liszt's confessor, Cardinal Hohenlohe-Schillingsfűrst, who on July 30, 1865, conducted the ceremony whereby Franz Liszt took minor orders as L'Abbé Liszt.[71]

Liszt had spoken very highly of Robert Schumann when he met Mikhail Viel'gorskii in Rome in 1839. (Viel'gorskii referred to him as "Schukman de Leipzig" in a letter to his children.)[72] In this way a seed was planted that bore fruit five years later when Clara and Robert Schumann visited Russia on a tour lasting from late February to early May 1844. The Viel'gorskii brothers extended their usual hospitality to the couple and received warm praise in return. Clara described them as "splendid people" who "live only for art and spare no expense in pursuit of it." Robert characterized them as "magnificent gentlemen" and in particular found Mikhail Viel'gorskii a person "with a genuine artistic temperament" who was "the greatest dilettante I have met."[73] Clara confided in her journal that Count Mikhail "is a man whom I truly love and respect," hastening to add that "Robert will not be angry with me over this confession because he loves and respects him as I do."[74] On her initial excursion about the city, Clara found the Gentry Club a "majestic site," remarking that "one does not see similar splendor even in Paris," but was disappointed to discover that the Engel'gardt House, where she was to perform, was "very ugly, dark and dirty."[75] Altogether she gave four public concerts in St. Petersburg and three in Moscow, made up variously of works by Bach, Beethoven, Chopin, Field, Liszt, Mendelssohn, Scarlatti, Schumann, and Thalberg. The Beethoven pieces included Sonatas no. 13 in E-flat, op. 27, no. 1; no. 17 in D minor (*The Tempest*), op. 31, no. 2; and no. 23 in F minor (*Appassionata*), op. 57. The critic Aleksandr Bulgakov praised Clara's ability to "make Beethoven come alive" through her freedom of expression, crystal clear articulation, and attention to detail.[76] Faddei Bulgarin, editor of the reactionary newspaper *Severnaia pchela* (*Northern Bee*), described her playing as being so full of grace, purity, and charm that "words cannot describe it," adding that "a certain kind of languor and melancholy is reflected in her beautiful and interesting face; her eyes burn with emotion and genius."[77] The Spanish mezzo-soprano Pauline García-Viardot also heard Clara in concert and declared that on the piano she "sings better than I do."[78]

On March 4 Clara substituted at the last moment for two ailing artists at a Philharmonia concert that included a performance of Beethoven's Ninth Symphony. Other music by Beethoven heard during the Schumann's stay were an unidentified quartet; the *Egmont* Overture, op. 84; and three of the four overtures to *Fidelio* (*Leonore*), op. 72. Certainly a high point of the trip was the opportunity for Robert to conduct his Symphony no. 1 in B-flat (*Spring*), op. 38, at the Viel'gorskii salon. Mikhail Viel'gorskii had scheduled a rehearsal of the composer's Piano Quintet in E-flat, op. 44, and was so taken by it that, on hearing Schumann also had a symphony with him, decided then and there to arrange for an orchestra to perform the work a few days later. After one rehearsal Robert successfully conducted the Russian premiere of the symphony on March 9 at a soirée that included Beethoven's *Leonore 1* Overture, a violin concerto by Wilhelm Molique performed by the artist, and a Mendelssohn piano concerto with Clara Schumann at the keyboard. Other activities of the Schumanns included additional private recitals by Clara, most notably one for Nicholas I and his family at the Winter Palace on April 12, much sightseeing, and a very heavy social schedule. While Clara noted in her journal that Robert occasionally suffered dizzy spells and experienced some "melancholy"—a tragic precursor of the deep depression that would manifest itself the following year, culminating in the suicide attempt of 1854—for the most part, Clara and Robert Schumann thoroughly enjoyed their Russian stay. They left for home on May 6 with Clara's newest acquisition, a St. Petersburg–made piano purchased at the Virt music store for twelve hundred rubles assignat, safely stowed away. They looked back on their sojourn "only with pleasure."[79]

Hector Berlioz's visit to Russia from late February to early May 1847 represented the last of the great composer-performer tours organized by Mikhail Viel'gorskii. In many ways this was the most spectacular one of all because Berlioz's "instrument" was nothing less than an outsize orchestra and chorus consisting of 160 players, 50 military musicians, and 180 singers, which he "played" (his word) like a Paganini of the baton. Vladimir Stasov noted as much following the first two concerts: "These were the most magnificent, most crowded, most brilliant (in terms of orchestra and applause), most deafening concerts that were presented this year."[80] This time there was no Beethoven, even though Berlioz considered Gluck and Beethoven the greatest of all composers. Rather the music was all Berlioz: the Overture to *Le carnaval romain*, op. 9; *Symphonie fantastique*, op. 14 (dedicated incidentally to Nicholas I); the "Apotheosis" from *Symphonie funébrè et triomphale*, op. 15; *Harold en Italie*, op. 16; concert excerpts and full production on April 23 of *Roméo et Juliette*, op. 17; and the first two parts of *La damnation de Faust*, op. 24. Except for a performance of the composer's *Requiem*, op. 5, at the Engel'gardt House on March 1, 1841, this was all new music for Russian concertgoers. The audiences responded enthusiastically, and the critics were favorable, Odoevskii writing an ecstatic review and Stasov, though voicing some misgivings at the outset, concluding that Berlioz was a "composer of genius."[81] The five concerts in St. Petersburg and one in Moscow yielded handsome box office receipts and enabled Berlioz to pay off his debts and return home with a tidy profit. All in all, the trip had proved a resounding success for performer and listener alike. "Believe me," Berlioz wrote Alexei L'vov in 1852, "I will never forget the reception Russian society in general and you in particular gave me and the favor the empress and entire family of your esteemed emperor showed me." He added, presumably entre nous, "What a shame the emperor doesn't like music!"[82]

In addition to patronizing foreign artists, Mikhail Viel'gorskii sought to further the interests of musicians at home. No one loomed larger in this regard than Mikhail Glinka (1804–57), the composer of Russia's first national operas, *A Life for the Tsar (Ivan Susanin)* (1834–36) and *Ruslan and Lyudmila* (1837–42). The poet Vasilii Zhukovskii had suggested the subject of *A Life for the Tsar* and penned the text for the epilogue, while Baron Egor Rozen, secretary to the future Alexander II, wrote the libretto. The singer Polina Barteneva arranged for a rehearsal of the orchestral part of act 1 at the Yusupov Palace, and in March 1836 Viel'gorskii held a full dress rehearsal at his salon. After this initial hearing, Viel'gorskii recommended that Glinka add an orchestral postlude to the choral introduction and, in scene 3, bring the chorus on stage with the arrival of Antonida's fiancé so as to render the homecoming a more festive and joyous occasion. Glinka extended his "sincere thanks" to Viel'gorskii for suggesting these changes and incorporated them into the score. Unfortunately, relations between the two men soured over Viel'gorskii's subsequent critique of *Ruslan and Lyudmila*, which he felt presented a number of musical and dramaturgical problems that rendered the work, in an oft-quoted phrase, "*un opera manqué*." Glinka broke off relations over this criticism and later inveighed against it in his memoirs. To his credit, however, the composer did not allow the dispute to affect his overall estimation of Viel'gorskii as both a friend and musician. On hearing of Viel'gorskii's death in 1856, Glinka wrote, "I do not want to dwell on our petty misunderstandings but remember only his friendship and goodwill toward me." He was "one of the finest musicians I ever met."[83]

Odoevskii characterized Mikhail Viel'gorskii as "the most learned musician of our day" and von Lenz wrote that the count possessed "universal encyclopedic knowledge."[84] Indeed Viel'gorskii's interests ranged from theology, medicine, and philosophy to technology and the law. His library of rare books comprised one of the most distinctive private collections in the country. He learned ancient Hebrew to study the Bible and was fluent in German, French, and English. His understanding of music was superb—as evidenced by the "historic concerts" he staged at his salon—while his knowledge of Beethoven's oeuvre was without peer. Lenz, who in 1852 wrote the Russian book on the subject, maintained that Viel'gorskii understood the "three styles" manner of Beethoven's life and work well before it had been articulated by the Belgian critic and composer François-Joseph Fétis in his *Biographie universelle des musiciens* of 1837.[85] In addition, Viel'gorskii knew most of the literary, musical, and artistic lions of his day. He was godfather to Aleksandr Pushkin's daughter Nataliia and served as one of the trustees of Pushkin's estate following the poet's untimely death in 1837. He assisted Aleksandr Griboedov in the revision of his drama *Woe from Wit* and secured Nicholas I's permission for the publication of Nikolai Gogol's play *The Inspector General*. He also wrote a good deal of music, ranging from chamber music to a five-act opera, *Tsigan* (*The Gypsy*), which lacked only the completion of several scenes and the orchestration of act 5 to reach performance stage. His two symphonies, composed no later than 1822, were Russia's first in the genre, rendering him, in the words of a Soviet scholar, the "pioneer of the Russian symphony."[86]

Mikhail Iur'evich Viel'gorskii died in Moscow the night of August 27–28, 1856, one day after the coronation of Alexander II. In an act signifying enormous respect for the deceased, the newly crowned emperor and his wife attended a private viewing of the body on August 28. The remains were then transported to St. Petersburg and buried on September 4 in the Lazaref Voskresen'e church at the Aleksandro-Nevskii monastery. Viel'gorskii's wife and two sons had preceded him in death; he left three daughters, the Countesses Apollinariia, Sofiia, and Anna.

Matvei Viel'goskii outlived his brother by ten years. In his lifetime he had served with distinction as an official in the Ministry of Foreign Affairs and at court and as a member of various St. Petersburg organizations devoted to assisting the poor and furthering the arts. He counted among his friends many of the leading musicians, writers, and painters of the era and enjoyed an international reputation as a virtuoso cellist for whom Felix Mendelssohn wrote his Second Cello Sonata, op. 58 (1843). He also proved instrumental in the founding of the Russian Musical Society (1859) and the St. Petersburg Conservatory (1862), detailed later in this study. While he sought to maintain the famous salon on Mikhailovskaia Square, the era of private music making among the aristocracy had largely passed. Late in life he emigrated to Nice, France, where he died on March 5, 1866 (New Style). His body was transported to Russia and buried alongside his brother. His valuable library and collection of stringed instruments were donated to the St. Petersburg Conservatory and a stipend for students was established in his honor.[87]

* * *

As for Matvei Viel'gorskii's famous cello, that in itself can serve as a fitting close to this discussion. The instrument was made in Cremona, Italy, in 1712 by the great master Antonio Stradivari. It was built for the Medicis in Florence but at some point disappeared from the Pitti Palace, probably during the Austrian occupation of 1737. It eventually came into the possession of Count Stepan Apraxin in Russia, who, spurning an offer from the Paris Conservatory, sold it to Matvei Viel'gorskii sometime after 1817 for thirty-four thousand rubles and four thoroughbred trotting horses. Viel'gorskii, in turn, to mark his own seventieth birthday in 1864, bequeathed the cello to the Russian virtuoso Karl Davydov. On the latter's death in 1889, the cello, now known as the *Davidov*, passed first to family heirs and then to various private owners via the auction houses of Paris, London, and New York. In 1964 a wealthy benefactress purchased the instrument for $90,000 on behalf of the English cellist Jacqueline du Pré. Du Pré bequeathed it to the American cellist Yo-Yo Ma, who has retained sole ownership of the instrument since 1987.[88]

A luthier familiar with the *Davidov* has remarked that "Antonio Stradivari made this cello to give us all a lesson in humility."[89] Part of the unique character of the instrument stems from the lustrous sheen of its varnish, but above all it is the cello's rich, resonant sound that has enthralled audiences over the years. "What an instrument!" an early-nineteenth-century listener enthused. "What can compare with its drawn-out tone! What can touch the soul with such sweetness!"[90] Yo-Yo Ma describes the sound this way: "The pianissimos float effortlessly. The instrument's response is instantaneous. The sound can be rich, sensuous or throbbing at every range, yet can also be clear, cultured, and pure. Each sound stimulates the player's imagination. However there is no room for error as one cannot push the sound, rather it needs to be released. I had to learn not to be seduced by the sheer beauty of the sound before trying to coax it from the cello."[91]

The *Davidov* can be heard to excellent effect in du Pré's classic 1965 recording of the Elgar Cello Concerto on the EMI label or Ma's 1994–97 remake of the Bach Cello Suites on the Sony Classical label. Either recording opens a door to a time long ago when the sound of a very special instrument signaled the start of yet another soirée in the heart of old St. Petersburg.

Notes

1. For an extended discussion of Razumovskii's palace, pleasure garden, and musical affairs, see Mark Ferraguto, "Representing Russia: Luxury and Diplomacy at the Razumovsky Palace in Vienna, 1803–1815," *Music and Arts*, XCVII, 3 (2016): 383–408. The Austrian Federal Geological Institute occupied the rebuilt portion of the palace from 1852 to 2005, at which point two private art collectors acquired the structure and converted it into an art foundation and private residence (address: Rasumofskygasse 23–25).

2. "Vesuvius" citation in David King, *Vienna 1814: How the Conquerors of Napoleon Made Love, War, and Peace at the Congress of Vienna* (New York: Harmony Books, 2008), 191. A highly believable, though fictitious, account of the fire is contained in Mark Aldanov, *The Tenth Symphony*, trans. Gregory Golubeff (New York: Scribner's Sons, 1948), 42–52. For colorful detail, see King, *Vienna 1814*, 190–92. On Razumovskii, see M. Alekseev, "Russkie vstrechi i sviazi Betkhovena," in *Russkaia kniga o Betkhovene: k stoletiiu so dnia smerti kompositora (1827–1927)*, ed. K. A. Kuznetsov (Moscow: Muzykal'nyi sektor, 1927), 79–85; Edward Dusinberre, *Beethoven for a Later Age: Living with the String Quartets* (Chicago: University of Chicago Press, 2016), 85–89, 107–9, 123–27; Patricia Grimsted, *The Foreign Ministers of Alexander I: Political Attitudes and the Conduct of Russian Diplomacy, 1801–1825* (Berkeley: University of California Press, 1969), 218–19; T. Livanova, *Russkaia muzykal'naia kul'tura XVIII veka v ee sviaziakh s literaturnoi, teatrom i bytom*, II (Moscow: Gosudarstvennoe muzykal'noe izdatel'stvo, 1953), 312–14; M. Razumovskaia, *Razumovskie pri tsarskom dvore: glavy iz rossiiskoi istorii, 1740–1815 gg.* (St. Petersburg: XXI Vek, 2004), chap. 13–16; *Thayer's Life of Beethoven*, ed. Eliot Forbes (Princeton, NJ: Princeton University Press, 1967), 400–2; A. A. Vasil'chikov, *Semeistvo Razumovskikh, III–IV* (St. Petersburg: Stasiulevicha, 1882–87).

3. King, *Vienna 1814*, 162.

4. Maynard Solomon, *Beethoven*, 2nd ed. (New York: Schirmer Books, 1998), 189. By "frying pan" Seyfried was referring to the resident Schuppanzigh Quartet.

5. Mark Ferraguto identifies the soldier's lament "Akh, talan li moi, talan" ("Ah, Whether It's My Luck, Such Luck") for Opus 59, no. 1 and the fortune-telling song turned tsarist hymn "Uzh kak slava Tebe Bozhe" ("Just as There Is Glory to Thee, O God on High") for Opus 59, no. 2. Mark

Ferraguto, "Beethoven *a la moujik:* Russianess and Learned Style in the 'Razumovsky' String Quartets," *Journal of the American Musicological Society*, LXVII, 1 (Spring 2014): 81, 92. See also Viacheslav Paskhalov, "Russkaia tematika v proizvedenniakh Betkhovena," in *Russkaia kniga o Betkhovene*, 185–90. "Restless brooding" quote from Joseph Kerman, *The Beethoven Quartets* (New York: W. W. Norton, 1979), 145; see also Jan Swafford, *Beethoven: Anguish and Triumph* (Boston and New York: Houghton Mifflin Harcourt, 2014), 446. Mark Ferraguto suggests that Beethoven may have drawn the melody of Opus 59, no. 3 from another Russian folk song, "Ty wospoi, wospoi, mlad Shaworontschek," which was published in the journal *Allgemeine musikalische Zeitung* in July 1804. Ferraguto, "Beethoven *a la moujik*," 112–16.

6. For a discussion of Opus 89 as it pertains to its composition, structure, and dedication, see Birgit Lodes, "'*Le congress danse*': Set Form and Improvisation in Beethoven's Polonaise for Piano, op. 89," trans. Sabine Ladislav, *Musical Quarterly*, XCIII, 3–4 (Fall–Winter 2010): 414–49.

7. The song is "Uzh kak po mostu mostochku." A. M., "Betkhoven i ego simfonii," *Muzyka i zhizn'* (August 1911): 14.

8. Alekseev, "Russkie vstrechi," 76–77. Swafford notes that Beethoven "liked to keep inspirational items on his desk and piano" to aid in the creative process. Swafford, *Beethoven*, 563.

9. Alekseev, "Russkie vstrechi," 84–85; A. Klimovitskii, "Betkhoven," *Muzykal'nyi Peterburg*, I (St. Petersburg: Kompozitor, 2000), 84–85; Solomon, *Beethoven*, 2nd ed., 81–82; Forbes, *Thayer's Life of Beethoven*, 191, 211–12, 307–8; Laura Tunbridge, *Beethoven: A Life in Nine Pieces* (New York: Penguin Random House, 2020), 33. Swafford claims that Countess Browne presented Beethoven with the riding horse. Swafford, *Beethoven*, 200.

10. Frau Bernhard (maiden name Kiesow) lived in the Klűpfeld household from thirteen to seventeen. She related this information to Ludwig Nohl in an interview of 1864. Klimovitskii, "Betkhoven," 128–33; Forbes, *Thayer's Life of Beethoven*, 401.

11. E. E. Liamina and N. V. Samover, *"Bednyi Zhozef": Zhizn' i smert' Iosifa Viel'gorskogo: opyt biografii cheloveka 1830-kh godov* (Moscow: Yazyki russkoi kul'tury, 1999), 18; T. Shcherbakova, *Mikhail i Matvei Viel'gorskie: ispolniteli, prosvetiteli, metsenaty* (Moscow: Muzyka, 1990), 14.

12. Richard Stites, *Serfdom, Society, and the Arts in Imperial Russia: The Pleasure and the Power* (New Haven, CT: Yale University Press, 2005), chaps. 2–3 . On sheet music in Moscow, see T. N. Livanova, ed., *Muzykal'naia bibliografiia russkoi periodicheskoi pechati XIX veka*, I (Moscow: Sovetskii kompozitor, 1960), item 1828; in St. Petersburg, see Klimovitskii, "Betkhoven," 126 and F. E. Purtov, "Peterburskie notoprodavcheskie katalogi pervoi chetverti XIX v.," in *Notnye izdaniia v muzykal'noi zhizni Rossii: sbornik statei*, III (St. Petersburg: Rossiiskaia natsional'naia biblioteka, 2007), 18–19, 24–25. On the 1828 Moscow concerts, see A. Khokhlovkina, "Muzykal'naia Moskva i Betkhoven: 20-ye i 30-ye gody," in *Russkaia kniga o Betkhovene*, 119; and Shcherbakova, *Mikhail i Matvei Viel'gorskie*, 30.

13. Adam Zamoyski, *Moscow 1812: Napoleon's Fatal March* (New York: Harper Collins, 2004), 346.

14. *Muzykal'naia bibliografiia*, I, items 38, 43–44, 46–47, 51–52, 1180, 1193, 1195, 1205–6, 1208, 1210, 1218.

15. Boris Berezovskii, *Filarmonichekoe obshchestvo Sankt-Peterburga: istoriia i sovremennost'* (St. Petersburg: Kul't Inform, 2002), 81; Alekseev, "Russkie vstrechi," 82; N. V. Gubkina, *Nemetskii muzykal'nyi teatr v Peterburge v pervoi treti XIX veka* (St. Petersburg: Dmitrii Bulanin, 2003), 284; *Muzykal'naia bibliografiia*, I, items 35–37, 41–42, 45, 48–49, 1060, 1062. The March 1813 performances of the *Choral Fantasy* and *Christ on the Mount of Olives* were Russian premieres staged only two years after the publication of the works in Leipzig. In

his discussion of the reception of Beethoven's music in America, Michael Broyles notes that *Christ on the Mount of Olives* also received a disproportionate number of performances in the early years of the republic and attributes this to the large role church choirs played in music making at the time. Michael Broyles, *Beethoven in America* (Bloomington: Indiana University Press, 2011), 5, [illegible]. Special thanks to Scott Messing of Alma College for information on early Russian Beethoven performances.

16. Carolyn C. Dunlop, *The Russian Court Chapel Choir, 1796–1917* (Amsterdam: Harwood Academic, 200[illegible]), 94.

17. Stites, *Serfdom, Society, and the Arts*, 97–98.

18. For extended commentary on the Kapella, see Dunlop, *The Russian Court Chapel Choir*, 5–55, 85–107, and Stites, *Serfdom, Society, and the Arts*, 96–98.

19. Iurii Arnol'd, *Vospominaniia*, I (Moscow: n.p., 1892), 22.

20. A. A. Gozenpud, *Dom Engel'gardta* (Moscow: Sovetskii kompozitor, 1992), 8.

21. The Engel'gardt concert hall in use today is not the original theater. The building was rebuilt following a devastating fire in 1856 and restored a second time as a result of extensive damage suffered during World War II. Gozenpud, *Dom Engel'gardta*, 234. On the St. Petersburg Philharmonic Society, see E. Al'brekht, *Obshchii obzor deiatel'nosti vysochaishe utverzhdennogo S.-Peterburgskogo filarmonicheskogo obshchestva* (St. Petersburg: Goppe, 1884), v–xxi; L. V. Beliakaeva-Kazanshaia, *Siluety muzykal'nogo Peterburga: putevoditel' po muzykal'nym teatram, muzeiam, kontsertnym zalam proshlogo i nastoiashchego* (St. Petersburg: Lenizdat, 2001), 124–39; Berezovskii, *Filarmonicheskoe obshchestvo*, 17–140; I. F. Petrovskaia, *Muzykal'noe obrazovanie organizatsii v Peterburge, 1801–1917: entsiklopediia* (St. Petersburg: Petrovskii fond, 1999), 296–99; Stites, *Serfdom, Society, and the Arts*, 90–96; *Stoletnii iubilei S.-Peterburgskogo filarmonicheskogo obshchestva, 1802–1901* (St. Petersburg: St. Peterburgskaia filarmoniia, [1902]), 7–21; P. Stolpianskii, *Muzyka i muzitsirovanie v starom Peterburge* (Leningrad: Muzyka, 1989), 106–8.

22. Alekseev, "Russkie vstrechi," 92–110; L. Ginzburg, *Istoriia violonchel'nogo iskusstva*, II (Moscow: Muzgiz, 1957), 223–77; L. S. Ginzburg, "Liudvig van Betkhoven i N. B. Golitsyn," in *Betkhoven: sbornik statei*, II, ed. N. L. Fishman (Moscow: Muzyka, 1972), 225–38; Lev Ginzburg, "Liudwig van Beethoven und Nikolai Fűrst [*sic*] Golitsyn," *Ősterreichische Musikzeitschrift*, XIX, 10 (October 1964): 523–29; Iu. S. Goriainov, *Liudvig van Betkhoven i kniaz Nikolai Golitsyn: k 200-letiiu so dnia rozhdeniia N. B. Golitsyna* (Belgorod: Bezelitsa, 1993); Ivan Maiham, *Beethoven: Naissance et renaissance des derniers quatuors* (Paris: Desclée De Brouwer, 1964), 26–38, 13[illegible]–35. A report of Golitsyn's murder on October 23, 1866, by an unknown assailant appeared in the *Journal de St.-Peterbourg* on June 15, 1883. Golitsyn's son, Prince Boris Nikolaevich, refuted the claim in a letter to the editor of the journal on June 17, 1883, and corrected the date of his father's death from October 23 to October 22, 1866. RNL, Otdel rukopisei, F. 12[illegible] (Vaksel'), ed. khr. 1220, l. 2.

23. Ginzburg, "Liudvig van Betkhoven," 225.

24. Golitsyn to Beethoven, November 29, 1823, in *Letters to Beethoven and Other Correspondence*, II (1813–23), trans. and ed. Theodore Albrecht (Lincoln: University of Nebraska Press, 1996), 28[illegible].

25. Forbes, *Thayer's Life of Beethoven*, 815–16. Dates conform to the New Style calendar.

26. Ginzburg, *Istoriia violonchel'nogo iskusstva*, II, 230–35; Goriainov, *Liudvig van Betkhoven*, 10, [illegible]4, 31–32; Kerman, *The Beethoven Quartets*, 223–25; Solomon, *Beethoven*, 2nd rev. ed., 347; Robert Winter and Robert Martin, ed., *The Beethoven Quartet Companion* (Berkeley: University of California Press, 1994), 215–16. The proper sequence of composition dates for the Golitsyn quartets is as follows: Opus 127—1823–25; Opus 132—1825; Opus

130—1825–26. Joseph Kerman and Alan Tyson, *The New Grove Beethoven* (New York: W. W. Norton, 1983), 163. See Kerman, *The Beethoven Quartets*, 224 for a clarification of this chronological confusion. There remains considerable controversy regarding Golitsyn's payment in full for the three quartets. For this tangled history, consult Ginzburg, *Istoriia violonchel'nogo iskusstva*, II; Goriainov, *Liudvig van Betkhoven*; and Forbes, *Thayer's Life of Beethoven*, 977–80, 1100–2.

27. Ginzburg, "Liudvig van Betkhoven," 229. The reference is to the Polish cellist Antoni Radziwiłł.

28. *La presse*, October 13, 1845, in Ginzburg, *Istoriia violonchel'nogo iskusstva*, II, 237.

29. *Otechestvennye zapiski*, LXV, 8 (August 1849): 272; LXVII, 12 (December 1849): 368–69. Golitsyn likely consulted the *Wielhorsky* Sketchbook, which contains the sketches for Opus 35 and the variation for the fourth movement of Opus 55. See Boris Schwarz, "Beethoveniana in Soviet Russia," *Musical Quarterly*, XLVII, 1 (January 1961): 7. On the *Prometheus* theme in the *Eroica*, see George Grove, *Beethoven and His Nine Symphonies*, 3rd ed. (New York: Dover, 1962), 81; and Thomas Sipe, *Beethoven: Eroica Symphony* (Cambridge: Cambridge University Press, 1998), 111–16.

30. *Letters to Beethoven*, III (1824–1828), 95–96. The Bernhard Romberg referenced in this quotation was the same Romberg who, on first playing the cello part of the Scherzo of Opus 59, no. 1, famously trampled the score underfoot because of the monotonously repetitive single B-flat note of the opening four measures. Presumably he found the jaunty melody beginning in the third measure of the Opus 127 Scherzo much more to his liking. See Lewis Lockwood and the Juilliard String Quartet, *Inside Beethoven's Quartets: History, Interpretation, Performance* (Cambridge, MA: Harvard University Press, 2008); Kerman, *The Beethoven Quartets*, 230; Winter and Martin, *The Beethoven Quartet Companion*, 181.

31. *La presse*, October 13, 1845, in Ginzburg, *Istoriia violonchel'nogo iskusstva*, II, 234.

32. *Letters to Beethoven*, III (1824–28), 152–53. The quartets remained in the possession of the Golitsyn family until 1862 when Golitsyn's son, Iuri N. Golitsyn (1823–72), bequeathed the autographs to the Hungarian violinist Joseph Joachim. Joachim in turn donated the manuscripts in 1889 to the newly established Beethoven Haus in Bonn. N. Fishman, *Etiudy i ocherki po betkhoveniane* (Moscow: Muzyka, 1982), 120.

33. Goriainov, *Liudvig van Bethoven*, 37–38. The reference to "science and art" echoes a deeply held sentiment Beethoven had expressed as long ago as 1812 to a young pianist by the name of Emilie M. "Persevere, do not only practice your art, but endeavor also to fathom its inner meaning; it deserves this effort. For only art and science can raise men to the level of the gods." Swafford, *Beethoven*, 589.

34. *La presse*, October 13, 1845, in Ginzburg, "Liudvig van Betkhoven," 236.

35. Opus 127 quote from Michael Steinberg, "Notes on the Quartets," in Winter and Martin, *The Beethoven Quartet Companion*, 217; Opus 130 quote from Maynard Solomon, "Beethoven: Beyond Classicism," in Winter and Martin, *The Beethoven Quartet Companion*, 68. For analysis of the controversy associated with the *Grosse Fuge*, see Kerman, *The Beethoven Quartets*, 367–74.

36. Kerman, *The Beethoven Quartets*, 192. For efforts to identify a unifying motif in Opus 130, see ibid., 304–5.

37. It is a remarkable fact that six of Beethoven's greatest quartets were the result of commissions from Russian patrons. In this regard, Kerman overstates the case when he includes Prince Joseph Max Lobkowitz, the dedicatee of the Opus 18 and 74 quartets, in this select company. Lobkowitz was a nobleman from Bohemia, not Russia. See Kerman, *The Beethoven Quartets*, 273; Paul Nettl, *The Beethoven Encyclopedia* (New York: Carol, 1994), 124–25.

38. Solomon, *Beethoven*, 403, Beethoven's italics. Beethoven reiterated this assessment on March 10, 1824 in a letter to the publisher Schott's Sons: "Difficult as it is to speak of myself, still I consider it [the *Missa solemnis*] my greatest work." Forbes, *Thayer's Life of Beethoven*, 915–16

39. Barry Cooper, ed., *The Beethoven Companion: A Guide to Beethoven's Life and Music* (London: Thames and Hudson, 1991), 256.

40. William Drabkin, *Beethoven: Missa solemnis* (Cambridge: Cambridge University Press, 1991), 11–18; Solomon, *Beethoven*, 343, 351–56; Forbes, *Thayer's Life of Beethoven*, 818–33.

41. *Letters to Beethoven*, II (1813–23), 283.

42. After the Philharmonia, Kapella, and court all turned down his request for support, Golitsyn paid one hundred ducats (eleven hundred silver rubles) of his own money to have performing parts of the score copied. Goriainov, *Liudvig van Betkhoven*, 23.

43. *Letters to Beethoven*, III (1824–28), 14. "Ten or more rehearsals" stands in stark contrast to the "typically one, sometimes none, rarely two" rehearsals that characterized concert preparation in Vienna at the time. Tunbridge, *Beethoven*, 97.

44. Boris Schwarz, "More Beethoveniana in Soviet Russia," *Musical Quarterly*, XLIX, 2 (April 1963): 14[illegible]. The same announcement appeared in the *St. Peterbourgische Zeitung* on March 18, 21, and 24 and in *Russkii invalid* on March 24.

45. Natan Fishman, "Istoricheskaia prem'era: k 200-letiiu so dnia rozhdeniia Betkhovena," *Sovetskaia muzyka*, XXXIV, 6 (June 1970): 100–2. Size of audience based on total ticket receipts of 2,25[illegible] rubles divided by a single ticket price of 5 rubles, as advertised in newspaper announcements. Ibid., 101.

46. *Letters to Beethoven*, III (1824–28), 23. Considerable confusion has arisen over the fact Golitsyn dated his letter April 8, 1824, and referred to the premiere as having taken place "the night before last" (*avant-hier soir*), meaning on April 6 (New Style) or March 25 (Old Style). Since newspaper announcements and a variety of credible Russian sources all give the date of the premiere as March 26, Golitsyn either inadvertently misdated his letter by one day or incorrectly used the French phrase. The date of the performance appearing in Thayer therefore needs to be advanced by one day (from April 6 to April 7, 1824). See Forbes, *Thayer's Life of Beethoven*, 831. For further details, consult Schwarz, "More Beethoveniana," 147–49.

47. Goriainov, *Liudvig van Betkhoven*, 26.

48. Fishman, "Istoricheskaia prem'era," 96.

49. Schwarz, "More Beethoveniana," 149.

50. Goriainov, *Liudvig van Betkhoven*, 35.

51. *Letters to Beethoven*, II (1813–23), 283, 289.

52. Alekseev, "Russkie vstrechi," 97.

53. Ginzburg, *Istoriia violonchel'nogo iskusstva*, II, 277.

54. I. F. Petrovskaia, *Konsertnaia zhizn' Peterburga* (St. Petersburg: Petrovskii fond, 2000), 110. On the Stray Dog, see W. Bruce Lincoln, *Sunlight at Midnight: St. Petersburg and the Rise of Modern Russia* (New York: Basic Books, 2000), 221–24; Liudmila Tikhvinskaia, *Povsednevnaia zhizn' teatral'noi bogemy Serebrianogo veka: kabare i teatry miniatiur v Rossii 1908–1917* (Moscow: Molodaia gvardiia, 2005), 112–55; Solomon Volkov, *St. Petersburg: A Cultural History*, trans. Antonina W. Bouis (New York: Free Press, 1995), 186–91; Charles A. Ward, *Moscow and Leningrad: A Topographical Guide to Russian Cultural History*, II (Munich: K. G. Saur, 1992), 217–18.

55. Iurii Viel'gorskii was married twice and sired eight sons and an undetermined number of daughters. Of the sons, by 1839 only Mikhail and Matvei were still alive.

56. *S.-Peterburgskie vedomosti*, 1803, as cited in Liamina and Samover, *Bednyi Zhozef*, 15–16; Stolpianskii, *Muzyka i muzitsirovanie*, 111, 212.

57. William von Lenz, "Graf Mikhail Iur'evich Viel'gorskii," trans. Aleksandr Serov, *Muzykal'nyi i teatral'nyi vestnik*, I, 49/51 (December 9/23, 1856): 917.

58. Viel'gorskii's first wife was the granddaughter of Ernst-Johann Biren (Biron), the infamous lover of Empress Anne (1730–40). There is indirect evidence to suggest that Leo Tolstoy modeled the character of Lisa Bolkonskaia in *War and Peace* after Ekaterina Karlovna Viel'gorskaia. Liamina and Samover, *Bednyi Zhozef*, 20–25.

59. On the Viel'gorskie's, in addition to the above, see Ginzburg, *Istoriia violonchel'nogo iskusstva*, II, 223–77; Liamina and Samover, *Bednyi Zhozef*, 7–516; T. Shcherbakova, *Mikhail i Matvei Viel'gorskie: ispolniteli, prosvetiteli, metsenaty* (Moscow: Muzyka, 1990); B. Shteinpress, "Mikhail Iur'evich Viel'gorskii, blagozhelatel' Glinki," in *M. I. Glinka: sbornik statei*, ed. E. Gordeeva (Moscow: Gosudarstvennoe muzykal'noe izdatel'stvo, 1958), 368–83; A. D. Skonechnaia, *Moskovskii Parnas* (Moscow: Moskovskii rabochii, 1983), 138–46; A. D. Skonechnaia, *Torzhestvo muz* (Moscow: Sovetskaia Rossiia, 1989), 166–76; T. Trofimova, "M. Iu. Viel'gorskii," *Sovetskaia muzyka*, VII, 5 (May 1937): 61–70; M. A. Venevitinov, "Frants List i graf Mikh. Iur'evich Viel'gorskii v 1839 g.," *Russkaia starina*, XVII, 11 (November 1886): 485–90.

60. *Istoriia russkoi muzyki*, ed. A. I. Kandinskii, IV (Moscow: Muzyka, 1986), 276–77.

61. "Memorial sensitive et raisonne des soirée musicales de Louisino, Anno 1822–1823," as cited in Liamina and Samover, *Bednyi Zhozef*, 39–40; Shcherbakova, *Mikhail i Matvei Viel'gorskie*, 30.

62. V. F. Odoevskii, *Muzykal'no-literaturnoe nasledie*, ed. G. B. Bernandt (Moscow: Gosudarstvennoe muzykal'noe izdatel'stvo, 1956), 87–88, 99–100. Mikhail Viel'gorskii was partly responsible for the eventual freeing of the serf violinist I. I. Semenov and the Ukrainian painter, poet, and musician Taras Shevchenko. Stites, *Serfdom, Society, and the Arts*, 80, 340–42.

63. Ward, *Moscow and Leningrad*, II, 56.

64. There is some confusion in the literature concerning the correct date and venue of the Russian premiere of the Ninth Symphony. Skonechnaia, *Moskovskii Parnas*, 140 and *Torzhestvo muz*, 169; and Trofimova, *M. Iu. Viel'gorskii*, 64 characterize the 1838 Viel'gorskii performance as the date and place of the premiere; Shcherbakova, *Mikhail i Matvei Viel'gorskie*, 43 asserts that the premiere took place in 1837 at the Viel'gorskii residence. Stites, *Serfdom, Society, and the Arts*, 65, argues correctly that the premiere occurred in 1836 but, like the above, locates it at the Viel'gorskii residence. Thus, for the record, the Russian premiere took place at the Gentry Club (Hall of the Nobility) on March 7, 1836, in a concert performed by the Philharmonia and Kapella with the participation of the soloists Eizrikh, Evseev, Usol'tsev, and Petrov. The "Autumn" and "Winter" portions of Haydn's *The Seasons* also appeared on the program. Al'brekht, *Obshchii obzor*, 11; and Berezovskii, *Filarmonicheskoe obshchestvo*, 186.

65. Arnol'd, *Vospominaniia*, III, 89–91; Ginzburg, *Istoriia violonchel'nogo iskusstva*, II, 289, 291–92; Liamina and Samover, *Bednyi Zhozef*, 219, 264, 277, 282, 306; Shcherbakova, *Mikhail i Matvei Viel'gorskie*, 44; T. Trofimova, "List v Rossii," *Sovetskaia muzyka*, V, 8 (August 1937): 56.

66. Arnol'd, *Vospominaniia*, III, 67–68; Ginzburg, *Istoriia violonchel'nogo iskusstva*, II, 289, 329–30; Shcherbakova, *Mikhail i Matvei Viel'gorskie*, 44–45; Stites, *Serfdom, Society, and the Arts*, 64, 439n31. On L'vov, see Dunlop, *The Russian Court Chapel Choir*, 15–26 and M. Alekseev, "Betkhoven v russkoi literature," in *Russkaia kniga o Betkhovene*, 159.

67. On Gogol and Iosif Viel'gorskii, see Liamina and Samover, *Bednyi Zhozef*, 381–516 passim and Henri Troyat, *Divided Soul: The Life of Gogol*, trans. Nancy Amphoux (New York: Minerva, 1975), 194–99. Gogol's unfinished story, "Nochi na ville" ("Nights in the Villa"), in which he gives expression to his deep love for Iosif and details the young man's final days, can be found in Liamina and Samover, *Bednyi Zhozef*, 470–72; portions are also translated in Troyat, *Divided Soul*, 197–98.

68. Shcherbakova, *Mikhail i Matvei Viel'gorskie*, 101. The critic Vladimir Odoevskii also praised Liszt's performances of Beethoven's piano sonatas, describing his technique as "surpassing all disciplines." Odoevskii, *Muzykal'no-literaturnoe nasledie*, 156.

69. Lenz's letter in Liamina and Samover, *Bednyi Zhozef*, 423–24. Liszt quote in Russell Martin, *Beethoven's Hair* (New York: Broadway Books, 2000), 32.

70. For a good description of Liszt as the first "modern day recitalist," see Paul Kildea, *Chopin's Piano: In Search of the Instrument That Transformed Music* (New York: W. W. Norton, 2018), 86. For a summary of press coverage and commentary by contemporaries on Liszt's opening concert in Russia, see V. Khvostenko, "List v Rossii," *Sovetskaia muzyka*, IV, 11 (November 1936): 30–48. For a listing of concerts and repertoire, see V. Natanson, *Proshloe russkogo pianizma* (Moscow: Gosudarstvennoe muzykal'noe izdatel'stvo, 1960), 217; Trofimova, "List v Rossii," 55–56; Elena Ukolova and Valerii Ukolov, *Gastroli Lista v Rossii: illiustrirovannaia khronika* (Moscow: Muzhdunarodnyi fond gumanitarnykh initsiativ, 2012). For color and analysis, see Arnol'd, *Vospominaniia*, III, 77–88; Gozenpud, *Dom Engel'gardta*, 104–13; A. Iablonskii, "List v Rossii," *Sovetskaia muzyka*, LIV, 12 (December 1986), 97–103; V. V. Stasov, *Izbrannye sochineniia*, ed. P. T. Shipunov (Moscow: Iskusstvo, 1952), II, 377–83; III, 410–22; Stites, *Serfdom, Society, and the Arts*, 117–19; Stolpianskii, *Muzyka i muzitsirovanie*, 64–67. Date of the premiere of the Sixth Symphony in Berezovskii, *Filarmonicheskoe obshchestvo*, 18[illegible].

71. Arnol'd, *Vospominaniia*, III, 88–91. Apparently Liszt had a habit of showing up late to concerts. Stites, *Serfdom, Society, and the Arts*, 118. On Liszt's womanizing during the Moscow tour, see I. A. Arsen'ev, "Vospominanie o Liste," *Russkaia starina*, VII, 9 (September 1886): 577. On the second tour, see Stasov, *Izbrannye sochineniia*, III, 422–32. On Liszt's decision to take orders in the Roman Catholic Church, see Derek Watson, *Liszt* (New York: Schirmer Books, 1989), 128. Liszt conducted a third valedictory tour to Russia (Kiev, Odessa, and Elizavetgrad) in 1847. Stasov, *Izbrannye sochineniia*, III, 432–34; and Stites, *Serfdom, Society, and the Arts*, 118–19.

72. Shcherbakova, *Mikhail i Matvei Viel'gorskie*, 102.

73. Stasov, *Izbrannye sochineniia*, III, 434–35.

74. Journal entry of March 9, 1844, in D. Zhitomirskii, *Robert i Klara Shuman v Rossii* (Moscow: Gosudarstvennoe muzykal'noe izdatel'stvo, 1962), 136–37.

75. Journal entries of February 22 and March 3, 1844, in Zhitomirskii, *Robert i Klara Shuman*, 122–23, 130. By the 1840s Engel'gardt Hall had fallen into considerable disrepair. The last concert held there in the nineteenth century was in 1846. Stites, *Serfdom, Society, and the Arts*, 94.

76. Gozenpud, *Dom Engel'gardta*, 148.

77. N. Findeizen, "Shuman v Rossii," *Russkaia muzykal'naia gazeta*, XIII, 27–28 (July 2/9, 1906): 624–25.

78. Natanson, *Proshloe russkogo pianizma*, 218.

79. John Worthen, *Robert Schumann: Life and Death of a Musician* (New Haven, CT: Yale University Press, 2007), 248. The Mendelssohn piano concerto performed by Clara Schumann on March 9 is not identified in the literature. On the Schumann's Russian tour, see Findeizen, "Shuman v Rossii," 623–29; Gozenpud, *Dom Engel'gardta*, 137–48; Stites, *Serfdom, Society, and the Arts*, 114; Stasov, *Izbrannye sochineniia*, III, 423–37; Worthen, *Robert Schumann*, 232–48; Zhitomirskii, *Robert i Klara Shuman*, 3–37. A Russian translation of Clara Schumann's travel journal is in Zhitomirskii, *Robert i Klara Shuman*, 94–176. The program of the March 4 Philharmonia concert is in Berezovskii, *Filarmonicheskoe obshchestvo*, 189.

80. Neil Cornwell, *The Life, Times, and Milieu of V. F. Odoyevsky, 1804–1869* (London: Athlone, 1986), 53.

81. Stasov, *Izbrannye sochineniia*, III, 30. Odoevskii, *Muzykal'no-literaturnoe nasledie*, 197–98; Cornwell, *The Life, Times, and Milieu*, 153. Regarding his love for Beethoven, Berlioz wrote the following in an undated letter to his sister Nanci: "The other day I heard one of the late quartets of Beethoven. . . . [T]here were nearly three hundred persons present, of whom six found ourselves half-dead through the truth of the emotion we had experienced, but we six were the only ones who did not find his compositions absurd, incomprehensible, barbarous. He rose to such heights that our breath began to fail us. . . . This is music [only] for him or for those of us who have followed the incalculable flight of his genius." Martin, *Beethoven's Hair*, 29–30.

82. Cited in Stasov, *Izbrannye sochineniia*, III, 448. On Berlioz and his Russian tour, see *Memoirs of Hector Berlioz from 1803 to 1865*, trans. Rachel (Scott Russell) Holmes and Eleanor Holmes (New York: Dover, 1966), 422–43; Cornwell, *The Life, Times, and Milieu*, 151–53; Gozenpud, *Dom Engel'gardta*, 224–30; Odoevskii, *Muzykal'no-literaturnoe nasledie*, 197–98, 220–25; Stasov, *Izbrannye sochineniia*, II, 27–34, III, 427–50; Stites, *Serfdom, Society, and the Arts*, 116–17; Stolpianskii, *Muzyka i muzitsirovanie*, 67–69. Berlioz returned to Russia in the winter of 1867–68. Cornwell, *The Life, Times, and Milieu*, 153–54. On travel conditions from Paris to St. Petersburg that Berlioz encountered on the two trips, see Kildea, *Chopin's Piano*, 120.

83. Shteinpress, "Mikhail Iur'evich Viel'gorskii," 379–80.

84. Skonechnaia, *Moskovskii Parnas*, 146; Lenz, "Graf Mikhail Iur. Viel'gorskii," 881.

85. Lenz, "Graf Mikhail Iur. Viel'gorskii," 882. Ownership and therefore presumed study of the 1802–3 Beethoven sketchbook now known as the *Wielhorsky* Sketchbook testifies as well to Viel'gorskii's deep understanding of Beethoven's compositional process. On the history and content of the sketchbook, see Schwarz, "Beethoveniana in Soviet Russia," 4–9. Interestingly, Beethoven's close friend Franz Oliva, who had emigrated to St. Petersburg in 1820, was a frequent visitor at the Viel'gorskii salon. Natanson, *Proshloe russkogo pianizma*, 214n4.

86. Trofimova, "M. Iu. Viel'gorskii," 69. In regard to Viel'gorskii's friendships, an anomaly is the lack of any mention of Nikolai Golitsyn in the literature. There is a report that Golitsyn and Matvei Viel'gorskii were occasionally seen playing together in the cello section of the St. Petersburg Philharmonia. Ginzburg, *Istoriia violonchel'nogo iskusstva*, II, 305. But in regard to a Golitsyn and Mikhail Viel'gorskii connection, the sources are strangely silent.

87. Ginzburg, *Istoriia violonchel'nogo iskusstva*, II, 292–330; Shcherbakova, *Mikhail i Matvei Viel'gorskie*, 69–82.

88. Tony Faber, *Stradivari's Genius* (New York: Random House, 2004), 137–47; Elizabeth Wilson, *Jacqueline du Pré: Her Life, Her Music, Her Legend* (New York: Arcade, 1999), 133–35.

89. Faber, *Stradivari's Genius*, 10.

90. Ginzburg, *Istoriia violonchel'nogo iskusstva*, II, 313, citing a listener's response to a performance by Matvei Viel'gorskii in 1824.

91. Faber, *Stradivari's Genius*, 9. Du Pré grew disgruntled with the instrument because it did not respond adequately to her forceful way of playing, and she eventually ceased playing it altogether. Wilson, *Jacqueline du Pré*, 286–87.

2

ENGAGING BEETHOVEN

Writer and Critic

As Beethoven's music came to occupy a more prominent place in Russian concert programming of the 1830s, 1840s, and 1850s, the initial period of performance gave way to a more complex one of criticism and analysis. Connoisseurs began talking about the music, critics brought it under the scrutiny of their pens, essayists ruminated on it, poets made allusions to it, and writers sprinkled their short stories, novels, and plays with references to it. The music enchanted some, appalled others, and mystified yet more. But no one could gainsay the fact Beethoven had arrived in Russia to stay.

The Literary Community

As a nineteen-year-old just setting out on his career, Mikhail Lermontov (1814–41) invoked Beethoven in shaping the opening paragraph of his "Panorama of Moscow" (1833): "Hardly has dawn broken before a harmonious hymn rings out from the bells of [Moscow's] gold-domed churches like a wonderful, fantastic overture by Beethoven, in which the thick growl of the bass viols, the crash of the kettledrums, and the singing of the violins and flutes are blended into one miraculous whole;—and it seems as if the incorporeal sounds acquire visual shape and the spirit of heaven and hell coil together beneath the clouds in an ever changing, immense, quickly revolving round dance!"[1]

In the unfinished story "Faro," written in 1841 near the end of a life cut tragically short, Lermontov recalled a musical gathering at the Viel'gorskii salon: "There was an evening soirée at the home of Count V. . . . The best artists of the capital paid with their art for the honor of an aristocratic reception. Among the guests one could catch fleeting glimpses of several writers and scholars, two or three fashionably dressed women, several young ladies and old women, and a guards officer. . . . [A] visiting singer approached the piano and opened the score. . . . [She] sang 'Erlkőnig,' Schubert's ballad to the words of Goethe."[2]

These examples bookend a body of writing that reflects deep immersion in the world of music. As a student, Lermontov learned to play the piano, flute, and violin, and he continued to play these instruments as an adult. He was also known for singing a large repertory of songs, composing the music to his poem "Cossack Lullaby," and enjoying abiding friendships with the singer Polina Barteneva and the critic Vladimir Odoevskii. He frequented the theater and regularly attended musical performances and literary discussions at the Viel'gorskii, Sologub, and Karamzin salons in St. Petersburg. On July 27, 1841, he died in a duel at just twenty-seven years of age.[3]

Lermontov's musicality in turn became a key characteristic of his writing. Song permeates the novel *A Hero of Our Time* (1840) through the voices of Bela and Kuzbich in "Bela," the mysterious "mermaid" in "Taman," and Mary in "Princess Mary." A conversation between Pechorin and Princess Mary is characterized as "meaningless on paper, which one cannot repeat or even remember exactly, for the tones and cadences change and heighten the meaning of the words, as they do in an Italian opera."[4] In the unfinished novel *Princess Ligovskaia* (1837), another Lermontov-like Pechorin figure displays alabaster busts of Paganini, Ivanov, and Rossini on his mantelpiece; a chapter of the novel takes place at the Aleksandrinskii Theatre in St. Petersburg during a performance of Daniel Auber's *La Muette de Portici* (*Fenella*) (1828) with the ballerina Mariia Novitskaia and tenor Konstantin Golland in the lead roles; and Vera's "meaningless smile" is likened to the smile "one sees on the face of a ballerina who has just completed a pirouette."[5] In the play *The Strange Man* (1831), a guest refers to the upcoming concert of a famous harpist from Paris, while two strings on an instrument creating "harmonious sounds" and "an equal number of possible dissonances" describes a problematic friendship.[6] And in the unfinished quasihistorical novel *Vadim* (1834), Lermontov repeats verbatim the famous remark of John Field on hearing Johann Nepomuk Hummel play the piano for the first time: "Either you are the Devil, or you are Hummel! Only he could play like that!"[7]

These and other references add up to an eclectic list of composers, performers, and works that gives little indication of Lermontov's personal tastes in classical music. Indeed, he never adumbrates his own preferences. As for Beethoven, a single reference in a substantial body of work does not seem especially noteworthy. But the use of a Beethoven overture as a metaphor in "Panorama of Moscow" is significant for two reasons. First, all of the majesty, mystery, and historical weight of Russia's medieval capital city is perfectly captured by such a multilayered and powerful piece of music, and it should not go unremarked that Lermontov specifically turned to Beethoven in an effort to capture the unique character of this citadel of Russian culture and civilization. One only misses the color and exultant sound of the brass section of the orchestra to complete this aural picture. Second, even an isolated reference is sufficient to make the point that, for musically astute Russian readers, Beethoven's music had already become a recognizable literary device only six years after the composer's death. This constitutes remarkably rapid acculturation and points toward the accelerating role Beethoven's music would come to play in Russian musical, intellectual, and political life in the years ahead.

Aleksandr Griboedov (1795–1829) was not only a poet, dramatist, and linguist but also a music lover, minor composer of waltzes, and author, with Petr Viazemskii, of a musical comedy (vaudeville). He counted Beethoven among his favorite composers and found in his music great power and beauty. Griboedov's masterpiece, the comedy *Woe from Wit* (1827), begins with a flute and piano playing a duet offstage and weaves references from music, ballet, and opera throughout its four acts.[8] Like Lermontov and most of the other writers of this era, Griboedov came from the aristocracy and thus obtained a solid grounding in music at an early age. He played the flute, harp, organ, and piano, becoming particularly adept on the latter instrument. The actor Petr Karatygin recalled, "I loved to listen to his playing on the piano. . . . He would sit down, gather himself, and begin to improvise. . . . How much taste, strength, glorious melodies there were! He was an excellent pianist and a great connoisseur of music; his favorite composers were Mozart, Beethoven, Haydn, and Weber."[9] The playwright Nikolai Polevoi remarked that Griboedov "passionately loved music" and was not at all bothered by the technical aspects of piano playing, rather he "studied music as a profound theorist." Mikhail Glinka also found Griboedov to be a "very good musician." In the winter of 1824–25 at his salon in St. Petersburg, Griboedov audaciously sight-read with P. N. Lasvrent'eva Beethoven's entire Fifth Symphony in a piano four-hand redaction. According to Lasvrent'eva, he "modestly said, 'Let's try,' adjusted his glasses and . . . played [Lasvrent'eva's ellipsis]."[10]

Arrested in conjunction with the roundup of alleged conspirators following the failed Decembrist Revolt of 1825, Griboedov was imprisoned in the General Staff Building on Palace Square in St. Petersburg—but even then managed to continue his piano playing. According to Dmitrii Zavalishin, who was arrested along with Griboedov, a music-loving guard would take the two prisoners at night to the Loredo confectionary shop on the corner of Nevskii

Prospekt and Admiralty Square, where, in a secluded back room, Griboedov would "unburden his soul" at a piano. In June 1826 the playwright was exonerated from complicity in the Decembrist affair and continued his career as a diplomat. Tragically, in his capacity as plenipotentiary minister to Persia, he was killed in an anti-Russian riot in Tehran on January 30, 1829. Griboedov had just turned thirty-four and left behind a Georgian bride, Princess Nina Chavchavadze, whom he had married only six months before. His remains were buried at the St. David Monastery outside Tbilisi, Georgia, in July 1829.[11]

The fabulist Ivan Krylov (1769–1844), one of Russia's most beloved writers, was an accomplished violinist who performed the chamber music of Boccherini, Haydn, Mozart, and Beethoven with some of the best artists of his day. He particularly valued Beethoven for the high idealism and emotional strength of his music. Born in Moscow into a nonnoble family, Krylov spent his formative years in Tver, where he studied at the local seminary, received private lessons on the violin, and took part in domestic music making. In 1782 he moved to St. Petersburg, worked for a time as a government clerk, and began his literary career as a playwright, librettist, and journalist. In the 1780s he wrote three comic operas and published several short-lived satiric and theatrical-musical journals. But his real métier was writing fables. A little over two hundred of the fanciful tales were published in nine books over the course of a long literary career. Several dealt with musical subjects. The practice of organizing choirs out of indentured servants is lampooned in "The Musicians," where a chorus of serfs sounds like a group of screeching animals.[12] The serf-performers in "The Village Band" can do no better, playing "mercilessly out of tune" and prompting the owner to lament, "I'd let them drink all day/If only they could play."[13] The fable "The Quartet" satirizes efforts at government reform that only result in the reorganization of the bureaucracy. A bear, a goat, a donkey, and a monkey attempt to perfect the playing of a string quartet by changing their seating arrangements. Achieving no success, they ask a passing nightingale for help:

> They pleaded, "Please, spare us some time
> To make of our quartet a paradigm:
> We have our instruments and scores
> Just tell us how to sit!"
>
> "For making music, you must have the knack
> And ears more musical than yours,"
> The nightingale comes back.
> "And you, my friends, no matter your positions,
> Will never be musicians!"[14]

Figure 2.1. Valentin Serov's sketch to Ivan Krylov's fable "The Quartet." I. Iampol'skii, *Krylov i muzyka, 1769–1969* (Moscow: Muzyka, 1970). Cover art.

Certainly this did not pertain to Krylov's own abilities as first violinist in a quartet that performed at the Imperial Court Chapel Choir (Kapella) and elsewhere. Petr Pletnev, rector of St. Petersburg University and a close friend, described the writer's playing of "such perfection [as to allow] the performance of the most difficult quartets with the best virtuosos of the time."[15] Krylov also regularly attended the main musical and literary gatherings in St. Petersburg—the Olenin Circle, the Kukol'nik "Wednesdays," the Odoevskii "Saturdays," and the Del'vig, Karamzin, L'vov, Shimanovskaia, and Viel'gorskii salons—and thus had ample opportunity to hear a broad range of music performed. The Russian Beethoven scholar Wilhelm von Lenz frequently encountered him at the L'vov salon and observed that he would "fall into the deepest reverie" whenever his favorite Beethoven quartet—no. 9 in C, op. 59, no. 3—was played. "Krylov loved to listen to the quartets of Haydn and Mozart but even more prized those of Beethoven," Lenz observed and quoted

Krylov as saying that "in Beethoven [quartets] one hears the voices of nature but one must know how to listen to them."[16] The last concert he attended took place on February 16, 1844, when the Spanish mezzo-soprano Pauline García-Viardot presented a recital at St. Petersburg University. Krylov died in the early morning hours of November 9, 1844, at seventy-five and was buried in the Tikhvin cemetery at the Aleksandro-Nevskii monastery.[17]

Russia's best-known satirist, Nikolai Gogol (1809–52), developed an early love for music, especially song, on his father's estate of Vasil'evka in the central Poltava region of Ukraine. He was also introduced to classical music at a relative's adjoining estate where chamber music, opera, and the symphonies of Mozart, Beethoven, and others were performed on a regular basis; his mother reminisced, "The double doors would open wide in room after room and some orchestra or quartet would begin playing."[18] Gogol's move to St. Petersburg in 1828 opened up the larger world of professional opera and ballet, in his words the "tsar and tsaritsa" of the St. Petersburg stage.[19] His friendship with Mikhail Viel'gorskii enabled him to attend performances of Beethoven's music at the Viel'gorskii salon, and while ministering to Iosif Viel'gorskii in Rome, he undoubtedly heard Franz Liszt play Beethoven sonatas. In an essay entitled "Sculpture, Painting, and Music" (1831), Gogol elevated music above the other arts as a powerful gift from God, granted "in order swiftly to turn us to Him." He closed by asking, "If music should leave us, what then will happen to our world?"[20] One scholar suggests that Gogol had Beethoven in mind in this reflection on the spiritual dimension of music. He describes the overall structural and expressive characteristics of Gogol's writing as "music itself."[21]

Song had been an integral part of Gogol's life from childhood, whether in the home, where his mother and grandmother frequently sang to him, or in the fields, where peasants labored to the rhythm of song. He had a fine voice and frequently delighted his friends with a large repertory he knew by heart. "I can't live without songs," he declared to a close friend in 1833.[22] It is not surprising, therefore, that song figures prominently in many of his stories, most notably in his masterful depiction of Russian provincial life in *Dead Souls* (1842). Toward the end of the novel, Gogol poses the question: "Russia! Russia! . . . Why does your mournful song, carried along your whole length and breadth from sea to sea, echo and re-echo incessantly in my ears? What is there in it? What is there in that song?"

A tentative answer is offered in the closing paragraph. Russia is likened to a troika that flies down the road at superhuman speed. The simple peasant driver with beard and mittens has "only to stand up and crack his whip and start up a song, and the horses rush like a whirlwind, the spokes of the wheels become one smooth revolving disc, only the road quivers and the pedestrian cries out as he stops in alarm, and the troika dashes on and on! And very soon all that can be seen in the distance is the dust whirling through the air."

At this point the song of the people becomes the voice of God: "[The horses] have caught the sound of the familiar song from above, and at once they strain their chests of brass and barely touching the ground with their hoofs are transformed almost into straight lines, flying through the air, and the troika rushes on full of divine inspiration."

But where is Russia rushing to? "She gives no answer. The bells fill the air with their wonderful tinkling; the air is torn asunder, it thunders and is transformed into wind; everything on earth is flying past, and, looking askance, other nations and states draw aside and make way for her."[23]

The riddle of Russia's future thus remains elusive. Gogol attempted to craft a solution in a sequel to *Dead Souls*, but all efforts proved futile. Twice he burned the partially completed manuscript, and after the second auto-da-fé, he took to his bed, refused to eat, and died after nine days on March 4, 1852. He was forty-two years of age.

Gogol idolized Aleksandr Pushkin (1799–1837), revered the world over as Russia's greatest poet. Pushkin wrote in a lean literary style tinctured with musical sound. As Avrahm Yarmolinsky notes: "There is something in Pushkin's poetry, irrespective of its substance, as Tchaikovsky observed, which enables it to penetrate to the depths of the soul—that something is its music."[24] Pushkin came from the aristocracy, obtained an outstanding education, knew all the leading artists of his day, participated in the affairs of the main literary salons in both capital cities, and regularly attended the theater, opera, and ballet as well as chamber and orchestral concerts. Aleksandra Smirnova-Rosset, maid of honor to Empress Aleksandra Fedorovna and an intimate of the cultural elite, commented in her memoirs that Pushkin "always attended" the Saturday concerts at the Engel'gardt House, where, among other works, he heard performances of Mozart's *Requiem*, Haydn's *Creation*, and symphonies by Beethoven, "in a word, serious German music."[25] Ivan Turgenev, the future novelist, saw him in the vestibule of the hall on January 24, 1837, just three days before the tragic duel that took the poet's life. Pushkin also frequented the salon of the critic Vladimir Odoevskii and praised the latter's short story "Beethoven's Last Quartet" when it was published in 1831. In turn, the poet Dmitrii Oznobishin observed that Pushkin "attended all the evenings" at the Viel'gorskii salon, "even those devoted exclusively to music."[26] Mikhail Viel'gorskii became a close friend, serving as godfather to Pushkin's daughter Nataliia and being appointed one of four trustees of the poet's estate following his death.

Pushkin rarely wrote about music in his letters and diaries, and when he did, he only provided the most rudimentary commentary. Such cursory notations might lead one to conclude that the poet was indifferent to the art form. Yet other letters and journal entries indicate that this was not the case. During his exile in Odessa from 1823 to 1824, for example, Pushkin frequently attended the Italian Opera, where he was "passionately" carried away by the operas of Rossini.[27] Vera Noshchokina, a close friend, commented in her memoirs that Pushkin "often asked me to play on the piano and listened for hours on end."[28] Others who knew the poet observed that he could talk about music as if he were a professional, citing his ability to discuss a Bach fugue with Vladimir Odoevskii immediately following a performance by the prince on the organ he maintained in his home.[29] Music also serves as a leitmotif in a number of Pushkin's poems and in the dramatic work *Mozart and Salieri* (1830), where Gluck, Piccini, and Haydn make cameo appearances and Salieri's opera *Tarare* (1787) is used as a literary device. Curiously, nowhere in the primary material, including Pushkin's diaries, does one encounter the name Beethoven. This is odd in that the poet was on intimate terms with eminent authorities, such as Vladimir Odoevskii and Mikhail Viel'gorskii, and heard Beethoven's music performed in the salons and concert halls of St. Petersburg and Moscow. But for whatever reason, he chose not to set down his thoughts on the composer. It may be, as recent scholarship argues, that Pushkin's life experiences and sensibilities as a poet shaped an attitude toward music that was more casual than committed, "more a pleasure than an art, more a part of play than of work."[30]

On one score, however, there is no ambiguity—like Lermontov and Gogol, Pushkin loved Russian popular song. The songs that his peasant nanny, Arina Rodionovna (d. 1828), sang stayed with him his whole life, and as an adult he systematically transcribed folk songs into a notebook he later gave to Petr Kireevskii, the Slavophile folk song collector. Several of Pushkin's acquaintances commented on his fine singing voice, a trait that is borne out by the following anecdote. One evening at the beginning of July 1833, a German tourist and his companion were walking on St. Petersburg's Krestovskii Island. They saw before them a lone figure leaning against a tree. They recognized the figure as the poet Aleksandr Pushkin. The account continues:

> From time to time the man raised his right arm high over his head as if he were an impassioned orator. . . . His words occasionally lapsed into the quiet singing of a touching folk song which, especially in the stillness of the night,

> produced an unimaginable effect on the listener's soul. . . . At this moment a boat carrying a large number of people passed down the Neva River. The musicians on board had just finished singing a popular song. Pushkin listened attentively to its waning echoes and instinctively moved his leg as if to a Russian folk dance. Several chords resounded on a guitar and a gentle male voice began singing Pushkin's beautiful song, "The Black Shawl." No sooner had the first verse ended than Pushkin, whose face seemed more ashen than usual, uttered to himself, "Since that day I have not known peaceful nights." With that he extended to us a short *Bon soir, messieurs*! and disappeared into the dark, green forest.[31]

Pushkin had rented a villa for the summer at the nearby suburb of Novaia Derevnia and was probably on one of his evening strolls when he encountered these German tourists. He resented intrusions into his private space, and this occasion proved no exception. But the explanation for such withdrawn behavior goes far beyond any irritation of the moment. While Pushkin enjoyed considerable popularity in the public arena, he faced serious problems in his personal life, problems that had destroyed his sense of equanimity. Not only were his daily affairs subject to the whims of a despotic emperor and the surveillance of a powerful secret police but also his debts continued to mount; his production of poetry, for whatever reason, began to fall off; his journalistic efforts generated only short-term success; and his beautiful but vapid wife—she of the "soul made of lace"—nonchalantly danced away the evenings with little regard for the consequences of her coquetry, which led, seemingly by design, to the tragic encounter with Baron Georges d'Anthès on January 27, 1837. That day dawned cold and windy. At approximately five o'clock in the afternoon, Pushkin strode out onto a field of honor blanketed in snow as the light began to fade, faced his rival at a distance of twenty paces, calmly walked toward the barrier with pistol raised, and was felled suddenly by a shot to the abdomen—the ball passing through the abdominal cavity, shattering the sacrum, and lodging in the bone. He died two days later in excruciating pain. "The sun of our poetry has set!" Odoevskii lamented. "Pushkin has died, died in the flower of his years, in the middle of his great career!"[32] He was but thirty-seven years of age.

Prince Vladimir Fedorovich Odoevskii (1804–69), writer, philosopher, musician, critic, and longtime government official, was passionate about music, championed Beethoven's art in his criticism, and devoted one of his stories to the composer. The last representative of an ancient noble family, Odoevskii attended Moscow University's Blagorodnyi Pansion (Noble Boarding School) from 1816 to 1822. While at university he developed an abiding interest in literature, music, philosophy, and science. In 1826 he

Figure 2.2. Vladimir Odoevskii. Portrait by A. Pokrovskii. M. R. Cherkashina, *Aleksandr Nikolaevich Serov* (Moscow: Muzyka, 1985), 17.

married Ol'ga Stepanovna Lanskaia and moved to St. Petersburg to enter government service. There he instituted his famous "Saturdays" salon, which from 1826 to the beginning of 1850 provided a vibrant intellectual setting for the rendezvous of the city's musical and literary elite. The novelist Vladimir Sollogub, son-in-law of Mikhail Viel'gorskii, noted: "On this divan [in Odoevskii's study], Pushkin listened in awe to Zhukovskii; Countess Rostopchina read her latest poem to Lermontov; Gogol eavesdropped on polite conversations; Glinka queried Count Viel'gorskii on how to resolve a problem in counterpoint; Dargomyzhskii contemplated a new opera and mused about a librettist."[33] During these years Odoevskii also established himself as Russia's first serious music critic and participated in the founding of the Russian Musical Society and St. Petersburg Conservatory. He published many stories, including the novella on Beethoven discussed below, and assisted in mounting the St. Petersburg premiere of Beethoven's Ninth Symphony. Appointed to the Moscow Senate in 1862, he returned to his birthplace, where he assisted Nikolai Rubinshtein in establishing the Moscow Conservatory in 1866. Odoevskii died from encephalitis on February 27, 1869. Shortly before his death, in a state of delirium, he was heard engaging in "some sort of soliloquy on music."[34]

Odoevskii came to Beethoven early in life—the "easy sonatas" were the means "by which we all learned how to play the piano," he noted in 1838.[35] In time Beethoven rivaled Bach as the prince's favorite composer, symbolized by a portrait that Odoevskii prominently displayed in his salon. But it was only in the wake of his participation in the Mozart-Rossini polemic of the late 1820s that he finally was able to get "to the heart of this man," as he phrased it in an 1833 letter to the composer Aleksei Verstovskii.[36] By this he was referring to the spiritual dimension of certain composers' works, which brings forth a "range of thoughts and ideas that cannot be expressed in words."[37] He drew the following distinction: "Going out of the theater after a Rossini opera you unwittingly hum the good tunes, as you do after French vaudeville; after Mozart's music you do the same, but beyond that there remains a deep and indelible impression in the soul."[38] And so it was with Beethoven, though now the spiritual component reflected the emotional distance music had traveled since Mozart's time. As Faust, Odoevskii's fictionalized alter ego, utters in tortured tones:

> No one's music impresses me so much as Beethoven's. It seems to touch every string of the heart; it raises in it all the forgotten, most secret sufferings and gives them shape; Beethoven's joyful themes are even more horrible; in them someone seems to laugh—out of despair. It is a strange thing: any other music, particularly that of Haydn, creates a pleasant, soothing impression in me. The effect Beethoven's music has is much stronger, but it disturbs you: through its wonderful harmony you hear some inharmonious cry. You listen to a symphony of his, and you are enraptured—yet your soul languishes. I'm sure that Beethoven's music must have been a torment to the composer himself.[39]

In this way "Beethoven's symphonies are the second generation of Mozart's symphonies," thus completing the progression from Monteverdi through Bach and Mozart that marked a "new epoch" in the history of music associated with the rise of "dramatic music," music that has the power to move the soul. After hearing a performance of *Tannhaüser* in Berlin in 1857 and a variety of other works in Moscow in 1863, Odoevskii added Wagner's name to this pantheon of composers.[40]

A penchant for writing fanciful tales bordering on the fantastic earned Odoevskii the sobriquet of the Russian E. T. A. Hoffmann. His novella "Poslednyi kvartet Betkhovena" ("Beethoven's Last Quartet") appropriately portrays Beethoven as a Romantic hero. The first piece of *Betkhoveniana* in the Russian language, Anton Del'vig's almanac, *Severnye tsvety* (*Northern Flowers*), first published the story in 1831 and reissued it in 1844 in an anthology of Odoevskii's tales entitled *Russkie nochi* (*Russian Nights*). As early as April 29, 1827, just one month and three days after Beethoven's death, Odoevskii had confided in a letter to Mikhail Pogodin that he was considering writing a literary work on the composer but complained that he could not find relevant biographical material in the St. Petersburg bookshops. In the end, he chose not to focus on the biographical features of Beethoven's life and career but on what he called the composer's "musical character." This took the form of a portrait of "an enfeebled genius" who, though a proud man certain of his gifts, was tormented by the inability to hear his own music and the failure of those around him to appreciate his late-style compositions.

The novella takes place in Vienna in the spring of 1827 and begins with a group of music lovers attempting to perform Beethoven's most recently published quartet. They play a few bars and then throw down their bows in despair over the "absurdity of the piece." However, they pick them up and try again out of respect for the former glory of the great composer. Beethoven, accompanied by his last student, a young girl named Louise, enters the room on the pretext of renting the apartment, pretends to listen to the playing for a while, and then meekly leaves at the girl's behest. They return to his one-room flat on the fourth floor of an old building on the outskirts of the city. A lengthy monologue ensues that recounts again and again the twin themes of Beethoven's hearing malady and the fate of the misunderstood artist in society at large. "I even noticed that some of them seemed to smile while playing my quartet; that's a true sign that they never understood me," Beethoven sadly observes. Then he shares with Louise the outline of a new symphony that had occurred to him on their walk home. "It will immortalize my name," he declares. "In it I'll change all the laws of harmony; I'll find effects no one has suspected until now. I'll build it on a chromatic melody and use twenty kettledrums; into it I'll introduce hundreds of chimes tuned to various pitches. . . . Into the finale I'll introduce drumbeats and gunshots—and I will hear this symphony, Louise!" It would be similar to *Wellingtons Sieg*, "my best work to date." He then goes to the piano, bereft of even a single intact string, and silently plays the most complex fugues in five and six parts. He suddenly strikes the keys with his whole hand and stops. "Do you hear?" he asks Louise. "Here is a chord no one has dared to use until now. That's it! I shall combine all the tones of the chromatic scale in one chord and I shall prove to the pedants that this chord is correct." His critics do not understand that he is "forestalling time and acting in accordance with laws of nature as yet unnoticed by ordinary men and at times incomprehensible even to myself. Fools! They compare him to Michelangelo—but how did the creator of 'Moses' work? In anger, in rage, with powerful strokes of his hammer he hit the motionless marble and made it impart a living idea, hidden beneath the stone. This is how I work too! I do not understand cold rapture! I understand only the kind of rapture when the whole world turns into harmony for me, when every feeling, every thought sounds within me; when all the forces of nature become my instruments; when blood boils in my veins, my body shivers, and my hair stands on end." Suddenly "harmonious sounds" are heard from the house next door, and Beethoven throws open the window. "I hear!" he shouts. "This is Egmont's symphony—yes, I recognize it: here are the wild battle cries, here the storm of passions; they flare up, they seethe; here they are at their fullest—and everything is quiet again; only the vigil light is left gleaming, but it is dimming, dying, but not forever. . . . Trumpets sound again: they fill the entire world, and no one can silence them. . . ." Then, "crowds of people were coming and going at a splendid ball given by one of the ministers in Vienna. 'What a pity!' someone said. 'The theater conductor Beethoven has died, and they say that there is no money for his burial.' But the voice was lost in the crowd; everyone was listening attentively to the words of two diplomats discussing an argument that had taken place between some people at the court of a German prince."[41]

This remarkable tale does indeed appear "Hoffmanesque" in character. However, if the title is to be believed, the quartet being played at the outset of the story could not have been no. 16 in F, op. 135, Beethoven's true last quartet, which was published posthumously in September 1827. The last quartet published in Beethoven's lifetime was no. 12 in E-flat, op. 127 (June 1826). Technically, then, the title of the novella makes no sense—though in a work of fiction poetic license is perfectly legitimate. In this light, it might be more suitable to identify the quartet in question as no. 13 in B-flat, op. 130, with its astonishing *Grosse Fuge* finale. References to "formless outbursts," "painstaking pedantry of an inept counterpointist," "incomprehensible dissonances," and "leaps and trills impossible on any instrument" indicate that Odoevskii may have had the *Grosse Fuge* in mind when crafting the story.

It is difficult to determine Odoevskii's own estimation of Beethoven's late string quartets since he did not comment on them in his articles and reviews. Only in 1863 did he make passing reference to the "celebrated" quartets no. 14 in C-sharp minor, op. 131, and no. 15 in A minor, op. 132, "whose performances are rarely satisfactory even though they surpass all heretofore existing quartet compositions."[42] But this taciturnity fell by the wayside when it came to the symphonic literature. He singled out the Third Symphony (*Eroica*) for the "remarkable energy" of its instrumentation and described the Fifth, with its repetitive four-note motif that "resounds throughout the entire symphony," as one of Beethoven's "loftiest works."[43] But Odoevskii reserved his highest praise for the Ninth, which he characterized as the "most original, grandiloquent composition that has ever existed in the history of art."[44] He queried Verstovskii in 1834: "Have you seen the score of Beethoven's Ninth Symphony? It is a miracle; in it Beethoven has chartered a new course for music that no one could have imagined."[45] Given the significance he attached to the work, Odoevskii unsurprisingly assumed a leading role in staging its first performance in the Russian capital. Toward this end he collaborated with the poet Vasilii Zhukovskii in translating the vocal text for the use of the chorus and soloists, a task that took several nights of concentrated effort due to the difficulty of identifying Russian words that could retain the original meaning of Schiller's poem and Beethoven's interpolations while syllabically matching notations in the vocal score.[46] On the eve of the premiere, Odoevskii sought to prepare concertgoers for what promised to be a unique listening experience:

> Do not search in this symphony for the usual singing, usual brilliant phrases, usual chords; here everything is new: a new combination of instruments, a new joining of melodies; here the orchestra is not a collection of instruments where each plays its solo and then joins the others; here there is one instrument—*the orchestra itself*; here singing is not for one or another instrument but belongs to the entire orchestra and is possible only on this living, organic instrument. The effect this symphony produces is beyond words: initially it staggers one by its immensity, as if it were the vault of a gigantic Gothic edifice; but a moment later—this horror is transmuted into a quiet, reverential feeling; you look carefully—and with amazement notice that the walls of the temple from top to bottom are covered with filigree tracery, that this entire frightful mass is light, airy, full of life and grace.[47]

A final rehearsal took place at the Engel'gardt House on the morning of March 7, 1836. Mikhail Glinka was there in the company of Wilhelm von Lenz and a host of other cognoscenti from the music world. Lenz subsequently penned this moving reminiscence: "During the scherzo Glinka, holding his head in his hands, cried out, 'I can't deal with this. Oh! This is simply unbelievable!' And he began sobbing."[48] That evening at the Noble Assembly Hall, in a grand concert that opened with two movements from Haydn's *Die Jahreszeiten* (*The Seasons*), the combined forces of the St. Petersburg Philharmonic Society and the Imperial Court Chapel Choir under the direction of Johann Keller, assisted by the soloists Eizrikh, Evseev, Usol'stev, and Petrov, performed Beethoven's Symphony no. 9 in D minor (*Choral*), op. 125.[49] This marked a milestone in the initial phase of Russian Beethoven reception. In time the *Choral* symphony became a fixture in the standard concert repertoire, emerging as a powerful anthem—an *Ode to Freedom*—for those engaged in the political struggle against the tsarist regime.

Westernizers and Slavophiles

Intense philosophical debate over the character of Russia's past and future historical development shaped Russian intellectual history in the second quarter of the nineteenth century. The Westernizer-Slavophile controversy had been awaiting resolution since Peter the Great forcibly turned Russia onto a Western path in the early eighteenth century. While maintaining many aspects of the traditional Russian system—above all the central role of the state in the life of the nation—the emperor adopted such features of contemporary Western European society as a modernized central administrative apparatus; state-directed economic development; secular education with an emphasis on technical subjects; modern dress, manners, and social practices; and subordination of the church to the state. This abrupt shift in national direction led over time to a rift, particularly in educated society, between those who welcomed the changes and those who sought to turn back the hands of time. Nationalists in the Slavophile camp viewed Peter as an Antichrist despoiler who had violated all they considered sacred in Russian national culture. They sought to dismantle this alien system and return to the presumed golden days of the pre-Petrine era, when, so it was argued, tsar and people lived in harmony with one another and shared a unique historical destiny. The more forward-looking Westernizers embraced Peter as a modernizing visionary who had finally turned Russia onto its proper historical course. They hoped to accelerate the process of westernization and hasten the day of Russia's complete reintegration into the larger European world of which it was considered an integral part. This bifurcated view of culture and history, touching on the most fundamental aspects of national consciousness, was never satisfactorily resolved and remains to this day a cardinal feature of Russian intellectual life.

In the realm of music, Richard Taruskin argues persuasively that attempts to view the activities of the Russian music community through the lens of the Westernizer-Slavophile controversy are essentially meaningless, for the very act of composing a work of music or writing a piece of criticism signified that "one's basic acceptance of and commitment to the musical Europeanization of Russia has been made."[50] The same holds true for Russian Beethoven reception in the Nikolaevan era in that, by definition, it reflected a Western orientation.

The Slavophiles evinced little interest in classical music in general or Beethoven in particular. This is surprising in light of the connections between Slavophilism and German Romanticism, but the Slavophile focus on Russian exclusiveness, the spiritual domain of the Orthodox faith, the unique sociology of the countryside, and pre-Petrine patterns of historical development all militated against any interest in the adoption of Western cultural norms or practices. The Westernizers, on the other hand, began discussing Beethoven's music early on among themselves and in their published works. They tended to view Beethoven as a kind of patron saint for those critically thinking individuals who saw no virtue in Russian backwardness and sought by every means possible, including the ultimate tool of revolution, to advance the cause of westernization that Peter the Great had begun. Many of the most prominent radical publicists of the time were to be found in the Westernizer camp.

The letters, essays, and other writings of such key figures of the Slavophile movement as Sergei (1791–1859), Konstantin (1817–60), and Ivan (1823–86) Aksakov; Ivan (1806–56) and Petr (1808–56) Kireevskii; Aleksei Khomiakov (1804–60); and Iurii Samarin (1819–76) yield nothing of value on Beethoven. Only Ivan Aksakov offered an occasional comment on the composer and then in a generally disparaging manner. Writing to his parents from Kaluga in 1846 about the music-loving Unkovskii family residing in his district, Aksakov noted on May 4 that he had dined with the family the previous day and "was very pleased that they played for me Beethoven's [Opus 13] *Pathétique* Sonata." However, on June 8 he tepidly commented that the Unkovskii daughters "sing Schubert and play Beethoven but all of this leaves me completely cold." By June 15 he closed the door on these soirées by giving vent to his "exasperation" over the Unkovskiis' "pitiful praise for Beethoven and other [composers]."[51] Sergei Aksakov kept a piano at his Abramtsevo estate and wrote lengthy commentaries on new vaudeville productions for leading theater publications; Stepan Shevyrev (1806–64), a Slavophile in all but name, knew Franz Liszt in Rome and wrote knowledgeably about his pianistic skills following the 1842 Russian tour. All of the Slavophiles were highly educated thinkers and writers steeped in Western idealistic philosophy. Ivan Aksakov, Aleksei Khomiakov, and both Kireevskii brothers had traveled and lived abroad during formative stages in their careers. But all of this proved of no avail when it came to cultivating a love for classical music. The Slavophiles looked elsewhere for inspiration, above all deep into the soul of Mother Russia.[52]

The Westernizers were not disinterested in the Russian soul but were much more concerned about the overall health of the body politic. Their inclination to look to the West for answers to problems of endemic Russian backwardness brought them into contact with Western cultural values. This in time led them to Beethoven. Interest in the composer's music began with the establishment in Moscow of the N. V. Stankevich Circle (1833–37), which drew together such future luminaries of the Westernizer camp as Vissarion Belinskii, Aleksandr Herzen, Nikolai Ogarev, and Mikhail Bakunin, among others. While the members of the circle primarily occupied themselves with the analysis and dissemination of German idealistic philosophy, they also sought to popularize the music of Beethoven through discussion groups and private and public music making. The Viel'gorskii salon in St. Petersburg complemented these efforts. Mikhail Viel'gorskii dismissed the Slavophiles as hopeless romantics, writing at one point, "It is a pity that people with minds and hearts and talents have traveled a crooked path, imagining a so called *Slav* who is not Russian but some kind of abstract construct that in fact cannot exist. Is it possible to rewrite history and reproach the Great Peter for the deformed structure of the Russian state?"[53]

Much has been written about the radical Westernizers of the 1840s, the first true generation of the Russian revolutionary intelligentsia. They came from varied backgrounds: Bakunin and Ogarev from the landed gentry, Belinskii from the emerging professional middle class, and Herzen from an out-of-wedlock union between a noble landowner and a young German woman from Stuttgart. These men were bright, well educated, steeped in the nuances of German idealistic philosophy, and destined to exercise enormous influence on Russian intellectual and political history in the decades ahead. Their biographies are well-known. The intent here is to examine the ways in which these "Men of the Forties" responded to the music of Beethoven.

Vissarion Belinskii (1811–48), Russia's first and greatest literary critic, placed Beethoven in the company of Homer, Shakespeare, and Goethe as one of the "paramount geniuses of art" and described his symphonies as creating a feeling of "rapturous awe" in the listener. He considered Beethoven the "Shakespeare of music."[54] Belinskii expressed his deep emotional response to Beethoven's music in letters to Mikhail Bakunin. On September 21, 1837, he commented that a single phrase in an unidentified piano sonata had exerted "the same powerful impression on me" as the performance by the great Russian actor Pavel Mochalov in Shakespeare's *Hamlet.* On June 20, 1838, he wrote that he had just listened to a recital of the Opus 20 Septet "with tears of rapture" in his eyes and "had trembled from the sounds that so unexpectedly and powerfully accosted my soul."[55] Belinskii's most memorable commentary came in response to an article by the reactionary Faddei Bulgarin, editor of *Severnaia pchela* (*Northern Bee*), a mouthpiece for Nicholas I's doctrine of Official Nationality. Bulgarin had chastised the city fathers of Bonn, Beethoven's birthplace, for their decision to erect a statue in honor of the composer and remonstrated in part, "When a monument is erected for the nation, a father can point it out to his son and say with respect, 'There is an example for you!' But what can one do in pointing out a monument to Beethoven? Only sing a motif from *Fidelio* (which, between us, is a boring opera) or recall some symphony or another!!! . . . I am prepared to name Beethoven an unusual, striking individual, even a famous one, but I will not call him a *great man*. Greatness is not in notes but in the soul, in the mind!"[56]

Belinskii was incredulous and, in keeping with his reputation as "Vissarion Furioso," responded with a sarcasm that was peculiarly his own: "It is necessary to erect a monument to [Justinus] Kerner, a mediocre poet—and not erect one to the greatest musical genius in the world! 'Greatness is not in notes but in the soul, in the mind'! Apparently the feuilletonist has not heard that the soul and the mind are sometimes found in notes, as they are in marble, paint, and the printed word!"[57]

As teenagers, Aleksandr Herzen (1812–70) and Nikolai Ogarev (1813–77), first cousins and fast friends, ascended the Sparrow Hills overlooking Moscow and solemnly swore to devote the remainder of their lives to continuing the struggle the Decembrists had begun. This of course is a well-known story. Not so well known is Herzen's view that the mood engendered by the experience was so powerful that only music could bring comfort and rest: "There are moments when one fully feels the inadequacy of speech, when one wants to express oneself with harmony, with music. Only music, the incorporeal daughter of tangible sound, can calm the agitated soul and suffuse it with peace and tranquility."[58] That music formed an important part of Herzen's worldview is attested to by the frequency with which he mentions it in his writings. That the music of Beethoven did not particularly engage him is also evident from the literature. In his characterization of the discussions among the young Romantic idealists in the Stankevich Circle, for example, one finds the following subtly disparaging commentary: "The philosophy of music had a place in the foreground. Of course no one ever spoke of Rossini; to Mozart they were indulgent, though they did think him childish and poor. To make up for this they carried out philosophical investigations into every chord of Beethoven."[59] As a rule, Herzen referred to Beethoven in his writings only in passing and on one occasion dismissed him as passé: "To be continually calling up the dead, to be repeating Beethoven . . . is all very well, but it says nothing for creativeness. . . . Where is the new art, where is the artistic initiative?"[60] If Herzen attached significance to any single composer, it would appear to have been Mozart. By secularizing art through his operas, Mozart had "created an epoch, a revolution in thinking, like Goethe's *Faust*, like the year 1789. . . . Mozart is Mirabeau . . . the Dantons of the future are to be found in his music."[61] It is unclear what Herzen meant by these attributions, which most commentators would assign much more readily to Beethoven than Mozart. Whatever the case, Herzen apparently found some unstated aspect of Beethoven's music wanting.

This most assuredly was not the case with Ogarev. The future poet grew up listening to his father's serf orchestra and developed a deep passion for music that remained with him his entire life. "Study music. . . . Live in art," he wrote his wife in 1842. "This is a reliable refuge for everything."[62] Herzen observed that Ogarev "passionately loved and knew music, especially that of Beethoven, and became violently indignant if someone performed his music inaccurately or carelessly. 'Beethoven,' he said, 'must first be mastered before one dares to play him.'"[63] Ogarev was also friends with Bettina Brentano von Arnim, a famous figure in the German Romantic movement who had known Beethoven and written voluminous (if not very intelligible) letters about his music. "Yesterday Bettina visited us," Ogarev wrote on October 17, 1844, "and she talked so much that my head swam. . . . In her *Correspondence with Goethe* she has recorded her conversations with Beethoven, before whom I am ready to fall to my knees. A few of Beethoven's words are enough for developing an entire philosophy of music."[64] Most importantly, Ogarev was the first member of the intelligentsia to link Beethoven's music directly to the revolutionary struggle. His poem "Beethoven's Heroic Symphony" (1841) was dedicated to the Decembrist Aleksandr Odoevskii and alluded to the powerful Third Symphony, with its depiction of the life, death, resurrection, and apotheosis of the universal hero as a poetic device to recall the "valiant warriors" of 1825 who had "sought freedom for people and country." In the same year he declared, "When the French Revolution sang *La Marseillaise*, did not Goethe strike a blow against the Christian world with the first part of *Faust*? Did not [Beethoven's] 'Heroic Symphony' thunder with triumphal cries? Note how the great masters relate to society, how they spring from it and speak for it. . . . [If] art remains aloof from social questions and lives only for itself, it will be without content and become worthless."[65]

Thus did Ogarev apply Belinskii's dictum of the social utility of literature to the music of Beethoven. For better or worse, the composer was brought out of the cloister of the temple precinct and erected on a pedestal in the colonnaded space of the agora. Or as the historian Peter Lang has written in a different context, "Apollo put down his lyre, donned a red cap, and picked up a trumpet."[66]

Unlike Belinskii, Herzen, and Ogarev, Mikhail Bakunin (1814–76) was in fact a revolutionary. "Future historians of revolutionary activity in Russia and Spain, in Sweden and Italy, in France, Germany, and Poland," a commentator noted in 1906, "will find [Bakunin's] hand everywhere."[67] Though he did not associate Beethoven's music directly with the revolutionary cause, it moved him so deeply that one can conclude he heard the battle cry in it. The "Storm" movement of the Sixth Symphony in particular profoundly affected the future anarchist. On March 1, 1833, Bakunin took a distant cousin, Mariia Voevskaia, to hear the St. Petersburg premiere of the symphony. In a letter of March 5 to his sister Varvara, he reported that Beethoven was his favorite composer and described his response to the concert as follows: "What magnificent music! How beautifully it was performed! It seemed as if my spirit, shaking off the envelope of its corporeal prison, soared to the heavens. I was so happy. Those people whose ambition and other concerns render them incapable of apprehending these marvelous sounds, which appear to descend from the sky, appeared so pitiable to me. Beethoven's 'Storm' especially enraptured me. Afterwards my cousin told me that she had become terrified at the expression on my face when I listened to this music. It seemed as if I were ready to destroy the whole world."[68] [YOUTUBE VIDEO 5]

Writing to his sisters from Berlin on January 4, 1840, Bakunin characterized his response to a performance of two Beethoven quartets he had just heard by declaring: "Beethoven is unique: his music is a true exultation of the spirit; listening to him, one understands what constitutes the true life."[69] On Palm Sunday in 1849, Bakunin attended a performance of the Ninth Symphony at the Dresden opera house with none other than Richard Wagner on the podium. Afterward he rushed up to the composer and melodramatically declared, "Should all the music that had ever been written perish in the [coming] world conflagration, we must pledge ourselves to rescue this symphony, even at the peril of our lives."[70] In Dresden Bakunin and the French socialist Pierre Proudhon frequently met at the home of the pianist Adolph Reichel to listen to Beethoven and discuss Hegelian philosophy. Reichel became Bakunin's friend for life and played Beethoven for him whenever he was in Dresden. This occurred for the last time on June 14, 1876, just two weeks before Bakunin's death. Bakunin's final words to Reichel were, "Everything will pass and the world will perish, but the Ninth Symphony will remain forever."[71]

The death of Herzen in 1870, Bakunin in 1876, and Ogarev in 1877 brought to a definitive close the period in which the first generation of the revolutionary intelligentsia had emerged as a real force in the intellectual and political history of Russia. It is fitting that, on his deathbed, Bakunin should have recalled Beethoven's Ninth Symphony, which invokes so eloquently the brotherhood of all humanity in its mighty choral conclusion. This message can be seen as both a vision of Russia's future and a call to action for those who sought to carry on the struggle the first generation had begun.

Figure 2.3. Aleksandr Serov. Painting by Valentin Serov. M. R. Cherkashina, *Aleksandr Nikolaevich Serov* (Moscow: Muzyka, 1985), 129.

Serov Decodes the Ninth

In the second quarter of the nineteenth century, Beethoven confounded Russian critics. Like their counterparts in the West, critics in Russia found a great deal to praise in the early- and middle-style works but much to censure in the late-style compositions. Late Beethoven "goes beyond the boundaries of art," one commentator groused in 1844.[72] But by the middle of the century, Russian critics began making their peace with the late-period style, many in fact coming to find in it the highest expression of Beethoven's art; this became the prevailing mode of interpretation to the Revolution of 1917. No one proved more instrumental in this midcentury shift than the esteemed music critic A. N. Serov (1820–71). The following discussion explores the life, milieu, and writings of this seminal figure in Russian Beethoven reception.

Aleksandr Nikolaevich Serov was born in St. Petersburg on January 11, 1820, and grew up in a highly respected and economically comfortable family. His father, Nikolai Ivanovich Serov, blessed with a bright mind and quick wit, enjoyed public favor as an important official in the Finance Ministry. His mother, Anna Karlovna Serova (née Gablits), came from Jewish ancestry and displayed a fine intelligence, warm personality, and what acquaintances termed a noble heart. Though neither parent evinced particular interest in music or the arts, they recognized the importance of a cultural education for their son and thus took him regularly to the theater, provided him with instruction on the piano and cello, promoted his interest in drawing and painting, and fostered his early love for literature. By age four he could read his native tongue and by nine was adept in French and German. He proved gifted in school as well, entering the gymnasium at ten and graduating ten years later from St. Petersburg's prestigious School of Jurisprudence.

After receiving his law degree in 1840, Serov began his government service, and for the remainder of his life, he held a variety of positions in the tsarist administration. But his real love was music. Like so many of his colleagues in the music world, Serov earned steady income in the public sector so that he could pursue his true passion as composer and critic in private life. His operas have been forgotten, although *Judith* of 1862 and *Rogneda* of 1865 enjoyed considerable success at the time. His transcriptions also proved popular. Displaying his early love for Beethoven, in 1847 Serov transcribed the *Coriolan* Overture for piano, an arrangement that won favor with Franz Liszt, and in 1848 he orchestrated the *Pathétique* Sonata for a performance at the St. Petersburg University concerts the same year. Other transcriptions included piano renditions of a variety of Beethoven's chamber and orchestral works, portions of *Fidelio*, and all five parts of the *Missa solemnis*. But it was Serov's criticism that proved of lasting value.[73]

Serov began writing music criticism in 1851, and before his death he had published a wide range of articles and reviews in twenty-seven different journals. Together with his wife, Valentina Semenovna Serova (1846–1924), he established the journal *Muzyka i teatr* (*Music and Theater*) in 1867; though short-lived, it raised the level of discourse on music in the Russian capital. Serov also gained fame in the 1850s and 1860s for the series of public lectures he delivered on a variety of music topics. In recognition of his reputation as the leading Russian authority on Beethoven, the Russian Musical Society elected him as its representative for the 1870 Beethoven centenary celebrations in Vienna. Tragically this proved his last service to music. Serov died from a heart attack on January 20, 1871, having just turned fifty-one. At the moment of death, he was engaged in his favorite pastime, reading about music—in this case Emil Naumann's *Die Tonkunst in der Kulturgeschichte* (1869), the volume opened to a discussion of Mendelssohn.

Serov became without a doubt the recognized authority on the music of Beethoven in late imperial Russia, establishing the framework within which virtually all subsequent criticism proceeded. His analysis impacted criticism in the Soviet period as well. He began airing his views at a time when Russian Beethoven criticism, though still displaying an amateurish quality, was coming into its own as a recognized scholarly discipline. The great debate over the meaning of the late style dominated the discussion, and Serov wasted no time in joining the fray.

Aleksandr D. Ulybyshev (1794–1858), who had published a three-volume study of Mozart in 1843, which testified to his love for Classical form, balanced argument, and the elegantly shaped line, led one side of the debate. While Ulybyshev found some things to praise in late Beethoven—above all the deep feeling expressed in the Piano Sonata in C minor, op. 111—his overall view that the late style marked the "decline" of contemporary music should not come as a surprise. "Beethoven," he argued, "constantly searching for the new and the unusual, which did not always accord with the beautiful, more and more fell into capriciousness and dilettantism, at times completely drowning in them. The late quartets demonstrate this." As for Beethoven himself, Ulybyshev viewed the late style as exhibiting "marks of mental disorder," which signified the "pitiful and terrible ruin of a great man."[74]

Wilhelm F. von Lenz (1809–83) stood on the other side of the debate as the main advocate of the late style. His writings examined a variety of genres in Beethoven's oeuvre but focused on the thirty-two piano sonatas, which he analyzed in the "three styles" manner, set forth by François-Joseph Fétis in 1837 and by Anton Schindler in his biography of the composer in 1840.[75] For Lenz, Beethoven's late style stood as the "highest expression of individual genius." The late quartets in particular represented the "microcosm of Beethoven's soul." "This is genius—to create heaven out of dreams," he declared. Beethoven's late style "opens a door to the cosmos."[76] This is a highly romanticized view, and indeed, Lenz characterized Beethoven as the "navigator" of Romanticism. While there are those who would disagree with this interpretation, Lenz's positive evaluation of the late style helped balance the perspective of Ulybyshev and pointed in the direction of the analysis Serov felt compelled to bring before the public.

Serov went straight to the point in his critique of Ulybyshev's broadside against Beethoven: "Don't measure Beethoven by Mozartian standards," he declared. "Don't dress him up in a suit he has outgrown!"[77] Serov's concern was not with Mozart's music, which he certainly admired, especially the operas, but with Ulybyshev's dogmatic insistence that music had reached its apogee with Mozart. Serov could not fathom an argument that amounted in effect to a declaration that the development of art had reached a dead end. "Art reflects ideas and ideas change as the life of mankind changes; therefore art, which is the expression of life, must continuously change as life itself does."[78] And certainly this was so in Beethoven's progress as a composer. His music had changed over time "not only in regard to form" but in the "philosophical-poetic conception of his compositions. . . . In general, the character of Beethoven's art more and more freed itself from the laws of scholasticism."[79] And if, as Ulybyshev charged, Beethoven's late works conveyed contrary states of emotion, why should this disconcert the critic? "In nature there are azure skies and frightful dark clouds; there are luxuriant flowering valleys with gardens and brooks and huge bare cliffs washed by stormy seas; and in man there are the smiles of infants and the scalding tears of jealousy and despair. Why cannot art, why cannot music, the language of the soul that is as endless as nature herself, not be reflected after Haydn and Mozart in no less a remarkable person and striking poet as Beethoven!"[80]

In the end, Serov concluded that Ulybyshev could not accept modern music in general, whether it concerned the new directions that had been chartered by Beethoven or the varied sound worlds of Chopin, Schumann, Liszt, and Wagner. He closed his long epistle on the following categorical note: "For you, *nunc et in saecula*, there is only one sun on the musical horizon—Mozart; all other great musical geniuses gravitate only towards this one, lone star. We are richer: in our musical firmament shine several stars of the first magnitude, each becoming a dazzling sun as we approach its aura and enter the radiance of its light."[81]

Since Lenz was favorably disposed toward Beethoven, Serov needed to walk a finer line in critiquing his work. He certainly found some things to praise and commended Lenz in particular for such observations as the following:

- Beethoven was able to give full expression to all that humanity apprehends in life, nature, and the world because he was a composer of true genius, not simply a learned musician.
- Harmony, contrapuntalism, orchestration, and innovations in rhythm were key technical features of Beethoven's art.

- The *idea* for Beethoven was everything, technique serving only to allow it to triumph.
- The Beethovenian motif, as seen for example in the first four measures of the *Pastoral* Symphony, contains within itself the embryo of all rhythmic, harmonic, and melodic combinations that subsequently arise from it.[82]

But Serov found much more to criticize. He considered Lenz to be every bit the fanatic in regard to Beethoven as Ulybyshev had been in terms of Mozart; as an intellectual interested in raising the level of critical discourse, this understandably concerned him. Moreover, he found Lenz's work too discursive, much more like a two-volume *feuilleton* than a serious scholarly investigation, and he considered Lenz's treatment of the piano sonatas to be the "weakest part of the study."[83] The lack of musical examples—not even one—also troubled him, again particularly in regard to the piano sonatas, where the discussion in places was "completely unclear" in the absence of such visual guides.[84] But above all, Serov took issue with Lenz's conclusion that the *middle*-period works, as exemplified above all by the *Pastoral* Symphony and the Piano Sonata in A-flat, op. 26, represented Beethoven's "truly great style." Serov was dumbfounded. As successful as the Sixth Symphony was in depicting life in the countryside, it was "only a picture, an episode" in the vast human cosmos that Beethoven had crafted in the late symphonies—beginning with the Seventh; the late piano sonatas, commencing with Opus 101; the late quartets from Opus 95 forward; and the resplendent *Missa solemnis* choral work. How could these timeless compositions begin to compare with such lighter fare singled out by Lenz, inspired and charming as it was?[85] Serov therefore concluded that, despite "serious thoughts on practically every page," Lenz's skills were unequal to the task of interpreting music as complex and profound as that offered by Beethoven. His study could be recommended only to those readers interested in a "conversation occasioned by Beethoven." Those searching for a "serious critical account of Beethoven and his three styles" would have to look elsewhere.[86]

In his review of Lenz's study, Serov noted that an adequate analysis of the critic's commentary would require "writing a book against a book" and that a review was obviously not the place for such an undertaking. Serov never wrote such a book, but from the mid-1850s to the late-1860s, he did advance his argument in articles and lengthy essays on Beethoven's symphonic music. Simultaneously, and in large part as a result of his influence, the polemical nature of Beethoven criticism that had characterized discussion in the 1840s and 1850s began to give way to more detached reflection as a consensus gradually emerged in Russian music circles over the greatness of Beethoven, including his late-period style. The concert programs of the Imperial Russian Musical Society and the recently established St. Petersburg and Moscow Conservatories, founded in 1862 and 1866 respectively, pointed toward a more sophisticated, unified view of Beethoven's art, as did commentary in the provincial press during the 1870 Beethoven centenary celebrations. Even the members of the "Mighty Handful" circle of Russian nationalist composers, who argued with Serov over practically everything, had to agree with him when it came to Beethoven.[87]

What were Serov's attitudes toward Beethoven's music in general? More than anything, he considered the composer a masterful symphonist: "No one can measure up to Beethoven in the composition of symphonies," he declared. Beethoven's symphonies are "one of the immortal miracles of art on a par with the plays of Shakespeare and the poetry of Homer." Beethoven "is everything . . . he is the entire world." Moreover, he argued that the late style had set the course for modern music as a whole: "Musician and scholar alike can easily trace the origin of contemporary music in the late compositions of Beethoven. . . . All of the beloved devices of Mendelssohn and the so-called innovations of Chopin and Liszt or the orchestral and harmonic inventions of Berlioz and Wagner are already to be found in Beethoven's late style, and not just in embryonic form but in a mature state." As for Beethoven's only opera, Serov initially tended to agree with Mikhail Glinka, who had once declared that he "would not trade *Fidelio* for all the operas of Mozart!" But in time Serov cooled to the work because of its awkward libretto, dramaturgy, and staging requirements. This did not affect his estimation of the music, however, as indicated by the praise he lavished on the *Leonore 3* Overture in an 1861 article.[88]

Serov's view of Beethoven as a symphonist above all is borne out by his criticism, which commented only *inter alia* on the sonatas, quartets, concertos, and other genres. Of the symphonies, Serov devoted his fullest attention to the Ninth, writing three lengthy essays over a twelve-year period from 1856 to 1868 on its structure and meaning. Commentary on the other symphonies is scattered throughout these and other essays and also appears in various concert reviews. Serov clearly admired the unique qualities of each of the symphonies—no two ever sounding alike—yet in the end, the Ninth caught and held his attention, in part because of his interest in elucidating the late-period style. Herein lies his major contribution to Russian Beethoven criticism.

Serov's first foray into the world of the Ninth Symphony was occasioned by a performance of the work at the second concert of the St. Petersburg

Concert Society's 1856 season.[89] Serov noted how rare an opportunity it was for a St. Petersburg audience to hear the symphony performed.[90] Unhappily, most of those in attendance apparently had found the performance difficult to bear. They appeared "as if under some great weight and were only able to relax when Mendelssohn's music to *A Midsummer Night's Dream* began playing."[91] Why was it, Serov wondered, "that this score, spun out of such priceless philosophical and artistic treasures in both thought and form, is like a sealed book for most listeners?" The answer, he suggests, lay in the fact audiences were not yet attuned to the world of late Beethoven. In terms of the piano sonatas, which ones were played? The *Pathétique*; the Sonata in A-flat, op. 26; the *Moonlight*; and sometimes the *Appassionata*. But rarely, if ever, did one hear the late sonatas. "They are not known at all and for a long time will remain unknown." Which of the quartets were performed? Those from the Opus 18 set, the *Razumovsky* set, or the *Harp* Quartet. "But the E-flat Quartet is only the *tenth* quartet Beethoven composed out of seventeen altogether. What of the final seven? 'Well, they are very difficult and somehow wild, incomprehensible.'"[92] Still, Serov could take heart that some progress had been made in the ability of Russian audiences to appreciate Beethoven's mature music. It used to be that the Opus 59 quartets were never performed, being viewed as "monstrosities"; now "any worthwhile quartet considers it obligatory to play them alongside those of Haydn and Mozart." Similarly with the symphonies. Until a few years ago, the Seventh and Eighth were rarely performed, as if orchestras were "shy of them"; now they have "entered into the permanent repertoire of all concert societies."[93]

Nonetheless the Ninth Symphony "scares audiences." It is a "Leviathan," the work of a "half mad musician," an "inaccessible monstrosity." How, then, could it be rendered intelligible to music lovers? Serov argued that an understanding of the symphony could only be derived from a "full and close familiarity with all of Beethoven's orchestral compositions." Listeners should study the scores or play piano arrangements to "learn what kind of music this is and how musical ideas alternate, how they are connected to one another, how they are worked out." Through such a close reading, the organic growth of Beethoven's ideas would be revealed and the listener would be in a better position to understand how orchestral sounds "bloomed with unheard of beauty" in Beethoven's late-period style as he used a "new palate" of tones to create "unprecedented miracles of musical color." Each of the symphonies showed progress over the preceding one, if not in a straight mathematical line (the Fifth is "stronger" than the Sixth, the Seventh "more vigorous" than the Eighth), then in terms of the "widening and spreading out" of symphonic form. This is the key to understanding the late-period style in general and the Ninth Symphony in particular. And what was it about the Ninth that made it unique in Beethoven's oeuvre? It was of course the joining of words to orchestral music. This "universally supreme idea," Serov commented by way of conclusion, was one of Beethoven's "greatest poetic inventions," the product of "an entire lifetime" devoted to music.[94]

Serov's second essay appeared in 1864 in response to an article by the German philosopher David Friedrich Strauss.[95] Strauss began his article by recalling a performance of the Ninth Symphony that had taken place in Bonn during the August 1845 music festival staged to celebrate the unveiling of the Beethoven monument:

> During the performance the audience became fatigued trying to escape from the gloomy labyrinth of the Allegro, drew away from the demonic horse race of the Scherzo, and had almost begun to waste away under the sounds of the deep, emotional sorrow of the Adagio when all of a sudden Beethoven, as it were, poured cold water on everyone—with the unexpected entry of a baritone vocal recitative! The *Ode to Joy* could not alleviate this horror for the listeners; on the contrary, they fled in terror and returned to the safety of their homes. Such fear, such fright! And everyone had counted on having such a fine time![96]

Strauss did note that in the years following that horrific night ("the hair stood up in fright"), the public had gradually warmed to the symphony and in 1853 it was one of the most popular of Beethoven's symphonic works. But not for Strauss. He could never forget that "tubful of cold water."[97]

What caught Serov's eye, however, was not the anecdotal nature of this article but the argument it presented concerning the blending of orchestral and vocal music. While the French critics Chrétien Urhan and Hector Berlioz and German writers Friedrich Kanne and Franz Fröhlich saw no contradiction between the vocal and instrumental portions of the Ninth Symphony, Strauss asserted that there was an "ancient boundary" between the two forms of music that could not be crossed.[98] Should words and music be combined in a single work, instrumental music could only be used to introduce vocal music, either as a prelude that swells naturally into the vocal part—Strauss cited the instrumental passage in Handel's *Messiah* just before the first number, "Comfort ye my people," as an example—or as an overture to an opera; it would of course be absurd for vocal to introduce instrumental music. The problem with the Ninth Symphony lay in the fact three-plus movements of instrumental music preceded the vocal portion of the fourth movement; obviously "neither a prelude nor an overture can be longer than the [vocal] music it precedes." But more than this, the instrumental portion could not be considered an overture at all, because "there is nothing of the finale in it . . . [rather] it rushes towards the finale, seeks it out." Nor could it be considered a prelude, because "it does not pave the way to the vocal music but develops a range of ideas and emotional states independent of it, as indeed does the finale itself in regard to what has gone before." For these reasons, Strauss concluded that the *Ode to Joy* was a deus ex machina, serving only to violate canonic principles. It was as if a sculptor had fashioned a human figure out of white marble and glazed its head with color: "Such an artist would certainly be considered mad. Does not the character of the Ninth Symphony have the same effect?"[99]

Serov obviously did not take kindly to such a negative view of a work he knew and loved so deeply. Since he had not examined the choral finale in relation to the symphony as a whole in his 1856 essay, he now used Strauss's article as a point of departure for engaging in such an inquiry. Serov asserted at the outset that nowhere more than in the Ninth Symphony can one detect the "triumph of the organic" in Beethoven's creative process: "*The entire Ninth Symphony, from beginning to end*, from the first Allegro ma non troppo, un poco maestoso to the last outbursts of the prestissimo in the finale, *in all parts, in all the various combinations, is based on only one musical idea, on one theme*. This theme—the *Ode to Joy*—is the single *foundation of the entire* symphony."[100] This unity finds expression in both the ideas of the composition and the music itself. Poetically, the first three movements convey states of "eternal rejection, everlasting loss, and universal sorrow," until the triumphant finale announces the "radiant brotherhood of all mankind." Musically, Serov observed that Beethoven alludes to the theme of joy (*Freudenlied* in D) for short periods of time, in various guises, and always in a major key in the instrumental portions of the symphony: in the 2/4 rhythm of the first allegro; the dactylic 3/4 rhythm in D that pulsates in the scherzo; the folk dance in D in 3/4 time in the trio; and the short, consoling D major and G major melodies in 3/4 meter that appear episodically in the adagio. Serov uncovered another musical secret of the symphony's organic unity: the extended "search for joy" of the first three movements is grounded in the material of the fourth movement but, the adagio aside, in minor key tonality; this is, as it were, "a *reverse* image of the blinding brilliance of the finale."[101]

So much for the lack of relation of the parts to the whole, a brilliant riposte to Strauss's critique. As for Strauss's dictum regarding the "ancient boundary" between instrumental and vocal music, Serov asserted that, whether one considers a sonata, toccata, quartet, serenade, suite, or symphony, every melody is also vocal in character; every harmony is like a chorus of voices. "The difference [between instrumental and vocal music] is only one of register, velocity, force of delivery, and so on. In point of fact, in terms of emotional impact on the listener, there is *no* difference. Music without words, if it is expressive, can carry away the listener as *dramatically* as a dramatic *song* can, just as music with words can captivate a listener as charming *sound*, melody, or timbre of voice without the slightest relationship to words and their meaning."[102]

Serov also declared that Strauss's analogy of the glazed head on the marble statue was in fact the *correct* way to view the finale of the Ninth. Unlike the symphonies of Haydn and Mozart, which called for "something serious in the first Allegro, something elegantly languid in the Adagio, something sedately joyful or humorous in the Minuet or Scherzo, and a rondo-dessert finale," Beethoven's symphonies from the Third on were "all adorned with glazed heads" in the sense that the finales represented the culmination of the entire orchestral arguments. By turning the classical symphony upside down, Beethoven had "established a different sequence in symphonic order . . . [whereby] the last part is without doubt the *main* part and all the preceding parts are preparatory in nature."[103]

But of greatest importance, Beethoven had created a new symphonic form that called for commendation, not censure: "This courageous seafarer elected to sail farther in order to open up new lands, unlock an entire new world! . . . He took the symphony to its highest level but felt that, properly speaking, *all instrumental music*, its whole mass, is *gravitating* towards a union with human speech, with song. . . . The transitional epoch of instrumental music ended with Beethoven."[104] Appropriately, Serov gave Richard Wagner the final word: "The last *symphony has already been written.* In it Beethoven found it necessary to join instrumental music *with song, with human speech.* Columbus was only seeking a passage to the Orient and discovered half a world. Beethoven felt the need of a *vocal* finale for his instrumental work and in the process showed up the *bankruptcy* of symphonic music. In essence, his symphony *prepared* the ground for the musical drama."[105]

Serov's final essay, published in 1868, presented his longest and most thorough explication of the structure and meaning of the Ninth Symphony.[106] In the opening pages, he summarized his by now familiar views on the development of symphonic form up to Beethoven, the ways in which Beethoven had modified the emotional content of that form, and the new form he had created in the Ninth Symphony. In complete contradiction to Strauss, Serov now asserted that "the entire Ninth Symphony breaks down into two main parts: *a cantata with words* (the finale) and a colossal 'prelude' or 'overture' in three movements (the Allegro, the Scherzo, and the Adagio)." The finale represents "the goal of all mankind—the Elysium of brotherhood, the kingdom of joy," while the instrumental portions are designed to "*gradually lead* the listener" along the difficult path humanity must tread as it journeys toward that goal.[107]

Consistent with his view that the finale constituted the most important part of the symphony and the choral conclusion "holds the key to an understanding of the preceding movements," Serov began his exegesis with the *Ode to Joy*.[108] In a close analysis of Schiller's poem and the corresponding musical text, he elucidated the poem's message of humankind's dual desire for fellowship ("Brűder") and spiritual comfort ("Vater"), the first earthbound, the second to be found in the celestial sphere; examined how these twin aspirations were expressed musically in two separate themes, one a song ("Freude, schőner Gőtterfunken"), the other a chorale ("Seid umschlungen, Millionen!"); and discussed how Beethoven fused these two themes in the agape of the coda's extended double fugue.[109] As for the path along the way, Serov observed that, with episodic major key exceptions, the first two movements are grounded in minor key tonality, signaling that "mankind must pass through darkness on its way to the light." The first movement represents the "darkest pages of human history, pages of everlasting struggle, doubt, *oppression*, and *sorrow*, relieved only momentarily by flashes of joy and happiness appearing fleetingly like lightning." In the scherzo, all is motion, but this restive music expresses only "resigned discontent"—one hears no joy here. The trio of the scherzo, though in the key of D, provides no real relief either, only repeating ad nauseum a trivial dance that indicates how "far away lies Elysium."[110] However, with the adagio in B-flat, "the best of all Beethoven adagios," the character of the argument begins to change. The movement conveys the "moving, peaceful gentleness" of the "religious" music of the finale that is "beyond all confessional distinctions, expressing the pure evangelical spirit of love." In this way, Beethoven prepares the listener for the solution offered by the finale. In the orchestral introduction to the fourth movement itself, the thematic germs of the first three movements are "cast away" by the orchestral cello and double bass recitative, and the phrase "O Freunde, nicht diese Tőne! Sondern lasst uns angenehmere anstimmen und freudenvoller," sung by the baritone soloist, announces the choral conclusion to Beethoven's grand symphony.[111]

Serov ended his essay by remarking that the Ninth Symphony was "such a *well composed, deeply philosophical* and, by its colossal structure, *amazing musical* composition that it remains, after almost half a century . . . *a book for seven publishers*." He added that his interpretation of the symphony, especially in regard to the organic unity of the work as a whole, was unique in the Beethoven literature. Even the noted German critic A. B. Marx had missed the point when he wrote that "between the *finale* of this symphony and its preceding movements, *there is no internal connection or common* cause—the finale is the arbitrary appendage of a capricious genius." In point of fact, Serov argued, the interpretation he had offered "*can be confirmed in every instance by the notes of Beethoven's score.*"[112]

In broad outline, then, this is Serov's view of late Beethoven. His criticism can be judged as inspired and informed, original in design, and guided by the highest standards of textual analysis. There are occasional lapses into hyperbole—the declaration that all post-Beethovenian musical innovation derives from late-style formulations, for example, is not systematically examined or illustrated with musical examples—and the focus on a single thematic element in the Ninth Symphony is too categorical for some tastes. But overall Serov presents cogent arguments that deserve careful consideration.

There is no question that Serov's view of the organic unity of the Ninth Symphony represents his most important and original contribution to Beethoven scholarship. A. B. Marx was not alone in denying any relationship between the first three movements of the symphony and its unorthodox finale. In 1898 George Grove observed the same: "It must be said here that no connection need be looked for between the first three movements of the Choral Symphony and the 'Ode to Joy' which inspired the *Finale*." Indeed, in language similar to that penned by Strauss, Grove termed the joy theme a "*deus ex machina*."[113] Further, while Donald Tovey noted in 1935 that "the general scheme of the whole symphony" pointing toward the finale is "simple and satisfactory enough," he did not analyze the work in its entirety from the perspective of a central unifying idea.[114] Only with more recent scholarship has Serov's view of the Ninth Symphony as an organic whole come into its own as a widely adopted mode of analysis. Rudolph Réti offers an interpretation of the work that is remarkably similar in scope, if not approach, to that advanced by Serov.[115] Lionel Pike defends the use of thematic elements in musical analysis and provides a close reading of the Ninth Symphony that parallels Serov's interpretation.[116] More recently, Maynard Solomon used Serov's analytical model in his own investigation of the symphony.[117] Hans Mersmann, Walter Engelsmann, and Feritz Cassirer argue as well for the isolation of a single motif or thematic element in clarifying the interconnectedness of the symphony's four movements.[118] While there is no universal agreement on the validity of this approach—Heinrich Schenker, for one, offers strong opposition—Serov's analysis of the Ninth Symphony's organic unity, a singular approach until modern times, has clearly become a cardinal feature of contemporary scholarship.[119]

In the context of Russian music history, Serov's legacy is evident. His view of Beethoven's art regarding its place in the canon and the significance of the late style in setting the course of modern music in general strongly influenced the attitudes of key members of the Russian music community in the last decades of tsarist rule, especially those who comprised the "Mighty Handful" group of nationalist composers. Nikolai Rimsky-Korsakov (1844–87) commented in his memoirs that the circle traced music of interest to it "no further back than to Beethoven."[120] Aleksandr Borodin (1834–87) styled the Third Symphony the "ancestor of contemporary symphonic music."[121] César Cui (1835–1918) asserted that "all aspects of contemporary music are combined in Beethoven" and the late style "set the limits to which modern music can aspire."[122] And Vladimir Stasov (1824–1906), the spiritual leader of the group, wrote in 1901 that Beethoven had "imprinted his personality and powerful, extraordinary innovations on music of the entire succeeding century."[123] On the other hand, Petr Tchaikovsky (1840–93), the perennial outsider among Russian musicians, respected but did not love Beethoven. For him, Mozart was the one and only "musical Christ."[124] It is not inconsequential that he entitled what is known as his Fourth Orchestral Suite *Mozartiana*.

Serov's writings also had considerable impact on the subsequent course of Russian Beethoven criticism as it concerned the important question of the relationship between art and politics. Serov himself was not an ideologue, yet he inadvertently set the stage for more politically driven interpretations by being the first Russian music authority to associate the Beethovenian muse with the ideals of the French Revolution.[125] From this perspective, it was a short step to the depiction of Beethoven as a revolutionary, the prevailing view of the composer in late-imperial critical writing. In the wake of the Russian Revolution, the communist regime in turn co-opted this revisionist view, transforming Beethoven's music into a propaganda weapon in the arsenal of the one-party state and the composer himself into an icon of Soviet power. This appropriation of both man and music most certainly would not have found favor with Serov. He had devoted his entire career to analyzing the miraculous interior world of ideas and tones embedded in the scores of Beethoven's masterful creations. He pursued his craft diligently and with skill. The conversation he discovered in the course of his investigations was as rich and compelling as life itself. Now that voice had been stilled, set aimlessly adrift in the moribund vacuum of ideology and power. In such a sterile environment, the critical analysis that Serov had brought to his investigations no longer had a place.[126]

Still, Aleksandr Serov remains the preeminent figure in nineteenth-century Russian Beethoven criticism and is arguably one of the world's great interpreters of Beethoven's late-period style. It is intriguing to speculate on the conversations he must have had with his colleagues from the West at the Beethoven centenary celebrations in Vienna. Did any of them show interest in his view of the "organic" character of Beethoven's music or the miraculous process by which divinely inspired art emerged from only the germ of an idea? One does not know. But Serov's collected writings, consisting of articles, essays, and reviews ranging across a wide spectrum of musical history and thought, are available to the scholar and reveal a brilliant mind at work. They contain scholarship of enduring worth, as fresh and compelling today as when it was crafted a century and a half ago.[127]

Notes

1. M. Iu. Lermontov, *Sobranie sochinenii*, IV (Moscow-Leningrad: AN SSSR, 1959), 503–04.

2. Ibid., 483–84. The guards officer is undoubtedly Lermontov himself.

3. Iraklii Andronikov, "Muzykal'nost' Lermontova," *Sovetskaia muzyka*, XXVIII, 10 (October 1964): 52–58; B. Glovatskii, *Lermontov i muzyka* (Moscow-Leningrad: Muzyka, 1964), 17–32.

4. Mikhail Yurevich Lermontov, *A Hero of Our Time*, trans. Philip Longworth (New York: New American Library, 1962), 20, 24–25, 76–77, 106, 115.

5. Guy Daniels, *A Lermontov Reader* (New York: Macmillan, 1965), 74–75.

6. Ibid., 284, 286.

7. Lermontov, *Polnoe sobranie sochinenii*, IV, 61; Patrick Piggott, *The Life and Music of John Field, 1782–1837: Creator of the Nocturne* (Berkeley and Los Angeles: University of California Press, 1973), 52.

8. The title of the play, one of Russia's most beloved to this day, is variously translated as *Woe from Wit* (the most common translation), *The Trouble with Reason*, and *The Misfortune of Being Clever*. A passable English translation can be found in F. D. Reeve, ed. and trans., *An Anthology of Russian Plays*, I (New York: Random House, 1961), 85–163.

9. V. A. Natanson, "Fortepiannye proizvedeniia Betkhovena v russkom kontsertnom repertoire (pervaia polovina XIX steletiia)," in *Betkhoven: sbornik statei*, II, ed. N. L. Fishman (Moscow: Muzyka, 1972), 214–15. See also M. Alekseev, "Betkhoven v russkoi literature," in *Russkaia kniga o Betkhovene: k stoletiiu so dnia smerti kompozitora (1827–1927)*, ed. K. A. Kuznetsov (Moscow: Muzykal'nyi sector, 1927), 158. Karatygin was the first to play Chatskii in the St. Petersburg premiere of *Woe from Wit* (January 26, 1831); in other performances, he played the roles of Farmusov and Repetilov. "'Gore ot uma' v spravkakh," *Teatr i iskusstvo*, 4 (January 25, 1904): 91. He also appeared in the St. Petersburg premiere (April 19, 1836) of Nikolai Gogol's play *The Inspector General*. Henri Troyat, *Divided Soul: The Life of Gogol*, trans. Nancy Amphoux (New York: Minerva, 1975), 137–38.

10. A. Voinova, "Griboedov-muzykant," *Sovetskaia muzyka*, XLIII, 5 (May 1979): 94. The scores of two waltzes in E minor and A-flat by Griboedov were published in 1832 in the journal *Liricheskii al'bom*. V. Botsianovskii, "Novaia rukopis' 'Goria ot uma,'" *Teatr i iskusstvo*, 4 (January 25, 1904): 90. There is evidence that Griboedov also composed a mazurka and sonata for piano. Voinova, "Griboedov-muzykant," 90.

11. The Tehran riot is discussed in detail in Laurence Kelly, *Diplomacy and Murder in Tehran: Alexander Griboyedov and Imperial Russia's Mission to the Shah of Persia* (London: Tauris Parke, 2006).

12. Richard Stites, *Serfdom, Society, and the Arts: The Pleasure and the Power* (New Haven, CT: Yale University Press, 2005), 76.

13. Nikolay Stepanov, *Ivan Krylov* (New York: Twayne, 1973), 110.

14. Ilya Kutik and Andrew Wachtel, *From the Ends to the Beginning: A Bilingual Anthology of Russian Verse* (Evanston, IL: Northwestern University, 2001). The poem in its entirety is available online at "Krylov: Quartet," From the Ends to the Beginning, accessed March 8, 2022, http://max.mmlc.northwestern.edu/mdenner/Demo/texts/quartet.htm?.

15. I. Iampol'skii, *Krylov i muzyka, 1769–1969* (Moscow: Muzyka, 1970), 21.

16. Ibid., 38–39.

17. On Krylov's directorship of the Russian Section of the Russian National Library (1812–14), see Yury Pamfilov, ed., *The National Library of Russia, 1795–1995* (St. Petersburg: Liki Rossii, 1995), 21–22.

18. Troyat, *Divided Soul*, 14.

19. G. A. Tiumeneva, *Gogol' i muzyka* (Moscow: Muzyka, 1966), 47.

20. N. V. Gogol', *Sobranie sochinenii*, VI (Moscow: Khudozhestvennaia literatura, 1986), 22.

21. P. Neelov, "Gogol' v muzyke (k stoletiiu so dnia rozhdeniia)," *Muzykal'nyi truzhenik*, III, 6 (March 15, 1909): 1–2.

22. Letter of November 9, 1833, to Mikhail Maksimovich, in Troyat, *Divided Soul*, 100.

23. Nikolai Gogol, *Dead Souls*, trans. David Magarshack (Baltimore: Penguin, 1961), 231, 258–59.

24. Avrahm Yarmolinsky, ed., *The Poems, Prose and Plays of Alexander Pushkin* (New York: Random House, 1936), 11.

25. A. O. Smirnova-Rosset, *Zapiski, dnevnik, vospominaniia, pis'ma* (Moscow: Federatsiia, 1929), 176. Smirnova-Rosset also recalled an evening in St. Petersburg when Pushkin, in the company of Vladimir Odoevskii and Mikhail Viel'gorskii, peppered a young protégé of Beethoven (Girt) with questions about the composer—"about his deafness, his melancholy, his original ideas, about the blind girl for whom he [allegedly] composed the 'Moonlight Sonata.'" Alekseev, "Betkhoven v russkoi literature," 158.

26. A. Glumov, *Muzykal'nyi mir Pushkina* (Moscow-Leningrad: Gosudarstvennoe muzykal'noe izdatel'stvo, 1950), 140.

27. Aleksandr Pushkin, *Polnoe sobranie sochineniia*, 2nd ed., VIII (Moscow: AN SSSR. 1958), 19; X, 64, 71–72. At the end of October 1824, Pushkin wrote an acquaintance that, during his exile at the family estate of Mikhailovskoe, the daughters of his neighbor Praskovia Osipova in nearby Trigorskoe had played Rossini for him and he had copied the music into a notebook. This indicates that he had some knowledge of musical notation. Ibid., X, 103.

28. Vas. Iakovlev, *Pushkin i muzyka*, 2nd ed. (Moscow: Gosudarstvennoe muzykal'noe izdatel'stvo, 1957), 59.

29. O. D. Golubeva, *V. F. Odoevskii* (St. Petersburg: Rossiiskaia natsional'naia biblioteka, 1995), 54–55.

30. Boris Katz and Caryl Emerson, "Pushkin and Music," *The Pushkin Handbook*, ed. David M. Bethea (Madison: University of Wisconsin Press, 2005), 597.

31. Fr. Tiez, "Ein russicher Dichter: Petersburger Erinnerung aus dem Jahre 1833," *Familien-Journal*, 606 (1865), cited in I. Eiges, *Muzyka v zhizni i tvorchestve Pushkina* (Moscow: Muzgiz, 1937), 15. The line attributed to Pushkin's song, "And from that day I have not known peaceful [*spokoinykh*] nights," should read, "And from that day I have not known joyful [*veselykh*] nights." Contrary to the account, the line does not appear in the first verse of the poem but in the penultimate couplet. Pushkin, *Polnoe sochinenie sochineniia*, II (1956), 17.

32. Odoevskii's necrologue appeared in the literary supplement to the journal *Russkii invalid* on January 30, 1837. T. J. Binyon, *Pushkin: A Biography* (New York: Alfred A. Knopf, 2003), 608–9. The "soul made of lace" attribution comes from Suzanne Massie, *Land of the Firebird:*

The Beauty of Old Russia (New York: Simon and Schuster, 1980), 234; the phrase is more properly rendered in its French iteration (*ame de dentelles*) as used in Serena Vitale, *Pushkin's Button*, trans. Ann Goldstein and Jon Rothschild (London: Fourth Estate, 1999), 54.

33. A. Sollogub, "Vospominanie o kniaze V. F. Odoevskom," in V. F. Odoevskii, *Poslednii kvartet Betkhovena: povesti, rasskazy, ocherki*, ed. V. Murav'ev (Moscow: Moskovskii rabochii, 1982), 342–43. Sollogub's description calls to mind the quip by the Viennese *salonnière* Berta Zuckerkandl, "On my divan Austria comes alive." Eric R. Kandel, *The Age of Insight: The Quest to Understand the Unconscious in Art, Mind, and Brain, from Vienna 1900 to the Present* (New York: Random House, 2012), 29.

34. Reminiscence by M. P. Pogodin, as cited in A. P. Piatkovskii, "Kniaz' V. F. Odoevskii: literaturno-biograficheskii ocherk v sviazi s lichnymi vospominaniiami," *Istoricheskii vestnik*, I, 4 (April 1880): 712.

35. V. F. Odoevskii, *Muzykal'no-literaturnoe nasledie* (Moscow: Gosudarstvennoe muzykal'noe izdatel'stvo, 1956), 156.

36. Ibid., 496.

37. Z. Savelova, "Betkhoven i Odoevskii," *Muzykal'noe obrazovanie*, 1–2 (January–March 1927): 115.

38. Neil Cornwell, *The Life, Times and Milieu of V. F. Odoevsky, 1804–1869* (London: Athlone, 1986), 147.

39. V. F. Odoevsky, *Russian Nights*, trans. Olga Koshansky-Olienikov and Robert E. Matlaw (New York: E. P. Dutton, 1965), 130–31.

40. G. B. Bernandt, *V. F. Odoevskii i Betkhoven: stranitsi iz istorii russkoi betkhoveniany* (Moscow: Sovetskii kompozitor, 1971), 48; G. B. Bernandt, "V. F. Odoevskii-muzykant," in Odoevskii, *Muzykal'no-literaturnoe nasledie*, 64. On Odoevskii and Wagner, see Odoevskii, *Dnevnik*, 28–31, 89–92, 250–52; and Rosamund Bartlett, *Wagner and Russia* (Cambridge: Cambridge University Press, 1995), 26–27, 32–33.

41. Odoevsky, *Russian Nights*, 123–29. For an alternate translation, see Carol Bailey Hughes, "'Beethoven's Last Quartet': A 'Hoffmannesque' Tale by Russian Critic Vladimir Fedorovich Odoevskii (1804–1869)," *Beethoven Newsletter*, IV, 2 (Summer 1989): 27–29.

42. *Nashe vremia*, 1863, no. 51 (March 8), in Odoevskii, *Muzykal'no-literaturnoe nasledie*, 648–49.

43. Bernandt, "Iz istorii russkoi betkhoveniany," 57; Odoevskii, *Muzykal'no-literaturnoe nasledie*, 219.

44. Odoevskii, *Muzykal'no-literaturnoe nasledie*, 113.

45. Ibid., 497.

46. For the translation of the choral parts, see *Nadstrochnyi perevod khora k 9-oi simfonii Betgovena na Odu Shillerea: k radosti (an die freude)* (St. Petersburg: St. Peterburgskoe filarmonicheskoe obshchestvo, 1836).

47. Odoevskii, *Muzykal'no-literaturnoe nasledie*, 115, Odoevskii's italics.

48. A. A. Gozenpud, *Dom Engel'gardta: iz istorii kontsertnoi zhizni Peterburga pervoi poloviny XIX veka* (St. Petersburg: Sovetskii kompozitor, 1992), 49. For the original citation, see Wilhelm von Lenz, *Beethoven et ses trois styles*, II (St. Petersburg: Bernard, 1852), 189.

49. Boris Berezovskii, *Filarmonicheskoe obshchestvo Sankt-Peterburga: istoriia sovremennost'* (St. Petersburg: Kul't Inform, 2002), 186.

50. Richard Taruskin, *On Russian Music* (Berkeley: University of California Press, 2009), 36.

51. Ivan S. Aksakov, *Pis'ma k rodnym, 1844–1849* (Moscow: Nauka, 1988), 243, 266, 269. The follow-up volume in this series, *Pis'ma k rodnym, 1849–1856* (Moscow: Nauka, 1994) contains no references to Beethoven.

52. N. Arsen'ev, "A. S. Khomiakov (ego lichnost' i mirovozrenie)," in A. Khomiakov, *Izbrannye sochineniia* (New York: Chekhov, 1953), 3–43; Abbott Gleason, *European and Muscovite: Ivan Kireevsky and the Origins of Slavophilism* (Cambridge, MA: Harvard University Press, 1972); V. Korel'nikov, "Literator-filosof," in I. V. Kireevskii, *Izbrannye stat'i* (Moscow: Sovremennik, 1984), 5–28; A. Pypin, "Kharakteristiki literaturnykh mnenii ot dvadtsatykh do piatidesiatykh godov: istoricheskii ocherk/Slavianofil'stvo," *Vestnik Evropy*, VII, 6 (June 1872): 47–97; Nicholas Riasanovsky, *Russia and the West in the Teaching of the Slavophiles* (Cambridge, MA: Harvard University Press, 1952); V. V. Stasov, *Izbrannye sochineniia*, III (Moscow: Iskusstvo, 1952), 420–21; Stites, *Serfdom, Society, and the Arts*, 137; N. I. Tsimbaev, "Iu. F. Samarin," in Iu. F. Samarin, *Izbrannye proizvedeniia* (Moscow: Terra, 1997), 5–14.

53. T. Shcherbakova, *Mikhail i Matvei Viel'gorskie* (Moscow: Muzyka, 1990), 27–28, Viel'gorskii's italics. On the Stankevich Circle, see Edward James Brown, *Stankevich and His Moscow Circle* (Stanford, CA: Stanford University Press, 1966); Edmund Kostka, "At the Roots of Russian Westernism: N. V. Stankevich and His Circle," *Slavic and East-European Studies*, VI, 3/4 (Autumn–Winter 1961): 158–76.

54. V. G. Belinskii, *Polnoe sobranie sochinenii*, II (Moscow: AN SSSR, 1953), 355; III (Moscow: AN SSSR, 1953), 432; V (Moscow: AN SSSR, 1954), 244.

55. V. G. Belinskii, *Polnoe sobranie sochinenii*, XI (Moscow: AN SSSR, 1956), 182; V. G. Belinskii *Izbrannye pis'ma*, I (Moscow: Khudozhestvennaia literatura, 1951), 128.

56. F. Bulgarin, "Fel'eton," *Severnaia pchela*, 219 (1845), Bulgarin's italics. See also *Severnaia pchela*, 81 (1846).

57. V. G. Belinskii, *Polnoe sobranie sochinenii*, IX (Moscow: AN SSSR, 1955), 377.

58. G. B. Bernandt, "Gertsen i muzyka," *Sovetskaia muzyka*, XXVI, 5 (May 1962): 78.

59. Alexander Herzen, *My Past and Thoughts*, trans. Constance Garnett (New York: Alfred A. Knopf, 1968), 400.

60. Ibid., 1686.

61. Bernandt, "Gersten i muzyka," 80.

62. N. I. Voronina, *Ogarev i muzyka* (Saransk, Russia: Mordovskoe knizhnoe izdatel'stvo, 1981), 27.

63. G. G. Elizavetina, ed., *N. P. Ogarev v vospominaniiakh sovremennikov* (Moscow: Khudozhestvennaia literatura, 1989), 223.

64. Letter of October 17, 1844, from Ogarev to N. Kh. Ketcher and V. G. Belinskii, cited in Voronina, *Ogarev i muzyka*, 63.

65. N. P. Ogarev, *Izbrannye proizvedeniia*, I (Moscow: Khudozhestvennaia literatura, 1956), 416; II (Moscow: Khudozhestvennaia literatura, 1956), 441.

66. P. Lang, "French Opera and the Spirit of Revolution," in *Irrationalism in the Eighteenth Century*, ed. H. Pagliaro (Cleveland, OH: Press of Case Western Reserve University, 1972), 108.

67. M. A. Bakunin, "Bakunin i Gertsen (k istorii russkogo dvizheniia)," in *Pis'ma M. A. Bakunina k A. I. Gertsenu i N. P. Ogarevu* (The Hague: Mouton, 1968 reprint), 321.

68. Mikhail A. Bakunin, *Sobranie sochinenii i pisem, 1828–1876*, I (Moscow: Vsesoiuzhnoe obshchestvo polit-katorzhan i ssyl'no-poselentsev, 1934), 84. E. H. Carr erroneously attributes this story to the premiere of the Ninth Symphony, which did not take place until March 7, 1836. E. H. Carr, *Michael Bakunin* (New York: Vintage, 1968 reprint), 321. Date of premiere of the Sixth Symphony is cited in Berezovskii, *Filarmonicheskoe obshchestvo*, 186.

69. Bakunin, *Sobranie sochinenii i pisem, 1828–1876*, II (Moscow: Vsesoiuzhnoe obshchestvo polit-katorzhan i ssyl'no-poselentsev, 1935), 282.

70. Carr, *Michael Bakunin*, 196. Shortly after this performance, the Revolution of 1848 broke out in Dresden, and the opera house burned to the ground. A guard watching the conflagration

turned to Wagner and quipped, "Well, Mr. Conductor, joy's beautiful divine spark has made a blaze." David Benjamin Levy, *Beethoven: The Ninth Symphony*, rev. ed. (New Haven, CT: Yale University Press, 2005), 165.

71. Carr, *Michael Bakunin*, 506.

72. T. N. Livanova, "Betkhoven i russkaia muzykal'naia kritika XIX veka," in *Betkhoven: sbornik statei*, ed. N. L. Fishman, II (Moscow: Muzyka, 1972), 175.

73. The following autograph transcriptions, dating from 1845–57, are housed in F. 693, op. 1 of the Manuscript Division of the Russian National Library in St. Petersburg: Septet, op. 20; Third Symphony, op. 55 (movements 1–3); *Coriolan* Overture, op. 62; *Fidelio*, op. 72 (duet, no. 8, and finale); Piano Sonata in A-flat, op. 110 (Fugue); Piano Sonata in C Minor, op. 111; *Missa solemnis*, op. 123; Overture in C (*Die Weihe des Hauses*), op. 124; Ninth Symphony, op. 125 (Scherzo); String Quartet in E-flat, op. 127. All of the transcriptions are for two pianos, four-hand, except for that of the Scherzo of the Ninth Symphony, which calls for four pianos, eight hand.

74. A. D. Ulybyshev, *Novaia biografiia Motsarta*, II (Moscow: Iurgenson, 1843; reprint 1891), 131–32; and *Novaia biografiia Motsarta*, III (Moscow: Iurgenson, 1843; reprint 1891), in Livanova, "Betkhoven i russkaia muzykal'naia kritika," 178. See also Ulybyshev, *Beethoven, ses critiques et ses glossateurs* (Leipzig: Brockhaus/Gavelot, 1857). For extended analysis, see Kristen M. Knittel, "Divining the Enigmas of the Sphinx: Alexander Oulibicheff as a Critic of Beethoven's Late Style," *Beethoven Newsletter*, VIII, 2 (Summer 1993): 34–37.

75. For an analysis of the tripartite system as originally conceived compared to the way we understand it today, especially in regard to the third-period style, see Kristen M. Knittel, "Imitation, Individuality, and Illness: Behind Beethoven's 'Three Styles,'" *Beethoven Forum*, IV (1995): 17–36.

76. W. von Lenz, *Beethoven et ses trois styles: Analyses des sonates de piano suivies de l'essai d'un catalogue critique, chronologique et anecdogique de l'ouvre de Beethoven*, in Livanova, "Betkhoven i russkaia muzykal'naia kritika," 183, 189. See also Lenz, *Beethoven: Eine Kunst-Studie*, 5 vols. (Kassel, Germany: E. Balde, 1855–60). Joseph Kerman offers a critical yet sympathetic view of Lenz in his introductory remarks in Wilhelm von Lenz, *Beethoven et ses trois styles* (New York: De Capo, 1980), v–xiv.

77. A. N. Serov, "Pis'mo k A. D. Ulybyshevu po sluchaiiu tolkov o Motsarte i Betkhovene," *Stat'i o muzyke*, I (Moscow: Muzyka, 1984), 255.

78. Ibid., 198.

79. Ibid., 210, 216.

80. Ibid., 218.

81. Ibid., 265.

82. A. N. Serov, "Betkhoven i tri ego stilia. Kniga V. F. Lentsa," *Stat'i o muzyke*, I (Moscow: Muzyka, 1984), 169.

83. Ibid., 141, 165.

84. Ibid., 148.

85. Ibid., 172.

86. Ibid., 179.

87. Livanova, "Bethoven i russkaia muzykal'naia kritika," 190.

88. Ibid., 190, 197. For the article on the *Leonore 3* Overture, see A. N. Serov, "Tematism (Thematismus) uvertiury 'Leonore': etiud o Betkhovene," *Stat'i o muzyke*, V (Moscow: Muzyka, 1989), 177–92.

89. A. N. Serov, "Deviataia simfoniia Betkhovena," *Stat'i o muzyke*, II-A (Moscow: Gosudarstvennoe muzykal'noe izdatel'stvo, 1985), 253–61.

90. The St. Petersburg premiere of the Ninth Symphony occurred on March 7, 1836. A second performance on March 4, 1844, was the last before the concert of 1856. E. Al'brekht, ed., *Obshchii obzor deiatel'nosti Vysochaishe utverzhdennogo S. Peterburgskogo filarmonicheskogo obshchestva*, II (St. Petersburg: Goppe, 1884), 13.

91. Serov, "Deviataia simfoniia Betkhovena," *Stat'i o muzyke*, II-A, 254.

92. Ibid., 254–55, Serov's italics. By referring to seventeen quartets, Serov is including the *Grosse Fuge*, op. 133, the original finale of Opus 130.

93. Ibid., 255. The Seventh Symphony premiered in St. Petersburg on March 6, 1840; the Eighth on February 24, 1849. E. Al'brekht, *Obshchii obzor*, 12, 15.

94. Serov, "Deviataia simfoniia Betkhovena," *Stat'i o muzyke*, II-A, 254–59.

95. A. N. Serov, "Zametka sovremennogo znamenitogo myslitelia (iz nemuzykantov) o deviatoi simfonii Betkhovena," *Stat'i o muzyke*, VI (Moscow: Muzyka, 1990), 212–25. The article by Strauss, entitled "Beethovens Neunte Simphonie und sein Verehrer," had appeared in the *Allgemeine Zeitung* in 1853 and reprinted in a collection of Strauss's writings in 1862. This publication came to Serov's notice and prompted the response examined herein. The portrait of Strauss that follows is a far cry from that of the notorious author of *The Life of Jesus, Critically Examined*, 2 vols. (1835–36) and *New Faith* (1872). See Peter Gay, *Schnitzler's Century: The Making of Middle Class Culture, 1815–1914* (New York: W. W. Norton, 2002), 160–61.

96. Serov, "Zametka," *Stat'i o muzyke*, VI, 213. The performance was conducted by Franz Liszt, who also conducted the Fifth Symphony and performed in the *Emperor* Concerto.

97. Ibid., 213.

98. Robin Wallace, *Beethoven's Critics: Aesthetic Dilemmas and Resolutions during the Composer's Lifetime* (Cambridge: Cambridge University Press, 1986), 74–77, 121–23.

99. Serov, "Zametka," *Stat'i o muzyke*, VI, 214–16. Gustav Mahler once told a friend that setting a perfect poem to music would be "as if a sculptor chiseled a statue from marble and a painter came along and colored it." Jonathan Carr, *Mahler: A Biography* (New York: Overlook, 1997), 128.

100. Serov, "Zametka," *Stat'i o muzyke*, VI, 217, Serov's italics.

101. Ibid., 219–20, Serov's italics. Because Serov did not provide musical examples, it is difficult to know precisely where some of the instrumental portions he references appear in the score.

102. Ibid., 221, Serov's italics. Serov observed that Russians were in love with Italian opera even though they did not understand a word of the language.

103. Ibid., 219, 224, Serov's italics.

104. Ibid., 223, 224–25, Serov's italics.

105. Ibid., 225, Wagner's italics. For an elaboration of Wagner's views, see Richard Wagner, *Pilgrimage to Beethoven and Other Essays*, trans. William Ashton Ellis (Lincoln: University of Nebraska Press, 1994), 21–45. For commentary, see William Meredith, "Wagner's Beethoven: A Posthumous *Pilgrimage to Beethoven* in 1840," *Beethoven Newsletter*, VIII, 2 (Summer 1993): 46–53.

106. A. N. Serov, "Deviataia simfoniia Betkhovena, ee sklad i smysl," *Izbrannye stat'i*, I (Moscow-Leningrad: Gosudarstvennoe muzykal'noe izdatel'stvo, 1950), 425–34. Serov's debt to Wagner in the interpretation that follows is not acknowledged. See Maynard Solomon, "The Ninth Symphony: A Search for Order," in *Beethoven Essays* (Cambridge, MA: Harvard University Press, 1988), 14.

107. Serov, "Deviataia simfoniia Betkhovena," 425–29.

108. Ibid., 429.

109. Ibid., 429–32. *Agape* is a nice choice of word, as is this description by Robert Winter: "In a single bold stroke Beethoven has synthesized the totality of human experience: joy and

awe, celebration and worship, faith and hope." Robert Winter, "A Close Reading," *Ludwig van Beethoven: Symphony No. 9*, computer software (Santa Monica, CA: Voyager, 1991), card 325.

110. At this point in the discussion, Serov noted how remarkable it was that not only were the major key episodic passages in the first allegro and scherzo taken "note for note" from the "hymn theme" of the finale but also the very movements themselves were "constructed *in the same way*," the major key tonality of the finale only being changed into minor key equivalents. ("This can be demonstrated only in reference to the score, but there it is graphic and beyond dispute.") All of this testified to the "*unity* of the idea" around which Beethoven built his symphony. Serov, "Deviataia simfoniia Betkhovena," 433, Serov's italics.

111. Serov, "Deviataia simfoniia Betkhovena," 432–34.

112. Ibid., 434, Serov's italics and paraphrase of Marx. For a fuller discussion of Marx, see Wallace, *Beethoven's Critics*, 45–64. Serov's reference to "a book for seven publishers" was one of his favorite expressions, which he employed when referring to a composition that, because of its meritorious character, warranted universal publication.

113. George Grove, *Beethoven and His Nine Symphonies*, 3rd ed. (New York: Dover, 1898; reprint 1962), 354, 373.

114. Donald Francis Tovey, *Essays in Musical Analysis*, II (London: Oxford University Press, 1935), 35.

115. Réti begins his analysis with the first allegro and systematically moves forward from there. Rudolph Réti, *The Thematic Process in Music* (New York: Macmillan, 1951), 11–30. Réti does not acknowledge Serov's groundbreaking work and in fact asserts that "to the best of my knowledge this book represents the first attempt to analyze the particular type of compositional process described in the following pages" (p. vii). For extended discussion on Réti's mode of analysis, see Scott Burnham, *Beethoven Hero* (Princeton, NJ: Princeton University Press, 1995), 102–10.

116. Lionel Pike, *Beethoven, Sibelius, and the "Profound Logic": Studies in Symphonic Analysis* (London: Athlone, 1978), 4–12, 59–78.

117. Solomon, *Beethoven Essays*, 14–18. See also Cook, *Symphony No. 9*, 81–82.

118. Maynard Solomon, *Beethoven*, 2nd rev. ed. (New York: Schirmer, 1998), 407.

119. Heinrich Schenker, *Beethovens neunte Sinfonie* (Vienna: Universal, 1912), in Cook, *Symphony No. 9*, 83–86. For extended discussion on Schenker's mode of analysis, see Burnham, *Beethoven Hero*, 89–102.

120. Nikolay Andreyevich Rimsky-Korsakoff, *My Musical Life*, trans. Judah A. Joffe (New York: Tudor, 1935), 242.

121. Livanova, "Betkhoven i russkaia muzykal'naia kritia," 198. See also Iu. Kremlev, *Russkaia mysl' o muyyke: ocherk istorii russkoi muzykal'noi kritiki i estetiki v XIX veke*, II (Leningrad: Gosudarstvennoe muzykal'noe izdatel'stvo, 1958), 260.

122. Ts. A. Kiui, "Neskol'ko slov o Betkhovene po povodu ego stoletnego iubileia," *Izbrannye stat'i* (Moscow: Gosudarstvennoe muzykal'noe izdatel'stvo, 1952), 180. See also Kremlev, *Russkaia mysl' o muzyke*, II, 220–26.

123. V. V. Stasov, "Iskusstvo XIX veka," *Stat'i o muzyke*, V-B (Moscow: Muzyka, 1980), 9. See also Kremlev, *Russkaia mysl' o muzyke*, II, 139–40.

124. David Brown, *Tchaikovsky: The Final Years, 1885–1893* (New York: W. W. Norton, 1991), 95. See also Kremlev, *Russkaia mysl' o muzyke*, II, 432–35.

125. Livanova, "Betkhoven i russkaia muzykal'naia kritika," 192–96; Serov, "Deviataia simfoniia Betkhovena," *Izbrannye stat'i*, I, 429.

126. To be sure, Russian Beethoven scholarship in the late-Soviet period became more professionally oriented and, for the most part, free of ideological bias. See especially N. L.

Fishman, ed., *Betkhoven: sbornik statei*, 2 vols. (Moscow: Muzyka, 1971–72); and N. L. Fishman, ed., *Etiudy i ocherki po betkhoveniane* (Moscow: Muzyka, 1982).

127. A. N. Serov, *Izbrannye stat'i*, 2 vols. (Moscow: Gosudarstvennoe muzykal'noe izdatel'stvo, 1950); A. N. Serov, *Stat'i o muzyke*, 6 vols. (Moscow: Muzyka, 1984–90). There is also a German translation of selections from *Izbrannye stat'i*, I: Alexander Serow, *Aufsatz zur Musikgeschichte* (Berlin: Aufbau, 1955). The volume includes the 1868 essay on the Ninth Symphony.

3

EVALUATING BEETHOVEN

From *Freude* to *Freiheit*

BEETHOVEN'S RECEPTION IN RUSSIA CAME FULLY INTO ITS own in the second half of the nineteenth century. The great novelists of the era and the composers and critics at the turn of the century offered a broad range of opinion on the character and meaning of Beethoven's music. The critics in particular heard a call to revolution in the composer's more dramatic works. Such a highly charged perspective represented a sea change in the reception of the master's music in late imperial Russia and indicated the degree to which Russian Beethoven reception had become politicized in the context of the ongoing struggle against tsarist rule.

The View from On High

Russia's literary giants all recognized and valued Beethoven's art. Ivan Turgenev (1818–83) enjoyed a lifelong love affair with music—aided no doubt by his equally long infatuation with the Spanish prima donna Pauline García-Viardot—and counted Beethoven among his favorite composers. The Piano Sonata no. 14 in C-Sharp minor (*Moonlight*), op. 27, no. 2, delighted him above all else. Though he received no formal musical training and never learned to play an instrument or sing, Turgenev acquired a deep feeling for music at an early age through the concerts staged at his parent's Spasskoe estate in Orel Province. He probably encountered Beethoven's music for the first time at the Engel'gardt House concerts he attended while studying at the University of St. Petersburg from 1834 to 1837. In 1840 he lived for a time with Mikhail Bakunin in Berlin, where the pair studied Hegel by day and took in performances of Beethoven's quartets and symphonies by night. He wrote later that this period of intense immersion in Beethoven's music marked the "beginning" of his "musical education."[1] Turgenev was back in St. Petersburg from 1843 to 1847 and frequently attended recitals at the Viel'gorskii and Odoevskii salons, where he heard much of Beethoven's music performed. Exiled to his estate at Spasskoe in 1852 and 1853 for having published an unauthorized necrology of Nikolai Gogol, the writer sought solace in four-hand piano arrangements of Beethoven's orchestral music played by his steward's wife and her sister. The *Coriolan* Overture in C minor, op. 62, particularly enthralled him: "What a marvelous composition!" he wrote Viardot. "I do not know of another overture that can compare with it."[2] A concert he attended on November 24, 1852, at a neighboring estate where the adagio of Beethoven's Ninth Symphony and an arrangement for orchestra of his favorite Mozart composition, the Piano Fantasia in C minor, K. 475, were performed also delighted him.

One evening in the summer of 1854, Turgenev asked Ol'ga Aleksandrovna Turgeneva, a distant cousin and the object of his affections at the time, to play the *Moonlight* Sonata for him. An accomplished pianist who had studied under Adolf von Henselt, the cousin readily agreed. After the performance he took both of her hands in his and thanked her effusively. "You have given me the greatest pleasure," he exclaimed. "I shall always remember it." Years later he asked one of Ol'ga Aleksandrovna's daughters if she could play the sonata and reminisced about "how beautifully your mother played this wonderful work."[3] From August to October 1856, all of Beethoven's piano sonatas and four-hand arrangements of the symphonies were played at Courtavenel, the chateau of Pauline and Louis Viardot, outside Paris. "We were as happy as trout in a clear stream when the sun strikes it," Turgenev wrote the art critic Vasilii Botkin that fall.[4] But a recital of the Piano Sonata no. 28 in A, op. 101, by Anton Rubinshtein in London in 1857 perplexed the writer. "I was unable to understand it," he complained later.[5] This most assuredly was not the case with a performance of the opera *Fidelio*, op. 72, which Turgenev attended in St. Petersburg in January 1864. "The music made an extraordinary impression on me; I applauded like a claqueur," he wrote Viardot.[6] And so it continued down through the years. A diary covering the period of December 9, 1882, to January 29, 1883, records a number of concert evenings. The music on offer? Works by Haydn and Beethoven. Turgenev died of bone marrow cancer in Bougival, France, on September 3, 1883 (New Style), and, at his request, was laid to rest next to Vissarion Belinskii at the Volkov Cemetery in St. Petersburg.

The majority of Turgenev's poems, stories, and novels where the protagonists either play music, listen to music, or talk about music reflects his love for the medium. A variety of composers, including Beethoven, Bellini, Chopin, Donizetti, Field, Herz, Meyerbeer, Mozart, Rossini, Schubert, Steibelt, Strauss II, Thalberg, Verstovskii, and Weber, figure in his writings. Beethoven appears in at least six of the works. In the long poem "Andrei" (1846), the heroine "plays the celebrated *Funeral March* of Beethoven."[7] In "The Two Friends" (1854), Boris Andreevich "could not utter the name of Beethoven without a display of enthusiasm" and considered the composer "a genius of the first rank" even though "he is not appreciated by everyone."[8] In "A Correspondence" (1854), Mar'ia Aleksandrovna's detractors chided her for "rid[ing] at night up and down by the river, singing Schubert's Serenade, or simply moaning, 'Beethoven, Beethoven!'" One night to tease an unwelcome suitor, she "sat down at the piano before the open window, in the moonlight, and played Beethoven," an account that prompted her correspondent, Alexei Petrovich, to quip, "If I had been in your place, I'd have kept him singing Beethoven's *Adelaida* and gazing at the moon the whole night long."[9] In *Rudin* (1855), Baron Muffel "talked of Beethoven with such eloquence that even the old Prince went into raptures," and Rudin "continually insisted on Pandalevsky playing Beethoven."[10] In *A House of Gentlefolk* (1858), Lisa's effort to play a Beethoven sonata four-hand with Panshin proved unsuccessful when her partner fell two bars behind at the twentieth bar of the second movement allegro, while, on another occasion, Mar'ia Dmitrievna retired to her bedchamber because Beethoven's music "was too agitating for her nerves."[11] And the semiautobiographical tale "An Unhappy Girl" (1869) conveys the profound effect Piano Sonata no. 23 in F minor (*Appassionata*), op. 57, had on Turgenev as a young man:

> I loved music from childhood but at that time did not understand it well, hardly knew the works of the great composers, and, had Ratch not grumbled with some displeasure, "Aha! *weider dieser Beethoven*!," would not have guessed what Susanna had selected to play. This was, as I learned later, the famous Sonata in F minor, op. 57. Susanna's playing affected me beyond words: I had not expected such force, such fire, such a bold range of expression. From the very first bars of the headlong and impassioned Allegro that launches the sonata, I felt that stupor, that chill and sweet terror of rapture that instantly seizes the soul when beauty breaks in upon it with an unexpected rush. I did not move a single limb until the very end; the whole time I wanted to take a breath but dared not. I was sitting behind Susanna and could not see her face; I only saw how her long, dark hair now and then flew about and swept across her shoulders, how her figure rocked violently, and how her delicate hands and bare elbows moved swiftly and somewhat awkwardly. The last reverberations died away. I took a breath at last. Susanna continued to sit at the piano.[12] [YOUTUBE VIDEO 6]

Nowhere more than in this sensitively drawn reminiscence does Turgenev capture his love for Beethoven's music and the spell it cast over him. Indeed this is one of the most poetic descriptions of the power of the *Appassionata* to move the human spirit in all of reception literature.

Fedor Dostoevsky (1821–81) was passionate about Beethoven's music, as he was of Mozart and Rossini—the Rossini of the *Stabat Mater*, not the operas—and considered Beethoven the "poet of love, happiness, and amorous longing."[13] He confided in a friend that, of all musical compositions, he loved best Beethoven's Piano Sonata no. 8 in C minor (*Pathétique*), op. 13, which "always bathed him in a whole world of forgotten sensations."[14] At an early age, Dostoevsky was introduced to literature, particularly the works of Ann Radcliffe, Walter Scott, and Friedrich Schiller, but there is no evidence that music formed a part of his upbringing. Only after arriving in St. Petersburg in 1837 to study at the Nikolaev Military Engineering Institute did he begin exploring the world of classical music through the concerts, operas, and ballets he attended, including historic performances by Pauline García-Viardot, Franz Liszt, Hector Berlioz, Ole Bull, and Heinrich Ernst. The publication of his first novel, *Poor Folk*, in 1846 opened the doors to the Odoevskii, Sollogub, and Viel'gorskii salons with their rich musical fare. The budding writer particularly enjoyed the company of Mikhail Viel'gorskii, who, it is said, served as the model for the kind prince in the unfinished novel *Netochka Nezvanova* (1849). Dostoevsky was arrested in 1849 for his involvement in the activities of the Petrashevsky Circle, subjected to an infamous mock execution, and then sentenced to four years' hard labor in Siberia to be followed by military service for life in Siberian exile. Pardoned by Alexander II in 1857, he returned to St. Petersburg in December 1859 and engaged in the cultural affairs of the capital once again. He visited Western Europe in 1862 and 1863 and sojourned there from 1867 to 1871 in the company of his second wife, Anna Grigoreevna Snitkina, whom he had married on February 15, 1867.

Anna wrote in her memoirs that "though not a connoisseur of music, my husband very much loved the compositions of Mozart, Beethoven's *Fidelio*, Mendelssohn's 'Wedding March' from *A Midsummer's Night Dream*, and Rossini's *Stabat Mater*, and experienced great pleasure when listening to his favorite pieces." She added that he "did not at all care for the works of Richard Wagner."[15] Anna's diary provides information on a number of open-air concerts the couple attended during their stay in Dresden in the summer of 1867. On June 17 they heard Mozart's Symphony no. 41 (*Jupiter*) ("It was all marvelously good. Fedia was in complete rapture."); on June 21 they took in Beethoven's *Fidelio* Overture and a Wagner potpourri; on June 23 they listened to Beethoven's Symphony no. 1 in C and "an exquisite Strauss waltz"; and on June 29 they were enthralled by Beethoven's Symphony no. 2 in D ("Such astonishing music that we simply cannot get enough of. Fedia was in rapture.")[16] The couple then traveled to Baden-Baden, where on July 25 they attended a "magnificent" concert that included a performance of Beethoven's Incidental Music to Goethe's *Egmont*, Ferdinand Hérold's *Zampa*, and some excerpts from Mozart's *Marriage of Figaro*.[17] In letters to Anna in the late 1870s, Dostoevsky commented on his continued concertgoing during visits to Ems, Germany, to relieve his chronic pulmonary emphysema. June 30, 1875: "The music has improved today (probably with the weather); they played two pieces by Beethoven—perfectly delightful." July 30, 1876: "My angel, this morning I heard the overture from Beethoven's *Fidelio*. Nothing grander has ever been created than this! It is in the light graceful manner, but it has passion; there is passion and love everywhere in Beethoven." August 19, 1879: "The music here is good, but they seldom play Beethoven and Mozart. It is always Wagner (a most dull German dog in spite of all his fame) and all sorts of rubbish."[18] Unfortunately, the rest provided only temporary relief. Dostoevsky died from his disease, exacerbated by an epileptic attack, on January 28, 1881, and was buried next to the poet Vasilii Zhukovskii in St. Petersburg's Aleksandro-Nevskii cemetery. Thirty thousand mourners accompanied the coffin while seventy-two delegations carried wreaths and fifteen choirs sang in the funeral service and at graveside.[19]

The Soviet musicologist Abram Gozenpud argues that Dostoevsky "intuitively" crafted his stories and novels according to "principles of musical composition." He cites the author's use of leitmotifs—for example, the bell in *Crime and Punishment* (1866) and the knife in *The Idiot* (1869)—the depiction of alternating periods of silence and sound as cyclic patterns of *piano* and *forte* expressiveness, the characterization of the changing psychological disposition of protagonists as the modulation from one tonality to another, and even the construction of "a singular ABBA" sectional form with "postlude" in the story "White Nights" (1848). Gozenpud uses such words as *symphonic*, *choreographic*, and *polyphonic* to describe Dostoevsky's prose and cites opera as a model for episodes that conjure up "solo, ensemble, and choral scenes." In sum, "the structure of the writer's works, the development of contrasting themes and images, their struggle and interplay, are akin to musical dramaturgy."[20] Technically, these claims make no sense. Dostoevsky received no formal musical training, and Anna Dostoevskaia observed that her husband was not an expert in music, though he "had a good musical ear."[21] He thus was not equipped to craft a work of fiction in the same way a composer would shape a piece of music. But such a narrow view misses the point. The creative process is a mysterious one that draws on a deep well of human experience; sparked by intuition, it engages both the mind and the heart in an intricate dance of nuance and surprise. So it was with Dostoevsky. His "good musical ear" enabled him to "hear" words or phrases as if they were notes and apprehend musical form as a template for dramatic expression. He based his writing as well on the same principles of design—unity, balance, proportion, emphasis, repetition, movement, and contrast—that shape all great art, including music. We will never know precisely to what extent all this played out, but it is apparent that at some level the language of music shaped the character of Dostoevsky's literary voice.

Gozenpud is not alone in noting similarities between Dostoevsky's prose style and aspects of musical discourse. The French poet, dramatist, and diplomat Paul Claudel cites the "ample crescendos in the manner of Beethoven," which characterize Dostoevsky's writing, and considers the first two hundred pages of *The Idiot* (1869) "a masterpiece of composition equal to Beethoven's masterpieces."[22] The American translator Michael Katz refers to the "richness of registers or tones" in *Crime and Punishment* (1866).[23] The Soviet literary scholar Mikhail Bakhtin, like Gozenpud, uses the term *polyphony* to describe Dostoevsky's many-voiced writing style: "*A plurality of independent and unmerged voices and consciousnesses, a genuine polyphony of fully valid voices is in fact the chief characteristic of Dostoevsky's novels.*"[24] The Soviet musicologist Arnol'd Al'shvang also adopted this approach in comparing Dostoevsky's novels to the symphonies of Tchaikovsky.[25] The term is used as well by Dostoevsky scholar Victor Terras to describe the various levels of discourse on which *The Brothers Karamazov* (1880) operates. Citing the motifs, themes, variations, and leitmotifs that form the narrative structure of the work, Terras concludes that "the various motifs of the novel are linked by a variety of syntagmatic as well as paradigmatic bonds, much as musical motifs are in a symphonic composition."[26]

Dostoevsky's love of music also prompted him to make references to a variety of composers in his works, including Beethoven on two occasions. In *The Insulted and Injured* (1861), Katerina Fedorovna asks the autobiographical figure of Ivan Petrovich if he is fond of music, to which he replies in the affirmative. She continues, "If there were time I'd play Beethoven's Third [Piano] Concerto for you. That's what I'm playing now. All those feelings are in it . . . just as I'm feeling them now. So it seems to me. But that must be for another time; now we must talk."[27] In *The Brothers Karamazov* (1880), Beethoven's *Choral* Symphony comes to mind when Dmitri says to Aleksei, "Alyosha, you alone will not laugh. I wanted to begin . . . my confession . . . with Schiller's hymn to joy *An die Freude!* But I don't know German, I only know it's *An die Freude.*"[28]

In both art and life, Dostoevsky was the Beethoven of Russian letters. Both artists created masterpieces while encountering great hardship—Beethoven

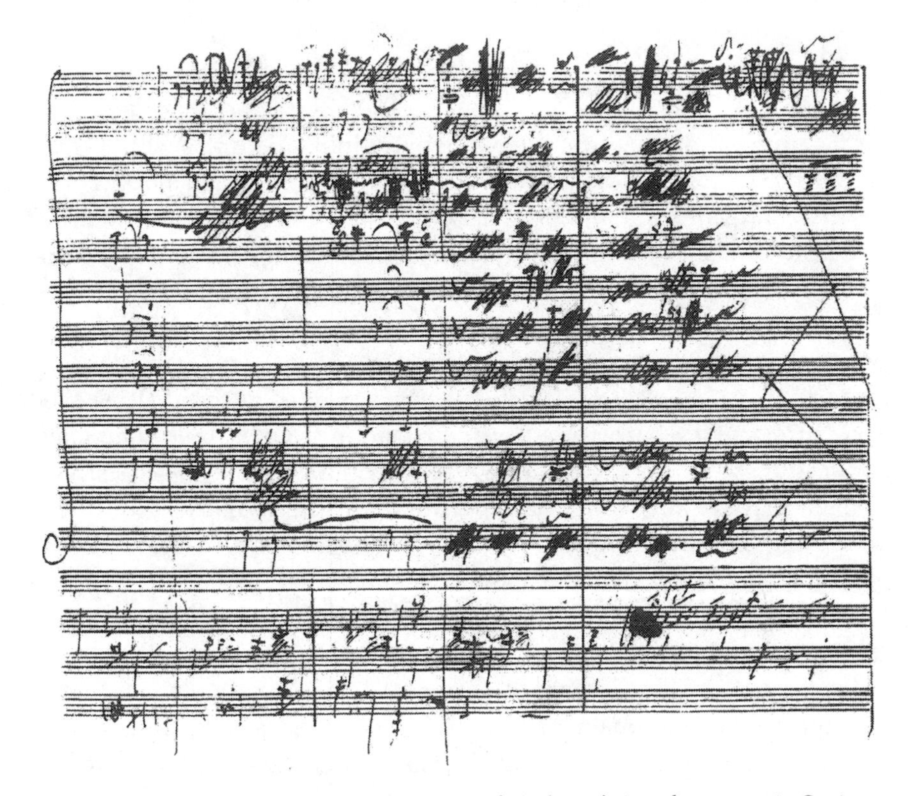

Figure 3.1. Page from original manuscript score of Beethoven's Symphony no. 5 in C minor, op. 67. Public Domain.

Figure 3.2. Page from Dostoyevsky's Notebooks for *The Brothers Karamazov*. Public Domain.

through his devastating hearing loss, failures in relationships with women, and increasing social isolation and Dostoevsky from his epileptic seizures, addiction to gambling, and persistent indebtedness. Both also had strong personalities that can charitably be described as difficult at best. Beethoven's irascible ways are legendary, while Dostoevsky said about himself, "I simply don't fit into the category of staid and conventional people. . . . In all things I go to the uttermost extreme; my life long I have never been acquainted with moderation."[29] Each engaged in titanic creative struggles in crafting their works. Dostoevsky burned the entire first draft of *Crime and Punishment* (1866) and revised *The Possessed* (1872) twenty times, telling his close friend Apollon Maikov that "never has any work cost me so much labor."[30] For Beethoven, the three different versions of the opera *Fidelio*, which occupied the composer from 1803 to 1814; the fourteen renditions of the main theme of the second movement of Symphony no. 5, which were written over an eight-year period; and the four-year effort to complete the *Missa solemnis* all testify to the enormous effort required to arrive at finished form. Leonard Bernstein observed that the manuscript of the Fifth Symphony "looks like a bloody record of a tremendous inner battle," something that could also be said of Dostoevsky's notebook for *The Brothers Karamazov* (1880).[31] Both artists also created large, emotionally charged, highly dramatic works that, in their late periods, assumed a deep spiritual dimension as well. And each crafted pieces of art that will forever remain universal in their appeal. Unlike the works of Lermontov, Pushkin, Gogol, Goncharov, Turgenev, Chekhov, Gorky, Pasternak, and Solzhenitsyn, to cite but the most prominent examples, Dostoevsky's novels, like those of Tolstoy, are not fixed in time and place but transcend the contextual to address fundamental issues of human behavior. Likewise Beethoven's music, while grounded in the late Classical / early Romantic era, speaks in a timeless fashion of humanity's desire for personal growth, freedom from oppression, and spiritual fulfillment. The universality of the Beethovenian message is exemplified by the Voyager 1 and 2 space probes, which continue to hurtle through space following their launches in 1977. Each carries a gold-coated copper recording of a variety of Western and non-Western music, including the first movement of Beethoven's Symphony no. 5 in C minor, op. 67, and the *Cavatina* from his String Quartet no. 13 in B-flat, op. 130, as a possible means of communicating with extraterrestrial life somewhere in the cosmos.[32]

Lev Tolstoy (1828–1910) grew up listening to and playing music and developed a profound if troubled attachment to it. *War and Peace* sparkles with the sound of music and dance in perfectly judged counterpoint to the cries and clamor of the battlefield. That Tolstoy could be deeply moved by Beethoven is evident from the following remarks he penned to his aunt Aleksandra Tolstaia on August 18, 1857: "For a long time I had to fight against a feeling of aversion for my country; now I am beginning to accustom myself to all the horrors that make up the human condition. . . . Fortunately, there is one salvation: morality, the world of the arts, poetry and human relations. There, nobody bothers me, policeman or town councillor. I am alone. Outside the wind howls, outside all is mud and cold; I am here, I play Beethoven and shed tears of tenderness."[33]

The violent emotions expressed in "The Kreutzer Sonata" (1889) offer testimony of a different sort. But by the time Tolstoy published *What Is Art?* in 1896 (or 1898), the master of the roman à clef had turned his back on Beethoven, as he had on all art—including his own—that he deemed artificial and devoid of genuine (that is, religious) feelings.[34] In his diatribe on aesthetics, Tolstoy attacked the Ninth Symphony as an "interminable, muddled and artificial work in which only one or two short passages manage to emerge from an ocean of incomprehensible sound."[35] How Tolstoy, despite the profundity of his changed worldview and antipathy to late Beethoven, could have rejected so completely a composer he once held so dear is a question that will never be satisfactorily answered.

Tolstoy came naturally to his love of music. His maternal grandfather habitually awakened to the opening bars of Haydn symphonies played by the serf orchestra he maintained on his estate at Yasnaya Polyana, and his mother was an accomplished pianist. One of the future writer's earliest childhood memories was of his mother playing Beethoven's *Pathétique* Sonata, which, as he recalled in his literary memoirs, caused him to feel "sad, heavy and gloomy."[36] Folk music sung by the serfs at Yasnaya Polyana also exerted a significant influence on the young boy's developing sensibilities. As a student at Kazan' University from 1844 to 1847, Tolstoy studied the piano informally and on April 17, 1847, wrote in his diary that over the next two years, in addition to a variety of ambitious tasks, he intended to "attain the highest degree of perfection in music and painting."[37] While little came of this resolve, in June 1849 he did hire a German piano tutor named Rudolph to teach him the rudiments of music theory and practice. The instructor, who shares character traits with the drunken violinist in the short story "Albert" (1857), stayed at Yasnaya Polyana for only a short time but succeeded in providing Tolstoy with a solid foundation in piano technique that served him well. Study of the piano understandably fell off from 1851 to 1856 during Tolstoy's military service, which included action in the Crimean War, but musical activities did not

Figure 3.3. Wanda Landowska playing for Tolstoy at Yasnaya Polyana, 1907. Photograph by Sophia Tolstaia. Courtesy of L. N. Tolstoy State Museum, Moscow.

cease altogether. His letters home indicate that he had access to a piano at his various billets in Bucharest, Kishinev, Simferopol', and the outskirts of Sevastopol' and continued to play music in his spare time. One of his first acts after being discharged from the army was to write his sister Mariia Nikolaevna on June 5, 1856, "I'm sending you the upright piano; send me the grand piano and *Don Giovanni* as you promised and some Beethoven and Mozart pieces which you perhaps don't need as well."[38]

From 1856 to 1862, Tolstoy lived primarily in St. Petersburg and Moscow and on two occasions traveled abroad. During his visit to Paris in 1857, he attended a performance of the Beethoven Piano Trios in D (*Ghost*) and E-flat, nos. 1–2, op. 70, and concluded that the French were "gods" when it came to playing Beethoven. During this time Tolstoy made the acquaintance of Vladimir Odoevskii and undoubtedly attended his "Saturdays" salon; he also befriended Nikolai Rubinshtein with whom he discussed the idea of founding a music conservatory in Moscow, which came to pass in 1866. From 1862 to 1910, with the exception of most of the winters of 1881 to 1901 when he lived in Moscow, Tolstoy spent the remainder of his life at Yasnaya Polyana. In the 1870s he played the piano three to four hours a day and performed four-hand with his wife, Sophia (Sonya), in repertoire ranging from Weber to early Beethoven. During these years eminent musicians from Russia and abroad concertized at the Tolstoy residences; in 1907 the Polish keyboardist Wanda Landowska, her two-manual harpsichord in tow, paid a celebrated visit to Yasnaya Polyana at Christmastime. The writer's death on November 7, 1910, in the rail master's house at the Astapovo station and burial two days later at Yasnaya Polyana are legendary. Not so well-known is that, on September 14, 1928, at the conclusion of the centenary celebrations of Tolstoy's birth, a choir of 250 Yasnaya Polyana schoolchildren sang the *Ode to Joy* from Beethoven's Ninth Symphony.[39]

Tolstoy was particular about what he liked and disliked in music. He preferred pieces in a major key with fast tempos, a pronounced rhythmic drive, and a clear, simple melodic line. He enjoyed instrumental over orchestral music and above all favored the piano and stringed instruments, including the guitar and balalaika. He liked vocal music but with a few exceptions—*Der Freischűtz, Don Giovanni, Il barbiere di Siviglia*, and *Orfeo*—did not care for opera. "Fat ladies in tights" lacked verisimilitude in his eyes.[40] He emphatically did not like Wagner, his one experience, a performance of *Siegfried* in Moscow on April 18, 1896, confirming his worst suspicions. "I couldn't even sit through one act, and rushed out like a madman," he wrote his brother Sergei the next day. "It's a stupid farce, not suitable for children over seven, pretentious, sham, utterly false and with no music."[41] On April 20 he fumed that the music made no sense: "You listen but you cannot tell whether the orchestra has already started to play or is still tuning up."[42] Tolstoy's favorite composers were Weber, Haydn, Mozart, Beethoven, Schubert, and Chopin. He also liked the masters of "old music," whom he identified for Wanda Landowska as Bach, Handel, Couperin, Rameau, and Scarlatti and confided that they helped "calm his nerves" and "transport him to another world."[43] As for the composers of his own era, he found several pieces by Schumann acceptable but was highly critical of Berlioz, Brahms, Liszt (except for some of his transcriptions), and Richard Strauss.

Regarding Beethoven, Tolstoy maintained what Dorothy Green terms a "love-hate relationship" with the composer's music.[44] He did not like the late compositions and argued that their "contrived and unpolished and therefore often musically meaningless and incomprehensible" character reflected, as Aleksandr Ulybyshev had claimed, the grievous results of the composer's descent into near-total deafness.[45] In *What Is Art?*, the Piano Sonata no. 28 in A, op. 101, came in for as much criticism as the Ninth

Symphony; he described it as one of those "shapeless improvisations" that characterized the late style and an "unsuccessful attempt at art, containing no definite feeling and therefore not infectious."[46] On the other hand, Tolstoy looked favorably on some of the compositions from the early and middle periods, including the *Pathétique*, *Moonlight*, and *Appassionata* piano sonatas; the *Kreutzer* Violin Sonata; the Opus 70 Piano Trios; and the Septet. On balance, one suspects that Tolstoy did not consider Beethoven a truly great composer. He at least left Petr Tchaikovsky this impression in 1876 when he declared to his face that Beethoven lacked talent. More than two years later, Tchaikovsky was still troubled by this encounter. Writing to his benefactress and friend Nadezhda von Meck on March 3, 1879, he recalled: "'I want to know you better,' [Tolstoy] said. 'I want to talk to you about music.' And he had barely shaken hands before he stated his own musical views. Beethoven was bereft of talent—this was the start. A great writer, a divinely-gifted searcher of hearts, began by giving utterance, in a tone filled with confidence, to nonsense that would have insulted any musician. What could I do? Argue back? Well, I did. I started a dispute. To tell the truth, he deserved a lecture, but how could I stand up and give him one, then and there?"[47]

Tchaikovsky finally put the matter to rest in an 1866 diary entry: "Among other things [Tolstoy] liked to run down Beethoven, and openly expressed doubt of his genius. This is a trait not at all characteristic of great men. To bring down to one's own lack of comprehension a genius who is recognized by everyone is a peculiarity of men of limited intellect."[48]

Whatever his estimation of Beethoven as a composer, Tolstoy certainly viewed his music as a central feature of the cultural world his literary figures inhabited. In *Childhood* (1852), as already noted, Tolstoy's mother, Mariia Nikolaevna plays the *Pathétique* Sonata to lugubrious effect on her young son's awakening sensibilities, while in *Boyhood* (1854) Liubov Sergeevna performs "several of Beethoven's sonatas with great precision," and in *Youth* (1857) she plays both the *Pathétique* and *Moonlight* Sonatas "in memory of *maman*."[49] In *Family Happiness* (1859), the playing of the *Moonlight* Sonata by Mariia Aleksandrovna bookends a relationship that extends from the passion of early courtship to the less heated but more secure world of settled married life.[50] Tolstoy's greatest novel, *War and Peace* (1869), does not mention Beethoven, yet there is a magnificent dream sequence that, if Ruth Rischin is to be believed, conjures up the fourth movement of the Ninth Symphony:

> And suddenly Petia heard a harmonious orchestra playing some unknown, triumphantly sweet hymn. . . . The melody grew and passed from one instrument to another. What was being played was what is known as a fugue. . . . Each instrument, now sounding like a violin, now like a horn . . . played its own part, and before having finished the melody, blended with another that began almost the same, and with a third, and with a fourth, and they all blended into one and again separated, and again all blended now into something triumphantly solemn, now into something dazzlingly brilliant and victorious. . . . He tried to conduct this enormous orchestra of instruments. "Now softer, softer, die away now." And the sounds obeyed him. "Now then, louder, merrier. Still more, still more joyful!" And from an unknown depth swelled ever more sonorous triumphant sounds. "Now, voices, join in!" commanded Petia. And at first from afar men's voices were heard and then women's. The voices swelled and swelled in balanced triumphant force and Petia listened to their extraordinary beauty with feelings of awe and joy.[51]

This "dream fugue" is not meant to be taken literally, of course, since at the time of the novel's action the Ninth Symphony had yet to be written, but it should be viewed as a "musical metaphor to symbolize a psychological state"—the euphoria Petia feels on the eve of the raid that tragically will take his life.[52] In *Anna Karenina* (1877), the protagonist's self-satisfied husband, Aleksei Aleksandrovich, though he lacks any understanding of art, poetry, and music, "liked to talk about Shakespeare, Raphael, Beethoven, about the significance of the new schools in poetry and music, which with him were all sorted out in a very clear order." To which Anna shrugs. "Well, God bless you."[53] In "The Kreutzer Sonata" (1889), the Violin Sonata no. 9 in A (*Kreutzer*) serves as the vehicle for Tolstoy's celebrated exploration of the psychopathic power of music, "that most refined lust of the senses," to incite a crime of passion.[54] And finally, in *Resurrection* (1899) Prince Nekhludov falls into a "state of perfect harmony with himself" while listening to a four-hand performance of the second movement of Beethoven's Fifth Symphony.[55]

The biographical literature is replete with references to Tolstoy's deep emotional response to music, and this is especially true concerning Beethoven's *Kreutzer* Violin Sonata. About a performance of the work at Yasnaya Polyana on July 3, 1887, Henri Troyat writes that Tolstoy "listened with tears in his eyes; then, during the [first] presto, unable to control himself, he rose and went to the window where, gazing at the starry sky, he stifled a sob. Sonya received the benefits of his transports later that same evening, when they were alone: as she wrote immediately afterward in her diary, under the influence of the music her husband had become 'the affectionate and tender Lyovochka of old.' A few weeks later she discovered that she was pregnant."[56] A. N. Wilson writes that,

Figure 3.4. Tolstoy listening to music, 1909. Sketch by Leonid Pasternak. B. A. Katz, comp., *Muzyka v tvorchestve, sud'be i v dome Borisa Pasternaka* (Leningrad: Sovetskii kompozitor, 1991), 59.

"as always," Tolstoy was "moved" by another performance of the sonata that took place in the spring of 1888 at his Moscow residence.[57] After this recital, attended by the painter Ilia Repin and the actor Vasilii Burlak-Andreev, Tolstoy suggested a collaborative project based on the music: he would write a story structured around the tale of a wronged husband that Burlak-Andreev had shared with him the previous year, Repin would paint a picture depicting a scene from the story, and Burlak-Andreev would read the story in public with the painting serving as a backdrop. While Burlak-Andreev died in May of that year and Repin apparently forgot about the project altogether, Tolstoy followed through on the suggestion and completed what is known as "The Kreutzer Sonata" in 1889. The novella, in a word, uses a performance of Beethoven's Violin Sonata no. 9 as the cause célèbre of the protagonist's descent into a state of insane jealousy that culminates in the murder of his innocent wife. The psychological build-up to the murder and the commission of the crime itself, recounted in excruciating detail, would have made for a very dramatic reading, and one can only imagine that Repin's projected painting would have been every bit as disturbing as the portrait of Ivan the Terrible and the dead tsarevich he had finished in 1885.[58] As it is, Tolstoy bequeathed to posterity a work that illuminates brilliantly the power of music to shape human emotions and, at least in literature, carve out a pathway to mortal destruction.[59]

Commentary by contemporaries also attests to the strong emotional effect music had on Tolstoy. Vasilii Alekseev, tutor to the Tolstoy children, remarked on how Tolstoy's eyes would well up with tears when he listened to Beethoven.[60] Stepan Bers, the writer's brother-in-law, observed, "I noticed that the sensations aroused in him by music were accompanied by a slight pallor to the face and a barely noticeable grimace expressing something akin to horror."[61] The French journalist Paul Boyer remarked, "Tolstoy sat down to play Chopin. At the end of the fourth Ballade, his eyes filled with tears. 'Ah, the animal!' he cried. And suddenly he rose and went out."[62] The conductor and double bass virtuoso Serge Koussevitzky, after performing with the Paris Quartet at Yasnaya Polyana in November 1909, wrote, "We played a long time. Tolstoy sat and cried the whole way through. The Concert Sinfonia by [Jean Baptiste] Lorenzetti for viola d'amore, double bass, and string quartet had an especially strong effect on him. Lev Nikolaevich asked that we repeat many parts of it."[63] To Maurice Kues, the Swiss tutor of his grandsons, Tolstoy growled, "My tears mean nothing. So what? There is some music I cannot listen to without weeping, that's all, just as my daughter Sasha cannot eat strawberries without getting hives! Anyway, sometimes I weep when I laugh too. It's nerves, nothing but nerves!"[64] Of course it was anything but nerves. As Tolstoy himself observed, "Music is the stenography of feeling," the "mute prayer of the soul."[65] Sergei Nikolaevich Tolstoy, the writer's musically gifted son, summed up the effect of music on his father this way:

> I have not known anyone in my life who reacted to music as strongly as my father did. Hearing music, Lev Nikolaevich could not avoid listening to it. Music that was pleasing to him would cause him to become agitated, something would catch in his throat and constrict his nose, he would sob and shed tears. . . . Sometimes music agitated him against his will, even tormented him, and he would say, "*Que me veut cette musique*?" . . . Such were the direct effects of music on Lev Nikolaevich over the course of his entire life, beginning with childhood and extending to his last years when he told V. F. Bulgakov that, if all European civilization were to collapse, he would only regret the loss of music.[66]

Beyond offering additional testimony to the impact of music on Tolstoy's emotional well-being, these observations shed light on a much more fundamental issue: Tolstoy feared music and its power angered him because he did not understand it and had no control over how it affected him. Pozdnyshev, the autobiographical narrator of "The Kreutzer Sonata," feverishly grapples with this problem in the following rambling monologue:

> Two people [Pozdnyshev's wife and her alleged lover] are taken up with the most noble of arts, music; for that a certain closeness is required, and there is nothing reprehensible in that closeness, and only a stupid, jealous husband could see something undesirable in it. And yet everybody knows that it is precisely by means of these same occupations, especially music, that the greater share of adulteries occur in our society. . . . They played Beethoven's *Kreutzer* Sonata. Do you know the first presto? Do you?! . . . That sonata is a fearful thing. Precisely that part. And music generally is a fearful thing. . . . What is music? What does it do? And why does it do what it does? They say music has an elevating effect on the soul—nonsense, lies! It affects one, affects one fearfully. . . . In China music is a state affair. And that's how it should be. As if it can be allowed that anyone who likes should hypnotize another or many others and then do what he likes with them. . . . Take, for instance, this *Kreutzer* Sonata, the first presto. How can that presto be played in a drawing room among ladies in décolleté? . . . These things can be played only in certain, important, significant circumstances, and when there's a demand to accomplish certain important actions in accordance with that music. . . . Otherwise the calling up of an energy, a feeling, that accords neither with the place, nor with the time, that is not manifest in anything, can only have a pernicious effect. On me, at least, this thing had a terrible effect.[67] [YOUTUBE VIDEO 7]

This, then, is the heart of the issue. "It was really fear that he felt," Romain Rolland writes, "fear inspired by the stress of those unknown forces which shook him to the roots of his being. In the world of music he felt his moral will, his reason, and all the reality of life dissolve."[68] This is likely why Tolstoy lashed out so vehemently against classical music in his treatise *What Is Art?* Better to take comfort in the simple harmonies of folk song, he seems to be saying, than suffer the emotional anguish of subjugation to a force one can neither control nor understand. Tolstoy goes further in "The Kreutzer Sonata" by suggesting that music not only shapes emotions at the personal level but also can unleash potentially destructive forces at the societal one. It is for this reason, as Pozdnyshev observes, that music is a state affair in China. But he is silent as to how such authority is to be exercised. Despite all the police power a state apparatus may have at its command, how can it control the residual effects of the listening experience once the concertgoer leaves the music hall? Perhaps there is but one way: co-opt the music, transform it into iconography, and use this ideological construct as a propaganda weapon in support of the regime itself. Although Tolstoy did not live to see the day, not long after his death this is precisely what happened to Beethoven and his music in the writer's now reconstituted homeland of Soviet Russia.

The Silent Underground

And how did the next generation of the revolutionary intelligentsia view music in general and Beethoven in particular? Hardly at all. A perusal of the literature reveals what at first glance is a surprising reticence on the part of key figures in the revolutionary movement of the 1860s and 1870s to reflect, as their Westernizer forebears had done, on the important connections between music and politics. Nikolai Chernyshevskii (1828–89), though he claimed to love music, acknowledged that he "knew it so poorly that he could not render a judgment on the merits of the great majority of well-known composers." He was certain, however, that he did not like Wagner.[69] As for Beethoven, Chernyshevskii considered his music "too obscure and often wild."[70] There is no mention of Beethoven in the criticism of Nikolai Dobroliubov (1836–61), except for two uninformative references in the philosophical essays.[71] There is a similar lack of commentary in the critical essays of Nikolai Mikhailovskii (1842–1904), perhaps due to the fact, as he admitted in 1874, he had "a very poor understanding of music in general and knew nothing at all" about contemporary Russian music.[72] Nor is there any discussion of note in the writings of Petr Lavrov (1821–1900) and Petr Tkachev (1844–85), though they surely had their views.[73] Dmitrii Pisarev (1840–68) did offer some thoughts but only to disparage Beethoven's art. He snidely remarked in one of his essays that those who find more pleasure in a toy than a Beethoven sonata should not be criticized for their "bad taste," since the issue is no more significant than "whether a sweet muscat or a robust sherry is the better wine."[74] Elsewhere he claimed that "liking music is as stupid as liking pickled cucumbers" and that "Beethoven was only as great as the chef at Dusseau's."[75] But then, as he boasted in another essay, music for himself and his cohorts was "terra incognita" in that they "did not know the difference between 'do' and 'fa' or a flat and a sharp and did not even glance at the works of music critics."[76]

How does one account for this uniform lack of interest in music on the part of the most radical members of the Russian intelligentsia? The answer has much to do with their attitude toward art in general—"as pretty as Brussels lace and almost as useless," to quote Pisarev again.[77] The newly emergent *raznochintsy* ("mixed rank"), with their more diversified social base, inflated sense of self, tough-minded realism, exclusive interest in the material world, and missionary zeal in promoting the doctrines of socialism, could find no place in their worldview for the abstract theories of literature, history, aesthetics, philosophy, and religion that had nurtured their parents' generation. "We still believed in the efficacy and importance of philosophical and metaphysical ideas," Turgenev reflected in commenting on his studies at Berlin

University in the 1840s.[78] But no more. The tilt away from the humanities and toward mathematics, economics, and the sciences that characterized trends in higher education, especially in the professional schools, had the effect of creating a new type of mentality attuned more to rational scientific investigation than to matters of the heart. In Turgenev's *Fathers and Children* (1862), Bazarov dissects frogs and collects rare beetles but can only laugh when he hears Arkady's father playing Schubert on the cello and finds Pushkin so much "rubbish." The world had ominously become a very cold, dehumanized, and, as events were to prove, violent place. If there was no room for art, there was no room for the finer sensibilities of the spirit as well.

In the Critic's Corner

Thus one must not look to the radical intelligentsia while examining the last phase of Beethoven reception in late imperial Russia. The trail has not grown cold, only taken a turn—onto the writing desks of the eminent music critics of the period. Russian Beethoven criticism had developed apace and, by the middle decades of the nineteenth century, had become a recognized scholarly discipline. As a result of this more sophisticated analysis and in the context of a rapidly changing political environment, a radical new image of Beethoven came into view: Beethoven as revolutionary, the "Shakespeare of the masses." Critics drew on half a dozen key works in fashioning this new trope: the Third, Fifth, and Ninth Symphonies with their unique blend of pathos and passion; the emotionally charged overture and incidental music to Goethe's tragedy *Egmont*, which conveys in musical terms the tragedy of the sixteenth-century eponymous hero who sacrificed his life in defense of Flemish liberty; the opera *Fidelio*—a classic example of the "rescue opera" genre popular during the French Revolution—which tells the story of the unjustly imprisoned Spanish nobleman Florestan, who gains his freedom through the bravery of his faithful wife, Leonore; and the heroic, pulse-driven *Leonore* and *Fidelio* overtures, especially the *Leonore 3* Overture, famously characterized by Richard Wagner as "not the overture to the drama [but] the drama itself."[79]

The origins of this new interpretation, which shifts the discussion from literature to musicology, can be traced to the writings of Aleksandr Serov, unquestionably the most highly regarded Beethoven authority in late imperial Russia. While Serov is best known for his astute scholarship on the late works of the composer, he was also the first Russian critic to draw attention to Beethoven's intellectual associations with the French Revolution. He initially made this connection in an 1858 essay that analyzed the meaning of the Ninth

Symphony in the context of the forces, "those cataclysms which, like the roar of underground thunder, resound to the present day and place their volcanic stamp on thought, poetry, and all modern spiritual life," unleashed by the year 1789. He declared that the entire premise of the Ninth Symphony was that the "realm of freedom and unity *must be conquered*."[80] Serov amplified these views in a public lecture in 1868: "A contemporary of the French Revolution, Beethoven from his youthful days was imbued with the principles of 1789; this epoch instilled in the hearts of such poets as Schiller and Beethoven those pure *ideals* toward which humanity was rushing. . . . The ideas of *freedom* . . . and *brotherhood*, the uniting of all mankind in a *single kiss*, remained Beethoven's most beloved and cherished dream that *demanded* to be incarnated in tones."[81]

Serov's remarks were mainly about music, but they pointed toward a more ideologically driven mode of analysis. Vladimir Stasov (1824–1906), leading advocate of Russian national music and a renowned critic in his own right, undoubtedly had something of the political in mind when he declared in 1901 that "Beethoven was not only a great musician and master of his craft but a great spirit, music serving him, as did the marvelous creations of that other giant of our age, Lev Tolstoy, as a means of communing with people, of giving expression to what filled his soul." Significantly Stasov argued that the Ninth Symphony's *Ode to Joy* (*Lied an die Freude*) should be renamed the *Ode to Freedom* (*Lied an die Freiheit*) in line with what he claimed to be the original intentions of Schiller and Beethoven. The Ninth Symphony was nothing less than a "picture of the history of the world" that cast a "bright sunbeam" on humanity's way forward. No one before had assigned to music "such a great role in the fate of mankind," Stasov declared. Thus Beethoven "completely changed the meaning of music," freeing it from the dictum of art for art's sake and transforming it into a "great and serious matter in the life of man." Beethoven also created a new orchestra, "a hundred times richer and more powerful, harmonious, and versatile than before," and a new instrumental form, the scherzo, which later composers used in introducing a new range of human emotions into their works. But Beethoven's greatness lay above all in the "outpouring of his immense soul," which found reflection in the late compositions and signified a new direction in modern music. "The whole musical world of the 19th century lives in Beethoven," Stasov concluded.[82]

Anton Rubinshtein (1829–94), composer, critic, and greatest living piano virtuoso after Franz Liszt, maintained, along with Serov, that Beethoven was the music envoy of the French Revolution. He hastened to add, "Not of the guillotine, of course . . . but of *Liberté, Égalité, Fraternité*." He therefore

Figure 3.5. Anton Rubinshtein. Portrait by Ilya Repin. Alamy Stock Photo E7G7JF.

agreed with Stasov that *Freiheit* should be substituted for *Freude* in the Ninth Symphony's vocal finale, firmly believing that the literary censors of Schiller's day had forced the poet to substitute "joy" for "freedom" in his poem and that Beethoven was well aware of this. As confirmation that Beethoven had freedom in mind when composing the *Ode*, Rubinshtein presented the following arguments. The sensation of joy "is not an acquired emotion but arrives suddenly and unexpectedly; freedom, on the other hand, can only be secured through struggle. Thus Beethoven's theme begins *pianissimo* in the bass viols and passes through many variations before finally ringing out triumphantly." In addition, "freedom is an extremely serious matter and for this reason the *Ode* theme exhibits a similar earnest character." Moreover, the choral line, "Seid umschlungen, Millionen" ("You millions, I embrace you"), repeated four times in the closing stanzas of the vocal material "is not compatible with one's understanding of joy for joy is a more individualized emotion and cannot embrace all of mankind." As for other arguments, Rubinshtein tantalizingly ended his commentary with a simple "and much more along these lines" without indicating what else he may have had in mind.[83]

Rubinshtein bore an uncanny resemblance to Beethoven and championed the composer's music in his criticism and long concert career. Franz Liszt called him Van II for his appearance and love of Beethoven. He certainly found much to praise in the master's works. Following a performance in 1888 of the Piano Sonata no. 1 in F minor, op. 2, as part of a lecture-recital series on the history of keyboard music, he turned to his audience and said, "Have you, thus far, heard anything like this finale? Here you feel our own century, our agitation and nervous excitement. I cannot get over my astonishment at this man of the eighteenth century who felt the modern spirit so far in advance."[84] [YOUTUBE VIDEO 8] Concerning key middle-period works, he declared in 1892, "What is the Inferno scene in Gluck's *Orfeo* compared to the second movement of Beethoven's Piano Concerto No. 4? What is any tragedy, with the possible exception of *Hamlet* and *King Lear*, in comparison to the second movement of the Piano Trio in D [*Ghost*]? What is a whole drama in comparison to the Overture to [Collin's] *Coriolan* in C minor?"[85] Regarding the symphonies, he valued all nine but after no. 1 in C and no. 2 in D reordered the others in accordance with his view of their increasing artistic merits: no. 4 in B-flat, no. 8 in F, no. 6 in F (*Pastoral*), no. 7 in A, no. 3 in E-flat (*Eroica*), no. 5 in C minor, and no. 9 in D minor (*Choral*).[86] And, contrary to prevailing opinion, he considered Beethoven's only opera, *Fidelio*, "the greatest opera written up to that time" because of its dramatic qualities, beautiful melodies, interesting orchestration, vocal expressiveness, and the fact "each sound emanates from the depth of the soul and must therefore penetrate the soul of the listener."[87] But Rubinshtein reserved highest praise for the late-style works, especially the piano sonatas, string quartets, and the Ninth Symphony, because the deaf Beethoven had to rely solely on "hearing with the soul's perception" and in this way crafted music of inestimable beauty and spiritual depth. "Oh! The deafness of Beethoven! What a terrible personal tragedy! What immense good fortune for art and mankind!"[88]

Critic and composer Iurii Engel' (1868–1927) likewise tied Beethoven to the French Revolution and argued that he stood as an exemplar of the "new man," which had appeared on the world stage in the wake of 1789. Such a person, "exhibiting to the highest degree possible the will, strength, and individuality of the man of honor," made Beethoven "our closest and most intimate ally." He praised the composer's symphonic music for the "limitless diversity, depth, and strength" of its thematic material, "broad sweep" of its melodic invention, "harmonic riches," "mastery of counterpoint," "unending rhythmic variety and flexibility," and "deep, intrinsic spirituality." But above all, Engel' argued, Beethoven's significance as a composer lay in his adherence to his own "sacred precept" that "music must strike fire from the heart of man" (*Die Musik soll dem Menschen das Feuer aus dem Geiste ausschlagen*).[89]

Sergei Bulich (1859–1921), a distinguished Orientalist, musicologist, and educator, published an article in 1909 entitled "Music and Ideas of Liberation" that included an extended discussion of Beethoven and his music. After providing some anecdotal information on Beethoven's political beliefs, Bulich explored key compositions by way of elucidating Beethoven's fidelity to the concept of freedom. The Third Symphony depicts a "titanic struggle" in the first movement, "deep grief" in the "Funeral March" of the second movement, and "magnificent freedom and life" in the last two movements. In the Fifth Symphony, a "great spirit" battles against the "blows of fate" (first movement) and an ominous "dark force" (third movement), experiencing only momentary "bright happiness" along the way (second movement), before gaining "new strength" (transition to the fourth movement) and "blazing forth" in "triumphant victory" (finale). Concerning *Fidelio*, Bulich summarized its main dramatic features and argued that the music expressed the twin themes of love and freedom standing at the heart of the work much more forcefully and directly than the "listless and saccharine libretto." This "profound and significant idea," he suggested, could be heard to best effect in the concluding section of the *Leonore* 2 and 3 Overtures. "Again the rapid passages of the first violins, playing initially *pianissimo*, are joined by the second violins, violas, cellos, and basses, everything becoming louder and louder, fusing at last into a stormy, triumphant torrent of sound celebrating the victory of love over hatred, freedom over tyranny." [YOUTUBE VIDEO 9] Similarly in regard to the overture to Goethe's tragedy *Egmont*, after all seems lost, "somewhere, as if from deep underground, an almost imperceptible sound is heard; it swells, gains strength, and is transformed into a powerful, raging torrent; the seemingly indestructible fetters of slavery and tyranny break asunder and the blazing sun of freedom floods the wreckage of the old order with its glorious light." [YOUTUBE VIDEO 10] Bulich ended his discussion with an analysis of the Ninth Symphony. Like his peers, he equated *An die Freude* with *An die Freiheit* but remarked especially on the finale's Turkish March in B minor, which he viewed as portraying "the liberated people celebrating universal brotherhood, embracing one another, sending a kiss to the entire world, and kneeling before the Almighty Creator, the incarnation of brotherhood, equality, love, and freedom." All ends with "universal rejoicing and a prayer to Joy-Freedom, daughter of Elysium, spark of divine light."[90]

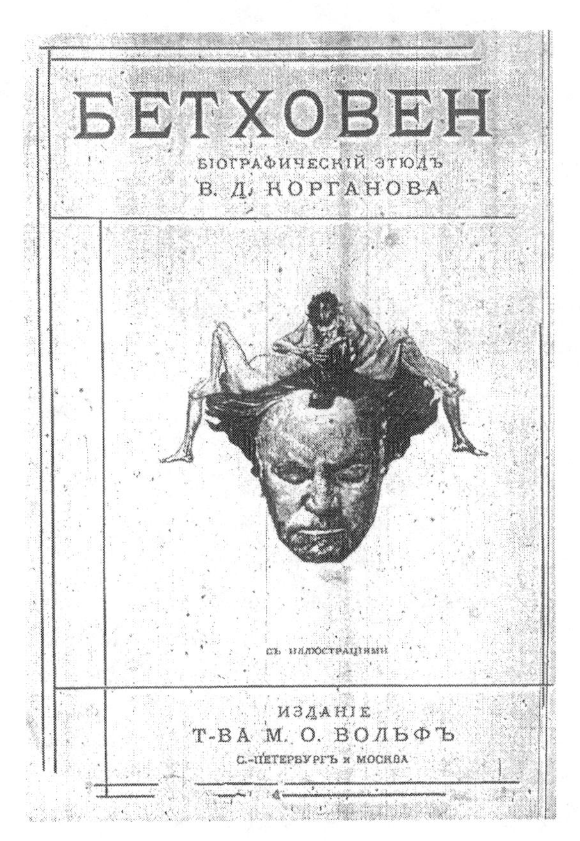

Figure 3.6. The Erotic in Beethoven Iconography, World of Art Era. B. D. Korganov, *Betkhoven: biograficheskii etiud* (St. Petersburg and Moscow: Vol'f, [1908]). Frontispiece.

Bulich observed at the close of his article that music obviously cannot convey a specific political message. Nonetheless, "for us [Russians] music is a powerful vehicle for the expression of emotions and, in spite of the most unfavorable social conditions, can reflect a whole range of feelings and attitudes that one way or another pertain to ideas of liberation." The "more powerful and inspired the music," the more it can "inflame the human soul with one of the most powerful motivating forces in history—the idea of freedom." Surely Bulich had Beethoven and the impending revolution in mind when penning these closing lines.[91]

Vasilii Korganov (1865–1934), composer, pianist, pedagogue, critic, and musicologist, published a study of Beethoven in 1909 that cited parallels between the tenets of the French Revolution and the composer's desire to see "freedom, equality, and brotherhood [established] everywhere." Romanticism had created a "cult of reason" that, among other phenomena, had focused the attention of composers on the "external, realistic world, primarily concerning social and even political events." And so it was with Beethoven. He was a "child of his epoch, a slave to his muse." Beethoven believed in the "possibility of realizing Plato's republic, in the brilliant future of a socialist order, in equality, in communism," Korganov asserted.[92] An intriguing feature of this study is the iconography adorning the work's frontispiece, where Beethoven is depicted in a dreamlike trance while two nude lovers locked in a tight embrace share a passionate kiss reclining on his own tousled mane! While the imagery may raise eyebrows, it is in fact representative of the element of eroticism in book design graphics that characterized the artwork of a variety of publications in the *Mir Iskusstva* (World of Art) movement of the late imperial period. The intention was to celebrate the sensual and beautiful, not the prurient or pornographic.[93]

In a fascinating comparative study of the final symphonies of Beethoven and Tchaikovsky published in 1912, the composer and critic Nikolai Miaskovskii (1881–1950) contrasted the "optimism" of Beethoven's Ninth Symphony with the "pessimism" of Tchaikovsky's Sixth (*Pathétique*). In Tchaikovsky's, "the individual appears in the finale as such a solitary person abandoned in outer space that the efforts in the middle two movements to join with humanity through momentary outbursts of heroism appear hopelessly in vain: man is alone and will forever remain alone in the face of pitiless, indifferent Fate." Beethoven's Ninth, on the other hand, reflects a "gripping optimism with a social coloration" to it. Beethoven was the first and perhaps only composer to "proclaim with such overwhelming force and convincing passion the powerful social principle that in unity lies strength, a precept that resounds all around us these days." In the Ninth Symphony, the "internal struggle" of the first movement, the "titanic attempt to gain both internal and external freedom by the still isolated individual" in the second movement, and the "tranquil peace" of the third movement are followed by the "intoxicating rejoicing" of the finale, in which the "fiery hymn, the *Ode to Joy* (that is, *Ode to Freedom*) expresses Beethoven's deepest conviction that mankind, united in purpose and holding to first principles, has unconquerable strength."[94]

In 1913 Victor Val'ter (1865–1935), violinist and music critic, published an article, "The Ideological Content of Beethoven's Music," in which he reviewed Paul Bekker's *Beethoven* (1911) as a vehicle for offering his own thoughts on the concept of freedom in Beethoven's music. Val'ter cited Bekker to the effect that a single "poetic idea" shaped Beethoven's artistic output—"the struggle of the individual for his freedom in the most unrestricted sense of the word." In the course of this struggle, Bekker continued, "the artist is enlightened and becomes a hero." Val'ter elaborated on this idea by citing as examples of the hero in Beethoven's music the figures of Napoleon—though eventually, if somewhat equivocally, disavowed by the composer—Leonore, Egmont, and Coriolan. But he declared that the "highest freedom is achieved by Beethoven himself, the main hero of his art, when he frees us together with himself from life's calamities and leads us to a higher, celestial happiness," the type of joy expressed in the finale of the Ninth Symphony, the *Missa solemnis*, and the late quartets. "There is no work of art, science, or philosophy," Val'ter proclaimed, "that fully frees us from the trifles of life, temporary misfortunes, and fear of death as much as the music of Beethoven!"[95]

In 1913 David Shor (1867–1942), eminent pianist, pedagogue, and Beethoven scholar, delivered a series of lectures in the Crimean town of Simferopol' on the history of music from Christian times to the age of Beethoven in which he argued that Beethoven had "fused music with social ideas." Inveighing against the "extreme materialism" of the modern age and the degree to which "pornography" had infiltrated literature and the theater, Shor reminded his audience that the function of art was to offer a moral compass to humanity and that Beethoven's music exemplified this fundamental principle. Significantly, in an earlier iteration presented in the Volga River town of Saratov in 1908, Shor had been accused by the provincial governor of "violating the charter and existing regulations [of the sponsoring organization] by deviating from the stated program in order to praise Beethoven not as an artist but as a revolutionary." Subsequently, in an essay on the composer published posthumously, Shor argued that Beethoven remained loyal to the "best ideals" of the Age of Enlightenment, including the "great principles of freedom" lying at the heart of Enlightenment thought. Unlike the composer's contemporaries, including Haydn and Mozart, who stood aloof from the main intellectual and social currents of their day and therefore "remained but great musicians," Beethoven was a true "son of his era and indeed went beyond it" by proclaiming the "perfection of man." He "believed so firmly in the ethical strength of his 'divine art' and valued his artistic calling so highly that he refused to bow his leonine head to crowned officials. . . . Service to mankind based on love and self-denial represented the sum total of his existence." Shor concluded that Beethoven's art continues still to "illuminate the path . . . to universal brotherhood."[96]

And in April and May 1917, on the heels of the February Revolution, which resulted in the collapse of the tsarist regime, Vsevolod Cheshikhin (1865–1934), critic, writer, translator, and author of the poem "Betkhoven" (1892), published a lengthy article entitled "Composers and Revolutions," which included references to Beethoven. Cheshikhin cited the Third, Fifth, and Ninth Symphonies and the opera *Fidelio* as examples of Beethoven's loyalty to "republican" political ideals. The Third Symphony enshrined the "hero" in Western musical literature, the Fifth depicted the individual in both "internal" revolt and "external revolutionary" struggle, and the Ninth, with its by now predictable *Ode to Freedom*, called for the creation of a "cosmopolitan republic" through the appeal, "You millions, I embrace you." And in *Fidelio*, Leonore personifies liberty by freeing her husband, Florestan, a "*political* felon, a Republican," from the clutches of the tyrannical Pizarro. As for Beethoven, Cheshikhin concluded that there was no distinction between his art and the way he lived his life. He was a "born and committed democrat, if not a revolutionary."[97]

* * *

Certainly the Russians did not invent this image of Beethoven as revolutionary. The view originated in the second quarter of the nineteenth century in the criticism of E. T. A. Hoffman and other leading exponents of German Romanticism.[98] Serov was familiar with the writings of Hoffman and undoubtedly drew on his criticism in shaping his own views of Beethoven. But Russian musicologists went well beyond their Western counterparts in the emphasis they placed on the presumed connections between Beethoven's music and fundamental tenets of the French Revolution, above all the concept of freedom that they uniformly embraced by substituting *Freiheit* for *Freude* in the finale of the Ninth Symphony. [YOUTUBE VIDEO 11] This much was new, and those who crafted these assessments were some of the most prominent scholars and musicians engaged at the time in serious writing on Beethoven. Moreover, tens of thousands of music lovers read their views and flocked to concert halls everywhere to experience Beethoven's music firsthand.

Notes

1. Letter to Pauline García-Viardot, September 12, 1850, in A. Kriukov, *Turgenev i muzyka: muzykal'nye stranitsy zhizni i tvorchestva pisateliia* (Leningrad: Gosudarstvennoe muzykal'noe izdatel'stvo, 1963), 17. On September 9, 1840, Bakunin wrote his sister from Berlin that he and Turgenev "listen to a Beethoven symphony every Wednesday—today we heard the *Pastoral*." In December of the same year, he wrote that "we frequently go together to hear symphonies, quartets (the majority by Beethoven), and oratorios." V. Iakovlev, "Muzykal'naia Moskva i Betkhoven: 40-ye i 50-ye gody," in K. A. Kuznetsov, ed. *Russkaia kniga o Betkhovene: k stoletiiu so dnia smerti kompozitora (1827–1927)* (Moscow: Muzykal'nyi sektor, 1927), 131.

2. Letter to Pauline García-Viardot, November 16, 1852, in Kriukov, *Turgenev i muzyka*, 18–19.

3. L. N. Nazanova, "Turgenev i O. A. Turgeneva," *Turgenevskii sbornik: materialy k polnomu sobraniiu sochinenii i pisem I. S. Turgeneva*, I (Moscow-Leningrad: Nauka, 1964), 294; E. S. Ilovaiskaia (Somovaia), "Vospominaniia o Turgeneve," *Turgenevskii sbornik: materialy k polnomu sobraniiu sochinenii i pisem I. S. Turgeneva*, IV (Leningrad: Nauka, 1968), 253. The encounter with Ol'ga Aleksandrovna's daughter occurred in March 1879.

4. Leonard Schapiro, *Turgenev: His Life and Times* (New York: Random House, 1978), 128.

5. Ibid., 126.

6. Letter to Pauline García-Viardot of January 31, 1864, in Kriukov, *Turgenev i muzyka*, 19.

7. I. S. Turgenev, *Sobranie sochinenii*, X (Moscow: Gosudarstvennoe izdatel'stvo khudozhestvennoi literatury, 1957), 215. The reference is to Piano Sonata no. 12 in A-flat ("Funeral March"), op. 26.

8. Ivan Turgenev, *The Two Friends and Other Stories*, trans. Constance Garnett (New York: Macmillan, 1921), 12, 48.

9. Ivan Turgenev, *The Story of a Superfluous Man, Etc.*, trans. Constance Garnett (New York: Macmillan, 1920), 297–98, 307–8.

10. Harry Stevens, trans., *The Vintage Turgenev*, II (New York: Vintage, 1960), 155, 191.

11. Ivan Turgenev, *A House of Gentlefolk*, trans. Constance Garnett (New York: Macmillan, 1920), 22–23, 31–34, 128.

12. Turgenev, *Sobranie sochinenii*, VII, 110–11.

13. F. M. Dostoevskii, *Pis'ma*, ed. A. S. Dolinin, III (Moscow-Leningrad: Academia, 1934), 231.

14. V. V. Grigorenko et al., ed., *F. M. Dostoevskii v vospominaniiakh sovremennikov*, I (Moscow: Khudozhestvennaia literatura, 1964), 358.

15. Ibid., II, 47. Henri Troyat egregiously misstates this declaration: "Feodor Mikhailovich had musical culture. . . . He liked Beethoven, Mendelssohn, Rossini, but couldn't stand Mozart." Norbert Guterman, trans., *Firebrand: The Life of Dostoyevsky* (New York: Roy, 1946), 292.

16. *Posledniaia liubov' F. M. Dostoevskogo: A. G. Dostoevskaia, dnevnik 1867 goda* (St. Petersburg: Andreev i synov'ia, 1993), 130; *F. M. Dostoevskii v vospominaniiakh sovremennikov*, II, 104, 107, 109.

17. Ibid., 116.

18. Dostoevskii, *Pis'ma*, III, 187, 231; Elizabeth Hilliand and Doris Mudie, trans., *The Letters of Dostoevskii to His Wife* (New York: Richard R. Smith, 1930), 277.

19. Konstantin Mochulsky, *Dostoevsky: His Life and Work*, trans. Michael A. Miniban (Princeton, NJ: Princeton University Press, 1967), 648.

20. A. Gozenpud, *Dostoevskii i muzyka* (Leningrad: Muzyka, 1971), 5, 133–42; A. Gozenpud, *Dostoevskii i muzykal'no-teatral'noe iskusstvo* (Leningrad: Sovetskii kompozitor, 1981), 60–62, 129–30, 148–52.

21. Gozenpud, *Dostoevskii i muzyka*, 90.

22. Henri Peyre, "The French Face of Dostoevski," in *Dostoevski and the Human Condition after a Century*, ed. Alexei Ugrinsky et al. (New York: Greenwood, 1986), 127–28.

23. Jennifer Wilson, "Floating in the Air: The World That Made Dostoyevsky's *Crime and Punishment*," *Nation*, CCCVI, 11 (April 16, 2018): 30.

24. Mikhail Bakhtin, *Problems of Dostoevsky's Poetics*, ed. and trans. Caryl Emerson (Minneapolis: University of Minnesota Press, 1984), 6, Bakhtin's italics. For a full discussion of the term, see ibid., 4–46. For its use as a literary device, see Robert Littell, *The Mayakovsky Tapes* (New York: St. Martin's, 2016), 74.

25. A. Al'shvang, *Izbrannye stat'i*, I (Moscow: Sovetskii kompozitor, 1964), 77–78, in Gozenpud, *Dostoevskii i muzyka*, 134.

26. Victor Terras, *A Karamazov Companion: Commentary on the Genesis, Language, and Style of Dostoevsky's Novel* (Madison: The University of Wisconsin Press, 1981), 104.

27. F. M. Dostoevskii, *Sobranie sochinenii*, III (Moscow: Gosudarstvennoe izdatel'stvo khudozhestvennoi literatury, 1956), 258–59. Dostoevsky's ellipsis.

28. Fyodor Dostoevsky, *The Brothers Karamazov*, trans. Richard Pevear and Larissa Volokhonsky (London: Quartet Books, 1990), 105–6. Dostoevsky's ellipses. A short while later, on page 107, Dmitri quotes the first two stanzas of Schiller's poem. For Schiller's influence on the writing of the novel, see Joseph Frank, *Dostoyevsky*, V (Princeton, NJ: Princeton University Press, 2002), 394–97, 436.

29. Richard Pevear, "Foreword," in Fyodor Dostoevsky, *Crime and Punishment*, trans. Richard Pevear and Larissa Volokhonsky (New York: Alfred A. Knopf, 1992), vii. See also Bertram Wolfe, *Three Who Made a Revolution*, 4th rev. ed. (New York: Dial, 1964), 32.

30. Fyodor Dostoevsky, *The Notebooks for the Possessed*, ed. Edward Wasiolek (Chicago: University of Chicago Press, 1968), 5. This penchant for excessive rewriting afflicted Tolstoy as well. The writer revised the opening chapter of his unfinished novel on Peter the Great twenty-seven times and still was unsatisfied. William L. Shirer, *Love and Hatred: The Stormy Marriage of Leo and Sonya Tolstoy* (New York: Simon and Schuster, 1994), 71. For the process as it affected the writing of *Anna Karenina*, see ibid., 74–75.

31. Leonard Bernstein, *The Joy of Music* (New York: Simon and Schuster, 1954), 81.

32. The recordings also contain greetings in 60 languages, 118 pictures, and a variety of other material. William Meredith, "The *Cavatina* in Space," *Beethoven Newsletter*, I, 2 (Summer 1986): 29–30. NASA announced on September 12, 2013, that Voyager 1 had left the solar system and was now traveling in interstellar space some eleven and a half billion miles from earth. Voyager 2 followed on December 10, 2018.

33. Letter to Aleksandra Tolstaia, August 18, 1857, in Henri Troyat, *Tolstoy*, trans. Nancy Amphoux (Garden City, NY: Doubleday, 1967), 187–88.

34. There is considerable confusion over the proper publication date of *What Is Art?* The book was originally published in Russian in 1896 by the Posrednik publishing house. However, Tostoy disavowed this edition after the book appeared in print for what he considered unwarranted revisions that had been dictated by the censorship board of the Russian Orthodox Church. He then endorsed Aylmer Maude's 1898 English translation of the original manuscript as the "true form" of the book, and it is this date that scholars frequently cite in their references to the work.

35. Troyat, *Tolstoy*, 555.

36. Leo Tolstoy, *Childhood, Boyhood, Youth*, trans. Judson Rosengrant (New York: Penguin, 2012), 38.

37. Ruth Rischin, "*Allegro Tumultuosissimamente*: Beethoven in Tolstoy's Fiction," in *In the Shade of the Giant: Essays on Tolstoy*, ed. Huge McLean (Berkeley: University of California Press, 1989), 13.

38. R. F. Christian, ed. and trans., *Tolstoy's Letters*, I (New York: Charles Scribner's Sons, 1978), 58. Later in the same year, Vasilii Botkin wrote Turgenev that Tolstoy was "reveling" in Beethoven's music. David Magarschack, trans., *Turgenev's Literary Reminiscences and Autobiographical Fragments* (New York: Farrar, Strauss and Giroux, 1958), 170.

39. Rosamund Bartlett, *Tolstoy: A Russian Life* (New York: Houghton Mifflin Harcourt, 2011), 439.

40. S. L. Tolstoi, "Muzyka v zhizni L. N. Tolstogo," *Muzyka*, 50 (November 12, 1911): 1134.

41. R. F. Christian, ed. and trans., *Tolstoy's Letters*, II (New York: Charles Scribner's Sons, 1978), 538.

42. Troyat, *Tolstoy*, 538–39. See also Rosamund Bartlett, *Wagner and Russia* (Cambridge: Cambridge University Press, 1995), 52–53.

43. V. N., "L. N. Tolstoi i muzyka," *Russkaia muzykal'naia gazeta*, XVII, 51–52 (December 19–26, 1910): 1154; N. Ianchuk, "K 80-ti-letiiu rozhdeniia L. N. Tolstogo," *Muzyka i zhizn'*, 8 (September 5, 1908): 2. The conductor Serge Koussevitzky engaged the writer in a long conversation about music in which it became apparent that Tolstoy "not only knew all premodern composers but was familiar with the schools and epochs to which they belonged." V. A. Iuzefovich, *Sergei Kusevitskii*, I (Moscow: Iazyki slavianskoi kul'tury, 2004), 162.

44. Dorothy Green, "'The Kreutzer Sonata:' Tolstoy and Beethoven," *Melbourne Slavonic Studies*, I, 1 (1967): 17.

45. Rischin, "*Allegro Tumultuosissimamente*," 50.

46. Tolstoy, *What Is Art?*, 134–35. By "infectious," Tolstoy meant art that transmits genuine ("religious") feelings versus "corrupt" feelings. For a good discussion of this distinction, see Caryl Emerson, "*What Is Art?* and the Anxiety of Music," *Russian Literature*, XL (1996): 437.

47. Catherine Drinker Bowen and Barbara von Meck, "*Beloved Friend:*" *The Story of Tchaikowsky and Nadejda von Meck* (New York: Random House, 1937), 308–9.

48. George Rapall Noyes, *Tolstoy* (New York: Duffield, 1918), 154. On the other hand, Tchaikovsky certainly agreed with Tolstoy when it came to Richard Wagner. He had this to say about Wagner's music in a letter to the composer Sergei Taneev: "Can it really be that this pretentious, heavy-handed and untalented rubbish will be enjoyed by future generations, as we now enjoy the Ninth Symphony [by Beethoven]? If so, it's a terrible prospect." Pauline Fairclough, *Classics for the Masses: Shaping Musical Identity under Lenin and Stalin* (New Haven, CT: Yale University Press, 2016), 212.

49. Tolstoy, *Childhood, Boyhood, Youth*, 38, 191, 325.

50. Leo Tolstoy, *Family Happiness*, in *The Death of Ivan Ilych and Other Stories*, trans. J. D. Huff (New York: Signet Classics, 1960), 11, 85.

51. Rischin, "*Allegro Tumultuosissimamente*," 30–31.

52. Ibid., 43. For full discussion and analysis of *War and Peace*, see ibid., 26–43.

53. Leo Tolstoy, *Anna Karenina*, trans. Richard Pevear and Larissa Volokhonsky (New York: Viking, 2001), 111–12.

54. Leo Tolstoy, "The Kreutzer Sonata," trans. Richard Pevear and Larissa Volokhonsky, in *The Death of Ivan Ilyich and Other Stories* (New York: Alfred A. Knopf, 2009), 149.

55. Leo Tolstoy, *Resurrection*, trans. Rosemary Edmonds (New York: Penguin, 1966), 549.

56. Troyat, *Tolstoy*, 497. This was to be Sonya's thirteenth and last completed pregnancy.

57. A. N. Wilson, *Tolstoy* (New York: Fawcett Columbia, 1988), 379.

58. "Ivan the Terrible and His Son Ivan on November 16, 1581" (1885), Tretyakov Gallery, Moscow.

59. There have a number of attempts to analyze "The Kreutzer Sonata" as a verbal rendering of Opus 47, either in terms of the composition's expressive character (Eguchi, Rishchin) or as the sonata allegro form in which its first movement presto is written (De Roeck, Emerson, Green, Papazian). While Tolstoy, unlike Dostoevsky, was a trained musician equipped to craft his novella as a literary sonata, there is no evidence that he consciously set out to do so. Nonetheless, for perceived parallels, see Emerson, Green, and Rischlin above and Galina L. De Roeck, "Tolstoj's *Krejcerova Sonata*: Music as Its Theme and Structure," *Russian Language Journal*, XLVI, 153–155 (1992): 111–18; Mahoko Eguchi, "Music and Literature as Related Infections: Beethoven's Kreutzer Sonata Op. 47 and Tolstoj's Novella 'The Kreutzer Sonata,'"

Russian Literature, XL (1996): 419–32; and Elizabeth A. Papazian, "Presto and Manifesto: The Kreutzer Sonatas of Tolstoj and Beethoven," *Russian Literature*, XL (1996): 491–516. Eguchi and Papazian provide musical examples. Interestingly, Tolstoy inserted the word *crescendo* into the text of the novella at the critical moment when rage erupts into an act of murder, something that is frequently lost on English readers due to the failure of translators, Pevear and Volokhonsky aside, to carry the word over. For the original, see L. N. Tolstoi, "Kreitserova sonata," *Sobranie sochinenii*, X (Moscow: Gosudarstvennoe izdatel'stvo khudozhestvennoi literatury, 1958), 337.

60. Wilson, *Tolstoy*, 329.

61. Daniel Rancour-Laferriere, *Tolstoy on the Couch: Misogyny, Masochism and the Absent Mother* (New York: New York University Press, 1998), 123.

62. *Le Temps*, November 2, 1902, in Romain Rolland, *Tolstoy*, trans. Bernard Miall (Port Washington, NY: Kennikat, 1972), 183.

63. Iuzefovich, *Sergei Kusevitskii*, 162–63.

64. Troyat, *Tolstoy*, 634.

65. First quotation in S. L. Tolstoi, "Muzyka v zhizni L. N. Tolstogo," 1132 and Rancour-Leferrere, *Tolstoy on the Couch*, 12; second quotation from the memoirs of the writer Maxim Gorky. When Gorky asked Tolstoy what he meant by the term "mute," he replied, "Because [music] is without words. In sound there is more soul than in thought. Thought is a purse with coins in it, but sound is not dirtied with anything, it is inwardly pure." Rancour-Laferriere, *Tolstoy on the Couch*, 125.

66. S. L. Tolstoi, "Muzyka v zhizni L. N. Tolstogo," 1100.

67. Tolstoy, "The Kreutzer Sonata," 142–47.

68. Rolland, *Tolstoy*, 179.

69. N. G. Chernyshevskii to A. N. Chernyshevskii, April 1, 1881, in N. G. Chernyshevskii, *Polnoe sobranie sochinenii*, XV (Moscow: Gosudarstvennoe izdatel'stvo khudozhestvennoi literatury, 1950), 324; Bartlett, *Wagner and Russia*, 50.

70. N. G. Chernyshevskii, "Esteticheskie otnosheniia iskusstva k deistvitel'nosti," in *Estetika i literaturnaia kritika: izbrannye stat'i* (Moscow: Gosudarstvennoe izdatel'stvo khudozhestvennoi literatury, 1951), 29. On at least one occasion, however, Beethoven's music exerted such a powerful influence on the critic that, despite his indifference, he could not dismiss it out of hand. Recalling a concert he had attended with his wife, he remarked, "They sang, they played, I read proof sheets. All of a sudden the orchestra began playing something entirely unique. This must be Beethoven, I thought. I checked the program and affirmed this was the case. Can you imagine, I listened to the whole piece all the way through!" Marina Raku, *Muzykal'naia klassika v mifotvorchestve sovetskoi epokhi* (Moscow: Novoe literaturnoe obozrenie, 201[illegible]), 236. For Chernyshevskii's views on music in general, see Chernyshevskii, "Esteticheskie otnosheniia iskusstva," 34–36.

71. N. A. Dobroliubov, *Selected Philosophical Essays*, trans. J. Fineberg (Moscow: Foreign Languages Publishing House, 1956), 72, 81.

72. Nikolai Mikhailovskii, *Sochineniia N. K. Mikhailovskgo*, II (St. Petersburg: Vol'f, 1896), 612.

73. On Lavrov, see P. I. Lavrov, *Historical Letters*, trans. James P. Scanlan (Berkeley: University of California Press, 1967). On Tkachev, see P. N. Tkachev, *Izbrannye sochineniia na sotsial'no-politicheskie temy*, V (Moscow: Izdatel'stvo vsesoiznogo obshchestva politika-torzhan i ssyl'no-poselentsev, 1935), 364; VI, 419.

74. D. I. Pisarev, "Posmotrim!," in *Sochineniia*, III (Moscow: Gosudarstvennoe izdatel'stvo khudozhestvennoi literatury, 1956), 470. The toy in question is the *van'ka-vstan'ka*, a wooden doll with a weight in its base that brings it to an upright position whenever tipped to one side or another.

75. Letter of July 3, 1877, from Peter Tchaikovsky to Nadezhda von Meck, in P. I. Tchaikovsky, *To My Best Friend: Correspondence between Tchaikovsky and Nadezhda von Meck, 1876–1878*, trans. Galina von Meck (Oxford, UK: Oxford University Press, 1993), 25.

76. D. I. Pisarev, "Obrazovannaia tolpa (Sochinenie F. M. Tolstogo)," in *Sochineniia*, IV (Moscow: Gosudarstvennoe izdatel'stvo khudozhestvennoi literatury, 1956), 261.

77. James H. Billington, *Mikhailovsky and Russian Populism* (Oxford: Oxford University Press, 1958), 14.

78. Ivan Turgenev, *Fathers and Sons*, trans. Rosemary Edmonds (Baltimore: Penguin, 1965), 6.

79. Vladimir Stasov coined the term "Shakespeare of the masses" in a letter of August 12, 1861, to Milii Balakirev. See *M. A. Balakirev i V. V. Stasov: perepiski*, I (Moscow: Muzyka, 1970), 170. Wagner quote is cited in Lewis Lockwood, *Beethoven: The Music and the Life* (New York: W. W. Norton, 2003), 261.

80. T. N. Livanova, "Betkhoven i russkaia muzykal'naia kritika XIX veka," in *Betkhoven: sbornik statei*, ed. N. L. Fishman, II (Moscow: Muzyka, 1972), 191, 196, Serov's italics.

81. A. N. Serov, "Deviataia simfoniia Betkhovena: ee sklad i smysl," *Izbrannye stat'i*, I (Moscow-Leningrad: Gosudarstvennoe muzykal'noe izdatel'stvo, 1950), 429, Serov's italics.

82. V. V. Stasov, "Iskusstvo XIX veka," *Stat'i o muzyke*, V-B (Moscow: Muzyka, 1980), 9–12. Leonard Bernstein substituted *Freiheit* for *Freude* at his historic December 25, 1989, concert in Berlin celebrating the fall of the Berlin Wall. It is now generally accepted that the *Freiheit* claim is a myth that found its way into the musicological literature via a novella, *Das Musikfest oder die Beethovener* (*The Music Festival, or the Beethovenists*), by Wolfgang Robert Griepenkerl and published in Leipzig in 1838. See Nicholas Cook, *Beethoven: Symphony No. 9* (Cambridge: Cambridge University Press, 1993), 94–95 and David Benjamin Levy, *Beethoven: The Ninth Symphony*, rev. ed. (New Haven, CT: Yale University Press, 2003), 165–67.

83. A. Rubinshtein, *Muzyka i ee predstaviteli: razgovor o muzyke* (Moscow and St. Petersburg: Iurgenson, 1892), 35, 38–39.

84. Catherine Drinker Bowen, *"Free Artist:" The Story of Anton and Nicholas Rubinshtein* (New York: Random House, 1939), 314.

85. Rubinshtein, *Muzyka i ee predstaviteli*, 39–40.

86. A. G. Rubinshtein, *Literaturnoe nasledie*, I, ed. L. A. Barenboim (Moscow: Muzyka, 1983), 183.

87. Rubinshtein, *Muzyka i ee predstaviteli*, 37.

88. Ibid., 40.

89. Iu. Engel', *Ocherki po istorii muzyki* (Moscow: Klochkov, 1911), 66–79.

90. S. Bulich, "Muzyka i osvoboditel'nye idei," *Vestnik Evropy*, XLIV, 2 (1909): 8–14.

91. Ibid., 26.

92. V. D. Korganov, *Betkhoven: biograficheskii etiud* (St. Petersburg and Moscow: Vol'f [1909]), 1–8.

93. On the World of Art movement, see John E. Bowlt, *Moscow & St. Petersburg, 1900–1920: Art, Life & Culture of the Russian Silver Age* (New York: Vendome, 2008), 161–99; A. Flegon, *Eroticism in Russian Art* (London: Flegon, 1976), 149–80; Yevgenia Petrova, ed., *The World of Art: On the Centenary of the Exhibition of Russian and Finnish Artists, 1898*, trans. from the Russian by Kenneth MacInnes and from the Finnish by Philip Landon (Helsinki: Finnish National Gallery Ateneum, 1998).

94. N. Miaskovskii, "Chaikovskii i Betkhoven," *Muzyka*, 77 (May 16, 1912): 436. The article also appeared in pamphlet form under the title, *Chaikovskii i Betkhoven* (Moscow: Muzyka, 1912).

95. Victor Val'ter, "Ideinoe soderzhanie Betkhovenskoi muzyki," *Russkaia muzykal'naia gazeta*, XX, 8–9 (February 24–March 3, 1913): 210–15; 10 (March 10, 1913): 241–45.

96. On the 1913 Simferopol' lectures, see O. S., "Simferopol' (korrespondentsiia)," *Russkaia muzykal'naia gazeta*, XX, 30–31 (July 28–August 4, 1913): 664–65. On the 1908 Saratov incident, see Ia. K. Evdokimov, "Muzykal'noe proshloe Saratova (do 1917 goda)," in *Iz muzykal'nogo proshlogo: sbornik ocherkov*, ed. B. S. Shteinpress (Moscow: Gosudarstvennoe muzykal'noe izdatel'stvo, 1960), 198. For the posthumously published essay on Beethoven, see David Shor, *Vospominaniia*, ed. Iulii Matveev (Moscow: Mosty kul'tury, 2001), 277–78.

97. V. Cheshikhin, "Kompozitory i revoliutsii," *Russkaia muzykal'naia gazeta*, XXIV, 13–14 (April 1–8, 1917): 289–90, Cheshikhin's italics. The full article extended over three issues of the journal: *Russkaia muzykal'naia gazeta*, XXIV, 13–14 (April 1–8, 1917): 282–92; 15–16 (April 16–23, 1917): 314–21; 17–18 (April 30–May 7, 1917): 338–46.

98. See especially Hoffmann's review of the Fifth Symphony in *Allgemeine musikalische Zeitung*, 12 (July 4/11, 1810): 630–42; English translation in *The Critical Reception of Beethoven's Compositions by His German Contemporaries*, II, trans. Wayne M. Senner, ed. Robin Wallace and William Meredith (Lincoln: University of Nebraska Press, 2001), 95–112. For commentary and analysis, see Matthew Guerrieri, *The First Four Notes: Beethoven's Fifth and the Human Imagination* (New York: Vintage Books, 2014), 88–123. For an overview of German Beethoven reception until 1918, see David B. Dennis, *Beethoven in German Politics, 1870–1989* (New Haven, CT: Yale University Press, 1996), 1–85.

4

EMBRACING BEETHOVEN

Concert Hall and Riverbank

BEETHOVEN'S MUSIC RESOUNDED THROUGHOUT THE EMPIRE IN LATE imperial Russia. The founding of the Russian Musical Society in 1859 and the formation of its attendant branches in a host of provincial centers in succeeding years contributed substantially to the progress of musical affairs. The establishment of the St. Petersburg and Moscow Conservatories in 1862 and 1866 respectively and the opening of a number of music schools elsewhere created the professional talent required for increased music making. These developments resulted in more frequent performances of Beethoven's music, reaching substantially larger audiences. The overture and incidental music to Goethe's tragedy *Egmont*; the Third, Fifth, and Ninth Symphonies; the *Fidelio* and *Leonore* Overtures; and concert arias and stagings of the opera *Fidelio* proved the most popular works. In this subtle yet telling way, Beethoven's more dramatic and politically suggestive music became part of the fabric of Russian life on the eve of the 1917 Revolution.

The Professionalization of Musical Life

The institutional framework responsible for Russia's musical progress in the late imperial period came into existence at the same time as the reform campaign launched during the reign of Alexander II (1855–81). While there was no direct link between the two—one dealing with the small world of music making, the other with broad issues affecting state and society—both were the product of the same impulse of modernization that shaped much of Russian public life in the last decades of tsarist rule. The debacle of Russia's ignominious defeat in the Crimean War (1854–56), a war lost at home to a coalition of smaller nations, served as the catalyst for the promulgation of the Great Reforms of the Alexandrian era, including the emancipation of the serfs (1861), enlargement of the prerogatives of provincial (1864) and municipal (1870) self-government, and liberalization of the legal (1864) and military (1874) systems. However, while of enormous significance in eliminating the worst abuses of past practices, these reforms proved insufficient to mollify the more radical elements in society at large and resulted in a number of attempts on the life of Alexander II that culminated in the assassination of the tsar on March 1, 1881. Efforts to stabilize the situation through the reactionary policies of the succeeding reigns of Alexander III (1881–94) and Nicholas II (1894–1917), coupled with rapid economic development, increasing social dislocation, and the disastrous effects of the Russo-Japanese War (1904–5) and World War I (1914–18), only exacerbated existing difficulties, contributing in their separate ways to the downfall of the monarchy in February 1917. During these same decades, however, Russian cultural life—from music to painting, literature to dance, architecture to the decorative arts—flourished in the renaissance of the Silver Age, facilitating Russia's rise to a position of primus inter pares in the avant-garde of fin de siècle Europe. The professionalization of the musical establishment at midcentury had much to do with this remarkable flowering of culture in the last decades of tsarist rule.

The name Anton Rubinshtein looms large in any discussion of the Russian Musical Society and St. Petersburg Conservatory, the spearhead of musical reform in the capital and, by extension, throughout the empire. By the time he was twenty-one, Rubinshtein had already studied under the best piano and composition teachers at home and abroad and acquired an enviable reputation as a world-class concert pianist. He had become friends with Franz Liszt, Felix Mendelssohn, and Robert Schumann and had even written an opera. But in Russia he discovered to his dismay that he was only "the son of a merchant of the second guild." As recounted with obvious pique in his memoirs, after having taken communion at Kazan' Cathedral during Holy Week services in 1850, Rubinshtein had to provide his name and rank to the deacon for notation in the confessional register. At this point, the following exchange took place:

> Your name and rank?
>
> Rubinshtein, artist.
>
> Artist, what does that mean? Are you an actor?
>
> No.
>
> Well, perhaps you are a teacher in some kind of institute?
>
> No.
>
> Then you are in government service?

> No, I do not work for the government.
>
> Well, then, just who are you anyway?

The questioning continued in this fashion before it occurred to the deacon to ask Rubinshtein who his father was:

> A merchant of the second guild.
>
> Well, there you have it—you are the son of a merchant of the second guild.[1]

Rubinshtein recorded this anecdote to illustrate the fact that, unlike painters, sculptors, and actors who obtained the special rank of free artist through their graduation from the Imperial Academy of Fine Arts or theater school, musicians did not enjoy this privilege, since there was no academic institution through which they could gain such recognition; unless they were in government service or worked in the imperial theaters or state schools, they were, as Rubinshtein's experience made clear, nobodies. One objective in establishing a conservatory as part of a national musical organization was to create a vehicle through which independent musicians could acquire professional status in the rigid hierarchy of the Russian ranking system. But a broader objective concerned reforming the overall state of musical affairs, especially in regard to the lack of symphonic societies that could offer orchestral and chamber concerts on a year-round basis and educational facilities that could provide professional training for aspiring composers, conductors, and performers. "Art was in the hands of a few dilettante-Maecenases who were enraptured above all by Italian opera and also composed in that manner," Rubinshtein complained. "Musician-artists, people who were skilled in the art of music, did not exist at all."[2]

Enter the Grand Duchess Elena Pavlovna, widowed sister-in-law of Nicholas I, an avid music lover, and as recounted in chapter 1, one of the royals responsible for Franz Liszt's celebrated performance of Beethoven's *Emperor* Concerto at the Viel'gorskii salon in 1843. The grand duchess had been favorably impressed by the premiere of Rubinshtein's opera *Dmitrii Donskoi* in 1852 and on this basis invited the composer into her employ as pianist for her court and supervisor of her musical soirées, or as Rubinshtein facetiously put it, "Palace Janitor for Music." She was also known for her liberal thinking on a range of topics, including the need to address the sorry state of musical affairs in the capital. In 1856 she invited Rubinshtein to her winter home in Nice, France, where he was able to discuss various reform ideas with her and the cellist Matvei Viel'gorskii, who was living nearby. "The concept of a Russian musical society and a conservatory was born in Nice," Rubinshtein wrote. "I talked with Matvei Viel'gorskii . . . about the fact that something needed to be done since the

Figure 4.1. Grand Duchess Elena Pavlovna. Unknown portraitist. Alamy Stock Photo WWK9DF.

state of music in Russia was lamentable no matter how one looked at it. Elena Pavlovna showed interest in this as well."[3] Rubinshtein subsequently brought the St. Petersburg reform advocates Dmitrii Kanshin, Vasilii Kologrivov, and Dmitrii Stasov (brother of the critic Vladimir Stasov) into the discussion. The group decided that instead of proposing the creation of an entirely new society that might disconcert officials jealous of their prerogatives in such matters, it would seek to resurrect a previously sanctioned but now defunct body, the Symphonic Society, which had been created in 1840 to perform occasional concerts for large orchestras. The ploy worked. On May 1, 1859, the state authorized the revival of the Symphonic Society, now to be called the Russian Musical Society; approved a revised charter prepared by Prince Vladimir Odoevskii; and confirmed a five-member directorship consisting of Kanshin, Kologrivov, Rubinshtein, Stasov, and Viel'gorskii. Elena Pavlovna provided some rooms in her Mikhailovskii Palace for music classes, while the grand duchess, the emperor and empress, other members of the royal family, and a number of wealthy aristocrats offered their financial support. In this way, the Russian Musical Society and a nascent St. Petersburg Conservatory came into being.[4]

The Russian Musical Society officially opened its doors on October 11, 1859, with a membership drive that attracted 20 "honored members," those paying a lump sum of one thousand rubles or one hundred rubles a year; approximately 490 "regular members" (fifteen rubles a year); and 86 choral performing members (five rubles a year). Rubinshtein became music director of the society (and in 1862 the St. Petersburg Conservatory) during his two terms on the board (1859–67 / 1887–91). Elena Pavlovna brought the organization under the protection of her patronage until her death in 1873, at which point her nephew the Grand Duke Konstantin Nikolaevich began shepherding its affairs. On April 6, 1873, the grand duke secured imperial status for the organization, thereby guaranteeing direct government financing of what had now become the Imperial Russian Musical Society.

The charter of the society stipulated that it was to (1) "develop musical education and the taste for music in Russia and encourage native talent" and (2) "perform as perfectly as possible the best works of instrumental and vocal music, to wit, symphonies, overtures, quartets, trios, oratorios, masses, cantatas, and the like, and provide an opportunity for native composers to hear their own works performed."[5] Rubinshtein immediately began pursuing the second objective by gathering together players from a variety of musical forces in St. Petersburg, rehearsing the ensemble at the Mikhailovskii Palace, and presenting the first concert on November 23, 1859, at the Gentry Club with some nine hundred in attendance. Given his obsession with Beethoven, Rubinshtein characteristically programmed a Beethoven symphony, no. 8 in F, op. 93, along with the overture to Glinka's *Russlan and Liudmila*, the finale of Handel's *Jephtha*, the finale of Mendelssohn's unfinished opera *Lorelei*, and his own Piano Concerto in G minor, op. 45, thus satisfying the injunction that works by native composers be included in the repertoire. Over the course of the subsequent nine concerts of the first season (1859–60), Rubinshtein programmed two more Beethoven symphonies, no. 4 in B-flat and no. 9 in D minor (*Choral*), and the *Emperor* Piano Concerto; excerpts from the incidental music to Kotzebue's *The Ruins of Athens*, op. 113; the song "Busslied" from Six Lieder to Poems by Gellert, op. 48; and the Romance for Violin and Orchestra in G, op. 40. Altogether, from 1859 to 1909, forty-two compositions by Beethoven were performed in 251 of the 512 regular and special concerts, signifying that Beethoven's music was heard in just under half of all concerts presented by the society. Significantly, works expressing the "revolutionary" spirit identified by late imperial critics received a credible number of performances: the overture and incidental music to Goethe's tragedy *Egmont* was presented twelve times; the Third Symphony twenty-one times; the Fifth Symphony eighteen times; the Ninth Symphony twenty-two times; and the *Leonore* and *Fidelio* Overtures twenty-eight times. By contrast, Mozart's music appeared on 107 concert programs (20%), Wagner's on 119 (23%), Mendelssohn's on 125 (24%), Liszt's on 138 (27%), Tchaikovsky's on 147 (28%), Rubinshtein's on 154 (30%), and Schumann's on 157 (30%). Beethoven thus emerged as the most frequently performed composer, and his more dramatic music, with its affirmation of the transformative power of the human spirit, gained repeated hearings at a time of increasing political unrest.[6]

Rubinshtein encountered greater difficulty in implementing the Russian Musical Society's other objective—the development of musical education. The teaching of a few classes in the Mikhailovskii Palace and in the homes of some of the instructors proved far from adequate and certainly did not measure up to his concept of a music conservatory. Rubinshtein thus turned to the Education Ministry with a fully developed proposal to establish what he called an Imperial Music School with graduates receiving the title of free artist on successful completion of their exit examinations, a proposal that the ministry flatly turned down as a "luxury" the country could ill afford. He then appealed to the public in an article entitled "About Music in Russia," published in the journal *Vek* (*Century*) in January 1861. Lamenting the fact that "in Russia there are hardly any artists-musicians in the usual sense of the term," Rubinshtein argued that "this of course results from the fact that our government at the present time does not grant to the musical profession those privileges that the other arts, such as painting, sculpture, and the like, enjoy, that is, it does not grant to musicians the *title of artist*." Rubinshtein concluded that "the only solution to this lamentable situation is the establishment of a conservatory."[7] This appeal did not generate the intended public support either and in fact backfired by sparking opposition among conservative elements who opposed the idea of a conservatory as a Western European innovation having no place in Russia. The critic Aleksandr Serov, for example, dismissed the proposal as "German guild-hall pedantry," while another opponent styled it "an amusing notion from those ancient tales where the hero is an artist."[8] As a last resort, in the spring of 1861, Rubinshtein turned once again to his benefactress, the Grand Duchess Elena Pavlovna, who used her influence with the Ministry of the Imperial Court to obtain official backing and financial support for the proposed institution. The ministry agreed to allocate an annual subsidy of five thousand rubles (increased in 1878 to fifteen thousand rubles) and on October 17, 1861, promulgated a charter establishing the St. Petersburg Conservatory. Among other provisions, the charter called for the government to appoint representatives to the graduation examination committee and issue diplomas, thereby creating a mechanism whereby the rank of free artist could be bestowed on all successful graduates. The conservatory officially opened

Figure 4.2. Nikolai Rubinshtein. Unknown photographer. Alamy Stock Photo EK2TF9.

its doors on September 8, 1862, with Rubinshtein as director. It certainly was no coincidence that the first diploma with the designation of free artist was awarded on February 23, 1863, to one Anton Grigor'evich Rubinshtein. The following citation from Elena Pavlovna accompanied the diploma: "It is especially pleasant for me to acknowledge that the first diploma with the rank of Free Artist will be adorned with the name of the individual who is associated with the founding of the [Russian Musical] Society and is justifiably deserving of fame throughout Europe. I confirm [the degree]. ELENA."[9]

Branches of the Russian Musical Society spread throughout the empire in the decades ahead, and a number of additional conservatories came into being as well. On February 28, 1860, Nikolai Rubinshtein, at the urging of his brother, established the Moscow branch of the society and assumed the position of music director. The Moscow Conservatory in turn opened its doors on September 1, 1866, again with Rubinshtein as music director. True to family form, works by Beethoven enjoyed pride of place in the offerings of the opening concert season (1860–61) of the Moscow branch. In addition to an unidentified overture, all of the following were performed that first year: *Appassionata* Piano Sonata, Third Piano Concerto, *Leonore* 3 Overture,

Fidelio Overture, overture to the incidental music to Kotzebue's *King Stephen*, and Symphonies nos. 4–8. The Third Symphony was presented on March 23, 1862, during the second concert season (1861–62), while the Ninth Symphony was performed on March 1 and 8, 1863, during the third concert season (1862–63). The March 1 performance represented the Moscow premiere of the work. Altogether, from 1860 to 1899, twenty-eight orchestral compositions by Beethoven were performed in 235 of the 500 regular and special concerts (47%). Among these performances, the overture and incidental music to Goethe's tragedy *Egmont* was presented ten times, the Third Symphony thirteen times, the Fifth Symphony eighteen times, the Ninth Symphony fourteen times, the *Leonore* and *Fidelio* Overtures thirty-two times, and excerpts from *Fidelio* two times. The scheduling of these politically sensitive works thus approximated the number of performances heard in St. Petersburg.[10]

In Kiev, the third major metropolitan city in late imperial Russia, a branch of the Russian Musical Society opened its doors on November 10, 1863. All told, from 1863 to 1913 twenty-six symphonic works and twenty chamber and choral pieces by Beethoven were performed in 87 of the 231 regular and special concerts (38%). The *Egmont* Overture was performed six times, the Third Symphony five times, the Fifth Symphony eight times, the Ninth Symphony two times, the *Leonore* and *Fidelio* Overtures five times, and excerpts from the opera *Fidelio* two times.[11] Other sections of the Russian Musical Society were formed in Kazan' and Khar'kov in 1864; Nizhnii-Novgorod, Saratov, and Pskov in 1873; Omsk in 1876; Tobol'sk in 1878; Tomsk in 1879; Penza in 1881; Tambov in 1882; Tbilisi (Tiflis) in 1883; and Odessa in 1886. By 1914, an additional forty-one sections had come into being, bringing the total number in the empire to fifty-six. New conservatories were also established in Saratov (1912), Kiev and Odessa (1913), and Tbilisi (Tiflis) and Khar'kov (1917). However measured, this was a remarkable record of music reform. "If the earliest branches of the [Russian Musical] Society were, as they liked to consider themselves, oases in a cultural desert," Lynn Sargeant writes, "by the outbreak of World War I, the Society's branches formed an archipelago of culture, linked by the railroad, the post, and the periodical press, that stretched from the Western Borderlands to the Sea of Japan."[12]

Performing around the Empire

By the late nineteenth century, in addition to the normal venues of St. Petersburg and Moscow, concerts featuring works by Beethoven were being presented across most of the empire—Poland, Finland, the Baltic provinces, central and southern Russia, Ukraine, the Caucasus, the Volga River basin, and western Siberia—and the number of performances increased correspondingly. A compilation of concert reports appearing in the provincial press for the period 1801 to 1880, while incomplete, offers some evidence: from 1801 to 1860, an average of only nineteen concerts per decade were staged in which works by Beethoven were performed; this number rose to seventy-eight from 1861 to 1870 and stood at seventy-six from 1871 to 1880. Significantly, the politically sensitive works cited above received their share of performances: the overture and incidental music to Goethe's tragedy *Egmont* was performed seven times, the Third Symphony nine times, the Fifth Symphony six times, the Ninth Symphony nine times, and staged performances of the opera *Fidelio* sixteen times.[13] That this data is incomplete is borne out by other evidence indicating that in St. Petersburg alone during the period of 1818 to 1905 *Fidelio* was presented at least forty-three times—three times in 1818 and 1819 (German Opera and Malyi Theater), ten times from 1834 to 1846 (German Opera), twelve times from 1863 to 1864 and in 1875 (Italian Opera), fourteen times in the 1870s and 1880s (venue not indicated), two or three times in 1889 (venue not indicated), once in 1891 (St. Petersburg Conservatory, first performance in Russian), and once in 1905 (Mariinskii Theater).[14] More complete data concerning performances of Beethoven's orchestral music in the period from 1859 to 1913 can be obtained from the concert programs of the St. Petersburg, Moscow, and Kiev branches of the Russian Musical Society. Altogether, these three societies presented 573 concerts, or on average eleven per year, in which works by Beethoven were featured. The overture and incidental music to Goethe's tragedy *Egmont* received twenty-eight performances, the Third Symphony thirty-nine, the Fifth Symphony forty-four, the Ninth Symphony thirty-eight, the *Leonore* and *Fidelio* Overtures sixty-five, and various arias from *Fidelio* four.

Centenary celebrations of Beethoven's birth in 1870 served to bring the composer to the attention of the concertgoing public as well. In St. Petersburg, the Russian Musical Society, in conjunction with the St. Petersburg Philharmonic Society, marked the occasion by performing the *Missa solemnis* in D, op. 123, at the Gentry Club on December 27, 1870. The work represented an unusual selection for a celebratory event and indeed the concert was poorly attended, a circumstance attributed by the press to the fact the mass was less popular with the public than other compositions by Beethoven. Nonetheless the entire royal family attended the performance and the violinist Leopold Auer was praised for his solo playing in the Benedictus, which "had a special effect" on the audience. The Overture in C, *Die Weihe des Hauses* (*Consecration of the House*), op. 124, opened the concert.[15] In Moscow, the Artist's Circle Hall staged a concert featuring three unidentified works by Beethoven on December 17, 1870. Around six hundred attended the event, which began with an address on the life of Beethoven by the critic and composer Iurii Arnol'd.[16] In Saratov the celebratory concert, in which some one hundred people participated, included the *Fidelio* Overture; one of the Romances for Violin and Orchestra; the finale of Symphony no. 5; and three pieces for chorus and orchestra comprising the Kyrie from the Mass in C, op. 86, the finale from *Christus am Ölberge* (*Christ on the Mount of Olives*), op. 85, and the march and chorus from *Die Ruinen von Athen* (*The Ruins of Athens*), op. 113.[17] In Tbilisi (Tiflis), the commemoration took place on December 14, 1870, at a concert that included several unidentified orchestral and choral works by the composer.[18] The Beethoven jubilee in Odessa was held on December 17, 1870, and offered performances of the *Egmont* Overture; Romances for Violin in G, op. 40, and F, op. 50; Scena and Aria *Ah! perfido*, op. 65; the *Emperor* Piano Concerto; and Symphony no. 5. Performance of the Fifth Symphony marked the premiere of the work in Odessa.[19] Warsaw repeated essentially the same program on December 17, 1870. The press reported that members of the audience "remained in a constant state of enthusiasm, filling the hall with outbursts of thunderous applause" at the conclusion of each work.[20]

By the turn of the century, as enumerated in table 1, Beethoven's music had become a fixture in concertizing throughout the empire. The geographical range of the programming is astonishing: from Congress Poland and the Baltic states in the west (Łodz, Warsaw, Riga, Vil'na [Vilnius]) deep into the heart of Siberia in the east (Tomsk, Irkutsk) and from Arkhangel'sk in the far north to Batum, Tbilisi, and Baku in distant Transcaucasia to the south. Only in America did the composer's music spread across a similarly vast expanse.[21] In the 1830s, only the cognoscenti in a few elite ensembles in St. Petersburg and Moscow performed works by Beethoven. By the turn of the century, these works had entered the mainstream of concert programming everywhere. The most popular pieces from 1895 to 1917 remained the same as before: the *Egmont* Overture was performed twenty-six times (plus one performance of excerpts from the incidental music), the *Leonore* and *Fidelio* Overtures thirty-six times (plus two full dress productions of the opera, one production of excerpts, and one concert aria), the Third Symphony forty-one times (plus two performances of the "Funeral March"), and the Fifth Symphony fifty-three times. Only the Ninth Symphony received fewer performances—ten altogether, six in Warsaw alone—undoubtedly due to the special difficulties the work posed for local orchestral and choral forces. But overall the same highly dramatic and emotive works that had engaged audiences in Russia's main urban centers since midcentury were being heard throughout the empire in the twilight years of the old regime.

Figure 4.3. Caricature of Sergei Koussevitzky. By Olga Koussevitzky. Courtesy of the Serge Koussevitzky Music Foundation, Library of Congress.

Down the Volga with Koussevitzky

The final chapter in Beethoven's reception in late imperial Russia centers on the remarkable life and career of Serge Koussevitzky, familiar to most readers as the longtime music director of the Boston Symphony Orchestra. Born into a poor Jewish family in Tver Province on July 26, 1874, Koussevitzky studied the double bass at the Moscow Philharmonic Society School, becoming a virtuoso on the instrument. Following graduation in 1894, he joined the Bol'shoi Opera Theater Orchestra and in 1901 succeeded his mentor as principal double bassist in the ensemble and professor of double bass at the Moscow Philharmonic School. From 1898 to 1905, he toured as a soloist in Russia and Germany, transforming the double bass into an admired recital instrument for which he transcribed a variety of standard concert pieces and composed several works of his own, including a concerto in F-sharp minor for double bass and orchestra (1902).

In 1905 Koussevitzky married Nataliia Konstantinova Ushkova, daughter of Russia's richest tea merchant. The couple moved to Germany so that Koussevitzky could study the art of conducting by observing the podium techniques of such giants in the field as Artur Nikisch, Felix Weingartner, Felix Mottl, Gustav Mahler, and Ernst von Schuch, all while honing his skills by guest conducting in London, Paris, Berlin, and Vienna. He also continued concertizing as a double bass soloist and in 1909 established the Russian

Music Publishing House (*Éditions Russes de Musique*) in Berlin to publish new works by Russian composers. In the same year, he returned to Russia and, in the 1909 to 1911 seasons, conducted an acclaimed series of concerts with the St. Petersburg and Moscow Imperial Russian Musical Society Symphony Orchestras.

In 1911 Koussevitzky acquired his own eighty-five-man orchestra with his wife's fortune, trained the ensemble over a three-month period by drilling it solely in the music of Beethoven, and began touring Russia in a series of fabled concerts that continued unabated until the spring of 1916, when wartime exigencies forced him to disband the ensemble. The New Symphony Concert Union, as the orchestra was called, debuted in the early autumn of 1911 with an ambitious one-week, four-program Beethoven festival that included Symphonies nos. 1–9, the Fourth Piano Concerto, and the Violin Concerto. The poet Osip Mandel'shtam captured the unique character of a Koussevitzky concert, the venue symbolically rumbling with revolutionary unrest:

> Here was no musical dilettantism but something threatening, even deadly, arose from the depths, something resembling a longing for action, an obscure prehistoric restlessness. In the hazy light of the gas-lamps the lordly edifice with many porticos was regularly besieged. The prancing mounted gendarmes, imparting to the atmosphere of the square a suggestion of civil disorder, clattered about and shouted, guarding the main entrance. Through the triple ranks carriages with springs and dim lamps crept in and arranged themselves in an imposing black camp. The cabmen did not venture to drive up to the building itself—they had been paid their fares on the way—and they slipped out, avoiding the wrath of the police. The St. Petersburger like a feverish little fish entered the marble ice-hole of the vestibule, disappearing into the glowing house of ice, rigged out with silk and velvet. The stalls and the seats behind them were crowded as usual, but the vast galleries off the side entrances were packed, and looked like baskets with clusters of human grapes. In the galleries a July temperature. In the air a perpetual shrilling, like cicadas on the steppe.[22]

Highlights of Koussevitzky's Russian concertizing included three steamship tours down the Volga River to the Caspian Sea and back in the spring seasons of 1910, 1912, and 1914 and four marathon all-Beethoven concerts in southern Russia in March and April 1913. The 1910 Volga tour, which transported the orchestra and invited guests twenty-three hundred miles from Tver to Astrakhan and back, included performances of Beethoven's *Egmont* Overture and Symphonies nos. 5–7, along with works by Rimsky-Korsakov, Scriabin (who performed his own Piano Concerto in F-sharp minor), Taneev, Tchaikovsky, Wagner, and a host of other composers. As the ship put down anchor on the last night of its return voyage, a passenger reflected, "It was

Figure 4.4. Koussevitzky's Third Volga River Tour, 1914. Sketch by Robert Sterl. Arthur Lourie, *Sergei Koussevitzky and His Epoch: A Biographical Chronicle,* trans. S. W. Pring (New York: Alfred A. Knopf, 1931), 111.

about 6:00 in the evening. . . . On the near bank birdsong could be heard coming from the woods. On the far bank a beautiful line of hills stood out in relief while some villages nestled together at the water's edge. A sunset cast a soft rosy glow over this splendid scene. . . . Thus the last evening spent on the Volga. The ship was its own Symphony that sailed away with it, but the memory of where the music had resounded will never be forgotten."[23]

The 1912 tour, from Yaroslavl to Astrakhan and back, included Beethoven's Symphonies nos. 5–6 in another broad-based program of Russian and Western music. The 1914 tour, again from Yaroslavl to Astrakhan and back, included Beethoven's Piano Concertos nos. 3–5 (Eduard Risler), the *Coriolan* Overture, and Symphonies nos. 3, 5, and 6, along with works by Debussy, Liszt, Richard Strauss, Tchaikovsky, and a half dozen Russian composers. The German musicologist and art critic Oskar Bie participated in the 1914 tour and reminisced as follows: "For a Russian, Beethoven is the beginning of the world. Beethoven and Russia are akin; both struggling, intense, eruptive. . . . We played the *Coriolan* Overture and the *Eroica* on the banks of the Volga. The effect was tremendous. From the bare earth arose music, the blessing of humanity, music for the humble and for the workers. A discovery, a new world arose for the people of Tsaritsyn . . . who heard the *Eroica* for the first time."[24]

The tours took from four to six weeks each, with ports of call at Tver (first tour only), Rybinsk, Yaroslavl, Kostroma, Nizhnii-Novgorod, Kazan',

Simbirsk, Samara, Saratov, Tsaritsyn, and Astrakhan. Along the way passengers had ample opportunity to picnic by the side of the river, take leisurely walks on the nearby steppe, visit native settlements and other points of regional interest, and explore the storied medieval towns cast like a handful of pearls along the banks of this majestic Russian waterway. Those who attended the concerts were treated in turn to a world of music few had ever experienced. One commentator wrote that workers in Tsaritsyn were so taken by a concert that they created their own amateur orchestra and named it after Koussevitzky. Another noted that the mayor of Nizhnii-Novgorod requested that the harp be placed next to the conductor's stand so that the audience could have a full view of the instrument and see how it was played. All in all, the Koussevitzky Volga River tours must rank as one of the highlights of Russian music making in the late imperial period.[25]

In a whirlwind of concertizing frenzy that probably has yet to be equaled anywhere in the world, Koussevitzky staged a "Beethoven Celebration" in the spring of 1913 in which his orchestra performed all nine symphonies, all five piano concertos, and the violin concerto in four concerts over four evenings in the following four cities: Odessa (March 7–10), Kiev (March 12–15), Khar'kov (March 25–26, 28–29), and Rostov-na-Donu (March 31 and April 1, 3–4). The local press, collectively catching its breath, responded with unabashed enthusiasm.[26]

Koussevitzky also conducted a series of Beethoven concerts in St. Petersburg from 1910 to 1914 that included the Violin Concerto (Auer/Kreisler/Marteau); Piano Concertos nos. 3 (Risler), 4 (Busoni/Dobrovein/Medtner), and 5 (Gol'denweiser); the *Coriolan*, *Egmont*, and *Leonore 3* Overtures; Symphonies nos. 1–9; and the *Missa solemnis*. Even during World War I when the regime banned the playing of all German music, Koussevitzky persisted in his Beethoven crusade, performing the Ninth Symphony in Petrograd in February 1915 and the Third Symphony in February 1916, together with an all-Beethoven program in Moscow in October 1916.[27]

Following the Bolshevik Revolution of October 1917, Koussevitzky was invited to head the music section of the Commissariat of Enlightenment in the newly formed Soviet government but declined in order to assume the directorship of the renamed State Philharmonic Orchestra of Petrograd. He served in this capacity from 1917 to 1920 before emigrating first to Berlin and then to Paris, where he staged his famous *Concerts Koussevitzky*, and finally to America, where he replaced Pierre Monteux as music director of the Boston Symphony Orchestra, a post he held with great distinction from 1924 to 1949. His deep experience, familiarity with a vast repertoire, and staffing decisions that brought significant new talent into the orchestra enabled him to transform a somewhat mediocre band into a top-tier ensemble that, according to Olin Downes of the *New York Times*, became the finest in the country by the end of the decade. In 1927 Koussevitzky marked the centenary of Beethoven's death with a performance of the late quartets, all nine symphonies, and the *Missa solemnis*, establishing Boston as the Vienna of America during that centennial year.

Koussevitzky's other achievements included assumption of the directorship of the Berkshire (now Tanglewood) Music Festival in 1936, establishment of its permanent performing venue (the Shed) in 1938, and formation of its music school in 1940—an institution that has trained an estimated 20 percent of America's orchestral musicians and 30 percent of its first-chair players. Koussevitzky selected Beethoven's Ninth Symphony to headline the inaugural concert in the Shed on August 4, 1938, "not only because it is the greatest masterpiece in musical literature, but because I wanted to hear the voice of Tanglewood singing Schiller's words calling all nations to the brotherhood of man."[28] Following his wife's death in 1942, he established the Koussevitzky Music Foundation in her memory. Significant works commissioned by the foundation during Koussevitzky's lifetime included Béla Bartók's Concerto for Orchestra (1942–43 / rev. 1945), Aaron Copeland's Symphony no. 3 (1944–46), Benjamin Britten's breakthrough opera *Peter Grimes* (1945), Olivier Messiaen's *Turangalîla-Symphonie* (1946–48), and Douglas Moore's opera *The Ballad of Baby Doe* (1956).[29]

In 1922 Koussevitzky commissioned Maurice Ravel to score the definitive orchestral arrangement of Modest Mussorgsky's piano work, *Pictures at an Exhibition*, and recorded it for the first time in 1930 with the Boston Symphony Orchestra. As a lifelong champion of new music, he also premiered a variety of avant-garde works, including Sergei Prokofiev's Violin Concerto no. 1 (1923) and Symphonies no. 2 (1925) and no. 4 (1930), Arnold Bax's Symphony no. 2 (1929), Igor Stravinsky's *Symphony of Psalms* (1930), Albert Roussel's Symphony no. 3 (1930), Arthur Honegger's Symphony no. 1 (1930), George Gershwin's Second Rhapsody (1931), Aaron Copeland's Appalachian Spring Suite (1945), Samuel Barber's *Knoxville: Summer of 1915* (1948), and Leonard Bernstein's Symphony no. 2 (*The Age of Anxiety*) (1949).[30] He was also a great Sibelian, earning praise from the composer for the "supreme mastery" with which he conducted the Finnish master's works.[31] Among Koussevitzky's pupils, undoubtedly the most famous was Leonard Bernstein, who studied at Tanglewood in the summers of 1940 through 1943. As a measure of the deep respect he held for his mentor, Bernstein unfailingly wore a pair of cufflinks

Koussevitzky had given him at every concert he conducted in a storied career lasting from 1943 to 1990.

Koussevitzky died in Boston on June 4, 1951, and was buried next to his wife, Nataliia. The Boston Symphony Orchestra that he fashioned over the years into one of the world's great ensembles remains his most lasting legacy.

* * *

In surveying the record of Beethoven performances in late imperial Russia, strikingly, no single work was presented more often than the opera *Fidelio*, either in full costume, concert arias, or the dramatic *Leonore* and *Fidelio* Overtures, which present in microcosm the main thematic elements of the work. Dealing as it does with the victory of justice over tyranny, it is tempting to draw appropriate conclusions concerning the impact of the opera on Russian audiences living through times of increasing political unrest. But the effects of music do not lend themselves to such tractable treatment. On the other hand, one can reasonably conclude that Beethoven's more powerful music both reflected and reinforced an existing climate of opinion that outstanding problems of state and society could only be resolved through violence. In this subtle yet telling way, Beethoven became an actor in the twilight years of tsarist rule. As Daniel Barenboim has commented in a different context,

> If you look at the role that music, and much more than music—theater and opera—played in societies and the totalitarian regimes, it was the only place that political ideas and social totalitarianism could be criticized. In other words, a performance of Beethoven, under the Nazis or under any kind of totalitarian regime, whether left or right, suddenly assumes the call for freedom, even becomes a very direct criticism of the policies of the regime and, therefore, is actually a much more disturbing and, at the same time, uplifting thing. This is a long way from the entertainment of Mozart divertimentos or Johann Strauss waltzes.[32]

Thus, when the double-headed eagle at last lost its bearings and plummeted thunderously to earth, Beethoven's fortissimo voice, like Florestan's in *Fidelio*, could be heard swelling in unison with the triumphant chorus as the curtain on the long drama finally came down. [YOUTUBE VIDEO 12]

Notes

1. A. G. Rubinshtein, "Avtobiograficheskie rasskazy (1829–1867)," in L. A. Barenboim, *Anton Grigor'evich Rubinshtein: zhizn', artisticheskii put', tvorchestvo, muzykal'no-obshchestvennaia deiatel'nost'*, I (Leningrad: Gosudarstvennoe muzykal'noe izdatel'stvo, 1957), 417.

2. Ibid.

3. Ibid., 415.

4. On the Russian Musical Society, see N. Findeizen, *Ocherki deiatel'nosti S.-Peterburgskogo otdeleniia Imperatorskogo Russkogo muzykal'nogo obshchestva (1859–1909)* (St. Petersburg: Glavnoe upravlenie udelov, 1909); N. Kashkin, "Piatidesiatiletie Russkogo muzykal'nogo obshchestva," *Muzykal'nyi truzhenik*, III, 10/11 (June 1, 1909): 5–10; 14/15 (August 1, 1909): 4–6; 16/17 (September 1, 1909): 8–11; Francis Maes, *History of Russian Music: From Kamarinskaya to Babi Yar*, trans. Arnold J. and Erica Pomerans (Berkeley: University of California Press, 2002), 34–48; I. F. Petrovskaia, *Muzykal'noe obrazovanie i muzykal'nye organizatsii v Peterburge, 1801–1917: entsiklopediia* (St. Petersburg: Petrovskii fond, 1999), 254–59, 269–71; A. I. Puzyrevskii, ed., *Imperatorskoe Russkoe muzykal'noe obshchestvo v pervye 50 let ego deiatel'nosti (1859–1909 g.)* (St. Petersburg: Milshtein, 1909); "50-letie Imperatorskogo Russkogo muzykal'nogo obshchestva," *Russkaia muzykal'naia gazeta*, XVI, 45 (November 8, 1909): 1026–29; Robert C. Ridenour, *Nationalism, Modernism, and Personal Rivalry in Nineteenth-Century Russian Music* (Ann Arbor, MI: UMI Research, 1981), 25–63; Lynn M. Sargeant, *Harmony and Discord: Music and the Transformation of Russian Cultural Life* (Oxford, UK: Oxford University Press, 2010), 53–81; Richard Stites, *Serfdom, Society, and the Arts in Imperial Russia: The Pleasure and the Power* (New Haven, CT: Yale University Press, 2005), 121–26, 389–98; Philip Taylor, *Anton Rubinstein: A Life in Music* (Bloomington: Indiana University Press, 2007), 82–122.

5. Findeizen, *Ocherki deiatel'nosti*, 14.

6. Ibid., appendix, 1–2, 58–68. The society also presented a chamber music series each year that offered at least one work by Beethoven at most concerts. For programs, see ibid., appendix, 76–107.

7. Ibid., 26–27, Rubinshtein's italics.

8. Ibid., 28 and Ridenour, *Nationalism*, 38.

9. Findeizen, *Ocherki deiatel'nosti*, 32. The conservatory, together with the offices of the Russian Musical Society housed within it, was located in a number of rented buildings until moving in 1896 to its permanent home at Theater Square 3 opposite the Mariinskii Theater. See Sargeant, *Harmony and Discord*, 108–12 and Stites, *Serfdom, Society, and the Arts*, 392. On the conservatory, see E. Al'brekht, *S.-Peterburgskaia konservatoriia* (St. Petersburg: Goppe, 1891); Iu. Kremlev, *Leningradskaia gosudarstvennaia konservatoriia, 1862–1937* (Moscow: Muzgiz, 1938); A. I. Puzyrevskii and L. A. Saketti, ed., *Ocherk piatidesiatiletiia deiatel'nosti S.-Peterburgskoi konservatorii* (St. Petersburg: Glazunov, 1912); Petrovskaia, *Muzykal'noe obraovanie*, 118–36; Sargeant, *Harmony and Discord*, 83–120; Taylor, *Anton Rubinstein*, 87–103; "50-letie S.-Peterburgskoi konservatorii (1862–1912)," *Russkaia muzykal'naia gazeta*, XIX, 51 (December 16, 1912): 1122–33.

10. N. A. Manykin-Nevstriev, *"Programmy," Simfonicheskie sobraniia 1–500 [Moskovskogo otdeleniia Imperatorskogo Russkogo muzykal'nogo obshchestva]: statisticheskii pravitel'* (Moscow: Iakovlev, 1899), 1–81. See also "K 50-letiiu Moskovskoi konservatorii," *Russkaia muzykal'naia gazeta*, XXIII, 36–37 (September 4–11, 1916): 634–37; N. D. Kashkin, *Pervoe dvadtsatipiatiletie Moskovskoi konservatorii* (Moscow: Iakovlev, 1891); Iurii Keldysh, *100 let Moskovskoi konservatorii* (Moscow: Muzyka, 1966); Gordon D. McQuere, "The Moscow Conservatory 1866–1889: Nikolai Rubinshtein and Sergei Taneev," *Canadian-American Slavic Studies*, XXXIV, 1 (Spring 2000): 33–61; G. A. Pribegina, ed., *Moskovskaia konservatoriia, 1866–1991: k 125-letiiu so dnia osnovaniia* (Moscow: Muzyka, 1991); N. D. Kashkin, ed., *Moskovskoe otdelenie Imperatorskogo Russkogo muzykal'nogo obshchestva: ocherk deiatel'nosti za piatidesiatiletie, 1860–1910 g.* (Moscow: n.p., 1910). On Beethoven performances in Moscow, 1840–60, see V. Iakovlev, "Muzykal'naia Moskva i Betkhoven: 40-ye i 50-ye gody," in *Russkaia kniga o Betkhovene: k stoletiiu so dnia smerti kompozitora (1827–1927)*, ed. K. A. Kuznetsov (Moscow: Muzykal'nyi sektor, 1927), 127–45.

11. Ios. Miklashevskii, *Ocherk deiatel'nosti Kievskogo otdeleniia Imperatorskogo Russkogo muzykal'nogo obshchestva (1863–1913)* (Kiev: Kul'zhenko, 1913), 93–181.

12. Sargeant, *Harmony and Discord*, 175–76; Iu. V. Keldysh, ed., *Muzykal'naia entsiklopediia*, II (Moscow: Sovetskaia entsiklopediia, 1974), 912–13.

13. Compiled from data in T. N. Livanova, *Muzykal'naa bibliografiia russkoi periodicheskoi pechati XIX veka*, I (1801–25) (Moscow: Gosudarstvennoe muzykal'noe izdatel'stvo, 1960), 58–59, supplementary items; II (1826–40) (Moscow: Gosudarstvennoe muzykal'noe izdatel'stvo, 1963), 57–59, supplementary items; III (1841–50) (Moscow: Muzyka, 1966), 63–65; IV (1851–60) (Moscow: Sovetskii kompozitor, 1967), 53–56, supplementary items; V (1861–70) (Moscow: Sovetskii kompozitor, 1971), 68–71, supplementary items; VI (1871–80) (Moscow: Sovetskii kompozitor, 1974), 61–65, supplementary items. These figures do not take into account the eighty-eight concerts for which there is no information on content. Total number of concerts should also include the thirty-one staged by the St. Petersburg Philharmonic Society from 1859 to 1897, in which twenty-one different works by Beethoven were performed. Boris Berezovskii, *Filarmonicheskoe obshchestvo Sankt-Peterburga: istoriia i sovremennost'* (St. Petersburg: Kul't Inform, 2002), 203–19. Locations of venues for the production of the opera *Fidelio*: Reval (Tallin), Riga, Moscow, and St. Petersburg. Location of concerts: Warsaw (Poland); Libav (Liepaja), Reval (Tallin), and Riga (Baltic provinces); Kronstadt and St. Petersburg (northwestern Russia); Khar'kov, Kursk, Mogilev and Moscow (central Russia); Chernigov and Odesssa (southern Russia); Kiev (Ukraine); Tbilisi (Tiflis) (Caucasus); Kazan' (Volga River basin); and Tobol'sk (western Siberia).

14. N. V. Gubkina, *Nemetskii muzykal'nyi teatr v Peterburge v pervoi treti XIX veka* (St. Petersburg: Dmitrii Bulanin, 2003), 284; "K 100-letiiu 'Fideliiu' Betkhovena (1805–1905)," *Russkaia muzykal'naia gazeta*, XII, 38 (September 17, 1905): 869–70; Russian National Library, Otdel rukopisei, f. 816 (Findeizen), op. 1, ed. khr. 581, l. 5.

15. "Muzykal'naia khronika," *Vechernaia gazeta*, 287 (December 30, 1870): 3; Berezovskii, *Filarmonicheskoe obshchestvo*, 210. See also Rostislav [F. M. Tolstoi], "Peterburgskaia khronika," *Golos*, 358 (December 29, 1870): 3; *Deutsche Blatt für Russland*, 150 (December 29, 1870 / January 10, 1871, New Syle); *Nordische Presse*, 281 (December 30, 1870 / January 11, 1871, New Style).

16. *Moskovskie vedomosti*, 103 (December 19, 1870): 3.

17. Ia. K. Evdokimov, "Muzykal'noe proshloe Saratova (do 1917 goda)," in B. S. Shteinpress, ed., *Iz muzykal'nogo proshlogo: sbornik ocherkov* (Moscow: Gosudarstvennoe muzykal'noe izdatel'stvo, 1960), 154.

18. *Kavkaz*, 144 (December 9/21, 1870).

19. *Odesskii vestnik*, 273 (December 15, 1870); 279 (December 22, 1870).

20. *Varshavskii dnevnik*, 262 (December 7/19, 1870).

21. See Michael Broyles, *Beethoven in America* (Bloomington: Indiana University Press, 2011), pt. 1.

22. Arthur Lourie, *Sergei Koussevitzky and His Epoch: A Biographical Chronicle*, trans S. W. Pring (New York: Alfred A. Knopf, 1931), 103–4.

23. Ellen fon-Tidebel', "Simfoniia na Volge," *Russkaia muzykal'naia gazeta*, XVII, 30/31 (July 25–August 1, 1910): 638–39.

24. Moses Smith, *Koussevitzky* (New York: Allen, Towne and Heath, Inc., 1947), 85. See also Oskar Bie and Robert Sterl, *Musik auf der Wolga, 1914* (Leipzig, Germany: Meissner and Buch, 1920).

25. B. N. Beliakov et al., *Opernaia i kontsertnaia deiatel'nost' v Nizhnem Novgorode-gorode Gor'kom* (Gor'kii: Volgo-Viatskoe knizhnoe izdatel'stvo, 1980), 195, 208–11; V. A. Iuzefovich, *Sergei Kusevitskii*, I (Moscow: Iazyki slavianskoi kul'tury, 2004), 303–18; Lourie, *Sergei*

Koussevitzky, 105–7; Smith, *Koussevitzky*, 73–86. The Tsaritsyn episode is recounted in Lourie, *Sergei Koussevitzky*, 107; the story about the harp in Smith, *Koussevitzky*, 78.

26. "Betkhovenskie torzhestva," *Russkaia muzykal'naia gazeta*, XX, 20–21 (May 19–26, 1913): 517–18; Iuzefovich, *Sergei Kusevitskii*, I, 317.

27. "Programmy simfonicheskikh kontsertov S. Kusevitskogo, 1910–1916," Arkhiv muzykal'noi biblioteki Gos. S.-Peterburgskoi filarmonii im. D. D. Shostakovicha, Inv. Nos 18229–34; Smith, *Koussevitzky*, 93. Koussevitzky was not alone in defying the tsarist ban on Beethoven performances during the war. Conservative critics accused Nikolai Mal'ko, perhaps the most distinguished conductor of the time, of furthering "criminal German propaganda" by performing the Ninth Symphony at Pavlovsk in the summer of 1917. A. S. Rozanov, *Muzykal'nyi Pavlovsk* (Leningrad: Muzyka, 1978), 134.

28. Smith, *Koussevitzky*, 281. The Berkshire Music Festival had been established by the American composer and conductor Henry Hadley in 1934.

29. For a listing of all commissioned works up to March 15, 1946, see Smith, *Koussevitzky*, appendix C, 376–77.

30. For a listing of all world premieres presented by the Boston Symphony Orchestra from 1924 to 1946, see Smith, *Koussevitzky*, appendix A, 363–69.

31. Quote, dated June 10, 1951, from back sleeve of "Koussevitzky Conducts Sibelius," Pearl Records, GEMM CDs, 9408.

32. Daniel Barenboim and Edward W. Said, *Parallels and Paradoxes: Explorations in Music and Society* (New York: Vintage Books, 2004), 44.

PART II
RUSSIA AFTER 1917

5

BEETHOVEN AS REVOLUTIONARY

Red Star Rising

FOLLOWING THE BOLSHEVIK REVOLUTION OF OCTOBER 1917 AND ensuing civil war of 1918–20, the communists emerged victorious as the sole rulers of an old empire shortly to be reconstituted as the Union of Soviet Socialist Republics. As before, Beethoven's music played a key role in shaping sensibilities in this new era of Russian history. But the way the public now heard the music was affected, at least outwardly, by the ideological constructs (and constraints) of the new regime. While there had been efforts before the revolution to equate Beethoven with the ethos of Russian revolutionary practice, nothing could compare with the wholesale appropriation of both man and music by the party-state apparatus in the communist era. Criticism now became tantamount to the recitation of dogma as Beethoven was transformed into a prophet of Soviet power.

Lenin and Beethoven

For those familiar with the literature on the Bolshevik Revolution and early Soviet history, Vladimir Lenin's reverence for Beethoven's *Appassionata* piano sonata is well-known. A reminiscence penned by the Soviet writer Maxim Gorky recalled an evening in Moscow, date unknown, when Lenin was listening to Beethoven sonatas performed by the pianist Isai Dobrovein. Turning to his hostess, Ekaterina Peshkova, he declared his love for the sonata as follows: "No one knows the *Appassionata* better than I. I can listen to it every day. It is amazing, superhuman music. I always think with pride, perhaps naively, what marvels human beings can create!" However, though Soviet sources remained forever silent on the point, this is not all Lenin had to say. Gorky quotes him further: "But I cannot listen to music too often. It affects one's nerves, makes one want to say kind, stupid things and stroke the heads of those who, living

Figure 5.1. Lenin listening to Isai Dobrovein playing Beethoven's Piano Sonata no. 23 in F minor *(Appassionata)*, op. 57; Gorky is to the right. Painting by G. Vasil'ev. *Sovetskaia muzyka*, XXXIII/5 (May 1969), frontispiece.

in such a foul hell, can create such beauty. Nowadays if one strokes someone's head, he'll get his hand bitten off! Better to beat the person unmercifully over the head, although ideally we oppose the use of force in human relations. Hm, hm, our task is infernally hard!"[1]

It was assuredly not in the interest of Soviet authorities to portray Lenin's darker side. And so throughout Soviet history, the anecdote remained at the level of benign praise and heartfelt affection, a nice way to portray both Lenin and Beethoven.[2]

Beyond this single truncated reference, scholarly writing on Lenin and indeed on Soviet history in general conveys no larger sense of the degree to which the architect of the Bolshevik Revolution and first Soviet head of state had bent his knee to the master from Bonn. Tucked away in the more specialized literature, however, are a number of references to Lenin's deep love for Beethoven's music.

Lenin's persona is so closely associated with the Bolshevik Revolution and early Soviet history that other aspects of his personality, including his broad range of cultural interests, are often ignored. A few words on his upbringing and educational experiences are therefore in order. Lenin was born in the Volga River town of Simbirsk on April 22, 1870, the second son of a cultivated family that held literature and the arts in high esteem. His father, Ilia Nikolaevich Ulianov, was a respected school inspector in the central Volga region and had been elevated to the ranks of the nobility for his exemplary service to the state. He owned a large library that testified to his love of the French classics, especially the works of Hugo, Molière, and Balzac. Lenin's mother, Mariia Aleksandrovna Ulianova (née Blank), came from a Germanic background and was a highly educated, though self-taught, woman. Her literary interests focused more on German authors, particularly the poetry of Heine, Goethe, and Schiller, but she also owned the complete Shakespeare in an English edition and Thiers's massive history of the French Revolution in the original French. Mariia Aleksandrovna inculcated a love of music in her children by teaching them to play the piano and often performed for them on the old-fashioned grand that still stands in the Ulianov parlor with a copy of a four-hand transcription of Bellini's *I Puritani* on the music stand.

Lenin showed an interest in music at an early age, playing four-hand with his sister Ol'ga and later escorting her to the opera in Kazan' and St. Petersburg during their university days. His younger brother, Dmitrii, recalled Lenin singing the songs of Heine and Valentin's second act aria *Avant de quitter ces lieux* from Gounod's *Faust*, indicating that Lenin had a baritone voice. Anatolii Lunacharskii, a close associate of Lenin and commissar for enlightenment in the early Soviet period, recollected that "Lenin sang. He sang with others. He sang alone while working and walking. He loved rhythm, melody, and prosody. Words and melodies became one with him."[3] The Muscovite singer Sarra Krylova recalled how much Lenin had enjoyed a recital she presented in his Kremlin apartment in the early 1920s in which she sang romances and arias by Tchaikovsky, Dargomyzhskii, Schubert, Grieg, Rimsky-Korsakov, and Beethoven.[4] Lenin was also an avid reader of literature, not only of that contained in his parent's library but also the works of the ancient Greeks and Romans—Homer, Xenephon, Cicero, Ovid, and Suetonius, above all—whom he read in the original, and of course the great Russian classics, especially the poetry of Pushkin and the novels of Goncharov, Turgenev, and Tolstoy. He proved to be a brilliant student in secondary school, winning the coveted gold medal on graduation and excelled at the universities of Kazan' and St. Petersburg, receiving from the latter institution a degree in law after only two years' extramural matriculation.

In his Kremlin office, Lenin boasted a library of over ten thousand volumes and found time in his busy schedule to meet with such notable figures from the West as Bertrand Russell and H. G. Wells. He wrote prolifically as well, his correspondence, essays, monographs, and ephemera filling forty-five volumes in the standard Soviet edition.[5] And he listened to music. Had it not been for the execution of his older brother, Aleksandr, in 1887 for his role in a conspiracy to assassinate Emperor Alexander III, an event that turned Lenin onto the path of revolution, he might have enjoyed an alternate career as an esteemed literary critic, economic theoretician, or university professor. In light of the foregoing, Lenin's love of Beethoven is perhaps not so surprising after all.[6]

An issue of an obscure party newspaper published in the northern Russian city of Arkhangel'sk on April 23, 1920, contained an article by Mikhail S. Kedrov with an eye-catching title: "Lenin and Beethoven." Kedrov, who was contributing to a series of articles commemorating Lenin's fiftieth birthday, began by noting that none of Lenin's biographers had written about the Soviet leader's devotion to classical music and that this was perhaps understandable since "one might assume that the leader of the working class had neither the desire nor the opportunity to spare time for music." In fact, Lenin "frequently attended musical concerts or called on individual comrade-musicians" during his exile in the West in the years from 1907 to 1917. Noting that Lenin had no use for music demanding acrobatic virtuosity and his dislike of sentimental music, such as songs without words, lullabies, and works containing saccharine melodies, Kedrov observed that Lenin did appreciate music requiring a sophisticated, well-trained ear. In this regard, he was attracted to Beethoven and "could listen for hours" to the composer. One evening in Switzerland, he came home in an excited state from a concert that included Beethoven's *Pathétique* Sonata and *Egmont* Overture, "rapturously" talked about the music with his wife, and insisted, "you absolutely must go hear this." In addition to these works, Lenin was awestruck by the *Coriolan* Overture in C minor, op. 62.[7]

On the same day that the party newspaper in Arkhangel'sk published this tribute to the Soviet leader, the Moscow party organization staged a "Communist Evening" to celebrate Lenin's birthday. A delegation of all leading government and party officials, headed by Leon Trotsky and Joseph Stalin, attended the event. Only the guest of honor, requesting to be excused from the inevitable litany of praise attending such affairs, was absent from the formal part of the program. The speeches began at 7:00 p.m. and lasted for three hours. They contained such encomiums as the following from Maxim Gorky: "In Russia there have been great men—Peter I, Leo Tolstoy, above all Lenin." The pianist David Shor, who was present as a member of the Moscow Trio, which performed later in the evening, was aghast that Gorky would compare Tolstoy with such avatars of state authority and considered it a betrayal of artistic sensibilities, especially coming from a writer. There followed an intermission during which guests retired to the buffet for a glass of sweetened tea, a slice of black bread, and a small piece of cheese, a welcome treat in times of privation brought on by the civil war. Finally, Lenin made his appearance. Looking agitated and waiting for the audience to settle down, he began by saying, "First of all, comrades, permit me to thank you for excusing me from your speeches." He then urged party and government workers not to "rest on their laurels" but continue "working indefatigably" to realize the goals of the revolution. Stalin interrupted him twice to announce that the party would be sending a gift of two wagonloads of flour to his residence, prompting Lenin, without breaking the flow of his remarks, to order that the flour be distributed instead to various workers' organizations in the city.

Finishing his speech around midnight, Lenin seated himself next to the piano to await the musical portion of the evening's program. As was customary in a concert performed before a Soviet head of state, Russian music predominated: Tchaikovsky's Piano Trio in A minor and Borodin's Quartet no. 2 in D. Given the late hour, Shor suggested to members of the Stradivarius Quartet that they play only the famous "Notturno" movement from the Borodin Quartet but the ensemble either did not hear him or chose to ignore his plea and played the entire four-movement work, which requires about thirty minutes. Shor and David Krein then played Beethoven's Violin Sonata in A (*Kreutzer*) followed by an encore of a Schubert violin sonata. Tellingly, the *Pathétique* Sonata, performed by Lenin's friend Isai Dobrovein, also appeared on the program. Lenin declared his satisfaction with the entire concert but especially praised the performance of the *Pathétique*. "Thank you, comrades, thank you," he said. "Beautiful music! I don't know about the speeches, which happily I didn't hear, but the music was lovely. And the best of all was Dobrovein. Delightful! Excellent! Wonderful!"[8]

It would appear that in contrast to the impression conveyed by the Gorky reminiscence, Lenin showed greater affection for the *Pathétique* than the *Appassionata* Sonata. Lydiia Fotieva, who performed on the piano in Geneva in 1904 and 1905 and later served as Lenin's personal secretary, confirms this in her memoirs: "Of the piano compositions that I played, Vladimir Il'ich loved to listen to Beethoven's *Pathétique* Sonata more than any other."[9] Nadezhda Krupskaia, Lenin's widow, repeats the same in her memoirs: "Il'ich especially loved the Sonata *Pathétique* and asked [Inessa Armand] to play it over and over again—he loved music."[10] On November 19, 1919, Lenin attended a celebrated performance of the *Pathétique* by the pianist Gavriil Romanovskii at the Kremlin residence of Aleksandr Tsiurupa. Krupskaia wrote that Lenin had gone to the recital "to hear how some famous musician performed this sonata."[11]

Lenin did not just admire Beethoven's *Appassionata* and *Pathétique* sonatas or the *Egmont* and *Coriolan* overtures, however. Unsurprisingly, he was also deeply moved by the Ninth Symphony. Galina Serebriakova, wife of a member of the party secretariat during Lenin's tenure in office, offers a touching reminiscence that recalls a performance of the *Choral* Symphony staged at Moscow's Bol'shoi Theater on February 20, 1921. Serebriakova was waiting for the performance to begin when she noticed Lenin and his wife coming into the hall unannounced. Lenin was dressed in a dark outer jacket and leaned unobtrusively against the wall next to a faded crimson curtain in an upper loge. He stood there for a long time, not wishing to disturb those around him. When other audience members noticed his presence, extra chairs were brought in, and Lenin and his wife were seated. Serebriakova continues,

> When the choir and soloists began singing the *Ode to Joy*, Il'ich leaned forward on the loge rail and I saw his elegant, tightly drawn face turn pale. He was entirely swept up in the power of the symphony whose triumphant, victorious sounds filled the huge hall, burst through the stone walls, and ascended to the heavens. Exultant, life-affirming chords crowned the finale and the music came to an abrupt end. Then, with the magical spell of Beethoven's great composition still lingering in the air, Lenin regained consciousness, as it were, rose from his seat, affably bowed to the audience and, making way for Nadezhda Konstantinovna, exited the hall.[12]

Lenin did not relish public display. That he had not only enjoyed but also been deeply moved by this performance of the Ninth Symphony is more than attested to by this sensitively drawn portrait of a world figure humbled by the power of Beethoven's magnificent creation.

Another reminiscence testifies even more poignantly to Lenin's high regard for Beethoven's music. On October 4, 1919, Elizaveta Drabkina, at the time a teenage shock worker in the Komsomol youth organization, and her mother attended one of Serge Koussevitzky's all-Beethoven concerts in the Large Hall of the Moscow Conservatory. On the program was the *Coriolan* Overture in C minor, *Leonore 3* Overture, Piano Concerto no. 4 in G (Isai Dobrovein), and Symphony no. 3 (*Eroica*). The autumn had turned unseasonably cold, and the cloakroom was closed. Elizaveta and her mother seated themselves in the fifth or sixth row of the parterre. The seat in front of Elizaveta was empty and to its left sat a gentleman wearing a cap with ear flaps trimmed in fur; the collar of his outer coat was turned up, and he sat "wearily drooping his shoulders." The orchestra players entered wearing fur coats and hats while Koussevitzky sported a gray sweater under his tailcoat. The concert began. Elizaveta wrapped herself tighter in her coat and prepared to listen to the music when her mother touched her hand and motioned with her eyes to the man sitting to their left. He had removed his cap and lowered his collar. It was Lenin. Elizaveta looked at him out of the corner of her eyes, the music of the overture fading in and out of her consciousness and noticed that "Vladimir Il'ich sat without stirring, absorbed by the music."[13]

This is a deeply engrossing account on several levels. One must be mindful of the fact that it was barely a year (August 30, 1918) since Lenin had been shot by a would-be assassin. Two bullets fired from a Browning revolver had entered his body at close range, one lodging itself deep in his left shoulder and the other, passing through the lungs and just missing the aorta, coming to rest in the right side of his neck, where it remained embedded until removed by a surgeon on April 23, 1922. Perhaps this accounted for the "drooping" body language Drabkina had noticed. In addition, Lenin was under a great deal of stress. In 1919 Russia found itself engulfed in a ruinous civil war that, by the time it came to an end in December 1920, had resulted in the loss of some two million lives and brought one of the world's great industrial powers to its knees. Famine and disease stalked the land while the original goals of the revolution had reached a dead end. The most dangerous hour for the regime was precisely in the same month and year that Lenin sat alone in that unheated Moscow theater. On October 14 White forces under the command of Anton Denikin captured Orel, just 120 miles south of the Red's main armory at Tula and but another 120 miles from Moscow, while on October 20 a White expeditionary force led by Nikolai Iudenich entered the outskirts of Petrograd and dug in only twenty miles from the city center. In this light, it might seem odd for a head of state to attend a concert, even if it did not begin until seven on a Saturday evening. But there was nothing Lenin could do but trust in the prowess of the Red Army under the leadership of its indefatigable war commissar, Leon Trotsky, to turn the tide on the battlefield. And perhaps he chose to listen to Beethoven on this particular occasion for a very personal reason. He may have felt that only the tonic of Beethoven's stirring music could provide him with the strength—or maybe the resolve—to persevere in the long struggle that assuredly lay ahead. However viewed, the image of Lenin listening to Beethoven in that place at that time is both poignant and surprisingly spiritual in its depiction of a lone individual seeking salvation through music.

For a man with such a complex, contradictory personality, one moreover who wrote so much and had so much written about him, it is frequently possible to find a passage somewhere in the literature that can support any number of points of view. So it is with the subject at hand. Anatolii Lunacharskii wrote that Lenin slashed the budget for the Bol'shoi Ballet because he considered it a "piece of pure landlord culture" and the budget for the Bol'shoi Opera because its "pompous court style" was "specifically landlord."[14] On another occasion Lunacharskii wrote that, while he always invited Lenin to the private concerts he held in his living quarters, Lenin would invariably respond, "Busy." Once Lenin said to him, "Of course, it's very pleasant to listen to music, but imagine, it affects my mood. Somehow, I cannot bear it."[15] Since Lunacharskii does not indicate when Lenin made this remark, it is impossible to know whether the response was uttered in the context of Lenin's failing health, which became a life-threatening issue beginning in 1922.[16] Whatever the case, Lenin clearly did not always maintain a consistent attitude toward music. On the other hand, there is no evidence that his love for Beethoven ever faltered.

As to the larger question of the relationship between Lenin's personal response to Beethoven and the role the composer's music came to play in Soviet history, one should proceed with caution. There is no question that the ideologists of the new regime transformed Beethoven into a veritable icon of Soviet power. Because of his dominant position in the party-state apparatus and role as its leading ideologist, one might logically assume that Lenin himself set the new tone. But there is no evidence to support such a view. Nor was there need of a Leninist imprimatur. For decades prior to the Revolution of 1917, Beethoven's great works had served as a cornerstone not only of Russian music making but also of Russian intellectual life in general. More to the point, the image of Beethoven as revolutionary, the idée fixe of Soviet commentary on the composer, long antedated the advent of Soviet power. In the communist era, the tone was set not by Lenin but by Anatolii Lunacharskii in his capacity as culture tsar. Lunacharskii's Beethoven emerges as a "representative of the democratic intelligentsia," who was "galvanized by the great French Revolution" to compose music of "resolute struggle" that now "finds reflection in our proletarian revolution."[17] The high watermark of this appropriation of art in the name of politics came on December 5, 1936, when the Extraordinary 8th All-Union Congress of Soviets adopted the so-called Stalin Constitution. A performance of the Ninth Symphony's *Ode to Joy* crowned these august proceedings, sending Beethoven's message of fellowship across the eleven time zones of the Soviet Union via the airwaves of Radio Moscow.[18] Ironically Stalin's Great Purge, which consumed the lives of three million innocent persons, had been launched with terrifying vengeance earlier the same year.

To return to Lenin by way of conclusion, there is nothing in the record to indicate that he required ideological justification to validate what was undoubtedly for him an intuitive response to very great music. Although an ideologue through and through, Lenin remained enough of a humanist—a true child of the Volga—to require no other intermediary than the notes themselves to apprehend the creative genius of Beethoven's noble art. As to what it was in particular that he found appealing in Beethoven, we will never know. Lenin did not write about the music or the man; his family, colleagues, and friends remained silent as well. Might not the emotional range of the *Pathétique* Sonata offer a clue? [YOUTUBE VIDEO 13]

Lunacharskii Charts the Course

Early Soviet culture found an able champion in Anatolii Vasil'evich Lunacharskii (1875–1933), linguist, philosopher, historian, playwright, music lover, and self-styled "poet of the revolution." Born in Poltava, Ukraine, on November 11, 1875, Lunacharskii attended the First Gymnasium—where his favorite subjects were foreign languages, literature, and music—in Kiev in the early 1890s. A voracious reader, he claimed to have read the whole of *Das Kapital* by thirteen (probably later) and then embraced Marxism as a revolutionary ideology. He joined a fledgling Marxist study circle at the gymnasium that he helped expand to some two hundred fellow classmates and agitated among artisans and railway workers in the city's working-class district. Completing his studies in 1895, he traveled to Zurich to study under the German positivist philosopher Richard Avenarius. There he met Pavel Aksel'rod and Georgi Plekhanov, founders, along with Vera Zasulich, of the Emancipation of Labor Group (1883), which coalesced into the Marxist Russian Social Democratic Labor Party (RSDLP) in 1898. Following a stay in Paris, where he roamed the museums and art galleries, Lunacharskii returned to Russia in 1898, joined the RSDLP, and engaged in underground revolutionary activity that led to arrest, imprisonment, and exile. In 1904, having sided with the Bolshevik wing of the RSDLP, he traveled to Paris to meet Lenin and then moved to Geneva to help edit the Bolshevik journal *Vpered* (*Forward*) and its successor *Proletarii* (*The Proletarian*). On Lenin's instructions, he returned to Russia in October 1905 during the later stages of the Revolution of 1905 to shepherd two legal Bolshevik journals through publication but was arrested in December in conjunction with the Moscow workers' uprising and spent two months in prison. In 1906 he found it increasingly difficult to exert any significant influence over the Byzantine course of internal party politics and by the beginning of 1907 elected to emigrate abroad once again.

Figure 5.2. Anatolii Lunacharskii, 1920. Portrait by Nicolai Fechin. Galina P. Tuluzakova, *Nicolai Fechin: The Art and the Life* (San Cristobal, NM: Fechin Art, 2012), 255.

Lunacharskii settled first in Italy before moving to Paris, where he immersed himself in the heady art, theater, and literary scene, wrote reviews for a number of Parisian and Russian newspapers, and founded a "circle of proletarian culture," as he called it, among Russian workers residing in the city. With the outbreak of World War I in August 1914, he fled first to Brittany and then to Switzerland, where he remained until the collapse of the tsarist regime in February 1917. On May 12 he left Zurich for Petrograd in the second trainload of Russian émigrés, arriving in the Russian capital on May 22 and throwing himself immediately into the cauldron of the ongoing revolutionary struggle. It is said that he ranked second only to Trotsky as "the great orator of Red Petrograd." Following the Bolshevik seizure of power on October 25, Lenin appointed him head of the Commissariat of Enlightenment (Narkompros), a post he held until September 1929, when he fell out of favor with Joseph

Stalin over education policies. He then served as a delegate to the League of Nations World Disarmament Conference and in August 1933 was appointed Soviet ambassador to Spain. While convalescing from heart disease prior to assuming this post, he died suddenly in Menton, France, on December 26 at fifty-eight. He had written the following epitaph shortly before his death: "If I die, I shall die well, quietly, as I have lived. As a philosopher, as a materialist, as a Bolshevik."[19]

Temperamentally, Lunacharskii and Lenin were polar opposites. As Lunacharskii observed after their first meeting in Paris in 1904: "Of course there was a great discord [of character] between myself and Lenin. He approached all issues as a man of political action with an immense audacity of spirit, as a tactician and indeed as a political leader of genius, whereas my approach was that of the philosopher, or, to put it more accurately, the poet of the revolution."[20] This difference was reflected in their opposing views of the positivist philosophy of empiriocriticism embraced by Lunacharskii in his studies with Avenarius and critiqued by Lenin in his *Materialism and Empirio-Criticism* (1909). Lunacharskii's "god-building" (*bogostroitel'stvo*) ideas, developed systematically in his two-volume study *Religion and Socialism* (1908–11), and Lenin's vehement rejection of any quasireligious aspect to Marxism represented yet another example of the deep philosophical differences dividing the two men.[21] Yet they genuinely liked one another, and to his credit, Lenin recognized that Lunacharskii's less doctrinaire outlook was precisely what the office of Narkompros needed. "In matters of culture," Lenin remarked, "nothing is as harmful and pernicious as hate, arrogance and fanaticism. In these matters great care and tolerance must be exercised."[22] It was in this spirit that Lunacharskii assumed direction of cultural and educational affairs in the crucial first years of Soviet power.

As both a traditionalist and an innovator, Lunacharskii endeavored to build on the past while furthering the progressive principles of the revolution. He sought to preserve the grand buildings, monuments, and museums of the tsarist era, which he viewed as an essential part of Soviet Russia's cultural heritage, at the same time that he supported the efforts of avant-garde artists to pursue their respective visions without hindrance from the state. The painters Natan Al'tman, Marc Chagall, Kasimir Malevich, and David Shterenberg; the architect Vladimir Tatlin; the film director Sergei Eisenstein; and the theater director Vsevolod Meyerhold all received encouragement from the commissariat during Lunacharskii's tenure in office. Writers and poets grouped in the acemist, futurist, imaginist, and symbolist movements benefitted as well from Lunacharskii's beneficent tutelage. In music, the conservatories received a large degree of administrative autonomy and managed to preserve their classical training programs despite the efforts of iconoclasts to do away with all vestiges of "bourgeois" pedagogy. "In view of the colossal organicity of music, in view of the fact that music as a whole is built on age-old traditions," Lunacharskii argued, "breaking away from these traditions will lead to barbarism and an abrupt downfall."[23]

These successes in the arts were not matched by similar progress in education, however. Lunacharskii sought to establish what he called "united labor schools," which would combine technical training with a traditional academic education—what was termed "polytechnic education"—but the increasing need for a skilled labor force meant that vocational training invariably won out over the united labor concept. Rather than lend his name to a policy he could not support, Lunacharskii resigned his post in the autumn of 1929. Overall, while he lacked the administrative skills and financial resources necessary to ensure complete success in all his endeavors, Lunacharskii proved an adept arbiter of cultural affairs during the formative years of communist rule. And in light of the cultural revolution Stalin launched in 1928, the Lunacharskii era must have appeared in hindsight as a golden age of creative thinking, artistic freedom, and cultural prosperity—like a flash of lightening in a darkening sky.

Lunacharskii was passionate about music, which he began studying at the gymnasium in his early teens and continued to explore while in Zurich and Paris from 1895 to 1898. His exile to Kaluga from 1900 to 1902 provided a surprisingly rich setting for his growing infatuation with the medium. There he became friends with Dmitrii Dmitrievich Goncharov, owner and director of the famed Linen Mill, which had been established by Peter the Great in 1718. Goncharov and his wife, Vera Konstantinovna, both singers and avid music lovers, had transformed their adjoining estate into a "miniature Athens," as Lunacharskii put it, with recitals and concerts, opera performances, dramatic productions, and poetry readings alternating with one another on a regular basis.[24] The poetry of Pushkin served as a kind of historical and cultural leitmotif to these proceedings in recognition of the fact the Linen Mill demesne had once been the childhood home of Pushkin's wife, Nataliia Nikolaevna Goncharova, Dmitrii Dmitrievich's great-aunt. It is said that Pushkin fell in love with the estate at first sight and enjoyed roaming through the woods and walking along the banks of the picturesque Sukhodrev River, which still flows through the property. As for Lunacharskii, he fell in love with Vera Konstantinovna, filling her gold-monogrammed notebook with impassioned poems, but the relationship, as well as can be determined, remained only platonic in nature—poetry and music apparently served as the sole vehicle for their flirtations.

In the summer of 1901, a young pianist by the name of Elena Fabianovna Gnesina, a protégé of Ferruccio Busoni, arrived at the estate as a houseguest of the Goncharovs. She was quite taken by Lunacharskii, whom she described as a "man of profound and broad opinions, a fine connoisseur of music, a witty and lively conversationalist, and an excellent reciter of poetry." In good weather the Goncharovs and their guests would go boating on the Sukhodrev River, with Lunacharskii standing in the craft and reciting from memory whole verses by Pushkin and Lermontov, along with his own poetry. "We never ceased to be delighted by the expressiveness of his recitations and by his staggering memory, which seemed to know no bounds," Elena Fabionovna recalled years later. "Anatolii Vasil'evich could recite poetry for hours on end and, astonishingly, we never tired of him or became bored." The evenings were devoted to music making. "The Goncharovs would sing, I would accompany them and play Chopin, and Anatolii Vasil'evich served as our splendidly attentive audience," Elena Fabionovna remarked.[25] Testifying to the fact that music was very much on his mind that summer, Lunacharskii wrote an epic poem entitled "Music, a Dithyramb to Dionysos" in just sixteen days in June and later penned two short stories with musical themes, "The Harp" and "The Violinist." By the end of the summer, the Goncharovs and Elena Fabionovna returned to Moscow, while Lunacharskii prepared to leave his idyll for the exile community of Vologda far to the north. He set pen to paper one last time, writing these wistful lines:

> My summer is gone and autumn
>   is come
> An autumn of distressful
>   parting.
> As the leaves change color,
>   these last few days
> Are filled with sweet torment.
> O, departing days let us
>   savor you like honey,
> Old honey, golden and sweet.
> Let us savor each moment
>   Enraptured
> Each moment fugitive and brief.[26]

Lunacharskii's sojourn abroad in the decade from 1907 to 1917 offered ample opportunity for further immersion in the world of music. He continued his study, regularly attended concerts, interacted with composers and performers, and wrote reviews on a variety of performances. The years in Paris from

1911 to 1914 proved especially productive in this regard. The French capital offered such disparate fare as Saturday-night concerts and charity balls for the émigré community, gatherings at Isadora Duncan's private dance studio, the new music of Claude Debussy and Maurice Ravel, workers' choral concerts at the Trocadero Museum, trade union festivals and concerts in Wagram Hall, and Sergei Diaghilev's Ballets Russes productions, which were revolutionizing the world of dance. All this and more caught Lunacharskii's journalistic eye. He got to know Diaghilev at this time and reviewed the premieres of a number of his historic ballets, including Igor Stravinsky's *Petrushka* (1911) and *The Rite of Spring* (1913).[27] He also frequented art galleries, museums, and exhibitions and spent considerable time in the bohemian art colony of La Ruche (The Beehive) on the Rue Danzig, where a large contingent of Russian painters was in residence, including Marc Chagall and David Shterenberg. In all of this, Lunacharskii was inadvertently preparing himself for his position as Commissar of Enlightenment.

Music continued to play an important role in Lunacharskii's life during his years in office. The private concerts he held in his living quarters attracted such eminent performers as the bass Fedor Chaliapin and contralto Aleksandra Meichik, the pianists Isai Dobrovein and Gavriil Romanovskii, the double bassist Serge Koussevitzky, and the Stradivarius Quartet. Other musicians in his circle of acquaintances included the lyric tenor Leonid Sobinov, the theorist and pedagogue Boleslav Iavorskii, the composers Boris Asaf'ev, Nikolai Miaskovskii, and Sergei Prokofiev, the English conductor Albert Coates, and the Hungarian violinist Josef Szigeti. Lunacharskii also patronized concerts by the Moscow Philharmonic and other orchestral groups in the city. Calling himself "a regular attendee of the Bol'shoi Theater," he considered "the best form of relaxation at the end of the week [to be] the opportunity to hear [Serge] Koussevitzky conduct rapturous music" in this renowned concert hall.[28]

Following his resignation from Narkompros in 1929, Lunacharskii and his wife lived primarily in Germany and France. Nataliia Aleksandrovna affirmed that "music acquired an especially large significance" for her husband in this last period of his life.[29] From September 1932 to January 1933, the Lunacharskiis resided in Berlin and frequently attended concerts by the Berlin Philharmonic under the baton of its permanent director, Wilhelm Furtwängler, and guest conductors Bruno Walter, Otto Klemperer, and Oskar Fried; they also heard Bronisław Huberman and Fritz Kreisler in concert. In the summer of 1933, they traveled to Paris and then settled in the French spa town of Evian-les-Bains on the shore of Lake Geneva. Here they heard the pianist Alfred Cortot in concert. Back in Paris in the fall, and ever mindful of his writing, Lunacharskii dictated to his wife the beginning of an article on Marcel Proust and two one-act plays, one of which was entitled *Nocturne for Solo Violin*. On November 29, the couple moved to Menton on the French Riviera and began attending afternoon concerts at Monte Carlo in nearby Monaco. "Music . . . . These last days of Anatolii Vasil'evich were permeated by music," Nataliia Aleksandrovna recalled. They heard Vladimir Horowitz, Nathan Milstein, and Gregor Piatigorsky in concert, and one day took in a performance of the tone poem *Death and Transfiguration*, op. 24, by Richard Strauss. "I noticed how intently Lunacharskii listened to this symphonic fantasia," Nataliia Aleksandrovna noted.[30] And indeed he died only a short time later, at 5:30 p.m. on December 26, 1933. A train transported his body back to Moscow, where it lay in state in the Hall of Columns, followed by cremation and burial of the urn in the Kremlin Wall Necropolis. For Soviet times, one supposes, this was as close to transfiguration as one could get.

* * *

No one did more than Lunacharskii to chart the course of Beethoven reception in Soviet Russia, particularly in terms of the hagiography that transformed the composer into a tribune of the Bolshevik Revolution. Lunacharskii wrote prolifically on a wide range of topics, with some forty-three hundred titles to his credit.[31] Of the 114 speeches, articles, and reviews dealing directly with music, fifty-eight are contained in the collection *V mire muzyki* (*In the World of Music*), published in Moscow in 1923 (reissued in 1958 and 1971). Commentary on Beethoven is scattered throughout these pieces, with five devoted exclusively to the composer.[32]

The Beethoven who emerges from these pages is an individual facing great difficulties in life, above all his loss of hearing, failures in love, and unhappy relationships with family and friends. Yet he did not despair; he struggled continually and persevered in his belief that victory would be his in the end. He was neither an optimist nor a pessimist but a "meliorist," someone who believes in progress and the ability of humanity to shape outcomes. "I am who I am," Beethoven mused in one of the essays. "I desire a happy and fulfilling life. Fate destroys this dream and renders me a wretched man. I summon it to battle. If I die, my downfall is all very well as I am repaid in other ways. But perhaps I will emerge victorious. Either way, the human spirit ultimately prevails."[33] In another piece, Lunacharskii observed:

> Beethoven was not one to view destiny, mankind, or his own life through rose tinted spectacles. He knew all the adversity of experience . . . . He did not embroider man's fate. With a courage bordering at times on despair, he would

Figure 5.3. Beethoven, c. 1800. Portrait by August Ludwig Stein. *Beethoven Journal*, XI, 3 (Spring 1995), 33.

> declare that it is terrible to live on earth, that falsehood still reigns in the world. But Beethoven did not surrender. He was not frightened by fate when it knocked on his door with a mailed fist . . . . He knew that struggle is difficult, that often the best will perish but he deeply and firmly believed in the certainty of victory in the end.[34]

There was of course another side to Beethoven. He enjoyed humor, was fond of jokes, and had a hearty laugh. Some of his music displays this lighter side, for example aspects of the scherzi (Italian for "jest") that he substituted for the more sedate minuets of his earlier works; the "premature" entry of the third horn just before the recapitulation of the first movement of Symphony no. 3 in E-flat, op. 55; the second and fourth movements of Symphony no. 8 in F, op. 93; and many of the canons and musical jokes, including the three-part canon "Ich bitt' dich, schreib mir die Es-Skala auf" ("Please write out an E-flat scale for me"), WoO172, rendered to the tune of an ascending E-flat scale! [YOUTUBE VIDEO 14] Other examples abound, and the correspondence offers ample additional evidence. The portrait by August Ludwig Stein (1732–1814), painted around 1800, uniquely depicts Beethoven with a slight smile gracing his face. Lunacharskii acknowledged this side of the composer's persona when he wrote, "All who have read [Beethoven's] letters and know his music recognize a distinctive sort of humor that invests his mirth with a kind of clumsy yet triumphant dance, an element that crowns his work in the great chorus of the Ninth Symphony."[35] Still, the scowl and set jaw depicted in most representations of the composer serve as a vivid reminder of the multiple issues affecting his sense of well-being.

A life beset by difficulties, committed to struggle, and validated by victory is emblematic of Beethoven's music as well. The essence of music, as reflected above all in the sonata-form construction of the Classical era, is the resolution of opposites, the realization through conflict of unity and harmony—joy through suffering, as it were. Lunacharskii evaluated Beethoven's oeuvre from this perspective, which accorded as well with his fidelity to Marxian dialectics. "The sine qua non of music," he argued, "is the disruption of equilibrium through the interaction of opposing themes, chords, and tones that are subsequently brought into balance through harmonization." Elsewhere he wrote, "There can be no music if there is no struggle. The internal laws that govern music concern the clash of one consonance with another. All music consists in the disruption and renewal of the equilibrium of sound." And again: "The basic dynamic of music is the summoning up in the listener's soul of various forms of fitfulness and dissatisfaction that are subsequently resolved in harmony. The resolution of dissonance is the fundamental feature of music's psychological effect."[36] And so it is with Beethoven's music. "In the symphonies and often in the sonatas one detects movement, solitary murmurs, the howl of the indignant crowd, a tension that quivers with the spirit of struggle. The very foundation of what can be called Beethoven's musical ethics is the consciousness of the deep and severe trials of existence posed by the terrible weight of social falsehoods and the indifference of nature, together with an awareness of the enormous possibilities for happiness that life offers in and of itself. Hence the primacy of struggle which, through suffering, culminates in victory and joy."[37]

In a narrative sense, "the hero, whom one senses in all of Beethoven's compositions, struggles with every sort of internal and external enemy. But in the end, he conquers, sometimes tragically, perhaps with the loss of his own life, but he always emerges victorious." Moreover, while "struggle is the predominant feature and spirit that permeates the main passages of Beethoven's music, this struggle must, in accordance with a firm conviction that never left the composer, ensure harmony and result in the victory of human reason over irrational forces." Such harmony, Lunacharskii hastened to add, "is not nirvana, some kind of placid classical repose, but joy, and to joy Beethoven intoned his last symphonic hymn." In these ways, art holds up a mirror to life. "The essence of human existence is encapsulated in the very structure of music: suffering, struggle, victory."[38]

In light of the main focus of Beethoven criticism in the late imperial period, the above analysis contains a glaring omission: Lunacharskii makes no reference to the word *freedom*. This seems odd at first reading. Recall that critics on the eve of the revolution had uniformly substituted the word *freedom* for *joy* in Schiller's great peroration that caps the Ninth Symphony. However, while appropriate in the age of struggle against tsarism, this was no longer the case. Political freedom had been won. The task now was to bring the collective will of society to bear on the building of the first socialist state in world history, an enterprise that could only be considered a joyful undertaking. Thus, though he did not acknowledge it as such, Lunacharskii restored the word *joy* to its original place in Beethoven's most famous composition while transforming the composer's music into an ideological construct that could serve the interests of the communist regime. The resurrection of this simple word might seem a trifle at best, yet it testified to a profound change in modern Russian history. Henceforth, despite the obvious parallels between tsarist despotism and a one-party dictatorship, a call for freedom could only be considered a counterrevolutionary act subject to prosecution under Article 58 of the Soviet penal code. For all intents and purposes, the word did not exist in the Soviet political lexicon and woe betide those who thought otherwise. Best, therefore, to embrace the joy and happiness of Beethoven's stirring music as an anthem to the construction of the new socialist order.[39]

As for all those "murmurs" and "howls" that Lunacharskii also heard in Beethoven's music, it is difficult in the absence of musical examples to determine precisely where they occur. In fact they can be heard almost anywhere as they can in the music of many other composers. What makes Beethoven's music unique are such technical features as abruptly alternating pianissimo and fortissimo passages, sudden tempo modulations and key changes, and, especially from the middle period on, the blazing extended codas that bring the works to a resounding close. Undoubtedly these effects, along with the inherent energy, strength, and vitality of the music itself, won Lunacharskii's praise. It probably also prompted him, like Nikolai Miaskovskii before the revolution, to dismiss the music of another great composer, Petr Tchaikovsky, as "effeminate" and a "narcotic" that had no place in the brave new world ushered in by the Soviet regime.[40]

If freedom was now a moot point, revolution certainly was not. From a Marxist perspective, the transition from socialism to a state of pure communism also involves struggle, albeit of a nonviolent character. From the perspective of modernization theory, the task was to overcome backwardness by instituting a program of rapid socioeconomic change. In either case, ongoing revolutionary struggle, what Stalin termed "building socialism in one country," remained the order of the day. In this sense Lunacharskii continued his analysis of Beethoven's music. He argued that, just as music reflects an individual's life story, so does it mirror the dynamics of world revolution. "Music can express practically all human experience—in small ways in terms of events, in large ways in terms of processes—because everything that occurs in society and nature concerns the destruction of equilibrium and its renewal. Above all, music is fit to be the language of revolution for revolution, in its very womb, as [Alexandr] Blok wrote, is musical, a process by which enormous world-wide discord is resolved into harmony, into something acceptable and positive for mankind."[41]

Time and again, Lunacharskii associated Beethoven's music with the French Revolution, the great predecessor to the Russian Revolution. In his words, Beethoven was the "firebrand" of the French Revolution, his music "fed on the same roots" as the French Revolution, his compositions reflected "in an unusually powerful way" the "storms" and "gigantic rhythms" of the French Revolution, and his very persona was "unthinkable" without the French Revolution.[42] Now that the French Revolution had been "superseded" by the Russian Revolution, those engaged in the crash industrialization campaign known as the "revolution from above" could in turn find inspiration in Beethoven's powerful music. The composer was "especially necessary at a time of seething activity full of contradictions such as ours," Lunacharskii declared. "There has not been and is no composer who is so beloved by the masses and so connected with humanity as Beethoven. The best of his compositions are hymns to universal unity and cooperation and express the joy of solidarity and the brotherhood of all mankind." Nowhere can one find "such militant vitality, such enthusiasm for struggle, such certainty in victory, such unbending resoluteness to fight to the end" as in Beethoven's compositions. The music of Beethoven, in sum, is a "call to courage, struggle, and brotherly unity."[43]

Lunacharskii's peroration exhibits all the hallmarks of a battle cry, and indeed this was its implicit intent. These were perilous times, full of danger and uncertainty. Workers by the tens of thousands would shortly be thrown into the "battle of ferrous metallurgy" on the "steel front" to carry out the directives of the draconian Five-Year Plans; millions in the rear would be called on to endure an enforced reduced standard of living to free up the vast resources needed for rapid economic development. In this context Lunácharskii transformed Beethoven's noble art into a propaganda weapon to be deployed in the great struggle against backwardness. In effect, the trinity of man, music, and message had been welded into a unified ideological construct designed to promote the strategic interests of the Soviet state. At the same time, it was in the interest of that same state authority to channel Beethoven's mighty music into productive, nonthreatening forms of social behavior. Leo Tolstoy had foretold as much in "The Kreutzer Sonata." Thus Beethoven's music became a state affair, its expressiveness now constrained by communist dogma, its message repurposed to serve ideological imperatives. As the Russian scholar Marina Raku observes, "Until the beginning of the 1920s, the Russian public still had a choice as to how to hear Beethoven but, beginning with the speeches of Lunacharskii, the possibility of such a choice narrowed conspicuously."[44]

Secularization of the Beethovenian muse to meet the needs of a totalitarian state proved to be Lunacharskii's greatest achievement, cementing his reputation as the Soviet Union's leading Beethoven critic in the early Stalin years. Overall, his contribution to Soviet Beethoven reception was considerable. While the analysis acquired a less doctrinaire tone over time, his view of Beethoven as a revolutionary remained a cardinal feature of critical writing for decades. Moreover, as the first musicologist of note to analyze Beethoven's music from an orthodox Marxist perspective, he laid the foundation for subsequent Soviet writing on the composer. Lunacharskii focused more on the large symphonic works than the more intimate chamber music in an effort to elucidate what he considered the "heroic" aspects of Beethoven's music and the connections he saw between Beethoven's art and the music of the French revolutionary era. In general, as he noted in the introduction to his collection of essays on music, he wanted to "build a bridge of sorts between the world of music and the world of socialism."[45] In this regard he enjoyed great success, significantly advancing the discipline of Soviet musicology and the more specialized field of Soviet Beethoven studies. No one did more to shape Beethoven reception in the Soviet era than this self-styled "poet of the revolution."

Celebrating Beethoven in 1927

The Soviet musicologist Konstantin Kuznetsov wrote in 1927, "One can declare without equivocation that, after the Germanic countries, our nation has embraced Beethoven with the widest reach and greatest passion, making him our own."[46] If concert programming of Beethoven's music in Petrograd and Moscow is any guide, Kuznetsov was not exaggerating. Already on March 6, 1918, the Petrograd State Philharmonic Orchestra under the baton of Serge Koussevitzky presented the *Leonore 3* Overture, the Violin Concerto, and Symphony no. 5; the "Turkish March" from Kotzebue's *Die Ruinen von Athen*, followed on June 15. In November 1918, on the occasion of the first anniversary of the Bolshevik Revolution, Symphonies nos. 4 and 5 and the finale of Symphony no. 9 were performed in Petrograd, while Symphony no. 9 and the opera *Fidelio* (renamed *Liberation* on this occasion) were staged in Moscow. In the 1918–19 concert season, Koussevitzky led the State Philharmonic Orchestra and soloists in Beethoven cycles, including all the symphonies and a variety of overtures and concertos, in both cities; he repeated the cycle, to include the *Missa solemnis*, in the 1919–20 concert season. Recitals of Beethoven's chamber music, canvassing sonatas, trios, quartets, and songs, were also performed in Moscow in 1919 and 1920.[47]

From 1920 to 1921, despite the enormous dislocations brought about by the civil war, a series of concerts was held in Moscow and Petrograd celebrating the 150th anniversary of Beethoven's birth. In Moscow, the Polish conductor Grzegorz Fitelberg conducted the Bol'shoi Theater Orchestra in performances of all nine symphonies, various concertos, and the *Missa solemnis*, while the Stradivarius Quartet performed the sixteen string quartets. In Petrograd, from December 16–18, 1920, Emil Kuper led the orchestra and soloists of the State Academic Theater of Opera and Ballet (formerly the Mariinskii Theater) in three all-Beethoven programs that included the Violin Concerto (Iosif Akron); the *Consecration of the House*, *Leonore 3*, and *Egmont* Overtures; the Third, Fifth, and Ninth Symphonies; and arias from the opera *Fidelio* (performed by Fedor Chaliapin, Ivan Ershov, and Nataliia Ermolenko-Iuzhina). In an essay published in conjunction with the concert series, the eminent musicologist Boris Asaf'ev, writing under his pen name Igor Glebov, declared that Beethoven's compositions represented the "seed from which the vital substance and meaning of our culture grows." Beethoven is the "symbol" of Soviet culture, his music the "expression of our identity." In troubled times such as the present, Asaf'ev assured his readers that Beethoven's music "gives us hope and brings us comfort."[48]

A more complete picture of the performances of Beethoven's music in the early Soviet period, as enumerated in table 2, can be obtained from the concert programs of the Petrograd State Philharmonic Orchestra / Leningrad State Academic Philharmonia for the years 1921 to 1927. Altogether, twenty-eight different works were heard in ninety-four concerts. As was true before the revolution, the more dramatic and compelling compositions predominated:

The Third Symphony was performed fourteen times (plus two performances of the "Funeral March"); the Fifth Symphony twenty-four times; the Ninth Symphony fifteen times (plus two performances of the *Ode to Joy*); the *Egmont* Overture and Incidental Music thirteen times; and the *Leonore* overtures eleven times. The highly dramatic Fifth Piano Concerto received thirteen performances as well. The range of programming and the predominance of the more popular works remained a constant feature of concertizing throughout Soviet history.

All of the foregoing served as prelude to the centenary celebration of Beethoven's death in 1927. The extraordinary amount of official attention devoted to the preparation of this event testified to the prominent role Beethoven and his music had come to play in Soviet Russia. In his capacity as head of Narkompros, Lunacharskii took the lead in organizing the series of lectures, concerts, broadcasts, and other events associated with the celebration. No other country, Germany and Austria included, went to such lengths in honoring the dead composer. Indeed, in their proclamation announcing the Beethoven festival, Lunacharskii and Pavel Novitskii, head of the organizing committee, intimated that, though international in scope, the centenary celebration was above all a Russian affair: "Beethoven's music is a call to courage, struggle, and the fraternal union of peoples. The main feature of his art profoundly relates to the fundamental aspirations of Soviet socialist culture." The proclamation ended on a declamatory note typical of official Soviet pronouncements: "Comrades! Glorify Beethoven, serve the cause of bringing musical culture to the broad masses, serve the cause of the revolutionary renewal of culture, serve the cause of the greatest of cultural revolutions!"[49]

In a separate essay entitled "Beethoven and the USSR," Novitskii explicitly contrasted the "Soviet" Beethoven with cultural norms he associated with the West. Beethoven, he declared, "has nothing in common with the sick despotic individualism of contemporary bourgeois culture. . . . His radiant courage has nothing in common with the decadent pessimism of contemporary bourgeois culture filled with forebodings of death. . . . His art has nothing in common with the lifeless, soulless, superficial technicism of contemporary bourgeois culture." On the contrary, Beethoven's music, with its "resolute rush, courageous inspiration, revolutionary passion, and sense of the fraternity of peoples, expresses the fundamental ethical and emotional forces of the proletarian revolution." It is for this reason that the Soviet Union can take pride of place in celebrating the centenary of Beethoven's death. Beethoven is "closer and more akin to the cause of the proletarian revolution and socialist creative work than all other musicians," Novitskii concluded.[50]

What is behind the crafting of what appears to be an emerging Soviet Beethoven cult? Certainly Russian national pride, always a sensitive issue whenever comparisons with the outside world are involved, can be considered a factor. So is the belief that the Bolshevik Revolution, the first "proletarian" revolution in human history, should be accorded special recognition as an event of worldwide significance. But above all, this was about a very unique and dangerous kind of Soviet-style politics then underway. In the short amount of time since Lenin's death, party propagandists had fashioned a cult of personality in his name that had elevated the former party leader to virtual demigod status. Joseph Stalin, general secretary of the party from 1922, was in turn cultivating his own personality cult in an effort to assume Lenin's mantle, a gambit that paid off at the 15th Party Congress in December 1927. There is of course nothing inherently sinister in the development of a Soviet Beethoven cult. But the fashioning of a cult of any kind, especially one of such magnitude, only conditioned the public that much more to view the language of adulation as a path to power and accept equivalencies as part of the natural order of things. One has only to substitute Stalin's name for Beethoven's in the declamatory citation noted above to understand how insidious this process could be. Significantly, though entirely coincidental, the celebration of the Beethoven centenary and the tenth anniversary of the Bolshevik Revolution occurred within a few short months of one another. This served only to reinforce the notion that music and politics were part of the same dynamic. The upshot of these and other factors was the creation of a modern-day *éminence rouge* standing at the very apex of Soviet power.[51]

In an appeal to all Soviet organizations and institutions, the Beethoven Committee charged with preparing the centenary celebrations announced the following: "In the country where the revolutionary dictatorship of workers and peasants has been achieved, the Beethoven celebrations acquire an *absolutely exceptional significance*. On the one hand, Beethoven's music is our most immediate fighting force for proletarian socialism; on the other, the Beethoven celebrations *coincide* with the cultural progress of the people, the *beginning* of the wide diffusion of musical culture, and the *first* shoots of proletarian music."[52]

In keeping with this rousing declaration, the committee presented an ambitious nationwide program to mark the centenary. Specific activities included:

- the publication and distribution of a variety of specialized and popular literature on Beethoven and his music, including the composer's complete works;
- radio broadcasts and theater productions;

- concert performances, including preconcert lectures on the international significance of Beethoven's music and, "most importantly," an analysis of the "revolutionary aspects" of the composer's works;
- establishment of a Beethoven Society to promote the study and appreciation of the composer and his music;
- the organization within institutions of higher learning of specialized seminars and research on Beethoven's music, including the awarding of prizes for publications emanating from such endeavors;
- inclusion of the opera *Fidelio* in the permanent repertory of the Bol'shoi Theater; and
- the formation of an all-Republic Beethoven committee to coordinate the celebration throughout the USSR, "even in the smallest outlying corners of the country."

It was decided to move the dates of the celebration from March to May 22–29 in accordance with the decision of German authorities to stage their celebration in Bonn at that time. The committee noted that advancing the calendar would also enable festival organizers to take advantage of warmer spring weather to mount demonstrations and other types of activities in outdoor venues—such as Moscow's Sokol'niki Park, the Hippodrome, and other public spaces—and invite neighborhood musical ensembles, choirs, and the like to participate in these open-air celebrations. The festival was to commence with an official conference held at the Bol'shoi Theater and attended by members of the government, delegations from foreign embassies, and representatives of party and professional organizations, including the music profession, scientific organizations, and various other societies. A performance of Beethoven's Ninth Symphony by the Bol'shoi Theater Orchestra and chorus under the direction of Otto Klemperer would bring the conference to a close. "Beethoven is the great leader of revolutionary art," the Beethoven Committee's appeal concluded. "The USSR must become Beethoven's second home! A great confluence of the ever increasing cultured masses with Beethoven's genius must be realized in the USSR! Through Beethoven to the mastery of all musical tradition! Beethoven is the path to proletarian music!"[53]

The most appropriate and compelling way to honor Beethoven was of course to perform his music. During the 1926–27 concert season, a number of all-Beethoven concerts were held around the country with this objective in mind. In Moscow (October 18, 1926–May 12, 1927), in addition to various piano sonatas, string quartets, and songs, the Violin Concerto (Lev Tseitlin), Piano Concertos nos. 4 and 5 (Egon Petri), the *Coriolan* Overture, the incidental music to the tragedy *Egmont*, and all nine symphonies were performed. In Leningrad

(March 9–May 8, 1927), two subscription series by the State Philharmonic Orchestra yielded up a rich fare in keeping with the city's reputation as the leading center of Beethoven reception in the country. Notable interpreters of Beethoven's art—including the Russian conductors Nikolai Mal'ko and Aleksandr Gauk; the German conductors Otto Klemperer and Hans Knappertsbusch; the Austrian pianist Artur Schnabel, who brought his own Bechstein piano with him; and the Hungarian violinist Josef Szigeti—provided star power. The concert series included a selection of the Opus 108 Scottish Songs, ten of the piano sonatas (Schnabel), the Violin Concerto (Szigeti), Piano Concertos nos. 1–5 (Schnabel), the *Coriolan* and *Leonore 2* Overtures, the incidental music to the *Egmont* tragedy, the *Choral Fantasy*, Symphonies nos. 1–9, and the *Missa solemnis*. In Khar'kov (February 2–April 14, 1927), chamber music took the stage in the form of two piano sonatas, all string quartets—except for the Opus 59 set—and eight-hand versions of Symphonies nos. 3, 4, and 6. In Odessa (March 7–May 7, 1927), two of the piano sonatas, Quartets nos. 2 and 9, and unidentified songs and symphonic music were heard. In Saratov (March 20–April 11, 1927), a variety of songs, chamber music, the Violin Concerto, the "Funeral March" from Symphony no. 3, and Symphonies nos. 1, 5, and 9 (the latter played twice) were performed. Finally, in a capstone "Beethoven Week" celebration in Moscow from May 27–June 2, 1927, the Beethoven Committee organized a series of concerts that included selections from the Scottish Songs, several of the violin sonatas, Quartets nos. 8, 9–11, and 14, the *Choral Fantasy*, and Symphony no. 5.[54]

Lunacharskii played an active role in many of these proceedings, including a preconcert address delivered on February 27, 1927, to hundreds of members of the Communist Youth League (Komsomol), who had been invited to hear a performance of Beethoven's Fifth and Seventh Symphonies. Lunacharskii talked at some length about the composer's life and art, his relationship to the French Revolution, and the central importance of his music to the course of Soviet history. He expressed the hope that these future leaders of the party-state apparatus would "feel this music with every fiber of their Komsomol heart." He cautioned, however, that this was "difficult music" that the uninitiated should not expect to comprehend fully in a single hearing. Nevertheless, citing architecture as an example, he observed that, while the untrained eye cannot take in all the detail and ornamentation contributing to the overall effect of a grand building designed by a great architect, it can appreciate in a general way the structure's magnificent beauty. So too with complex symphonic music—the general impression it makes on the listener is "enormous." Still, the music deserves "earnest attention." Lunacharskii then provided a short description of the two works on the program. The Fifth Symphony represented the "fundamental music of the revolution" in its celebration of "mankind's heroic answer to the predicament of fate." The Seventh Symphony stood for the "apotheosis and glorification of action" and depicted the "immense flight of joy"—the "joy of victory that we long for." He concluded his address by urging his young listeners to "bind themselves firmly to Beethoven and, through him, to the great world of music that we must know and understand."[55]

In addition to the concerts and other programs, a variety of commemorative articles and books appeared in 1927 that reflected Lunacharskii's view of Beethoven as a revolutionary. Representative of this criticism was that of the noted musicologist Evgenii Braudo (1882–1939). Braudo characterized Beethoven as an early adherent of "republican ideas" who was "in full agreement with the slogans of liberation of the French Revolution." With his move to Vienna in 1792, the composer became known for his "radical political views" and began writing music that reflected the "struggle for human freedom." In the Third Symphony, for example, "military-revolutionary rhythms run like a red thread through the composition, signifying the storming of the Bastille by an electrified crowd." In a technical sense, the creative use of the sonata form, "dynamic and dramatic by nature, based on the struggle of contrasting themes, accompanied by extremely varied and free rhythms, [and] eliciting the maximum intensification of tones," enabled Beethoven to compose orchestral music of "unbelievable expressive energy and extraordinary rhythmic power" that had "nothing in common with the smooth linearity of the compositions of his predecessors." Rather his music had a "monumentality" all its own, and it "rendered his works accessible to a mass audience." Herein lies the "great sociological significance of Beethoven's art," Braudo concluded.[56]

A number of other critics echoed these sentiments. They uniformly praised Beethoven as both a revolutionary and a poet and found in his art a source of great strength in times of trouble and political uncertainty. The slogan that had been coined after Lenin's death to comfort a distraught people—*Lenin zhil! Lenin zhivet! Lenin zhiv!* ("Lenin lived! Lenin lives! Lenin will live!")—could just as easily be applied to Beethoven. Thus the composer too would provide a guiding hand to an anxious nation in the perilous years that lay ahead.[57]

* * *

In light of the large figure Lunacharskii has cut in these pages, it is appropriate that he make a final appearance as this discussion draws to a close. One would do well to remember that, like Lenin, Lunacharskii was both an ideologue and a humanist who genuinely loved the arts and treasured music. His favorite composers were Beethoven and the Russian mystic Aleksandr Scriabin. In both, he found a deep spirituality that remained a constant source of inspiration over a lifetime devoted to music. In Paris in 1913, on the eve of the cataclysm that would change the world forever, and Lunacharskii with it, the future Commissar of Enlightenment experienced such a moment of transcendence at the home of the great violinist Lucien Capet. He had been invited to attend a private rehearsal by the Capet Quartet of Beethoven's immortal Quartet no. 14 in C-sharp minor, op. 131.

As Lunacharskii entered Capet's study, a high-ceilinged but rather small room decorated in blue damask with oak trim, he noticed a bust of a "powerful Beethoven" prominently displayed on the fireplace mantelpiece. The room was softly lit by cubically shaped lamps hanging from the ceiling. In the center of the room stood four illuminated music stands. The opened score of Opus 131 rested on them. Capet and his colleagues entered the room and seated themselves. While the others tuned their instruments and practiced short passages, Capet briefly engaged Lunacharskii in conversation. "Music!" he declared. "This word must be pronounced with the same reverence as the words 'wisdom,' 'religion,' 'prayer.'" He continued, "As performers of the whole range of music from historic times to the present, we have hardly found anything that can compare in tone, rhythm, and beauty to the music of Beethoven." Acknowledging his role as the high priest of France's Beethoven cult, Capet remarked, "We have discovered our cause—Beethoven. We work unceasingly for him. Sometimes we succeed." With that, he nodded to his companions, and they commenced playing Opus 131, the quartet Beethoven considered his greatest in the genre.

"And so," Lunacharskii recalled, "in that austere study a miracle unfolded. A mystery play incarnated in tones engendered, through trembling nerves, ecstasies of the soul that once had been experienced by Beethoven himself. The incomprehensibly logical sequence of sacred images of the Fourteenth Quartet unfolded majestically. Here is its imposing Gothic portal and, beyond it, the entire fantastic world of a land transformed. Silver nights, blood-red sunsets, luxuriant rose gardens and cypress groves. Sighs of happy sorrows, moans of agonizing delights." A whole range of images passed before the listener's eyes—a procession of monkish figures with their cowls thrown back singing tonelessly, their candles flickering in the dark; knights singing boldly, their banner and the magnificent plumage on their helmets fluttering in the breeze; minstrels singing a strange song to early spring, sensual in its mysticism and voluptuousness, that culminated in a kind of demure but graceful round dance; happy creatures singing through tears about love. The music conjured up many other images as well. Then, after what must have seemed an eternity, three staccato chords played fortissimo announced the sudden close of the quartet. Capet turned to Lunacharskii. "This is the whole world," he said.[58] [YOUTUBE VIDEO 15]

Notes

1. M. Gor'kii, *Sobranie sochinenii*, XVII (Moscow: AN SSSR, 1952), 39–40. See also his *Izbrannoe* (Leningrad: Lenizdat, 1984), 441. For extended discussion of Lenin and the *Appassionata* sonata, see A. A. Al'shvang and V. A. Tsukkerman, "Liubimye muzykal'nye proizvedeniia V. I. Lenina ('Appassionata' Betkhovena i Shestaia simfoniia Chaikovskogo)," *Sovetskaia muzyka*, XIII, 1 (January 1949): 8–18. The pianist Isai Dobrovein is better known in the West as Issay Dobrowen, music director of the San Francisco Symphony and a number of European orchestras between the wars. He died in Oslo, Norway, in 1953.

2. For examples of the quotation in its excised form, see A. Al'shvang, *Betkhoven* (Moscow: Gosudarstvennoe muzykal'noe izdatel'stvo, 1952), 305; S. E. Feinberg, *32 sonaty Betkhovena* (Moscow: Moskovskii rabochii, 1945), 3; B. Kremlev, *Betkhoven* (Moscow: Molodaia gvardiia, 1961), 4; A. V. Lunacharskii, "Pochemu nam dorog Betkhoven," *V mire muzyki: stat'i i rechi* (Moscow: Sovetskii kompozitor, 1958), 522n2.

3. S. Dreiden, "Muzyka i revoliutsiia (iz vyskazyvanii A. V. Lunacharskogo)," *Sovetskaia muzyka*, XL, 3 (March 1976): 55–56.

4. S. Krylova, "Spasibo za vashi pesni," *Komsomol'skaia pravda*, April 22, 1956, in M. Gol'denshtein, *Muzyka v zhizni Vladimira Il'icha Lenina* (Leningrad: Sovetskii kompozitor, 1959), 37–38.

5. V. I. Lenin, *Collected Works* (Moscow: Progress, 1960–70).

6. For biographical information on Lenin's family, see Louis Fischer, *The Life of Lenin* (New York: Harper and Row, 1964); Robert Payne, *The Life and Death of Lenin* (New York: Simon and Schuster, 1964); Robert Service, *Lenin: A Biography* (Cambridge, MA: Harvard University Press, 2000); David Shub, *Lenin: A Biography*, rev. ed. (Baltimore: Penguin Books, 1966); Adam Ulam, *The Bolsheviks* (New York: Collier Books, 1965); Dmitri Volkogonov, *Lenin: A New Biography*, trans. Harold Shukman (New York: Free Press, 1994); Bertram D. Wolfe, *Three Who Made a Revolution: Lenin, Trotsky, Stalin*, 4th rev. ed. (New York: Dial, 1964).

7. M. Kedrov, "Lenin i Betkhoven," *Izvestiia Arkhangel'skogo gubrebkoma i Arkhgubkoma RKP(b)*, April 23, 1920, 3. See also his *Iz krasnoi tetradi ob Il'iche* (Moscow: Gosudarstvennoe izdatel'stvo politicheskoi literatury, 1957), 10, where the songs without words are identified as those by Mendelssohn. Kedrov observed that Lenin also enjoyed Beethoven's Sonata no. 17 in D minor (*The Tempest*), op. 31, no. 2; some Schubert-Liszt transcriptions; and the Chopin Preludes. Kedrov, *Iz krasnoi tetradi*, 10. According to Robert Service, Lenin was also a "passionate admirer" of Richard Wagner. Service, *Lenin*, 136. David Shub reports that while convalescing following his first stroke on May 26, 1922, Lenin would ask the party official Grigorii Piatakov, an excellent pianist, to play for him. He "would play various selections by Chopin, Brahms and Bach. While playing, Piatakov often noticed that Lenin's face would completely change, become calm, simple and childishly earnest. The usual cunning gleam in his eyes disappeared entirely." Shub, *Lenin*, 437.

8. Lenin quote on the concert cited in S. Vinogradskaia, *Iskorka: rasskazy o V. I. Lenine* (Moscow: Detskaia literatura, 1965), 136. Description of the birthday celebration in D. Shor, *Vospominaniia*, ed. Iulii Matveev (Moscow: Mosty kul'tury, 2001), 222–23. This is the same David Shor whose Beethoven criticism informs part of the discussion in chapter 3.

9. L. A. Fotieva, *Iz zhizni V. I. Lenina* (Moscow: Gosudarstvennoe izdatel'stvo politicheskoi literatury, 1967), 12.

10. N. K. Krupskaia, *Vospominaniia o Lenine* (Moscow: Gosudarstvennoe izdatel'stvo politicheskoi literatury, 1968), 230. Armand was a coworker of Lenin and according to some sources his mistress. See, for example, Payne, *The Life and Death of Lenin*, 236; Service, *Lenin*, 199. Krupskaia described Armand as a "good musician who urged all of us to attend Beethoven concerts and played many compositions by Beethoven very well." Krupskaia, *Vospominaniia*, 230. In a letter of December 26, 1913, to Lenin's mother, Krupskaia wrote that Armand had been in "ecstasies" over a Beethoven quartet they had heard at a concert in Krakow. V. I. Lenin, *Collected Works*, XXXVII (Moscow: Progress, 1967), 507. Inessa Armand died from cholera in 1920.

11. Iu. V. Keldysh, ed., *Muzykal'naia entsiklopediia*, IV (Moscow: Sovetskaia entsiklopediia, 1978), 694; Krupskaia, *Vospominaniia*, 230. According to Anatolii Lunacharskii, Lenin heard Romanovskii perform the sonata twice at Tsiurupa's residence. S. Dreiden, "Lenin slushaet Betkhovena," *Sovetskaia muzyka*, XXVII, 4 (April 1963): 6n3 (left column).

12. Galina Serebriakova, *Svet neugasimyi* (Moscow: Gosudarstvennoe izdatel'stvo politicheskoi literatury, 1962), 3. See also Dreiden, "Lenin slushaet Betkhovena," 9–11.

13. Elizaveta Drabkina, *Chernye sukhari: povest' o nenapisannoi knige* (Moscow: Sovetskii pisatel', 1963), 371–73; V. Shikov, *Muzykanty verkhne-volzh'ia* (Moscow: Moskovskii rabochii, 1984), 91. It was also in 1919, that Lenin attended a performance of Beethoven's opera *Fidelio* at the Bol'shoi Theater. I. Sollertinskii, "'Fidelio' Betkhovena," in *I. Sollertinskii: muzykal'no-istoricheskie etiudy*, ed. M. Druskin (Leningrad: Gosudarstvennoe muzykal'noe izdatel'stvo, 1956), 63.

14. Fischer, *The Life of Lenin*, 491. See also A. V. Lunacharskii, *Vospominaniia i vpechatleniia* (Moscow: Sovetskaia Rossiia, 1968), 195.

15. A. V. Lunacharskii, "Lenin i iskusstvo: vospominaniia," *Sobranie sochinenii*, VII (Moscow: Sovetskaia literatura, 1967), 404.

16. Lenin suffered from arteriosclerosis, was beset by a series of strokes, and died on January 21, 1924, at fifty-three. The "Funeral March" of Beethoven's Symphony no. 3, together with the "Internationale" and music by Chopin and Wagner, was performed at the funeral on January 27, 1924. Leonid Maksimenkov, comp., *Muzyka vmesto sumbura: kompozitory i muzykanty v strane sovetov, 1917–1991* (Moscow: Mezhdunarodnyi fond "Demokratiia," 2013), 53–54.

17. Lunacharskii, "Chto zhivo dlia nas v Betkhovene," *V mire muzyki*, 341; "Pochemu nam dorog Betkhoven," *V mire muzyki*, 192.

18. A. Khokhlovkina, "Betkhoven i russkaia muzykal'naia kul'tura," *Sovetskaia muzyka*, XVI, 3 (March 1952): 48; Iu. A. Kremlev, *Fortepiannye sonaty Betkhovena* (Moscow: Gosudarstvennoe muzykal'noe izdatel'stvo, 1953), 21; N. Nikolaeva, "Deviataia simfoniia Betkhovena—puti v budushchee," *Sovetskaia muzyka*, XXXV, 8 (August 1971): 119; Iu. Vainkop, *L. Betkhoven i ego tvorchestvo* (Leningrad: Triton, 1938), 14.

19. Robert C. Williams, *Artists in Revolution: Portraits of the Russian Avant-Garde, 1905–1925* (Bloomington: Indiana University Press, 1977), 58. Phrase "great orator of Red Petrograd" from Isaac Deutscher, "Introduction," in Anatoly Vasil'evich Lunacharsky, *Revolutionary Silhouettes*, trans. Michael Glenny (New York: Hill and Wang, 1968), 17.

20. Deutsher, "Introduction," 13.

21. Despite official strictures, "god-building" as an ancillary element in Bolshevik thought shaped a variety of practices in early Soviet history. See Richard Stites, "Bolshevik Ritual Building in the 1920s," in *Russia in the Era of NEP: Explorations in Soviet Society and Culture*, ed. Sheila Fitzpatrick, Alexander Rabinowitch, and Richard Stites (Bloomington: Indiana University Press, 1991), 295–96.

22. Deutscher, "Introduction," 18.

23. Amy Nelson, *Music for the Revolution: Musicians and Power in Early Soviet Russia* (University Park: Pennsylvania State University Press, 2004), 181.

24. Lunacharskii, *Vospominaniia i vpechatleniia*, 27.

25. E. Gnesina, "Vospominaniia o Lunacharskom," *Sovetskaia muzyka*, XXXI, 3 (March 1967): 71; A. I. Tait, *Lunacharsky: Poet of the Revolution (1875–1907)* (Birmingham, UK: University of Birmingham, 1984), 46.

26. "Zolotoe utro" ("Golden Morning"), in ibid., 50. Tait's translation. On Gnesina, see E. Gnesina, "Iz moikh vospominanii," *Sovetskaia muzyka*, XXVIII, 5 (May 1964): 44–52; M. E. Rinikh, *Elena Fabianovna Gnesina: vospominaniia sovremennikov*, 2nd ed. (Moscow: Praktika, 2003). Pushkin visited the Linen Mill in May 1830 and from late August to early September 1834. On his impressions and activities, see Aleksandr Sredin, "Polotnianyi zavod," *Starye gody*, July–September 1910, 101–8; Grigorii Kogan, *Polotnianyi zavod: po Pushkinskim mestam* (Moscow: Gosudarstvennoe izdatel'stvo kul'turno-prosvetitel'noi literatury, 1951), 41–55, 70–91.

27. Lynn Garafola, *Diaghilev's Ballets Russes* (Oxford: Oxford University Press, 1989), 248; Sjeng Scheijen, *Diaghilev: A Life*, trans. Jane Hedley-Prole and S. J. Leinbach (London: Profile Books, 2009), 413. On Diaghilev's production of the Stravinsky ballets, including *The Firebird*, see Stephen Walsh, *Stravinsky: A Creative Spring: Russia and France, 1882–1934* (New York: Alfred A. Knopf, 1999), 140–43, 161–64, 201–11.

28. A. Lunacharskii, "Pis'mo v redaktsiiu," *Vestnik teatra*, 1920, no. 60, in S. Dreiden, *Muzyka-revoliutsii*, 2nd ed. (Moscow: Sovetskii kompozitor, 1970), 549.

29. N. A. Lunacharskaia-Rozenel', *Pamiat' serdtsa: vospominaniia*, 3rd ed. (Moscow: Iskusstvo, 1975), 433.

30. Ibid., 448. Ellipsis in first quote by Lunacharskaia-Rozenel'.

31. Tatiana V. Gryaznukhina and Alexander G. Gryaznukhin, "Triumph and Tragedy of People's Commissar A. V. Lunacharsky," *Byloe gody*, 2014, no. 31 (1): 43. These ranged from speeches, essays, brochures, plays, and translations to articles and books in the fields of philosophy, history, music, drama, art, and literature.

32. The essays on Beethoven include "Betkhoven" (1921), "Eshche o Betkhovene" (1921), "Betkhoven i sovremennost'" (1927), "Chto zhivo dlia nas v Betkhovene" (1927), and "Pochemu nam dorog Betkhoven" (1929). Lunacharskii, *V mire muzyki*, 77–81, 82–85, 331–33, 334–42, and 384–95 respectively. Lunacharskii's writings on music are listed chronologically in K. D. Muratov, comp., "Bibliografiia literaturnykh rabot A. V. Lunacharskogo o muzyke," in Lunacharskii, *V mire muzyki*, 482–88.

33. Lunacharskii, "Sotsial'nye istoki muzykal'nogo iskusstva," *V mire muzyki*, 375. The passage is a conceit on the part of the author. The term *meliorist* comes from Lunacharskii, "Eshche o Betkhovene," *V mire muzyki*, 85.

34. Lunacharskii, "Pochemu nam dorog Betkhoven," *V mire muzyki*, 391.

35. Lunacharskii, "Betkhoven," *V mire muzyki*, 80. On humor in Beethoven's music, see William Kinderman, *Beethoven: A Political Artist in Revolutionary Times* (Chicago: University of Chicago Press, 2020), 48–55, 183–85.

36. Lunacharskii, "Chto zhivo dlia nas v Betkhovene," *V mire muzyki*, 341; "Pochemu nam dorog Betkhoven," *V mire muzyki*, 392; "Eshche o Betkhovene," *V mire muzyki*, 83.

37. Lunacharskii, "Vosslav'te oktiabr'," *V mire muzyki*, 320.

38. Lunacharskii, "Eshche o Betkhovene," *V mire muzyki*, 83; "Betkhoven i sovremennost'," *V mire muzyki*, 333; "Sotsial'nye istoki muzykal'nogo iskusstva," *V mire muzyki*, 375.

39. It is true that Beethoven scholars in the Stalin era occasionally made reference to the "joy/freedom" conundrum but only in the context of citing, with little or no commentary, the observations of such pre-Soviet commentators as Vladimir Stasov and Anton Rubinshtein. See, for example, Al'shvang, *Betkhoven*, 301; A. Khokhlovkina, *Betkhoven* (Moscow: Muzgiz, 1955), 66–67.

40. Lunacharskii, "Muzyka i revoliutsiia," *V mire muzyki*, 127; "Chaikovskii i sovremennost'," *V mire muzyki*, 361–63.

41. Lunacharskii, "Pochemu nam dorog Betkhoven," *V mire muzyki*, 393. Aleksandr Blok, the great poet of the Russian Revolution, described the revolution as the "new music" that would sweep away all the problems evident in society. "With every cell of your body, with every beat of your heart, with every stirring of your conscience—listen to the Revolution," he urged. Alexander Blok, *The Spirit of Music*, trans. I. Freiman (Westport, CT: Hyperion, 1973), 19. For the original, see Aleksandr Blok, "Intelligentsiia i revoliutsiia," in *Sobranie sochinenii*, VI (Moscow-Leningrad: Gosudarstvennoe izdatel'stvo khudozhestvennoi literatury, 1962), 20.

42. Lunacharskii, "Sotsial'nye istoki muzykal'nogo iskusstva," *V mire muzyki*, 375; "Romantika," *V mire muzyki*, 358; "Taneev i Skriabin," *V mire muzyki*, 136; "Kul'turnoe znachenie muzyki Shopena," *V mire muzyki*, 35.

43. Lunacharskii, "Pochemu nam dorog Betkhoven," *V mire muzyki*, 394; "O Skriabine," *V mire muzyki*, 96; "Ko vsem rabotnikam muzykal'noi kul'tury v SSSR," *V mire muzyki*, 519.

44. Marina Raku, *Muzykal'naia klassika v mifotvorchestve sovetskoi epokhi* (Moscow: Novoe literaturnoe obozrenie, 2014), 216.

45. M. Priashnikova, "A. V. Lunacharskii o Betkhovene (iz istorii propagandy betkhovenskogo tvorchestva v Sovetskoi Rossii 20-kh godov)," in *Liudvig van Betkhoven, estetika, tvorcheskoe nasledie,ispolnitel'stvo: sbornik statei k 200-letiiu so dnia rozhdeniia*, ed. V. S. Fomin (Leningrad: Muzyka, 1970), 254.

46. K. A. Kuznetsov, "Predislovie," in *Russkaia kniga o Betkhovene: k stoletiiu so dnia smerti kompozitora (1827–1927)*, ed. K. A. Kuznetsov (Moscow: Gosudarstvennoe izdatel'stvo muzykal'nyi sektor, 1927), 1.

47. Concert programming in Petrograd in March and June 1918 from Arkhiv muzykal'noi biblioteki Gosudarstvennoi S.-Peterburgskoi filarmonii im. D. D. Shostakovicha/Papka no. 1 (1904–1919); concert programming in Petrograd and Moscow from 1918 to 1920 from N. V. Nest'ev, "Muzyka Betkhovena v Sovetskoi Rossii (1917–1927)," in *Betkhoven: sbornik statei*, ed. N. L. Fishman, II (Moscow: Muzyka, 1972), 243–49. See also Raku, *Muzykal'naia klassika*, 206–7.

48. Igor Glebov, "Betkhoven (1770–1827)," in *Pamiati Betkhovena* (Petrograd: n.p., 1920), 10, 17. For concert programs, see ibid., 2–7. For Glebov's essay, see also Russian National Library, Otdel rukopisei, f. 816 (Findeizen), op. 4, ed. khr. 3153, ll. 5–9.

49. "Ko vsem rabotnikam muzykal'noi kul'tury v SSSR," *Betkhovenskii biulleten'* 1 (Moscow: Betkhovenskii komitet pri Narkomprose RSFSR, 1927), 3–4. On the 1927 celebrations in Germany and Austria, see David B. Dennis, *Beethoven in German Politics, 1870–1989* (New Haven, CT: Yale University Press, 1996), 101–4, 111–14.

50. Pavel Novitskii, "Betkhoven i SSSR," *Betkhovenskii biulleten'* 1, 5–6.

51. On the Lenin cult, see Nina Tumarkin, *Lenin Lives! The Lenin Cult in Soviet Russia* (Cambridge, MA: Harvard University Press, 1983). On the Stalin cult, see Robert C. Tucker, *Stalin as Revolutionary, 1879–1929: A Study in History and Personality* (New York: W. W. Norton, 1973), 279–88.

52. "V komitete po podgotovke Betkhovenskikh torzhestv," *Muzykal'noe obrazovanie*, 1–2 (1927), 108. Italics in original.

53. Ibid., 168–69; Nikolai Shuvalov, "O Betkhovenskikh dniakh v Soiuze," *Betkhovenskii biulleten'* 1, 9–14. See also Pauline Fairclough, *Classics for the Masses: Shaping Soviet Musical Identity under Lenin and Stalin* (New Haven, CT: Yale University Press, 2016), 31–32; Nelson, *Music for the Revolution*, 185–90; Raku, *Muzykal'naia klassika*, 242–51.

54. "Betkhovenskaia khronika," *Betkhovenskii biulleten'* 1, 21–25; Gosudarstvennaia akademicheskaia filarmoniia, *Betkhoven (1827–1927)* (Leningrad: Gosudarstvennaia akademicheskaia filarmoniia, 1927), prilozheniia; Nelson, *Music for the Revolution*, 186. Centenary concerts were also held in Ukraine, Georgia, Armenia, and Azerbaijan. Nest'ev, "Muzyka Betkhovena," 253.

55. Lunacharskii, *V mire muzyki*, 394–95. The concert was performed by a conductorless orchestra known as Persimfans, a term derived from *Pervyi simfonicheskii ansembl' bez dirigera* (First Symphonic Orchestra without a Conductor), an ensemble established by the Moscow Soviet in 1922 that reflected the new egalitarian spirit of the age. On the Persimfans, see Nelson, *Music for the Revolution*, 42, 193–95; Richard Stites, *Revolutionary Dreams: Utopian Vision and Experimental Life in the Russian Revolution* (Oxford: Oxford University Press, 1989), 135–40; Marina Frolova-Walker and Jonathan Walker, *Music and Soviet Power, 1917–1932* (Woodbridge, UK: Boydell, 2012), 73.

56. E. Braudo, "Betkhoven," *Bol'shaia sovetskaia entsiklopediia*, VI (Moscow: Sovetskaia entsiklopediia, 1927), 79–88; "Betkhoven—grazhdanin," *Muzyka i revoliutsiia*, no. 3(15) (March 1927): 23. See also E. M. Braudo, *Betkhoven i ego vremia* (Moscow: Gosudarstvennoe izdatel'stvo muzykal'nyi sektor, 1927); Fairclough, *Classics for the Masses*, 32.

57. Among the commemorative works, see N. Briusova, "Betkhoven i sovremennost'," in *Russkaia kniga o Betkhovene*, ed. K. A. Kuznetsov, 3–12; Sergei Bugoslavskii, *Dva etiuda o Betkhovene* (Moscow: Moskovskoe obshchestvo dramaticheskikh pisatelei i kompozitorov, 1927); M. V. Ivanov-Boretskii, *Betkhoven: biograficheskii ocherk* (Moscow: Gosudarstvennoe izdatel'stvo muzykal'nyi sektor, 1927); V. Korganov, *Betkhoven (1770–1827)* (Erivan, Russia: Izdatel'stvo Gosizdata S.S.R. Armenii-513, 1927); S. M. Maikapar, *Znachenie tvorchestva Betkhovena dlia nashei sovremennosti* (Moscow: Gosudarstvennoe izdatel'stvo muzykal'nyi sektor, 1927); E. K. Rozenov, "Tvorcheskie dostizheniia Betkhovena v oblasti muzykal'noi formy," *Muzyka i revoliutsiia*, no. 3(15) (March 1927): 24–27; Iu. Vainkop, *Pamiatka o Betkhovene, 1827–1927* (Leningrad: Triton, 1927).

58. Lunacharskii, "U muzykanta," *V mire muzyki*, 42–45. At the time of Lunacharskii's visit, the Capet Quartet consisted of Lucien Capet on first violin, Morris Hewitt on second violin, Henri Casadesus on viola, and Marcel Casadesus on cello. For a unique description of how a modern-day quartet rehearses and performs Opus 131, see Edward Dusinberre, *Beethoven for a Later Age: Living with the String Quartets* (Chicago: University of Chicago Press, 2016), 1–14. The ensemble in question is the Takács Quartet, in residence at the University of Colorado-Boulder since 1986.

6

BEETHOVEN AS ICON

Cult and Canon

Appropriation of Beethoven and his music to serve the interests of the state—the hallmark of Beethoven reception in Soviet Russia—reached its apogee during the dictatorship of Joseph Stalin. Interpretations and extramusical modes of expression ranged across the board from the curious to the ridiculous to the sublime. The music resounded in concert halls across the land and was heard to special effect during World War II, while commentary in the press praised Beethoven as a stalwart soldier of socialist construction. The overall effect raised the composer to virtual iconographic status as a patron saint of the communist regime. The cult of Beethoven became part of the canon of Stalinist Russia.

Stalin and Beethoven

The word *perelom* is fraught with meaning in Russian history and rarely connotes a happy outcome. It can be translated variously as "break," "fracture," "great change," "turning point," or "crisis." Nineteen twenty-seven was such a year. Following the celebration of the tenth anniversary of the Bolshevik Revolution in October, the 15th All-Union Congress of the Communist Party of the Soviet Union convened in December. There Joseph Stalin defeated his main opposition and initiated the process that led to his emergence as the undisputed leader of the party and, by extension, the world communist movement. In conjunction with this consolidation of political authority, the self-styled Man of Steel wielded enormous influence over the ongoing course of the revolution that in turn shaped, and all too often destroyed, the lives of millions of Soviet citizens.

Born Iosif Vissarionovich Djugashvili in the Georgian town of Gori on December 6, 1878, Stalin came from the very lowest strata of imperial Russian society. His father, who is said to have beaten his son and wife in drunken rages, was a cobbler by trade, while his mother took in washing and sewing to augment the meagre family income. The boy began his schooling in 1888 at the Gori Ecclesiastical School and then, prompted by his mother's desire that he become a priest, entered the Tbilisi (Tiflis) Theological Seminary in 1894. He voluntarily quit the seminary in 1899, however, due to its harsh disciplinary regimen and his growing disillusionment with the Russian Orthodox faith. Next he joined the underground as a budding revolutionary. This took him in and out of prison followed by Siberian exile from 1902, the year he declared himself a Bolshevik, to 1917. Having as a youth adopted the nom de guerre Koba, the Georgian Robin Hood–like outlaw in Aleksandre Q'azbegi's popular story "The Patricide" (1883), Stalin won his spurs in the early years of the new century by organizing a number of bank robberies, euphemistically called "expropriations," to help fill the coffers of the Bolshevik Party. In 1912 he was co-opted onto the party's Central Committee and began calling himself Stalin, adapted from the Russian word for steel (*stal'*). Lenin was pleased to have found such a "wonderful Georgian" and set him the task of writing on the nationality question.

Freed from Siberian exile by the collapse of the Romanov monarchy in February 1917, Stalin returned to Petrograd on March 12 to engage in the ongoing revolutionary struggle. Following the Bolshevik victory in October, he was appointed People's Commissar for Nationality Affairs in the new Soviet government. Of greater importance was his election in 1922 as head of the Secretariat of the Communist Party of the Soviet Union, a post he adroitly put to his own use by placing his supporters in key positions of authority in the highest reaches of the party-state apparatus. With the death of Lenin in January 1924, Stalin engaged in an intraparty struggle that saw his faction emerge as the sole center of political power by 1929. From this vantage point, he launched a massive "revolution from above," consisting of the rapid development of industry and collectivization of agriculture, the latter campaign alone resulting in the death of 14.5 million peasants. Concurrently he waged a reign of terror against his former oppositionists and alleged spies and saboteurs in society at large, culminating in the Great Purge of 1936–38, which led to the arrest of eight million persons, of whom one million were executed and two million died in labor camps. This bloodbath was followed by the carnage of World War II (1941–45), in which some twenty-seven million Soviet soldiers and civilians perished and the Soviet Union, for all intents and purposes, gained control over half of Europe by war's end. Stalin's last years were marked by the outbreak of the Cold War and renewed repression at home. The dictator died on March 5, 1953, at seventy-four from complications stemming from a massive stroke he had suffered on March 1. On March 9 his embalmed body was laid to rest in a glass-enclosed casket next to Lenin's bier in the Lenin Mausoleum on Moscow's Red Square.[1]

Stalin displayed a genuine, if conservative, interest in classical music. He attended concerts, operas, and the ballet, always sitting at the back of his box, where he could see but not be seen. With the exception of Bizet and Verdi, he favored works by Russian masters—the Mighty Handful in music, Glinka and Mussorgsky in opera, Tchaikovsky in ballet (above all *Swan Lake*). He also enjoyed listening to classical music as performed by the pianists Emil Gilels and Sviatoslav Richter, the violinist David Oistrakh, and the cellist Mstislav Rostropovich. On the other hand, the damning critique of Dmitrii Shostakovich's opera, *Lady Macbeth of the Mtsensk District*, which appeared in the party newspaper *Pravda* on January 28, 1936, under the title, "Muddle Instead of Music," widely believed to have been written by David Zaslavskii at Stalin's behest, represents a famous attack on modern music. Stalin's conservative views extended as well to painting and sculpture, literature, drama, architecture, and film, and he even embraced such arcane matters as the proper way to play chess.[2] He took his direction of cultural affairs seriously. Robert Service writes, "Stalin was determined to get the kind of culture, high and low, appropriate to the state and society he was constructing. He increased his contacts with intellectuals. He watched plays and the ballet more than previously. He kept on reading novels, history books and conspectuses of contemporary science. He got his associates to do the same. Cultural transformation had to be directed just as firmly as the basic changes in economics and politics."[3] His active participation in the annual Stalin Prize Committee deliberations offers ample testimony to his genuine interest in cultural affairs—and his role as the ultimate arbiter of artistic expression in the Soviet Union.[4]

As for Beethoven, Stalin's views are difficult to assess. He did not keep diaries, his letters reveal very little of a personal nature, and his collected writings, like Lenin's, offer nothing of value.[5] An interview Stalin granted to a journalist from the Finnish workers' paper *Finskii vestnik* (*Finnish Herald*) in 1928—in which he argued that in history certain visionaries, often leading a lonely existence, paved the way to a better future for humankind through their works or actions—provides some evidence. Among this select company of "genius-heroes," he cited Democritus, Spartacus, Michelangelo, Newton, Lomonosov, Goethe, Babeuf, Beethoven, Pushkin, Darwin, Marx, and Lenin.[6] It is also alleged that Stalin ordered the inclusion of the *Ode to Joy* movement of the Ninth Symphony in the concert of 1936, discussed below, that was performed

Figure 6.1. Fedor Lopukhov, *The Grandeur of the Universe,* Scene 1 ("Creation of Light"). Silhouette by Pavel Goncharov. Fedor Lopukhov, *Velichie mirozdaniia: tantsimfoniia* (Petrograd: G. P. Liubarskii, 1922), 1.

Figure 6.2. Fedor Lopukhov, *The Grandeur of the Universe,* Scene 2 ("Creation of the Sun"). Silhouette by Pavel Goncharov. Fedor Lopukhov, *Velichie mirozdaniia: tantsimfoniia* (Petrograd: G. P. Liubarskii, 1922), 2.

to celebrate adoption of the so-called Stalin Constitution.[7] Beyond this, the record is silent on what else the dictator may have thought about Beethoven and his music. One must therefore look elsewhere for a broader understanding of Beethoven reception in the Stalin era.

Extramusical programming of the composer's music represented one aspect of early Soviet performance practice. This unusual approach originated in 1922 with Fedor Lopukhov (1886–1973), a noted dancer, ballet master, and pedagogue who coined the term *tantssimfoniia* ("dance symphony") to describe an original ballet he had choreographed to all four movements of Beethoven's Symphony no. 4 in B-flat, op. 60. The ballet, *Velichie mirozdaniia* (*The Grandeur of the Universe*), consisted of twenty tableaux in five scenes that depicted the origin of light and the sun, the creation of life, the birth of man and woman, the happiness of existence, and the perpetual motion of the universe. The premiere took place at the Mariinskii Theater in Petrograd on March 7, 1923, and was instantly panned by critics, causing Lopukhov to withdraw the production after this single performance. He wrote later that the problem stemmed above all from the music itself, which displayed an inherent artistic logic that had nothing to do with dance or balletic principles. He acknowledged that colleagues with whom he had discussed the project before the premiere, including the musicologist Boris Asaf'ev and conductors Aleksandr Gauk and Emil Kuper, correctly pointed out that an entirely new score should be composed for the ballet. Still, despite the fiasco, Lopukhov's ballet represented an honest artistic effort to update Beethoven to meet the requirements of a new age.[8]

A more prosaic programming effort was designed for propaganda purposes only and displayed little if any artistic merit. O. Timushev, a member of the Moscow Association of Rhythmists, published a pamphlet in 1930 that presented a gymnastic exercise set to the "Funeral March" movement of Beethoven's Piano Sonata no. 12 in A-flat, op. 26. The verbal instructions and accompanying graphics indicated that during the playing of the main melody and its succeeding iterations, seven columns of gymnasts of varying numbers would enter the stage one at a time and ascend a series of risers to create the outline of the Lenin Mausoleum on Red Square. On the fourth repetition of the melody, a large banner bearing Lenin's name would be unfurled above an open space representing the entrance to the "tomb." During the playing of the trio, four gymnasts dressed as Red Army soldiers would march into view and take up positions in front of the "mausoleum." Finally, during the reprise of the main melody, those in the assemblage would assume various poses, including a solemn salute to their fallen leader. As the music gradually faded away, the curtain would slowly lower or be drawn across the stage. Three thousand copies of the pamphlet were printed, probably intended for trade schools because the document bore the imprimatur of the state agency responsible for extracurricular education. The degree to which *Mavzolei* was actually staged is unknown. Certainly it represented one of the more peculiar aspects of Soviet *Betkhoveniana* in the Stalin era.[9]

The performance of Beethoven's music to mark an important state occasion represented a much more appropriate programming device. Such was the case on December 5, 1936, when the fourth movement of the Ninth Symphony was performed at the conclusion of the Extraordinary 8th All-Union Congress of Soviets of the USSR, which had just adopted the Stalin Constitution. The constitution reflected Stalin's claim that the Soviet Union had passed from the socialist to communist phase of its historical development, thereby ushering in an era of social equality and justice consonant with the end of class conflict. To celebrate this momentous event, the Symphonic Orchestra of the USSR, under the direction of Aleksandr Gauk, together with a variety of other instrumental, choral, and dance ensembles, presented a festive concert at the Bol'shoi Theater attended by Stalin and the entire entourage of Soviet high officialdom. In addition to the *Internationale*, which had become in effect the Soviet national anthem, and the *Ode to Joy* movement of Beethoven's Ninth Symphony, the concert consisted of a sequence of Russian, Ukrainian, Georgian, Bashkir, and Tatar folk songs and dances, an excerpt from a Georgian opera, a set of Red Army songs and dances, some classical ballet, and a reading of a scene from a popular play. The party newspaper *Pravda* praised the "joining of the inspired song [the *Internationale*] of [Pierre] de Geyter with the brilliant composition of Beethoven" as a fitting tribute to the adoption of the new constitution, while the army newspaper *Krasnaia zvezda* (*Red Star*) declared that the Beethoven work had enjoyed "exceptional success."[10]

In terms of regular programming of Beethoven's music, the debate between the populist and progressive camps of the Soviet musical establishment over proper concert repertoire in an era of proletarian rule need not concern readers of this study.[11] The canonization of Beethoven had been sufficient to allow the master to weather these ideological storms of the 1920s and early-1930s and maintain his position as primus inter pares among non-Russian composers whose works were performed in Stalin's Russia. Programming of Beethoven's music in Moscow and Leningrad from 1927 to 1953 illustrates this point.

In Moscow, while the lack of an established symphonic orchestra until 1936 hampered regular concertizing, ad hoc groups and visiting ensembles allowed for some performance of Beethoven's music. On January 29, 1922, for example,

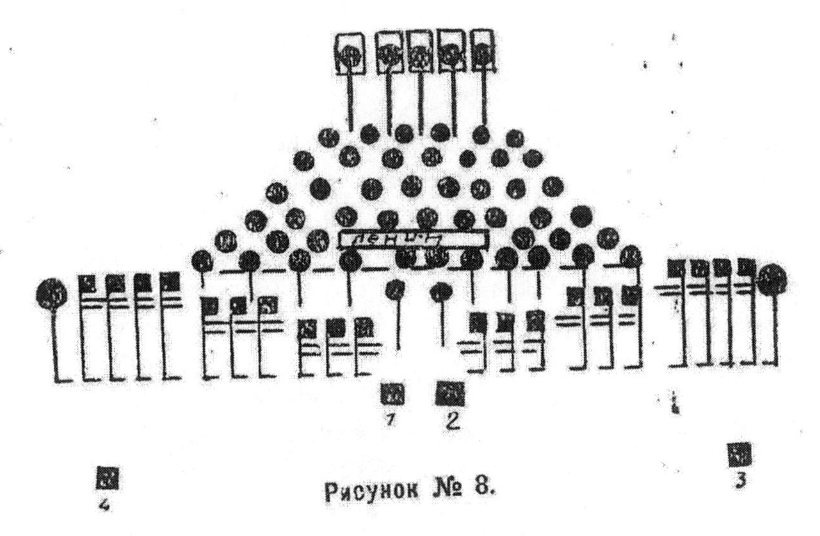

Figure 6.3. Outline of the Lenin Mausoleum. Stylization by O. Timushev. O. Timushev, *"Mavzolei:" ritmicheskoe shestvie. Muzyka Betkhovena* (Moscow: Muztorg PRO MONO, 1930), fig. 8.

Figure 6.4. Reduced score of the "Funeral March" Movement of Beethoven's Piano Sonata no. 12 in A-flat, op. 26. Insertions on score by O. Timushev. O. Timushev, *"Mavzolei:" ritmicheskoe shestvie. Muzyka Betkhovena* (Moscow: Muztorg PRO MONO, 1930), appendix.

a private orchestra, misleadingly calling itself the State Philharmonia, presented a huge inaugural concert that included Beethoven's Ninth Symphony along with Aleksandr Scriabin's *Poem of Ecstasy*, a Rachmaninov piano concerto, and some lesser works by Sergei Taneev and Mikhail Ippolitov-Ivanov. A week later the conductor-less Persimfans orchestra performed Beethoven's Symphony no. 3, *Egmont* Overture, and Violin Concerto to rave reviews. In January 1932 Oskar Fried and Eugen Jochum conducted what was probably the Bol'shoi Theater Orchestra in a series of Beethoven concerts that included the Fifth Symphony. Then, on October 5, 1936, the Symphonic Orchestra of the USSR, henceforth Moscow's permanent orchestral ensemble, made its appearance with the first of five concerts featuring all nine Beethoven symphonies. Erich Kleiber presided over the inaugural concert, consisting of the *Internationale* and the First and Third Symphonies, while the orchestra's permanent director, Aleksandr Gauk, conducted the remaining four over the following three weeks. Astonishingly, in the wake of this musical marathon, Gauk and his roster of guest conductors led the orchestra in twenty-five performances of the Ninth Symphony alone in a space of just two and a half months (the second half of December 1936 through March 1937). This heavy diet of Beethoven became a fixture of Moscow concert life during the remainder of the Stalin era. Data for the years 1938 to 1953, while incomplete, indicate that the composer's symphonies were performed twenty-three times, concertos six times, overtures six times, and fragments from the opera *Fidelio* once. However measured, this is an impressive record of the performance of works by a single composer, even if that composer was Beethoven.[12]

In their study of musical life in the Soviet Union until 1932, Marina Frolova-Walker and Jonathan Walker correctly identify the Leningrad Philharmonia as "the most distinguished of all Russian orchestras."[13] The orchestra had been the premiere performing ensemble in tsarist times and retained this reputation during the Soviet period as well. Led by Emil Kuper until his emigration in 1924, the composer and pedagogue Aleksandr Glazunov and a series of guest conductors (Oskar Fried, Otto Klemperer, Heinz Unger, and Hermann Abendroth) subsequently directed the Philharmonia until Nikolai Mal'ko assumed the permanent directorship in 1926. Pauline Fairclough provides an excellent summary of Russian and Western repertoire performed by the Leningrad Philharmonia at this time.[14] Table 3 summarizes the frequency of performance of Beethoven's music by individual work and years of performance for the period 1928 to 1953. The table indicates that there were, on average, twenty-eight Beethoven performances per year, a remarkable record made even more so by the reduced level of concertizing from autumn 1941 to summer 1944, when the

Philharmonia decamped to Novosibirsk during World War II. As had been the case both before and after the revolution, Beethoven's large-form orchestral works predominated: the Third, Fifth, and Ninth Symphonies received 197 performances; the *Coriolan*, *Egmont*, and *Leonore 3* Overtures had 144 performances; and the incidental music to Goethe's *Egmont* had 44 performances. The standout was Symphony no. 5, which received a total of 101 performances, about 15 percent of all Beethoven repertoire performed during this twenty-five-year period. Also notable, as was evident in 1921 through 1927 as well, is the incidence of lesser performed Beethoven, for example the earlier piano concertos, the other orchestral overtures, and such relative rarities as the Triple Concerto, *Choral Fantasy*, and the *Missa solemnis*. This suggests that, despite the ideological rigors of performance practice under Stalin, more balanced concertizing characteristic of the post-Stalin era was beginning to manifest itself in this period as well.

While the data is nowhere near as complete, scattered commentary in the Beethoven reception literature indicates that performance of Beethoven's chamber music also flourished during the Stalin era. For example, over the course of six recitals in 1945, all thirty-two piano sonatas were performed in Moscow.[15] Similarly the Beethoven Quartet performed all sixteen string quartets in Moscow during each of the 1927–28, 1931–32, 1936–37, 1939–40, 1946–47, 1949–50, and 1951–52 seasons. The Borodin, Bol'shoi, Glazunov, Glière, Stradivarius, and Taneev Quartets, among others, also performed the Beethoven quartets on a regular basis, as did ensembles in Azerbaijan, Georgia, Latvia, Lithuania, and other non-Russian localities scattered around the periphery of the Soviet Union.[16]

On the other hand, with the exception of an amateur production in 1928, the opera *Fidelio* did not receive a single staged performance in the Stalin era. This despite Lenin's injunction in 1919 that the Bol'shoi Theater perform the work as "one of the most immediate tasks of our musical theaters" and the 1927 party declaration, issued in conjunction with the centenary celebrations of Beethoven's death, that *Fidelio* be included in the Bol'shoi's permanent repertory.[17] As late as 1937, the musicologist Aleksandr Shaverdian declared that the opera, with its "lofty moral-philosophical ideas of struggle against darkness, emancipation of the human personality, and the ultimate triumph of reason and light," could only be "fully revealed, understood, and appreciated" by Soviet musical circles. The task was to "create an authentic realization of a monumental musical drama."[18] Yet in 1938 *Pravda* bemoaned the fact such universally acclaimed operas as *Fidelio*, Mozart's *Don Giovanni*, and Verdi's *Falstaff*, among others, "do not interest the artistic directorships of [our] opera companies."[19] While not discounting the five concert performances of *Fidelio* that did take place (Leningrad 1931, 1941, 1951 and Moscow 1936, 1938), this omission in Soviet Beethoven programming is remarkable, especially in light of the frequency of staged performances of *Fidelio* in the late imperial period. Might the subject matter have struck too close to home? The Soviet musicologist Anna Khokhlovkina, writing in 1961, implied as much when she noted that undisclosed "distortions of the ideological intentions of the composer" were responsible for the failure of the work to gain a permanent footing in the repertory. This strongly suggests that depictions of political tyranny and the ultimate victory of the oppressed over the forces of repression were not to be tolerated on the opera stages of Stalin's Russia.[20]

In addition to the concert hall, Beethoven programming in the Stalin era reached many listeners via the new medium of radio. Lenin early on had recognized the significance of radio, a medium he dubbed a "paperless newspaper," in reaching the masses. The first station was established in Moscow in early 1921 and broadcast a few hours of news and propaganda each day. The All-Union Radio began broadcasting in November 1924 under the auspices of the People's Commissariat for Posts and Telegraphs. The radio receiver, consisting of a round black loudspeaker mounted on the wall and attached to a cable wired to a single station, quickly became a ubiquitous feature of daily life throughout the Soviet Union. All industrial enterprises, state and collective farms, apartments, dormitories, hotel rooms, government and party offices, educational institutions, restaurants and canteens, commercial establishments, and the like sported the device—whose volume could be modulated but not switched off entirely. Loudspeakers were also set up in public spaces to bring important news broadcasts to the citizenry at large.

Known as the "people's university" and "people's conservatory," radio transmitted a wide variety of programming to Soviet citizens, ranging from children's fare to live broadcasts of theater productions, concerts, and opera, including virtually the entire repertory of the Bol'shoi Theater. The first radio broadcast of a piece of music occurred on September 17, 1922. Regular music transmissions five times per week began on October 12, 1924. In 1930 the Large Symphony Orchestra, the performing arm of the All-Union Radio (and later of Central Television), was established to bring live performances to the listening public. In its first year of broadcasting, the orchestra performed the complete Beethoven symphonic cycle, starting with the Ninth Symphony at its inaugural concert. Over time the orchestra and affiliated soloists presented all of the Beethoven concertos, the *Coriolan*, *Egmont*, *Fidelio*, *Leonore 3*, and *Prometheus* Overtures, a concert version of *Fidelio*, and a variety of lesser works. Families traditionally gathered in the evenings on holidays and nonworking days to listen to these and other broadcasts. Beethoven and Tchaikovsky proved the most popular composers among devotees of classical music.[21]

"Comrades! With this broadcast we inaugurate a cycle of concerts devoted to the art of Beethoven." Thus did the Large Symphony Orchestra of the All-Union Radio initiate a series of three broadcasts in 1936 that explored, through analysis and performance, a broad range of music by the composer. The broadcasts introduced listeners to the following compositions, listed in the order in which they appeared on the programs:

Program 1
Symphony no. 1 in C, op. 21 / movement 1
Adelaide, op. 46
Symphony no. 2 in D, op. 36 / movement 2
Dance in E-flat, WoO 83
Symphony no. 3 in E-flat (*Eroica*), op. 55 / movements 1–4

Program 2
Leonore 3 Overture, op. 72
2 Scottish Songs
  "Enchantress, farewell," op. 108, no. 18
  "Dim, dim is my eye," op. 108, no. 6
1 Irish Song
  "The pulse of an Irishman," WoO 154, no. 4
Symphony no. 6 in F (*Pastoral*), op. 68 / movements 3–5
Symphony no. 7 in A, op. 92 / movements 1–4

Program 3
Piano Sonata no. 17 in D minor (*The Tempest*), op. 31, no. 2
4 Goethe Songs
  "The joy of suffering," op. 83, no. 1
  "Yearning," op. 83, no. 2
  "The anguish of parting," op. 83, no. 3
  "Mignon," op. 75, no. 1
Violin Sonata no. 9 in A (*Kreutzer*), op. 47 / movements 1–3

As examples of Beethoven reception at the time, these broadcasts are interesting for a variety of reasons. First, they were almost entirely free of ideological bias. To be sure, the broadcaster made the obligatory reference at the outset of program 1 to Beethoven as "the most courageous of all composers" (Romain Rolland) and his art as "amazing, superhuman music" (Vladimir Lenin), but this is usual boilerplate frequently encountered in the literature. Overall the broadcasts focused on the music itself and presented a rather sophisticated analysis for a general audience. Secondly, the broadcasts canvassed a variety of genres and presented works that, for the most part, were less familiar to the listening public—most certainly in terms of the dance and song literature—than that offered in the concert hall. This facilitated a greater understanding of the complex character of Beethoven's oeuvre and opened up new avenues for exploration. Finally, the use of orchestral examples to illustrate the musical structure and character of a piece of music before performance of the work as a whole provided the listener with aural signposts to enhance the listening experience. Prior to a performance of the Third Symphony, for example, three distinguishing characteristics of movement 1 (1st theme, 2nd theme, reprise of 1st theme), two of movement 2 ("Funeral March" theme, C major B-section), two of movement 3 (main theme, trio horn fanfare), and one of movement 4 ("Prometheus" theme) were discussed and then played by the full orchestra. Overall, the three programs represented a sophisticated approach to musical discourse and testified that, in addition to serving as an ideological tool of the regime, radio had indeed become a true "people's conservatory." Other broadcasts included cycles devoted to Bach's preludes and fugues, Beethoven's string quartets and piano sonatas, Liszt's rhapsodies, and works by Mozart, Chopin, and Grieg.[22]

As for Beethoven reception literature published in the Stalin era, a 1950 article by composer and musicologist Arnol'd Al'shvang that appeared in the *Bol'shaia sovetskaia entsiklopediia* (*Great Soviet Encyclopedia*), 2nd ed., the authoritative source on all things Soviet (and Stalinist) at the time, is a good place to begin. As a highly qualified Beethoven scholar, Al'shvang presented a solid analysis of Beethoven's life and career and offered astute observations on the distinguishing characteristics of his music. At the same time, he displayed his ideological bias as a Soviet critic by describing Beethoven as a "musician-citizen," whose art reflected the general principal of "victory through struggle." He argued that "the best of Beethoven's symphonic compositions—the Third ('Heroic'), Fifth, and Ninth Symphonies, the *Egmont*, *Leonore No. 2*, *Leonore No. 3*, and *Coriolan* Overtures, the Fifth Piano Concerto, and others—resound with the theme of the struggle of heroic individuals and the masses against despotism and tyranny in pursuit of liberty and the happiness of mankind." In particular, the Ninth Symphony "must be placed on the same level of significance as the greatest revolutionary-heroic works of world art" through its depiction of the "provident future of mankind, animated by the joy of courageous defiance [and] the idea of the equality of all peoples." Al'shvang contrasted the views of "bourgeois formalist aestheticians" in the West, who dismissed Beethoven's music as "vulgar and out of fashion," with the outlook of "progressives" in the socialist world, who considered Beethoven "one of the greatest revolutionary artist-citizens who seamlessly unites his interests with those of the people." Referencing Friedrich Engels' comment in 1841 that Beethoven's Third and Fifth Symphonies were his favorite compositions and Lenin's oft-quoted description of Beethoven's *Appassionata* Sonata as "amazing, superhuman music," Al'shvang asserted that "Soviet musicologists, basing their analysis on Marxist-Leninist methodology, broadly investigate the philosophical and artistic content of Beethoven's creative work from the perspective of its socialist conditionality." In sum, the composer's art "occupies a significant place in the musical life of the country and is deeply enjoyed by listeners."[23]

A variety of commentators in the 1930s had prefigured Al'shvang's characterization of Beethoven and the role of his music in Soviet history. In 1934 the musicologist Iulian Vainkop attributed the enormous popularity of Beethoven's music in the Soviet Union to the fact it was associated with the "epoch of the construction of socialist culture" and the "aspiration for a new, free, and happy life" on the part of the Soviet people. Beethoven, "revolutionary musician and musician of the Revolution, belongs to that class which is realizing the results of the greatest of revolutions—the proletarian revolution. That is why, with few exceptions, the legacy of Beethoven must be and in fact is so valuable and significant for the country that is building the foundations of a socialist society and socialist culture."[24] In 1936 the writer and translator Nikolai Karintsev declared that "the music of Beethoven, courageous and calling for the emancipation of mankind and victory, resounds only in the country of the victorious proletariat. This music is closest and dearest to us because of its revolutionary heroism, inflexible will, and striving for the elimination of all that prevents mankind from living freely and happily. . . . On school benches, in concert halls, in open squares, and in theaters the music of Beethoven lives on because the human element of heroism that this music is famous for is grasped by a socialist country."[25]

In 1938 the musicologist Aleksandr Dolzhanskii described Beethoven and his music as follows: "This music is healthy, cheerful, and steadfast for Beethoven strongly believed in life, in the best socialist order, in the future of happy, humane existence. He called for a decisive struggle against all dark, hostile forces and demanded from people will power, consciousness, self-control, self-sacrifice. Heroism is one of the leading ideas in the entire art of Beethoven. One of his favorite musical images is of the hero leading the people through struggle to liberty and happiness."[26] And in 1940 the musicologist

Tat'iana Popova asserted that "only in our day, in the Soviet Union, has Beethoven found his authentic homeland and true listening public." In a study that focused primarily on the music, Popova argued that such works as the Third and Fifth Symphonies, the opera *Fidelio*, and music to Goethe's drama *Egmont* "seek to convey large socialist ideas." The best of Beethoven's compositions consist of "heroic struggle, acute, intense, and full of dramatic clashes, in search of a bright future, the end goal of which is the victory of the liberation of mankind. . . . Beethoven's greatest symphonies—the Third ('Heroic'), Fifth, and Ninth—chart a path from darkness to light, to victory through long, persistent, and heroic struggle."[27]

And so it went. A kind of formulaic redundancy—hyperbolic, chauvinistic, for the most part lacking in original ideas, and highly repetitive—shaped the character of Beethoven reception literature in the Stalin era. The commentary differed little from official propaganda. The image of a "grey blur," often used to describe both Stalin and his regime, could just as easily be applied to much of the discourse on Beethoven and his music at the time. There were of course exceptions, but for the most part, analysis lacked the sophistication of the Lunacharskii era.[28] As for Stalin, his views on Beethoven, as on virtually any other matter touching the human heart, remained as opaque as the man himself. On the other hand, the course chartered by Lunacharskii in the 1920s had clearly led by the 1930s to the fashioning of an iconography that elevated Beethoven to virtual supernatural status. As Marina Raku succinctly concludes, "By the middle of the decade Beethoven had been canonized once and for all."[29]

Nine Hundred Days

At approximately 0300 hours on June 22, 1941, Nazi Germany launched a massive three-pronged attack on the Soviet Union code-named "Operation Barbarossa" after the twelfth-century Holy Roman Emperor Frederick Barbarossa. The German and Allied forces, some 3.2 million strong, established an eighteen-hundred-mile front and set their sights on the strategic cities of Leningrad to the north, Moscow in the center, and Kiev to the south. While they succeeded in encircling Leningrad, they failed to take Moscow, eventually retreating to Ukraine, where they regrouped with the forces that had captured Kiev. In the spring and summer of 1942, they drove east as far as Crimea, the oilfields of the Caucasus, and the outskirts of Stalingrad on the Volga River. In vicious fighting from August 23, 1942, to February 2, 1943, Soviet forces eventually gained the upper hand at Stalingrad and forced the remnants of the German army to surrender. This marked the turning point in the war that, combined with Allied victories in the west, resulted in the fall of Berlin on May 2, 1945. What Hitler had predicted would be a short blitzkrieg became instead a grinding military campaign against a formidable foe. Ironically, Napoleon's 1812 invasion of Russia also had been launched on June 22 and crossed the Niemen River in roughly the same area as Hitler's forces in 1941. It is also significant that the winter of 1941–42 proved the coldest on record since the winter of 1812–13, which in turn had been the coldest on record since record keeping began during the reign of Catherine the Great in the late eighteenth century. For both would-be conquerors, Russia's vast expanses and extreme winters contributed significantly to their eventual defeats.[30]

With the outbreak of the war, Beethoven became a soldier on the front lines. An authoritative source observed in December 1945 that "from October-December 1941, during the heroic defense of the capital and the routing of the Germans from the environs of Moscow, the music of Beethoven resounded by radio throughout the country."[31] Such broadcasts became a staple of programming during the war, perhaps no more so than in Leningrad, which was subjected to a nine-hundred-day siege as a result of the German encirclement. While the Leningrad Philharmonia was evacuated to Novosibirsk in southwestern Siberia at the outset of the conflict, the Leningrad Radio Symphony Orchestra (LRSO), under the direction of Karl Eliasberg, remained in the city, where it performed a great many concerts, including seventeen performances of Beethoven's music, from October 1941 to January 1944. The concerts, along with broadcasts of classical music by Radio Leningrad, brought some measure of solace to those trapped in the city. "During the blockade," a survivor recalled, "Leningrad was filled with music. At any time of the day or night on the lonely squares and streets of the city, the symphonies of Beethoven, Tchaikovsky, and Shostakovich rang out from the loudspeakers. All of this made Leningrad seem more beautiful and majestic."[32] Still, over a million people perished from the bombardments, disease, hunger, and cold.[33]

On June 22 Leningraders gathered at loudspeakers throughout the city to listen to initial reports of the invasion. They then prepared defenses against the impending attack, which began in earnest on August 8. For three months a massive effort to dig trenches, lay mines, and erect tank barriers was undertaken by some five hundred thousand residents (mainly women) and military personnel. Simultaneously five hundred thousand children and those adults considered "cultural treasures" by the regime were evacuated from the city. On September 7 the Germans captured the Shlisselburg fortress on the banks of the Neva River, the last defensive bastion of Leningrad, and proceeded to sever all land routes to Russia's interior. They also cut the rail lines to Moscow

Figure 6.5. Leningrad, June 22, 1941. Unknown photographer. Announcement of Germany's invasion of the Soviet Union. In addition to official pronouncements, loudspeakers throughout the city broadcast a great deal of classical music during the ensuing nine-hundred-day siege. Andrei Kriukov, *Muzyka v efire voennogo Leningrada* (St. Petersburg: Kompozitor, 2005), 49.

and Murmansk, headquarters of the Soviet Northern Fleet on the Barents Sea. Yet they were unable to seize the city itself. Hitler finally grew impatient and ordered the withdrawal of two Panzer divisions to augment German forces outside Moscow. The fűhrer declared that, in lieu of capturing Leningrad, the objective now would be to starve the residents into submission. Thus was established the *kol'stso* or "ring" around the city. Except for Lake Ladoga to the east, which served as a perilous "Road of Life," enabling some provisions and military reinforcements to be trucked into the city over the ice in winter and transported by barge during the rest of the year, Leningrad was left largely to its own devices for the duration of the siege. Starvation reached catastrophic levels and even drove some to the desperate act of cannibalism. No city in modern times has suffered more at the hands of an enemy bent on annihilating an entire resident population, which at the outset of the war numbered more than three million persons.[34]

Despite the suffering and grim prospects for the future, Leningraders continued to indulge their love for music. Eliasberg and his forces, along with other ensembles in the city, offered a wide range of works by both Western and Russian/Soviet composers.[35] Table 4 tabulates compositions by Beethoven that the LRSO and guest artists performed at this time. Altogether, the Fourth Symphony was performed two times, the Fifth Symphony three times, the Ninth Symphony four times, the Fifth Piano Concerto two times, the *Diabelli Variations* one time, and unidentified piano works five times. The performances of October 1941 (Ninth Symphony), November 9, 1941 (Ninth Symphony), July 4, 1942 (Fifth Symphony), December 1, 1942 (Fifth Symphony), June 2, 1943 (Fourth Symphony), and January 15, 1944 (Fifth Piano Concerto) were broadcast over the airwaves of Radio Leningrad, the significance of which is discussed below.

Of the seventeen performances, the Ninth Symphony's undoubtedly resonated most immediately with city residents. A member of the orchestra offered the following reflections on the concert of November 9, 1941, held in the unheated hall of the Leningrad Philharmonia: "We had heard the Ninth Symphony time and again—for many of us its tones had been with us since childhood—but all of a sudden we interpreted and experienced the work as if it were brand new. We heard the symphony differently than before. . . . It was as if Beethoven had written the symphony in our own day, directing it straight at us, its themes touching on matters of immediate and vital importance." The concert elicited an enthusiastic response from the audience. Afterward Eliasberg and some of the players gathered in the green room. Sof'ia Preobrazhenskaia, the soprano soloist, rushed through the room to tend to her children at home; they had been frightened shortly before the concert began by an air-raid strike on a neighboring building. "We are proud that your voice resounds in Leningrad at this time," someone shouted. She waved her hand and departed. "A fearless Russian woman," someone said. Eliasberg, showing the strain of the performance, sat on a couch in his coat, hat, and gloves. "I'm cooling down," he joked. Concertgoers passed through the room to thank the performers for "delivering joy through music." One was

Figure 6.6. Leningraders attending a concert, October 26, 1941. Unknown photographer. Andrei Kriukov, *Muzyka v efire voennogo Leningrada* (St. Petersburg: Kompozitor, 2005), 49.

overheard remarking, "It is indeed an act of real heroism to stage a concert like this under our current conditions."[36]

Without a doubt the most significant musical event of the siege years was the Leningrad premiere of Dmitrii Shostakovich's Symphony no. 7 in C (*Leningrad*), op. 60, on August 9, 1942. Concert organizers had purposely selected this date to mock Hitler's boast that he would celebrate his victory over Leningrad with a banquet at the city's prestigious Astoria Hotel on that day. Shostakovich began composing the symphony in Leningrad and had completed the first three movements by the time he was evacuated to Moscow on

Figure 6.7. Leningraders purchasing concert tickets, Spring 1942. Unknown photographer. Andrei Kriukov, *Muzyka v efire voennogo Leningrada* (St. Petersburg: Kompozitor, 2005), 145.

October 1, 1941, and then to Kuibyshev (now Samara) on the Volga River. He completed the work on December 27, 1941, and oversaw its world premiere in Kuibyshev on March 5, 1942, when it was performed by the Bol'shoi Theater Orchestra under the direction of Samuil Samsud. The symphony was next performed in Moscow on March 29 by those players of the Bol'shoi Theater Orchestra who had not been evacuated and the Large Symphony Orchestra of the All-Union Radio, which had remained in the city. At the same time the 252-page conductor's score was flown over German lines into Leningrad in preparation for the symphony's premiere by the LRSO. When Eliasberg first saw the score, each movement bound in a thick notebook in dark binding, he reportedly thought to himself, "We will never be able to play this."[37] The score called for an outsize orchestra of over one hundred players, while the ranks of the LRSO had been reduced from ninety players to fifteen due to the privations of the siege and conscriptions for the war effort. Undaunted, Eliasberg went about the city searching out retired orchestra members and those on furlough, pleading with them to return to the orchestra for this one performance. He also rounded up some players from the front lines, especially trumpet and trombone players, to augment his diminished brass section. In this way, an orchestra of some forty members was cobbled together and rehearsals began in March.

Prior to the premiere late in the afternoon on August 9, Soviet defensive batteries launched a massive artillery barrage to silence the German guns aimed at Philharmonic Hall. Loudspeakers also broadcast the performance to Soviet and German frontline troops. Emotions ran high as ticket holders gathered for the concert. "When I entered the hall," survivor Tatiana Vasil'eva recalled, "tears came to my eyes because there were many people, all elated. We listened with such emotion, because we had lived for this moment, to come and hear this music. This was a real symphony which we lived. This was our symphony, Leningrad's." Oboist Ksenia Matus reflected, "Music was everything. Never mind the kasha, or that we were hungry. No one could feed us, but music inspired us and brought us back to life. In this way, this day was our feast." Trombonist Mikhail Parfionov remarked, "We were stunned by the number of people, that there could be so many people starving for food but also starving for music. Some had come in suits, some from the front. Most were thin and dystrophic." At the end of the performance, the applause lasted for about an hour. Eliasberg remarked later that "people just stood and cried and cried. They knew that this was not a passing episode but the beginning of something. We heard it in the music. The concert hall, the people in their apartments, the soldiers at the front—the whole city had found its humanity. And in that moment we triumphed over the soulless Nazi war machine." This sentiment found an echo of sorts among a squadron of German soldiers encamped outside the city who had listened to the concert over the loudspeakers. "Who are we bombing?" they asked. "We will never be able to take Leningrad. These people are selfless."[38]

If Shostakovich could lift the spirits of a city facing extinction, Beethoven could comfort the dying. The following vignette, so poignant in its imagery, was recorded in a diary by the pianist Aleksandr Kamenskii, who had remained in Leningrad during the siege and frequently performed for the public, including a great deal of Beethoven (see table 4). One day during the starvation winter of 1941–42, a tall female figure approached him and asked, "Aleksandr Danilovich, will you come with me?" Kamenskii was taken aback. The woman was young, but it was difficult to determine her age. Her skin was like parchment paper, her eyes colorless, her lips blue and dry, her voice faint and husky. She continued, "I plead with you, hear me out. We are living under such incredible conditions that the line between the possible and the impossible has been obliterated. Is that not true? You are therefore astonished by my request." She explained that her mother was dying from dystrophy and her final wish was to listen to the music she had always loved. As the only concertizing pianist in the city, would he fulfill her request? "Is

Figure 6.8. Karl Eliasberg rehearsing Dmitrii Shostakovich's Symphony no. 7 ("Leningrad"), op. 60. Unknown photographer. Alamy Stock Photo EK392X.

it far?" he asked. She indicated one of the streets crossing Liteinyi Prospekt. They left.

On entering the room to which he had been escorted, Kamenskii first noticed a lovely female portrait rendered in pastel hanging in an oval frame on the wall. Afternoon light passing through half a window—the rest of it having been boarded up with a piece of plywood—suffused the room. The living quarters seemed crammed with furniture. He spied a low couch strewn with pillows and what appeared to be a fur coat. He hesitated to stare in that direction. "Mama, Aleksandr Danilovich Kamenskii has come to play for you," the daughter announced. "Is this a dream?" the mother asked in a barely audible hollow voice. "Where is the piano?" he inquired. The daughter pointed to a formless mass in the middle of the room covered with pillows, wrapped in quilted jackets and warm shawls, and secured on top by a heavy carpet. After these items were removed with some difficulty, a perfectly polished black piano lid without a scratch on it came into view. Two piano books lay on top—one of Bach partitas, the other of Beethoven variations.

Kamenskii sat down and played a chorale and then a prelude and fugue by Bach-Liszt. Pausing to reflect on what he had just played, he did not hear the women behind him who seemed to be holding their breaths. Then one of them whispered quietly, "More." And with that he played all three movements of Beethoven's *Moonlight* Sonata. When he finished, he heard a deep sigh and then the same hollow, almost spectral voice whispering clearly and somehow rapturously, "What happiness!" and again more quietly, as if the voice was almost spent, "Happiness." The daughter, sitting at the head of her mother's bed, clasped her hands and glanced pleadingly toward the piano. Kamenskii played yet a third time and then lowered the lid and stood up. The daughter raised herself from the bed and, before he could stop her, bowed down low before him. "There are no words," she whispered, "to express our thanks to you. Mother has fallen asleep. . . . She is happy. . . . There is a smile on her face."[39] [YOUTUBE VIDEO 16]

Beethoven could also unnerve the enemy. The Radio Committee in charge of performances by the LRSO purposely programmed music by Beethoven, Schubert, and Schumann to wage psychological warfare against the Germans. Beethoven's music in particular resounded throughout the city and over the airwaves. Years after the siege, a former German soldier described for Eliasberg how he and his comrades in the *kol'tso* periodically listened to Radio Leningrad over their shortwave receivers. While they did not understand the Russian language, the "language" of the symphony was clear to them all. One day the soldier caught an LRSO radio broadcast of a Beethoven concert and, like those who had heard the premiere of Shostakovich's *Leningrad* Symphony in 1942, thought to himself, "If a city finding itself in such a monstrous position can broadcast concerts of classical music, it can never be defeated." And so the soldier surrendered. "Thanks to you," he told Eliasberg, "I am alive." There is of course no way of knowing how many other German soldiers may have followed suit, but it is apparent that Beethoven's voice had the power to shape outcomes with as telling an impact as the artillery shells that rained down daily on the German front lines.[40]

Piskarevskoe Memorial Cemetery on the outskirts of St. Petersburg is one of the saddest places on earth. It consists of 186 mounded mass graves containing the remains of some four hundred and twenty thousand civilians and seventy thousand soldiers who perished during the siege of Leningrad. Visitors pass down a 480-meter-long pathway extending from an eternal flame at one end to a huge bronze statue of *Rodina-mat'* (Mother Motherland) holding a wreath and looking out over the vast burial site at the other. Each mound holds the remains of some twenty-five hundred people and is identified by a simple block of granite engraved with the year of burial and either a hammer and sickle for civilians or a star for military personnel. Somber music constantly issues forth from loudspeakers located throughout the grounds. Many of the visitors are elderly, carrying posies and bent low with ageless grief and suffering. It is virtually impossible to grasp the enormity of the crime Nazi Germany committed against the city of Leningrad. The graves of half a million of its citizens help place the tragedy into perspective.

Midnight on the Fontanka

Ironically many Russians considered the quality of life during the war to be higher than what they had known in peacetime. This can be attributed to Stalin's early decision to take a number of steps designed to promote a greater degree of patriotism and social cohesion among the general population. He eased up on the terror, permitted somewhat freer discussion in the press, relaxed controls on cultural expression, allowed greater contact with the outside world, restored the Patriarchate of the Russian Orthodox Church, and looked the other way as some collective farms reverted back to individual farmsteads. In general, most people felt freer than at any time since the mid-1920s, and some even anticipated the creation of a genuine civil society in the postwar years. With the conclusion of hostilities, however, the old ways returned with a vengeance. Stalin became increasingly more paranoid at home and pursued policies in Eastern Europe that led to the outbreak of the Cold War abroad. In retrospect, the wartime years were seen as but an interlude in the ongoing saga of the Stalin dictatorship.

On November 15 and 16, 1945, a midnight conversation took place in Leningrad between a British envoy in the British Legation by the name of Isaiah Berlin—who would become one of the twentieth century's most eminent historians, critics, and political philosophers—and Anna Akhmatova, without a doubt the Soviet Union's most famous poet. The conversation occurred in Akhmatova's flat on the Fontanka Canal and ranged across a host of topics. Unfortunately, a commotion in the courtyard alerted authorities to Berlin's presence in the building. As a result, Akhmatova was accused of harboring a spy and was blacklisted by the regime until 1956, while Berlin's diplomatic status protected him, and he returned to Great Britain in early January 1946. Akhmatova always maintained that her meeting with Berlin sparked the outbreak of the Cold War, an outlandish notion, but it is fair to say that this midnight meeting between a Soviet citizen and a visitor from abroad exacerbated Stalin's worst fears and contributed to his inherent distrust of the West,

Figure 6.9. Isaiah Berlin, 1947. Unknown photographer. Courtesy of the Anna Akhmatova Museum at Fountain House, St. Petersburg.

prompting him to launch a new period of repression at home that continued unabated until his death in 1953.

Isaiah Berlin was born in 1909 in the Latvian capital of Riga at a time when the Baltic state was still part of the Russian Empire. His family, Russian by ethnicity, moved to Petrograd in 1917, back to Riga in 1920, and then to Great Britain in 1921. He studied at Oxford University and, among many other academic appointments, taught there from 1932 to 1941 and 1950 to 1967. He also served as the first president of Wolfson College from 1966 to 1975. Berlin loved Russian literature, spoke half a dozen languages, and was passionate about Beethoven's music, especially the string quartets and the opera *Fidelio*. Of his voluminous writings, probably the most popular is the extended essay,

"The Hedgehog and the Fox: An Essay on Tolstoy's View of History" (1953). "The fox knows many things, but the hedgehog knows one big thing," a line from the Greek poet Archilochus, became the prism through which Berlin examined the views of a broad range of Western writers and thinkers, extending from Plato to Marcel Proust, before analyzing Tolstoy's view of history as set forth in the epilogue to *War and Peace*. Berlin was appointed CBE in 1946 and received a knighthood in 1957. He died in 1997 at eighty-eight.[41]

Anna Akhmatova was born Anna Andreevna Gorenko in 1889 at Bol'shoi Fontan near the Black Sea port of Odessa. She began writing poetry at an early age, adopting as her nom de plume Akhmatova after the Tatar name of her maternal grandmother. During the Silver Age, she became a central figure in the St. Petersburg arts scene, especially at the Stray Dog (*Brodiachaia sobaka*) cabaret, where she gave famous poetry readings. Together with Osip Mandel'shtam and several other poets, Akhmatova founded the Acmeist anti-Symbolist school in 1911. She then published five books of poetry from 1912 to 1922. From 1935 to 1940, she wrote the cycle *Requiem*, the great set of poems detailing her personal response to the Stalinist terror. From 1940 to 1962, she assembled her other celebrated collection, *Poem without a Hero*, which she dedicated to "my friends and fellow citizens who perished in Leningrad during the siege." Akhmatova herself had been evacuated from the city in 1942 and lived in Tashkent, Central Asia, until her return in June 1944. In the postwar years, she struggled to maintain some semblance of a successful professional life in the context of a rapidly changing, and frequently unforgiving, political environment. Akhmatova died in 1966 at seventy-six. The complete texts of *Poem without a Hero* and *Requiem* were not published in the Soviet Union until 1976 and 1987 respectively.[42]

The midnight colloquy between Berlin and Akhmatova touched on many subjects, including the rewards of music and the character and meaning of Beethoven's last three piano sonatas. Music had been a part of Akhmatova's world since childhood and offered a deep source of consolation as she struggled with unbelievable hardships as an adult. "Music," a poem written in 1957 and 1958 and dedicated to Dmitrii Shostakovich, captures this well:

> Something miraculous burns in her,
> Edges are faceted before her eyes.
> She alone speaks to me
> When the rest are afraid to come near.
> When the last friend averted his gaze,
> She was with me in my grave,
> As if the first thunderstorm were singing,
> Or as if all the flowers broke into words.[43]

Figure 6.10. Anna Akhmatova, 1946. Photograph by L. Zivert. Courtesy of the Anna Akhmatova Museum at Fountain House, St. Petersburg.

The second poem in the *Midnight Verses* series (1963) conveys a similar sentiment:

> And it was so good this summer
> To become unaccustomed to my name
> In that almost vineyard silence
> And that reality imitating dream.
> And music shared the stillness with me,
> No one in the world is more compliant.
> Often it would lead me
> To the end of my existence.
>
> And I returned alone from there,
> And I knew, indeed, that for the last time

I am carrying with me a feeling like a miracle,
That . . . [Akhmatova's ellipsis][44]

A poem from *The Fifth Rose* series (1963) offers yet a third perspective:

Leave me alone with music,
We will soon strike an accord:
She is a bottomless reservoir—
I am a ghost, the shadow of reproach.
I don't meddle with her melodies,
And she will help me—to die.[45]

Anatoly Naiman (b. 1936), poet, translator, and writer who was a confidant of Akhmatova in her later years, commented on Akhmatova's love for music as follows:

> She listened to music frequently and for long periods; she listened to various kinds of music, but sometimes she would be especially interested in a particular piece or pieces for a certain time. In the summer of 1963 it was the Beethoven sonatas, in the autumn—Vivaldi; in the summer of 1964—Shostakovich's Eighth Quartet, in the spring of 1963—Pergolesi's *Stabat Mater*, and in the summer and autumn—Monteverdi's *L'incoronazione di Poppea* and especially often, Purcell's *Dido and Aeneas*, the British recording with Schwarzkopf. She liked listening to Beethoven's *Bagatelles*, much of Chopin (played by Sofronitskii), *The Four Seasons* and other Vivaldi concertos, and also Bach, Mozart, Haydn, and Handel.[46]

Regarding Beethoven, Berlin wrote that Akhmatova "spoke at length about music, about the sublimity and beauty of Beethoven's last three piano sonatas. Pasternak thought them greater than the posthumous quartets and she agreed with him. She responded with her whole nature to the violent changes of feeling within their movements."[47] Akhmatova's love of Beethoven found reflection in her poetry. The first poem (1944) in the *Apparition of the Moon* series, for example, makes a direct reference to the *Moonlight* Sonata:

From mother-of-pearl and agate,
From smoked glass,
So suddenly it slanted
And so festively it floated—
As if "Moonlight Sonata"
Had just crossed our path.[48]

In addition, when she penned the last line of the second poem in *The Fifth Rose* series (1963), Akhmatova most likely had in mind her conversation with the musicologist and pianist Heinrich Neuhaus, who placed the highest value on Beethoven's Piano Sonata no. 31 in A-flat, op. 110:

You shone with an otherworldly light
A reminder of the garden of paradise,
You might be a Petrarchan sonnet
Or the best of the sonatas.[49]

Akhmatova seemed particularly taken by Opus 110. In the initial version of her poem "The Call," the first two lines read, "And in the penultimate sonata / I carefully concealed you." In the final version, published in 1963, the lines were altered to read, "And in which of the sonatas / Will I carefully conceal you."[50] It is unclear why Akhmatova intentionally obscured the identity and, more importantly, the meaning of Opus 110. She penned two different epigraphs to a poem highlighting the *Arioso dolente* (*Lamenting Song*) section of the sonata's third movement. Might this explain the emotional significance the piano piece held for her? In his analysis of Opus 110, Neuhaus cited Anton Rubinshtein's characterization of the *Arioso dolente* to the effect that "even in the world's best operas, it is virtually impossible to find an aria of such beauty that expresses with so much power and feeling the depth of human sorrow."[51] Neuhaus probably shared this sentiment with Akhmatova. Perhaps this explains why she obscured its true meaning for the reader, and perhaps subconsciously for herself as well. [YOUTUBE VIDEO 17]

Berlin noted that, whatever the topic, Akhmatova throughout "spoke without the slightest trace of self-pity, like a princess in exile, proud, unhappy, unapproachable, in a calm, even voice, at times in words of moving eloquence. The account of the unrelieved tragedy of her life went beyond anything which anyone had ever described to me in spoken words; the recollection of them is still vivid and painful to me." He later recalled to Anatoly Naiman, "The whole evening was filled with a magic atmosphere. . . . I've never spent an evening like that with anyone." And on January 23, 1995, just two years before his death, he wrote to an acquaintance, "My visit [with Akhmatova] was, I think, the central event of my entire life."[52]

Berlin and Akhmatova fell in love that night. When he staggered back to his hotel room late in the morning of November 16, Berlin threw himself on the bed and declared to his travel companion, "I am in love! I am in love!" Akhmatova turned naturally to poetry. In the second poem of the *Cinque* series, written on December 20, 1945, she declared her love in language of delicate beauty:

Sounds die away in the ether.
And darkness overtakes the dusk.
In a world become mute for all time,
There are only two voices, yours and mine.
And to the almost bell-like sound

Of the wind from invisible Lake Ladoga,
That late-night dialogue turned into
The delicate shimmer of interlaced rainbows.[53]

The hope that the encounter might lead to a more permanent union persisted for some time. Berlin became the "Guest from the Future" in *Poem without a Hero*:

The guest from the future!—Is it true
That he really will come to me,
Turning left at the bridge?[54]

But this was not to be. Akhmatova answered her own query in the thirteenth poem (1953) of the *Sweetbriar in Blossom* series:

And that heart no longer responds
To my voice, exulting and grieving.
Everything is over. . . . And my song drifts
Into the empty night, where you no longer exist.[55]

Finally, in 1956, on learning that Berlin had married, she reconciled her conflicting emotions in the third and final dedication to *Poem without a Hero* and put the matter to rest:

Long enough I have frozen in fear,
    Better to summon a Bach Chaconne,
    And behind it will enter a man,
He will not be a beloved husband to me
    But what we accomplish, he and I,
    Will disturb the Twentieth Century.[56]

When news of the meeting between Berlin and Akhmatova reached Stalin, he is said to have quipped, "So now our nun is consorting with British spies, is she?"[57] This prompted an investigation into the "unsatisfactory situation" of two literary journals in Leningrad that had published some of Akhmatova's poetry. On August 16, 1946, Andrei Zhdanov, head of the party apparatus in Leningrad during the siege and now a secretary of the Central Committee, and Stalin's watchdog on cultural affairs, delivered a report in the form of a three-hour lecture to the Leningrad branch of the Union of Soviet Writers. In the course of this harangue, he savagely attacked Akhmatova as "one of the standard bearers of a hollow, empty, aristocratic-salon poetry, which is absolutely foreign to Soviet literature." He continued,

Anna Akhmatova's subject matter is thoroughly individualistic. The range of her poetry is pitifully limited—this is the poetry of a feral lady from the salons, moving between the boudoir and the prayer stool. It is based on erotic motifs

> linked with motifs of mourning, melancholy, death, mysticism and isolation. . . . She is half nun, half whore, or rather both whore and nun, fornication and prayer being intermingled in her world. . . . Such is Anna Akhmatova, with her petty, narrow private life, her trivial experiences and her religious-mystical eroticism. Akhmatova's poetry is totally foreign to the people.[58]

In the wake of this attack, the Writers' Union—the only means of livelihood for writers—expelled Akhmatova, and further publication of her work was banned. There is some evidence she thought Stalin's anger stemmed from the standing ovations she had received at readings of her work in Moscow on April 3, 1946, and Leningrad on August 7, 1946. When apprised of the ten-to-fifteen-minute ovation Akhmatova had received in Moscow, Stalin reportedly asked, "Who organized the standing?" György Dalos clarifies: "There was a strictly regulated hierarchy of applause at public meetings in the Soviet Union: applause, tumultuous applause, prolonged and tumultuous applause, tumultuous applause with the audience half-rising from their seats, and the high-point of all, wild tumultuous applause that went on without end, eventually turning into a standing ovation. . . . At political meetings in the 1950s teams of applause-leaders often stood in readiness, performing their task at a sign from the chair. This was commonly known as 'guided spontaneity.'"[59]

Wounded pride may have been a factor in light of Stalin's early efforts at writing poetry. But much more was at stake here, and Akhmatova was fortunate to have escaped with her life. As it was, she did not regain membership in the Writers' Union until 1951 and received permission only in 1956 to publish her work again. Looking back, Akhmatova seems to have accepted her fate with equanimity, commenting to Korney Chukovsky, "I was famous, then I was very infamous, and I am convinced that essentially it's one and the same thing."[60]

The crusade against Akhmatova, which was directed against the humorist Mikhail Zoshchenko as well, represented the tip of a dangerous new iceberg floating in the Gulag Archipelago. It would go down in history as the *Zhdanovshchina*, a short but vicious new reign of terror designed to rid the country of the disease of "cosmopolitanism," Stalin's term for alleged infatuation with Western cultural norms and practices on the part of the Russian intelligentsia. All the old machinery of terror came back: denunciations and forced confessions, secret trials, summary executions, and banishment to the gulag. The purge began with literature but quickly spread to ensnare leading figures in such disparate fields as history, economics, geography, physiology, linguistics, philosophy, the natural sciences, and cinematography. Even circus managers were caught up in the hysteria. Nor were musicians immune from the general crackdown. A number of high-ranking composers, including Dmitrii

Shostakovich, Sergei Prokofiev, and Aram Khachaturian, were charged with practicing "formalism," which meant engaging in art for art's sake rather than adhering to the norms of socialist realism.[61] A party resolution of February 10, 1948, accused the composers of writing unintelligible "dissonant" music that had nothing to do with the peoples' desire for "beautiful music, refined music." The accused lost the right to publish and perform their works, a situation that endured until the lifting of the decree in 1955. Shostakovich in particular suffered terribly from this ordeal, in part due to his natural nervous disposition but also because of the "Muddle Instead of Music" fiasco of 1936. He allegedly kept a packed suitcase by the door to his flat for the anticipated midnight knock from the secret police that fortunately never came.

The *Zhdanovshchina* technically ended in August 1948 with the sudden and rather mysterious death of its namesake and architect, Andrei Zhdanov. But the terror persisted in other ways, manifesting itself next in the so-called Leningrad Affair of 1949–50. Stalin detested the former northern capital for its Western ways, baroque architecture, effete intellectualism, and superior attitude toward the rest of the country, so unlike Moscow with its more provincial "Russian" character, cozy streets, and the storied history of its crenellated battlements. Like Ivan the Terrible in the sixteenth century, he saw plotters and schemers everywhere and in 1949 uncovered a "plot" by Leningrad officials to seize control of the government. Retribution followed swiftly with over two thousand municipal and regional officials arrested and found guilty of treason against the state. The terror also swept up an unknown number of the city's intellectual and professional class and either liquidated them or incarcerated them in the prison camp system.

The purge exhibited a pronounced anti-Semitic tone as well that stemmed from Stalin's paranoia over the establishment of the state of Israel in May 1948. The term "rootless cosmopolitanism" was coined to refer to those Russian Jews who now presumably desired to emigrate to the new Jewish state. This anti-Zionist drive, initially restricted to Leningrad, shortly erupted into a virulent national campaign orchestrated by Stalin. Untold numbers of Jews and others were arrested by the end of 1952. Then, on January 13, 1953, nine Kremlin doctors, six of them Jewish, were charged with having assassinated Zhdanov and other high officials and plotting to poison the remaining Soviet leadership, including Stalin himself. This "Doctors' Plot," as it came to be known, appeared to be the opening salvo of an all-out assault on Russian Jewry. However, Stalin's (natural) death on March 5 brought the matter to a swift end. The doctors were exonerated on March 31, 1953, by order of the Minister of Internal Affairs, who admitted that the charges had been fabricated. Fortuitously, yet another purge, this one with overtly anti-Semitic overtones, was averted.

* * *

Following his death on March 5, 1953, Stalin's embalmed body lay in state in the Trade Union's Hall of Columns from March 6 to 9. Throngs of mourners passed by the casket, many weeping openly. Joseph Stalin was the only ruler most had ever known. On March 9 the glass-enclosed casket was taken to the Lenin Mausoleum on Red Square and placed next to Lenin's bier. Then, at precisely 12:05 p.m., a sprightly little tune, unremarkable in its own right, suddenly displaced the dirgelike music that Radio Moscow had been broadcasting all morning. Though no one could have guessed it at the time, a new era had just dawned in Soviet history.

Notes

1. At the height of Nikita Khrushchev's de-Stalinization campaign in 1961, Stalin's body was removed from the mausoleum on October 31 and reburied in a plot between the tomb and the Kremlin wall. In his official biography, published in 1938, Stalin falsely listed his birth date as December 21, 1879; parish records in Gori indicate, however, that the actual date was December 6, 1878. For discussion of this anomaly, see Robert Service, *Stalin: A Biography* (Cambridge, MA: Harvard University Press, 2005), 14. Data on cost of collectivization from Robert Conquest, *The Harvest of Sorrow: Soviet Collectivization and the Terror-Famine* (New York: Oxford University Press, 1986), 306; information on the Great Purge from Robert Conquest, *The Great Terror: A Reassessment* (Oxford: Oxford University Press, 1991), 485–86; fatalities in World War II from Nicholas V. Riasanovsky and Mark D. Steinberg, *A History of Russia*, 7th ed. (Oxford: Oxford University Press, 2005), 518.

2. Stalin objected to the "hypermodern" school of chess as practiced by the chess master Alexander Alekhine. Alekhine was famous for attacking the board with bold, asymmetrical moves that focused on the far queen's side rather than adhering to the more conventional step-by-step approach, favored by Stalin, which concentrated on the center of the board. See Francis B. Randall, *Stalin's Russia: An Historical Reconsideration* (New York: Free Press, 1965), 255.

3. Service, *Stalin*, 302.

4. The Stalin Prizes were awarded from 1940 to 1954 for achievements in literature, music, painting, sculpture, architecture, drama, cinema, and science and technology. For Stalin's direct participation in the selection process, see Marina Frolova-Walker, *Stalin's Music Prize: Soviet Culture and Politics* (New Haven, CT: Yale University Press, 2016), 25–29, 106–7, 174, 187, 203–6, 333n55, 341n1. Since the Stalin Music Prize was awarded only to living Soviet composers and musicians, Beethoven's name appears only indirectly in the transcripts of the selection committee's deliberations. Ibid., 42, 50, 83, 92, 116, 280.

5. I. V. Stalin, *Sochineniia*, 13 vol. (Moscow: Gosudarstvennoe izdatel'stvo politicheskoi literatury, 1946–51). The closest reference to anything of a cultural nature is Stalin's oft cited characterization of proletarian art as "socialist in content, nationalist in form." Ibid., VII:138.

6. Randall, *Stalin's Russia*, 72–73. For a discussion that calls into question the authenticity of this source and Randall's response to the critique, see Rimo Vihavainen, "A Note on a Spurious Source: *Finskii vestnik*," *Russian Review*, XLIV, 1 (January 1985): 69–70.

7. Solomon Volkov, *Shostakovich and Stalin: The Extraordinary Relationship between the Great Composer and the Brutal Dictator*, trans. Antonina W. Bouis (New York: Alfred A. Knopf, 2004), 107. Volkov writes, "When the program of light music [for the forthcoming program] was shown to Stalin for his approval, he personally wrote in the finale of Beethoven's Ninth Symphony with its famed 'Ode to Joy,' replacing some of the lighter fare." Ibid., 107. Volkov provides no attribution for this statement. Since much of the book is based on uncited interviews with cultural figures the author knew in the Soviet Union before emigrating to the United States in 1976, it is difficult to determine if this is based on hearsay or fact. For the identity of the interviewees, see ibid., xii.

8. The performance of Beethoven's symphonic music for extramusical purposes was reflected as well in an unrealized 1921 project by the theater director Vsevolod Meyerhold to stage Beethoven's Third or Ninth Symphony as a "magical pantomime" of Lenin's electrification program. It was to be called "Dithyramb of Electrification." Marina Raku, *Muzykal'naia klassika v mifotvorchestve sovetskoi epokhi* (Moscow: Novoe literaturnoe obozrenie, 2014), 221. On Lopukhov's ballet, see Fedor Lopukhov, *Velichie mirozdaniia: tantsimfoniia Fedora Lopukhova muz. L. Betkhovena/4-aia simfoniia/s avtolitosiluetami Pavla Goncharova* (Petrograd: G. P. Liubarskii, 1922); Raku, *Muzykal'naia klassika*, 221–24; Mary Grace Swift, *The Art of the Dance in the U.S.S.R.* (Notre Dame, IN: University of Notre Dame Press, 1968), 62; Marina Frolova-Walker and Jonathan Walker, *Music and Soviet Power, 1917–1932* (Woodbridge, UK: Boydell, 2012), 90–91. Raku notes that a second performance of the ballet was staged at the Musorgsky Malyi Theater of Opera and Ballet (now Mikhailovskii Theater) in St. Petersburg in the spring of 2001 but does not indicate whether it fared any better with critics. Raku, *Muzykal'naia klassika*, 222n81.

9. O. Timushev, *"Mavzolei:" ritmicheskoe shestvie. Muzyka Betkhovena* (Moscow: Muztorg PTO MONO, 1930).

10. *Pravda*, December 6, 1936, no. 335, 6; *Krasnaia zvezda*, December 6, 1936, no. 280, 4; Raku, *Muzykal'naia klassika*, 281–92; Leonid Sidel'nikov, *Gosudarstvennyi akademicheskii simfonicheskii orkestr Soiuza SSR* (Moscow: Muzyka, 1986), 15–17. The eclectic nature of this concert might seem odd, but it reflected a fundamental feature of Russian/Soviet popular entertainment where "high" and "low" culture were often presented side-by-side on the same program. See Richard Stites, "Frontline Entertainment," in *Culture and Entertainment in Wartime Russia*, ed. Richard Stites (Bloomington: Indiana University Press, 1995), 126. On the 1936 constitution, see Donald W. Treadgold, *Twentieth Century Russia*, 9th ed. (Boulder, CO: Westview, 2000), 216–19.

11. The populist camp was represented primarily by the RAPM (Russian Association of Proletarian Musicians), which opposed what it considered the bourgeois music of the concert hall, opera house, and ballet studio in favor of new proletarian music that could be appreciated by the masses. The progressive camp, on the other hand, was represented by the ACM (Association for Contemporary Music), which favored modern trends in classical music and called for close links with Western composers. Consult standard works on Soviet cultural history for elaboration.

12. Pauline Fairclough, *Classics for the Masses: Shaping Soviet Musical Identity under Lenin and Stalin* (New Haven, CT: Yale University Press, 2016), 63–64; Frolova-Walker and Walker, *Music and Soviet Power*, 72–73; A. Morov, *Moskovskaia muzykal'naia* (Moscow: Moskovskii rabochii, 1964), 39–42; L. Grigor'ev and Ia. Platek, ed., *Moskovskaia gosudarstvennaia*

filarmoniia (Moscow: Sovetskii kompozitor, 1973), 52–53; "Otkritie kontsertnogo sezona v Moskve," *Pravda*, October 7, 1940, in *Muzykal'naia publitsistika raznykh let: stat'i, ocherki, retsenzii*, ed. Georgii Khubov (Moscow: Sovetskii kompozitor, 1976), 201–4; "Iubileinye kontserty," *Sovetskoe iskusstvo*, December 14, 1945; L. S. Sidel'nikov, *Bol'shoi simfonicheskii orkestr tsentral'nogo televideniia i vsesoiuznogo radio* (Moscow: Muzyka, 1980), 57–68; Sidel'nikov, *Gosudarstvennyi akademicheskii simfonicheskii orkestr*, 1–17, 23–87.

13. Frolova-Walker and Walker, *Music and Soviet Power*, 59.

14. Fairclough, *Classics for the Masses*, 59–63.

15. S. E. Feinberg, *32 sonaty Betkhovena: k tsiklu kontsertov* (Moscow: Moskovskaia gosudarstvennaia filarmoniia, 1945). Feinberg performed Sonatas nos. 1–6 in the first recital, nos. 7–11 in the second, nos. 12–16 in the third, nos. 17–22 in the fourth, nos. 23–28 in the fifth, and nos. 29–32 in the sixth.

16. L. Ginzburg, "K istorii ispolneniia kvartetov Betkhovena v Rossii," *Issledovaniia, stat'i, ocherki* (Moscow: Sovetskii kompozitor, 1971), 327.

17. Fairclough, *Classics for the Masses*, 45; Raku, *Muzykal'naia klassika*, 259; I. Sollertinskii, "'Fidelio' Betkhovena," in *I. Sollertinskii: muzykal'no-istoricheskii etiudy*, ed. M. Druskin (Leningrad: Gosudarstvennoe muzykal'noe izdatel'stvo, 1956), 63; "V komitete po podgotovke Betkhovenskikh torzhestv," *Muzykal'noe obrazovanie*, 1–2 (1927), 167–68. The Beethoven centenary planning committee had wanted the Bol'shoi to stage a performance of *Fidelio* in conjunction with the main events of the May 1927 festivities but was informed that the theater "found it impossible" to comply. The Bol'shoi offered instead to perform the *Missa solemnis*. Nikolai Shuvalov, "O Betkhovenskikh dniakh v Soiuze," *Betkhovenskii biulleten'* 1 (Moscow: Betkhovenskii komitet pri Narkomprose RSFSR, 1927), 13.

18. A. Shaverdian, *Fidelio: opera Betkhovena* (Moscow: Moskovskaia gosudarstvennaia filarmoniia, 1937), 29–30.

19. "Dela i plany opernogo teatra," *Pravda*, July 29, 1938, in *Muzykal'naia publitsistika raznykh let*, ed. Georgii Khubov, 100. *Fidelio* did not appear on the Leningrad stage until 1959. M. Druskin, "Torzhestvo muzyki ("Fidelio" v Malom Opernom Teatre)," *Sovetskaia muzyka*, XXIII, 3 (March 1959): 105–9.

20. A. Khokhlovkina, *Fidelio L. Betkhovena* (Moscow: Gosudarstvennoe muzykal'noe izdatel'stvo, 1961), 20. Khokhlovkina went on to note that a 1954 performance of *Fidelio* by the Bol'shoi resulted in a "brilliant artistic renewal" of the opera, thus allowing the work to "gain its rightful place in our life and struggle." Ibid., 20.

21. Katherine B. Eaton, *Daily Life in the Soviet Union* (Westport, CT: Greenwood, 2004), 274–75; Morov, *Moskva muzykal'naia*, 54–67; Sidel'nikov, *Bol'shoi Simfonicheskii Orkestr*, 5–202; Yuri Slezkine, *The House of Government: A Saga of the Russian Revolution* (Princeton, NJ: Princeton University Press, 2017), 509; Richard Stites, *Russian Popular Culture: Entertainment and Society since 1900* (Cambridge: Cambridge University Press, 1992), 81–83. For the early history of radio broadcasting in Leningrad, see Iu. Kalganov, "Pervye gody Leningradskogo radio," in *V pervye gody sovetskogo muzykal'nogo stroitel'stva: stat'i, vospominaniia, materialy*, ed. V. Bogdanov-Berezovskii and I. Gusin (Leningrad: Sovetskii kompozitor, 1959), 205–30. For the importance of radio in World War II, see James von Geldern, "Radio Moscow: The Voice from the Center," in *Culture and Entertainment*, ed. Richard Stites, 44–61.

22. Iu. Keldysh, *Betkhoven* (Moscow: Gosudarstvennoe izdatel'stvo po voprosam radio, 1936), 3–28; Morov, *Moskva muzykal'naia*, 63.

23. A. Al'shvang, "Betkhoven," *Bol'shaia sovetskaia entsiklopediia*, 2nd ed., V (Moscow: Bol'shaia sovetskaia entsiklopediia, 1950), 118–22. For extended discussion, see A. Al'shvang, *Betkhoven* (Moscow: Gosudarstvennoe muzykal'noe izdatel'stvo, 1952). Additional commentary

can be found in N. L. Fishman, ed., *Iz istorii sovetskoi betkhoveniany* (Moscow: Sovetskii kompozitor, 1972), 50–55, 70–73, 208–30. On Al'shvang, see G. Bernandt, "A. A. Al'shvang," *Sovetskaia muzyka*, IX, 9 (September 1941): 59–65.

24. Iu. Vainkop, *Betkhoven i ego tvorchestvo*, 2nd rev. ed. (Leningrad: Triton, 1934), 3, 20.

25. N. Karintsev, *Betkhoven (kartiny iz zhizni)*, 4th ed. (Moscow: Muzgiz, 1936), 66.

26. Cited in Raku, *Muzykal'naia klassika*, 300.

27. T. Popova, *Liudvig van Betkhoven: zhizn' i tvorchestvo* (Moscow: Komitet po delam iskusstv, 1940), 14, 24, 50.

28. While displaying some of the characteristics of the works cited above, the following studies of Beethoven's symphonic music exhibit a much higher level of professionalism: N. Ryzhkin, *Betkhoven i klassicheskii simfonism* (Moscow: Moskovskaia filarmoniia, 1938), 5–32; A. Shaverian, *Simfonii Betkhovena (putevoditel')* (Moscow: Moskovskaia gosudarstvennaia filarmoniia, 1936) 7–28.

29. Raku, *Muzykal'naia klassika*, 314.

30. For commentary on the way Leningraders perceived similarities between the campaigns of 1812 and 1941, see Alexis Peri, *The War Within: Diaries from the Siege of Leningrad* (Cambridge, MA: Harvard University Press, 2017), 217–22.

31. D. Tsyganov, V. Shirinskii, V. Borisovskii, and S. Shirinskii, "Proizvedeniia Betkhovena na konstertnoi estrade," *Sovetskoe isskustvo*, December 14, 1945. The authors were members of the Beethoven Quartet, which, among many other wartime activities, performed for the Soviet Northern Fleet in the Barents Sea in the autumn of 1943. On the occasion of the sinking of a huge Nazi transport ship displacing ten thousand tons, the authors observed: "During the heroic days of the battle with Hitler's pirates, Beethoven's music was heard to great effect on the Soviet battleships." Ibid.

32. Andrei Kriukov, *Muzyka v efire voennogo Leningrada* (St. Petersburg: Kompozitor, 2005), 118. For additional commentary by Kriukov, the recognized Russian authority on all things musical during the siege—and himself a survivor of the ordeal—see his *Muzyka v kol'tse blokady: ocherki* (Moscow: Muzyka, 1973); *Muzyka v gorode-fronte* (Leningrad: Muzyka, 1975); *Muzykal'naia zhizn' srazhaiushchegosia Leningrada: ocherki* (Leningrad: Sovetskii kompozitor, 1985); *Muzyka v dni blokady: khronika* (St. Petersburg: Kompozitor, 2002).

33. Technically the siege lasted 872 days (September 8, 1941–January 27, 1944). For the classic account, see Harrison Salisbury, *The 900 Days: The Siege of Leningrad* (New York: Harper and Row, 1969). For other commentary, in addition to Alexis Peri's study, see Leon Goure, *The Siege of Leningrad* (Stanford, CA: Stanford University Press, 1962); Brian Moynahan, *Leningrad: Siege and Symphony* (New York: Atlantic Monthly, 2013); Dmitri V. Pavlov, *Leningrad 1941: The Blockade*, trans. John C. Adams (Chicago: University of Chicago Press, 1965); Anna Reid, *Leningrad: The Epic Siege of World War II, 1941–1944* (New York: Walker, 2011).

34. Worker brigade and evacuation figures from Peri, *The War Within*, 23–24. On cannibalism, see ibid., 106–9.

35. For specific composers, see Kriukov, *Muzyka v efire*, 398–410. In the autumn and early winter of 1941–42, the LRSO performed six to twelve concerts per week. Ibid., 115. For 1942 as a whole, the orchestra performed some seventy times. Kriukov, *Muzyka v gorode-fronte*, 96.

36. D. Shen, "V osazhdennom Leningrade: zametka muzykanta," in *V gody velikoi otechestvennoi voiny*, ed. V. M. Bogdanov-Berezovskii and I. Gusin (Leningrad: Sovetskii kompozitor, 1959), 105–11.

37. Moynahan, *Leningrad: Siege and Symphony*, 2.

38. Vasil'eva and Matus quotes from "Shostakovich against Stalin," youtube.com [39:53–40:18]; Parfionov quote from Sophy Roberts, *The Lost Pianos of Siberia* (New York: Grove, 2020), 238; Eliasberg quote from Moynahan, *Leningrad: Siege and Symphony*, 487; German soldiers'

quote from Wikipedia, s.v. "Leningrad Première of Shostakovich's Symphony No. 7," last edited December 16, 2021, 01:29, https://en.wikipedia.org/wiki/Leningrad_premi%C3%A8re_of_Shostakovich%27s_Symphony_No._7. In the caption to the photo preceding p. 335, Moynahan asserts that the picture is of Eliasberg conducting the LRSO premiere of the "Leningrad" Symphony. In fact, as attested by Andrei Kriukov, the photo is of Eliasberg conducting the Leningrad Philharmonia on May 1, 1941, during the opening concert of the orchestra's new season. Kriukov, *Muzyka v efire*, photo insert fol. p. 144. For additional commentary on the symphony and the Leningrad premiere, see ibid., 164–70; Moynahan, *Leningrad: Siege and Symphony*, 1–6, 476–88; Harlow Robinson, "Composing for Victory: Classical Music," in *Culture and Entertainment*, ed. Richard Stites, 68–72. For excerpts from the diary that Ksenia Matus kept during the siege, see Peri, *The War Within*, 99, 137–38, 142, 152; for her photo with the oboe she played during the premiere, see ibid., photo insert fol. p. 125.

39. S. Khentova, *"Lunnaia Sonata" Betkhovena* (Moscow: Muzyka, 1975), 36–37. See also (but without the Kamenskii reminiscence) the author's earlier work, *Rasskaz o "Lunnoi Sonate": Sonata L. Betkhovena soch. 27 No 2 i ee ispolniteli* (Leningrad: Gosudarstvennoe muzykal'noe izdatel'stvo, 1961). Liteinyi Prospekt is one of the main avenues in Leningrad / St. Petersburg that intersects Nevskii Prospekt east of the Fontanka Canal.

40. Kriukov, *Muzyka v efire*, 70; quotes cited in Kriukov, *Muzyka v gorode-fronte*, 43.

41. For Berlin's correspondence and reminiscences, see Isaiah Berlin, *Letters 1928–1997*, 3 vol., ed. Henry Hardy et al. (Cambridge: Cambridge University Press, 2004).

42. For Akhmatova's poetry, consult Roberta Reeder, ed., *The Complete Poems of Anna Akhmatova*, expanded ed., trans. Judith Hemschemeyer (Boston: Zephyr, 1997).

43. Ibid., 476.

44. Ibid., 739.

45. Ibid., 742.

46. Anatoly Naiman, *Remembering Anna Akhmatova*, trans. Wendy Rosslyn (New York: Henry Holt, 1989), 147.

47. Isaiah Berlin, *Personal Impressions*, 3rd ed., ed. Henry Holt et al. (Princeton, NJ: Princeton University Press, 2014), 411.

48. Reeder, *The Complete Poems of Anna Akhmatova*, 436.

49. Ibid., 740. For an analysis of the relationship between Opus 110 and the last line of this stanza, see B. Kats and R. Timenchik, *Akhmatova i muzyka: issledovatel'skie ocherki* (Leningrad; Sovetskii kompozitor, 1989), 148–52. On Neuhaus, see Maria Razumovskaya, *Heinrich Neuhaus: A Life beyond Music* (Rochester, NY: University of Rochester Press, 2018).

50. Kats and Timenchik, *Akhmatova i muzyka*, 148; Reeder, *The Complete Poems of Anna Akhmatova*, 472.

51. G. G. Neigauz, "O poslednikh sonatakh Betkhovena," in *Iz istorii sovetskoi betkhoveniany: sbornik statei*, ed. N. L. Fishman (Moscow: Sovetskii kompozitor, 1972), 242. See also William Kinderman, *Beethoven: A Political Artist in Revolutionary Times* (Chicago: University of Chicago Press, 2020), 203–4.

52. Isaiah Berlin, *Personal Impressions*, 412–13; Anatoly Naiman, "Akhmatova and Sir," in *The Book of Isaiah: Personal Impressions of Isaiah Berlin*, ed. Henry Hardy (Washington, DC: Brookings Institution, 2004), 77; Isaiah Berlin, *Letters 1928–1997*, 617.

53. Reeder, *The Complete Poems of Anna Akhmatova*, 454.

54. Ibid., 552.

55. Ibid., 465. Akhmatova's ellipsis.

56. Ibid., 547.

57. Michael Ignatieff, *Isaiah Berlin: A Life* (New York: Metropolitan Books, 1998), 167.

58. György Dalos, *Guest from the Future: Anna Akhmatova and Isaiah Berlin*, trans. Antony Woods (New York: Farrar, Straus and Giroux, 1998), 56–57.

59. Ibid., 67.

60. Roberta Reeder, *Anna Akhmatova: Poet and Prophet* (London: Allison and Busby, 1994), 324.

61. Sheila Fitzpatrick observes that Beethoven's Ninth Symphony, especially the *Ode to Joy*, "was probably the ideal socialist-realist work in the minds of many Soviet opponents of formalism." Sheila Fitzpatrick, *The Cultural Front: Power and Culture in Revolutionary Russia* (Ithaca, NY: Cornell University Press, 1993), 213.

7

BEETHOVEN AS BEETHOVEN

The End of Ideology

THE FINAL PHASE OF RUSSIAN BEETHOVEN RECEPTION, extending from the end of the Stalin era to the present, witnessed a gradual return to a less ideological, more professionally oriented approach to the study of both man and music. While a certain hagiography persisted, there was a great deal less emphasis on political interpretations of the composer's art and much more focus on the music itself. In this way political correctness gave way to more nuanced analysis as musicologists began returning to nineteenth-century Russian (and European) critical traditions. This had the effect of freeing Beethoven's music from the shackles of political bias and allowing the composer to regain his integrity as an autonomous creative spirit. As had been the case at the outset, Beethoven was once again Beethoven.

De-Stalinization and Thaw

Born to poor peasants in the southern Russian village of Kalinovka on April 5, 1894, Nikita Khrushchev rose through the ranks to become first secretary of the Communist Party of the Soviet Union in September 1953. In March 1958 he became head of the government as well, through his elevation to the post of premier.[1] The Twenty-Second Party Congress of October 1961—when a new party program was adopted and the final phase of the de-Stalinization campaign he had initiated in 1956 was launched—marked the high point of his career. His authority began to wane in the autumn of 1962, however, following a failed effort to emplace intermediate-range nuclear missiles in Cuba. This, coupled with erratic efforts to promote economic development at home, led to his ouster on October 14, 1964. The party newspaper *Pravda* accused the former leader of "subjectivism and drift in Communist construction, harebrained scheming, half-baked conclusions and hasty decisions and actions divorced from reality, bragging and bluster, attraction to rule by fiat, [and] unwillingness to take into account what science and practical experience have already worked out."[2] Khrushchev spent the remainder of his life in comfortable retirement at his dacha outside Moscow. He died from a heart attack on September 10, 1971, and was buried at Novodevichy Cemetery three days later. A recording of music by Beethoven and Chopin was played at his funeral prior to graveside services.

Along with his erratic personality, Khrushchev displayed contradictory attitudes toward the arts. On the one hand, he liked classical music and the theater and enjoyed opera and (to a lesser extent) ballet. He loved to read, especially novels by Kuprin, Leskov, Saltykov-Shchedrin, Tolstoy, and Turgenev as well as works on nature and technology, and complained that he did not have more time for this pursuit. A grand piano stood in the dining room of his villa in Kiev during his tenure as head of the Ukrainian Party (1938–46 / 1948–49), at which time his children took music and English lessons. He displayed a special fondness for Russian and Ukrainian folksongs and dances and would invite guests to listen to them, along with opera arias, on his phonograph. In his retirement he avidly watched music performances on TV and listened to classical music and the news over the airwaves of the VOA and BBC. On the other hand, Khrushchev engaged in celebrated verbal attacks on authors and poets, detested jazz (listening to it was like having "gas on the stomach"), and had little if any understanding of modern art ("It's dog shit! . . . A donkey could smear better . . . with his tail."). The sculptor Ernst Neizvestny, who the family commissioned to design the bust on Khrushchev's graveside memorial, once described Khrushchev as "the most uncultured man I've ever met." And his American biographer, William Taubman, concluded that "no matter how hard he tried, even the self-made Khrushchev couldn't undo what Kalinovka had made of him."[3]

Yet, despite the barnyard language, boorishness, and occasional bout of outlandish behavior, Khrushchev's interest in the arts was genuine. His son-in-law, Aleksei Adzhubei, noted that Khrushchev's love for the theater and music should not be understood as "some sort of effort at adult self-education." Rather, this was his means of "exercising his feelings and the way he relaxed." Even during dangerous moments in the Cold War, Khrushchev repaired to the theater. During the height of the West Berlin Crisis in June 1961, for example, he attended a performance by Margot Fonteyn at the Bol'shoi Ballet—although he also summoned the British ambassador to his box during intermission to warn that should nuclear war result from the US military buildup, six hydrogen bombs would be "quite enough" for Britain and nine would do for France. During the even more dangerous Cuban Missile Crisis of October 1962, he attended three separate theater productions in the space of that critical week, taking in respectively an American performance of Mussorgsky's *Boris Godunov* at the Bol'shoi Opera, a performance by a Cuban touring group, and a concert by a Bulgarian ensemble. This and other evidence suggest that Khrushchev, like Lenin, sought to gain at least a measure of equanimity and spiritual enrichment through music.[4]

Khrushchev is best known for the so-called Secret Speech he delivered the night of February 25, 1956, at a closed-door session of the Twentieth Party Congress. The speech, lasting four hours with one intermission, served as a platform for the inauguration of Khrushchev's de-Stalinization campaign, which was designed to expose the consequences of the "personality cult" Stalin had fostered during his rule. The intention was to bury the terror along with the already entombed tyrant, a risky gamble in light of the broad complicity by many of those in the hall that night, above all Khrushchev himself. When asked late in life if he had any regrets about his career, Khrushchev replied, "Most of all the blood. My arms are up to the elbows in blood. That is the most terrible thing that lies in my soul."[5] But the gamble paid off. Though the speech did not disclose the full extent of the terror, it proved sufficient to put to rest the use of violence as an administrative tool in the conduct of party affairs. As Khrushchev quipped to his wife following his removal from office, "Well, that's it. I'm retired. If I accomplished nothing else, at least I provided for the non-violent transfer of power." That indeed was a considerable achievement.[6]

Stalin's death and Khrushchev's de-Stalinization campaign ushered in a temporary relaxation of controls over intellectual and artistic expression known as the Thaw, a term coined from the title of Ilya Ehrenburg's 1954 novel of the same name. Among those who took advantage of this easing in cultural relations was Elizaveta Drabkina, the same Drabkina who found herself sitting behind Lenin at that all-Beethoven concert in the fall of 1919. At that point she had already served as a machine gunner in the Red Guards, participated in the storming of the Winter Palace the night of the Bolshevik Revolution, and worked as secretary for Iakov Sverdlov, the first Soviet head of state, until his death in March 1919. She then served in the Red Army as a medical aide and machine gunner during the later stages of the civil war. After the war she engaged in party work in Moscow until her arrest in December 1936 on trumped-up charges of Trotskyism, for which she was sentenced to twenty years' hard labor as an "enemy of the people." She was sent first to the

Figure 7.1. Elizaveta Drabkina. Unknown photographer. Alamy Stock Photo B9P4MW.

Yaroslavl prison deep in the heart of central Russia before being transported to the notorious Noril'sk mining camp in northwestern Siberia, one of the most dreaded prisons in the gulag labor camp system, located two hundred miles north of the Arctic Circle. She was freed in either the general amnesty of March 27, 1953, or the broader release of political prisoners in 1954. Drabkina wrote her memoirs from 1956 to 1961 in the interval between the Twentieth and Twenty-Second Party Congresses, a period she described as making it "easy to breath, work, and create." She ended her memoir, which dealt primarily with the formative years of the Soviet Union, by declaring, "Once again the battle cry resounds, once again the battle begins! The battle for the realization of the Party program adopted by the 22nd Party Congress, the battle for Peace, Work, Freedom, Equality, Brotherhood and the Happiness of all

Figure 7.2. Aleksandr Solzhenitsyn. Unknown photographer. Alamy Stock Photo BPARKG.

peoples so that the Golden Age that the best minds and hearts of humanity have dreamed of can be realized!" It is difficult to judge whether this was a heartfelt sentiment or the obligatory language of one who had been rehabilitated. Nonetheless, it conveys the optimism associated with what was viewed as a new springtime of reform in the Soviet Union.[7]

Another beneficiary of the Thaw was the writer Aleksandr Solzhenitsyn. Solzhenitsyn had been serving as an officer in the Red Army during World War II when he was arrested in February 1945 for having written an impolitic letter, intercepted by Soviet intelligence agents, in which he spoke disparagingly of Stalin's wartime policies. For this offense he was sentenced in July of that year to eight years in the gulag, first in Moscow and its environs and then at a "corrective labor camp" at Ekibastuz in eastern Kazakhstan. After completing his prison sentence on February 9, 1953, he was exiled "in perpetuity" to a village near the Kazakh town of Kok-Terek, where he became a schoolteacher. Then in June 1956, in the wake of Khrushchev's de-Stalinization initiative, he was suddenly released from internal exile and permitted to return to Russia. From 1957 to 1959, he wrote his first novel, *One Day in the Life of Ivan Denisovich*, which Khrushchev personally read and sanctioned for publication. The work appeared in the literary journal *Novy Mir* (*New World*) on November 20, 1962, and rendered Solzhenitsyn an overnight literary sensation. His other major works appeared in remarkably rapid succession: *Cancer Ward* (1966), *The First Circle* (1968), and *The Gulag Archipelago* (1973–76). Both *Cancer Ward* and *The First Circle* were published in the West, virtually assuring Solzhenitsyn the Nobel Prize in Literature, which was awarded to him in 1970. As the political environment worsened following Khrushchev's ouster, however, Solzhenitsyn became more and more suspect in the eyes of the authorities. In 1969 the Writers' Union expelled him, and on February 13, 1974, following publication of parts of *The Gulag Archipelago* abroad, he was arrested, stripped of his citizenship, and forcibly deported from the Soviet Union. He and his family lived in Zurich, Switzerland, until July 1976, when they immigrated to America and settled on a fifty-acre farmstead in Cavendish, Vermont. There Solzhenitsyn worked for the next eighteen years on what he called the "chief artistic design of my life," *The Red Wheel*, a ten-volume semifictionalized account of the Russian Revolution. Solzhenitsyn returned to Russia in 1994, became increasingly more disillusioned with the post-Soviet order, and died in Moscow on August 3, 2008, at eighty-nine.

Solzhenitsyn displayed a special affinity for the music of Beethoven. The cultural historian Solomon Volkov described Solzhenitsyn's prose in *The Red Wheel* as being "all painstakingly organized, particularly with the help of rhythmically active prose. Solzhenitsyn manipulates the narrative rhythm, constantly changing it, juxtaposing contrasting sections and small episodes. This is musical prose, comparable not to *War and Peace*, as it sometimes is, but to the operas of Mussorgsky or Rimsky-Korsakov." When Volkov queried Solzhenitsyn on this aspect of his writing style, he received the following reply: "You felt it very correctly: frankly my favorite 'literature' teacher is Beethoven, I somehow always hear him when I write."[8] The Hungarian composer Béla Bartók considered Beethoven's greatest achievement to have been in revealing the "possibilities of progressive form." Such was the case with Solzhenitsyn, who was able to weave a massive amount of disparate material into a coherent narrative structure, creating in the process highly charged and multifaceted works of art.[9]

According to his first wife, Nataliia Reshetovskaia, Solzhenitsyn listened to radio broadcasts during his confinement in a special gulag research facility outside Moscow to broaden his understanding of classical music. One night he wrote her that he had just encountered two "marvelous sonatas" he had not heard before: Beethoven's Piano Sonata no. 17 in D minor (*The Tempest*), op. 31, no. 2 and the Piano Sonata no. 1 in F-sharp minor, op. 11, by Robert Schumann. This suggests that Solzhenitsyn already had a good understanding of the keyboard literature.[10] On another occasion he attested to his love of the German musical tradition by asserting in an interview that he could not imagine life "without Bach, Beethoven, and Schubert."[11] Solzhenitsyn's son Ignat also recalled walking into his father's workshop as a boy and "hearing a Beethoven symphony for the first time. . . . I just stopped and said, 'What is this?' And my father said, 'This is Beethoven' and he showed me the boxed set. He had tapes of one of Karajan's cycles, the one from the 1970s, which he used to listen to when he was writing or thinking. I was just blown away."[12] There is also a poignant reminiscence from the gulag years. One night Solzhenitsyn and his fellow prisoners were rousted out of their bunks to be "counted," a particularly invidious form of harassment since the prisoners obviously had nowhere to go. As they gathered for inspection, Solzhenitsyn heard dimly in the distance what he recognized as the *Largo e mesto* movement of Beethoven's Piano Sonata no. 7 in D, op. 10, no. 3. Someone in a village close by must have been listening to a recording or radio broadcast. The experience made an indelible impression on Solzhenitsyn, who penned the following poem to memorialize the event:

> Helpless to prise open eyelids weighted with sleep
> [Drawn out into] dazzling moonlight majesty.
> We come outside in comic capes, our blankets,
> We come boiling, come out cursing.
> All of a sudden, from a speaker weeping,
> There faintly wafts toward us a dour Beethoven *largo*.

According to Ignat Solzhenitsyn, his father suddenly "began to behave and act as a free man. . . . He was living in a completely unfree society, but the real freedom was inside." This mournful music could have had a deeply depressing effect on someone suffering the hopelessness of prison confinement. Beethoven himself described the *Largo e mesto* as depicting "a soul in the grips of melancholy." But not Solzhenitsyn. For him the experience marked a blinding moment of spiritual insight and reaffirmation of his integrity as an individual: the confines of a gulag prison, as constraining as they were, must have seemed infinitesimally small compared to the limitless horizons conjured up by Beethoven's immortal music. For anyone who doubts the power of Beethoven's art to move the human spirit and shape outcomes, Solzhenitsyn's life story provides an unequivocal response.[13] [YOUTUBE VIDEO 18]

Like Solzhenitsyn, Boris Pasternak evinced a deep interest in music that in turn shaped the tone and character of much of his writing. He was born in 1890 to parents of high artistic accomplishment. His father, Leonid Pasternak, was a leading impressionist painter and portraitist who taught for many years

Figure 7.3. Boris Pasternak, 1958. Unknown photographer. B. A. Kats, comp., *Muzyka v tvorchestve, sud'be i v dome Borisa Pasternaka* (Leningrad: Sovetskii kompozitor, 1991), 254.

at Moscow's School of Painting, Sculpture and Architecture. His mother, Roza Kaufman, was a highly regarded pianist who had studied under Anton Rubinshtein and taught at the Odessa Conservatory before leaving the concert stage to raise her family; she resumed her concertizing in 1907. Pasternak himself seriously considered a career in music but gave up the idea after six years due to what he called his lack of perfect pitch and pedestrian keyboard technique. He then elected to study philosophy, which he pursued at the University of Moscow and Marburg University in Germany, but eventually rejected this discipline as well to embrace literature as his permanent calling. Pasternak became one of the great poets of the twentieth century, for which, together with his novel *Doctor Zhivago*, he was awarded the Nobel Prize in Literature in 1958. He died of lung cancer on May 30, 1960, at seventy and was buried near his dacha at the writers' colony of Peredelkino outside Moscow.

While Pasternak's favorite composers were Chopin and the Russian visionary Aleksandr Scriabin, he showed an early interest in Beethoven as well. Contemporaries noted his "high esteem" for the music of Beethoven and Mozart, and his brother, Aleksandr, wrote that, during the family's stay in Berlin in 1905, the two "frequently and seriously" attended concerts by the Berlin Philharmonic of works by Beethoven, Brahms, and Wagner.[14] As a young man, Pasternak penned the following poem, entitled "Sounds of Beethoven in the Streets":

> How eloquent the sky-glow where
> Through melt-holes flares the stone.
> Above the roadway someone else
> Blows out the evening flame.
>
> Sometimes beneath the joists a tenant
> Resonating shifts the floor,
> And suddenly Beethoven hauls
> Sonatas' shackles on the square.
>
> Above one's temples hangs the spring.
> The window's shut, the flight erased.
> A cleft in throngs of stone is cut
> By music's philharmonic test.[15]

In the early 1920s, the poet Dmitrii Petrovskii dedicated a poem to Pasternak entitled "Betkhoven" in honor of Pasternak's piano improvisations at a poetry meeting.[16] And it has been argued that poems three through six of the *Themes and Variations* collection (written 1918 and published 1923) were constructed after Beethoven piano sonatas.[17] Also, Pasternak's second wife, Zinaida Eremeeva, had been married previously to the Beethoven specialist Heinrich Neuhaus and undoubtedly brought the latter's learned perspective on Beethoven to bear on conversations touching on the composer she shared with her husband.

The musicologist Munir Sendich has identified over twenty scholarly articles and books analyzing Pasternak's poetry from a musical perspective, an indication that, in spite of the early disappointments and failures, the grounding in the theory and practice of music had long-term positive effects.[18] Henry Gifford noted the "affinities with keyboard music" of Pasternak's early poetry.[19] The American conductor Leonard Bernstein attested as well to Pasternak's knowledge of and deep feeling for music. In 1959, in conjunction with a tour of the Soviet Union by the New York Philharmonic Orchestra, Bernstein and his wife were invited to lunch with Pasternak at Peredelkino. "We hit it off, straight away," Bernstein reminisced. "We talked for hours about art and the artist's view of history. . . . Very often, authors talk rot about music. But Pasternak talks with a musician and has something to say." Bernstein had invited Pasternak to the Philharmonic's final Moscow concert on September 11, which included performances of Beethoven's Seventh Symphony and Shostakovich's Symphony no. 5. Pasternak tracked down Bernstein in his dressing room during intermission to thank him for the performance of the Seventh Symphony. Calling the Second Movement allegretto "a tragic expression of the tragedy of existence," he enthused, "I have never felt so close to the aesthetic truth. When I hear you I know why you were born. I only want to listen, not speak." At the conclusion of the concert, with the resounding coda of Shostakovich's Fifth Symphony still ringing in his ears, Pasternak once again thanked Bernstein for sharing his art with the Moscow public. "You have taken us up to heaven," he said. "Now we must return to earth."[20]

In his 1957 autobiography, Pasternak described *Doctor Zhivago* as his "chief and most important work, the only one I am not ashamed of and for which I can answer with the utmost confidence."[21] He began writing the novel in the summer of 1946 and completed it in December 1955. The reader encounters the following felicitous passage late in the work. Yuri, Lara, and Katenka have returned to Varykino, it is night, and Yuri is writing poetry by lamplight:

> After two or three easily poured-out stanzas and several similes that he was struck by himself, the work took possession of him, and he felt the approach of what is known as inspiration. . . . Language, the homeland and receptacle of beauty and meaning, itself begins to think and speak for man and turns wholly into music, not in terms of external, audible sounds, but in terms of the swiftness and power of its inner flow. Then, like the rolling mass of a river's current, which by its very movement polishes the stones of the bottom and turns the wheels of mills, flowing speech itself, by the force of its own laws, on its way, in passing, creates meter and rhyme and thousands of other forms and constructions, still more important, but as yet unrecognized, unconsidered, unnamed.[22]

This marvelous description of the creative process points to the key role "The Poems of Yuri Zhivago," comprising the concluding chapter 17, play in the work as a whole. Pasternak described the twenty-five poems as "preparatory steps" and a "supplement in verse" to the novel itself. "The plan of the novel is outlined by the poems accompanying it," he added. The verses should therefore be viewed as an integral part of the entire work, its true final chapter, rather than a somewhat curious appendix of no immediate concern to the reader, as they often are made to appear in Western translations.[23]

At least nine of the poems can be traced directly to incidents or circumstances encountered in the novel itself, thereby highlighting, albeit in nonchronological order, key moments in the work.[24] The poems also underscore the cyclical nature of time in the novel, either in terms of the changing seasons or the ever-turning wheel of life.[25] The novel begins with the burial of the young Yuri's mother and closes in a foretelling of Christ's resurrection. The overarching theme is one of rebirth, symbolized above all by Zhivago's very name (*zhivoi* means "living" or "alive") and his profession as a poet-physician. Overall, in its synthesis of prose and poetry, the novel is unique in Western literature. One is reminded of another unique work of art: Beethoven's Ninth Symphony. Might not "The Poems of Yuri Zhivago" be considered Pasternak's *Ode to Joy*? Not only do the verses, like the opening measures of the symphony's fourth movement, look back to significant moments in the text, reminding the reader of the long journey just taken, but also, like the white light of the symphony's extended coda, they close with the Easter promise of Christ's ascent into heaven, the most joyous moment in the Christian calendar. Similarity of manner and message in the two works is remarkable.[26]

Early in 1956 Pasternak submitted the manuscript of *Doctor Zhivago* to the editors of *Novy Mir* for publication consideration. In September he received an eight-page rejection letter, signed by all five members of the editorial board, denouncing the novel for its "spirit of non-acceptance of the socialist revolution" and "pathological individualism . . . hypertrophied to unbelievable proportions."[27] In anticipation of this probable rejection, Pasternak in March of that year had handed over a copy of the manuscript to the Italian journalist Sergio d'Angelo, who was in Moscow working at Radio Moscow and representing the Giangiacomo Feltrinelli publishing house, which had published Solzhenitsyn's *Cancer Ward* and *The First Circle*. "You are hereby invited to watch me face the firing squad," Pasternak quipped as he turned over the manuscript.[28] Feltrinelli published the novel in Italian on November 15, 1957; its first printing of six thousand sold out in one day. The English translation followed in September 1958.

Pasternak was awarded the Nobel Prize in Literature on October 23, 1958, for his "important achievement both in contemporary lyrical poetry and in the field of the great Russian epic tradition." He cabled the Swedish Academy the next day: "Immensely thankful, touched, proud, astonished, abashed." But the award generated a virulent backlash in the Soviet Union, where authorities viewed it as a Cold War provocation. The Writers' Union expelled Pasternak on October 27. Two days later he cabled the Swedish Academy: "In view of the meaning attributed to this award in the society to which I belong, I must refuse the undeserved prize that has been bestowed on me. Do not take my voluntary rejection with any ill will."[29] It was not until December 1989 during the heyday of Mikhail Gorbachev's perestroika campaign that Pasternak's son was able to travel to Stockholm to collect his father's Nobel Prize medal and diploma. Fittingly, *Doctor Zhivago* had been serialized in the pages of *Novy Mir* the year before.

A thousand or more mourners attended Pasternak's funeral on June 2, 1960. On an old upright piano in the music room, some of the country's leading pianists—Stanislav Neuhaus, Andrei Volkonskii, Maria Yudina, and Sviatoslav Richter—played music by Beethoven and other composers favored by Pasternak. Richter concluded the recital with the *Marche funèbre* movement from Chopin's Piano Sonata no. 2 in B-flat minor, op. 35. At the graveside ceremonies, the philosopher and University of Moscow professor Valentin Asmus, a longtime friend of Pasternak, delivered the eulogy. "We have come to bid farewell to one of the greatest of Russian writers and poets, a man endowed with all the talents, including even music," Asmus began. "One might accept or reject his opinions but as long as Russian poetry plays a role on this earth, Boris Leonidovich Pasternak will stand among the greatest."[30] About fifty young people stayed until sundown reciting Pasternak's poetry over the gravesite. "A happy, tender sense of peace . . . filled them and enveloped them in an inaudible music of happiness, which spread far around."[31]

* * *

During his retirement, Nikita Khrushchev asked his son Sergei to obtain a copy of *Doctor Zhivago*. Sergei located a dog-eared typewritten copy that had circulated underground. Khrushchev took a long time reading the manuscript and never talked about it with his family. He only said, "We shouldn't have banned it. I should have read it myself. There's nothing anti-Soviet in it."[32]

The New Scholarship

Luba Brezhneva, niece of former Soviet leader Leonid Brezhnev (1906–82), began her family memoir by quoting the nineteenth-century Russian writer Saltykov-Shchedrin: "A gray sky, gray horizons filled with wandering gray phantoms, gray birds soaring through the gray air." While it is unclear whether Brezhneva intended this epigraph to depict her uncle or the times over which he presided, it is an apt description of both. Brezhnev was called the "efficient organization man, a Communist in a gray flannel suit," while his times were characterized as the "era of stagnation." Yet, regarding Soviet

Beethoven reception history, Brezhnev's eighteen-year rule (1964–82) yielded a rich trove of new scholarship largely free of communist clichés and ideological pretensions. Beneath the glacial shield of the era, the underpinning of rock and ice clearly had begun to give way.[33]

The celebration in 1970 of the two hundredth anniversary of Beethoven's birth inaugurated the new era. Like previous celebrations, the gala concert of December 16, 1970, featured the Ninth Symphony, performed on this occasion by the Symphonic Orchestra of the USSR under the direction of Evgenii Svetlanov. The Bol'shoi Theater held the concert, and Leonid Brezhnev, Aleksei Kosygin, Nikolai Podgorny, and other leading party and government officials attended. Dmitrii Shostakovich delivered a preconcert address in which he hailed Beethoven as a "genuine reformer in art" whose compositions reflected "humanistic ideals inspired by the ideas of the French Revolution."[34] A ten-kopek maroon-and-pink postage stamp depicting Beethoven and the opening bars of the *Appassionata* Sonata was also issued, and Melodiya, the Soviet recording label, released a four-LP set of Beethoven's piano music performed by Sviatoslav Richter.[35]

Most importantly, a commemorative publication issued by the Leningrad State Institute of Theater, Music, and Film consisted entirely of essays that reflected a much more nuanced and professional approach to the study of Beethoven and his music. While there certainly had been technical and biographical studies published in the Stalin era, nothing could compare with the broad range of scholarly essays contained in this compendium. Arnol'd Sokhor analyzed the aesthetic basis of Beethoven's ethical outlook as reflected in letters, diaries, the Conversation Books, and reminiscences of contemporaries; Iulii Kremlev explored the value of Beethoven's music in terms of the synthesis of intonation (melody, rhythm, harmony, timbre, dynamics, agogics) and logic (the ever-fluctuating character of human emotions and experience); Georgii Orlov examined Beethoven's compositions from the perspective of program music, both in a conventional sense and in terms of the dialectics of symphonic discourse; Lev Raaben summarized performances of Beethoven's piano, chamber, and orchestral works in the twentieth century by both Russian and non-Russian performers; Arkadii Klimovitskii provided a technical study of the so-called new theme in B-minor encountered in the first movement exposition of Symphony no. 3; Nina Iudenich discussed the element of folksong in Beethoven's string quartets; Klimentii Veksler examined the three little-studied and underperformed Opus 12 Violin Sonatas in D, A, and E-flat; Georgii Blagodatov offered remarks on the nature of the orchestra in Beethoven's day and how this shaped the composer's large-form

Figure 7.4. Natan Fishman, from the Project Personalities website, accessed March 8, 2022, https://persons-info.com/persons/FISHMAN_Natan_Lvovich.

compositions; Semen Levin presented a valuable essay on Beethoven in Soviet musicology; and Margarita Priashnikova summarized Anatolii Lunacharskii's views on Beethoven and his music. Except for the piece on Lunacharskii that, by definition, was ideological in nature, the essays in this compendium were refreshingly free of the polemical posturing of the Stalin era and pointed in the direction of a much more productive chapter in Russian Beethoven reception history.[36]

A two-volume study of Beethoven edited by Natan Fishman and published in 1971–72 confirmed that this was in fact the case. Fishman (1909–86) has been described as the "most renowned Beethoven scholar of modern Russia" who unfortunately is little known in the West.[37] Born in Baku, Azerbaijan, Fishman studied piano there, then performed as a concert pianist in Leningrad from 1927 to 1950, served as principal conductor of the Malyi Theater Orchestra in Moscow (1943–50), was a senior research fellow at the

Moscow State Central (Glinka) Museum of Musical Culture (1951–78), and taught piano at the Ippolitov-Ivanov School of Music (1935–38) and the Moscow Conservatory (1938–76). In 1962 he published a transcription and study of the *Wielhorsky* Sketchbook of 1802 and 1803, which had come into the possession of Mikhail Viel'gorskii by unknown means and eventually ended up in the holdings of the Glinka Museum, where it had been gathering dust until Fishman stumbled across it one day. "He was stunned," his coworker Larissa Kirillina wrote. "No facsimile could convey the effect made on him by the original, with its yellowed paper, faded ink, hasty handwriting, and oil spots—perhaps from the very lamp that illuminated the lines of the Heiligenstadt Testament!" Fishman received his doctorate in musicology in 1968 for his work on this valuable document.[38] Another large research project concerned the compilation of Beethoven's letters in Russian translation that resulted in the publication from 1970 to 1986 of three volumes covering the years 1787 through 1822.[39] And in 1971 Fishman edited an album of Soviet *Betkhoveniany* that included facsimiles of the program of the all-Beethoven concert conducted by Serge Koussevitzky on October 4, 1919, and the multifaceted concert celebrating adoption of the new constitution on December 5, 1936. The album also included photos of performances of the Ninth Symphony marking the 125th anniversary of Beethoven's death in 1952 and the 200th anniversary of his birth in 1970.[40]

Fishman's two-volume study of 1971–72 included a wide variety of essays by some of the leading Soviet Beethoven scholars of the day. In addition to such technical subjects as harmony (Viktor Berkov), modulation (Iurii Kholopov), rhythm (Miron Kharlap), dynamics (Viktor Tsukkerman), and polyphony (Vladimir Protopopov), the researchers focused their attention on such disparate topics as Russian Beethoven reception in the nineteenth and twentieth centuries (Lev Ginzburg, Tamara Livanova, Vladimir Natanson, Israil Nest'ev), Beethoven and his successors (Valentina Konen), the late-period compositions (Iurii Tiulin), Beethoven's influence on new stylistic trends in nineteenth-century music (Nadezhda Nikolaeva), the *Moonlight* (Viktor Bobrovskii) and *Appassionata* (Dmitrii Blagoi) Sonatas, the main theme of the first allegro of Symphony no. 3 (Arkadii Klimovitskii), the compositional history of *Fidelio* (Boris Iarustovskii), problems of tempo in performance of the piano sonatas (Sergei Pavchinskii), aspects of theme and structure in the early and middle periods (Lev Mazel'), sonata form in the late period (Vladimir Protopopov), the dramatic element in Symphonies nos. 5 and 9 (Iosif Ryzhkin), the significance of the kettledrum as a rhythmic device (Paul' Mis), the impact of the Ninth Symphony on later Western and Russian symphonic music (Nadezhda

Nikolaeva), and the idea of fate in Beethoven's oeuvre (Givi Ordzhonikidze). Of usefulness to scholars of Russian Beethoven reception history was the inclusion of a bibliography of Russian-language material on Beethoven for the years 1803–1970 (Nataliia Grigorovich). Aside from brief boilerplate references to the impact of Beethoven's music on socialist construction in the Soviet Union and East Germany, an indication that old habits die hard, there was not a single political note in any of these essays.[41]

Fishman edited a third collection of essays in 1972 that surveyed the course of Soviet musicology from the 1920s forward. In addition to investigations of a variety of technical issues, the volume included Anatolii Lunacharskii's main articles on Beethoven; reminiscences and commentary by the composers Aleksandr Glazunov, Nikolai Miaskovskii, and Sergei Prokofiev; a wide range of writings by the musicologists Boris Asaf'ev, Boleslav Iavorskii, Mikhail Ivanov-Boretski, Aleksandr Rabinovich, and Ivan Sollertinskii; and reflections by the pianists Samuil Feinberg, Aleksandr Gol'denweizer, and Heinrich Neuhaus.[42] In 1982, Fishman issued yet a fourth collection consisting primarily of revised versions of his own writings on Beethoven and including his study of the *Wielhorsky* Sketchbook, autographs of all Beethoven works and letters in Russian collections, and the St. Petersburg premiere of the *Missa solemnis*.[43] Overall, Fishman's contribution to Soviet Beethoven studies was enormous, both in terms of the volume of material he made available to the scholarly community and the high degree of professionalism he brought to the practice of his craft. He was, as Larissa Kirillina observed, the "first and best" of modern Russian Beethoven scholars.[44] As such, he placed Russian Beethoven reception on a new and much firmer foundation that has endured.

Perestroika in the Concert Hall

Despite the erratic politics of the Khrushchev years, glacial stasis of the Brezhnev era, and convulsive character of the Gorbachev reform campaign, music, as Gorbachev himself declared, represented a universal language that spoke to "everyone everywhere." It remained a constant in times of uncertainty, conflict, and change. In the process, it eventually freed itself from political strictures, resonating simply as sound according to its own inner logic and laws of expression. As the musicologist Leonid Gakkel' noted in 1997, music critics now were able to "draw conclusions without resort to rigid sociological analysis." The backs of LP dustjackets, CD liner notes, and concert programs reflected this as well. Commentators seemed much more intent on assisting listeners in understanding the historical background and artistic character of the music they were about to hear than in weaving an ideological web that had no real bearing on the listening experience. "The measure of the world is much larger than politics," Gakkel' concluded.[45]

Beethoven reception history in the post-Stalin era reflected these positive changes. Among Western composers performed in Russia, Beethoven continued to occupy the "resplendent first place in performance practice."[46] As before, the Leningrad (St. Petersburg after 1992) State Academic Philharmonia took the lead in performing the composer's music. During the fifty-year period, 1954–2004, extending from the first full year after Stalin's death to the end of the first half-decade of Vladimir Putin's rule, the Philharmonia gave a total of 1,370 performances of Beethoven's compositions, ranging from songs and dances to the blockbuster symphonic and choral literature, for an average of twenty-eight performances per year. Table 5 (see appendix) itemizes frequency of performance of key Beethoven works for this period. In comparing the data for the Stalin period (1928–53), as contained in table 3 (see appendix), with that of the post-Stalin period (1954–2004), as outlined in table 5, and making allowance for the twenty-five-year disparity in the two accounts by dividing the data for 1954–2004 in half to acquire an approximate equivalency, one can draw the following conclusions. First, in terms of overall number of performances, the two periods are remarkably similar (699 for 1928–53 compared to 1,370 ÷ 2 = 685 for 1954–2004). Thus, on average, twenty-eight performances took place annually over the entire period of 1928–2004, indicating that concert organizers adhered to a more or less rigid set of Beethoven (or Brahms or Tchaikovsky) performances in establishing their repertoire for the coming concert season. This is also true concerning the number of symphonies performed during this period (319 for 1928–53 compared to 614 ÷ 2 = 307 for 1954 to 2004). On the other hand, there is a noticeable disparity between the two periods in terms of the number of performances of the concerto literature and the overtures. The Violin Concerto received twenty-two performances from 1928 to 1953, compared to 74 ÷ 2 = 37 from 1954 to 2004. David Oistrakh performed most of the concerts from 1928 to 1953, while he was joined by Leonid Kogan, Gidon Kremer, Yehudi Menuhin, Wolfgang Schneiderhan, and other artists from 1954 to 2004, thereby allowing for an increased number of performances of this popular work. The disparity was even more pronounced in terms of the five piano concertos. From 1928 to 1953, there were eighty-two performances compared to 362 ÷ 2 = 181 in the period from 1954 to 2004. Undoubtedly this reflected the large number of guest artists in the post-Stalin era. From 1928 to 1953, performances were provided

Figure 7.5. Evgenii Mravinsky. Unknown photographer. Alamy Stock Photo B9RGAF.

almost entirely by Soviet pianists, above all Vladimir Ashkenazy, Emil Gilels, Sviatoslav Richter, and Maria Yudina. From 1954 to 2004, these local artists, supplemented by Yefim Bronfman, Vladimir Feltsman, Heinrich Neuhaus, and Mikhail Pletnev, were joined by such luminaries from abroad as Claudio Arrau, Paul Badura-Shkoda, Daniel Barenboim, Arturo Benedetti-Michelangeli, Alfred Brendel, Van Cliburn, Barry Douglas, Annie Fischer, Glen Gould, John Ogden, Maurizio Pollini, Artur Rubinstein, and Ignat Solzhenitsyn. Finally, regarding the overtures, a reverse disparity is evident. From 1928 to 1953, there were 172 performances compared to $193 \div 2 = 97$ in the period from 1954 to 2004. Since the message of most of the overtures is highly political in nature, these works more than likely proved more popular in the Stalin era of socialist construction than in subsequent years when politics held much less sway in the interpretation of Beethoven's more dramatic music. Today it is fair to say that while this visceral and evocative music will always move the listener in fundamental ways, it will do so more as a tonic to the soul than as a call to action.

Evgenii Mravinsky (1903–88), one of the giants of the Soviet conducting school, oversaw much of this performance activity. Born in St. Petersburg on June 4, 1903, Mravinsky attended the Leningrad Conservatory from 1927 to 1931 where he studied under the conductors Nikolai Mal'ko and Aleksandr Gauk. From 1932 to 1938, he was conductor of the Kirov Theater of Opera and Ballet (now, once again, the Mariinskii Theater) and in November 1938, following a number of guest appearances beginning in 1932, was appointed chief conductor of the Leningrad Philharmonia, a post he held for fifty years until his death in 1988. He is perhaps best known in the West for the premieres he conducted of six of Dmitrii Shostakovich's symphonies (nos. 5, 6, 8 [dedicated to Mravinsky], 9, 10, and 12) and the composer's *Song of the Forests* oratorio, Festive Overture, Violin Concerto no. 1 (David Oistrakh), and Cello Concerto no. 1 (Mstislav Rostropovich). Altogether, Mravinsky conducted 303 performances of Shostakovich's music. He also favored works by Béla Bartók, including thirty-three performances of the Music for Strings, Percussion, and Celesta; Arthur Honegger, including thirty-three performances of the Symphony no. 3 (*Liturgique*); and Igor Stravinsky, including ninety-three performances of the *Apollon musgète* ballet music. In addition, together with his young conducting assistants Igor Blazhkov (b. 1936) and Eduard Serov (b. 1937), Mravinsky introduced concertgoers to a variety of new works by rising (now well established) Soviet composers, among them Edison Denisov, Sophia Gubaidulina, Giya Kancheli, Alfred Schnittke, Rodion Shchedrin, Georgii Sviridov, and Galina Ustvol'skaia.[47] As for Beethoven, Mravinsky conducted a total of 196 performances of the maestro's works: 159 of the symphonies, 20 of the overtures, 12 of the concertos, 4 of the *Missa solemnis*, and 1 of the *Choral Fantasy*. His last concert, held on March 6, 1987, consisted of Schubert's Symphony no. 8 in B minor (*Unfinished*) and Brahms Symphony no. 4 in E minor. Mravinsky died of a heart attack on January 19, 1988, at eighty-four and was buried at the Bogoslovskoe cemetery in Leningrad. In 1992 a marble bas-relief of the conductor was affixed to the outside wall of the Philharmonia in honor of his long and illustrious career.[48]

The US-USSR cultural exchange agreement of January 27, 1958, together with similar agreements between the Soviet Union and other Western nations, contributed significantly to the rich diversity of musical life in post-Stalin Russia. Tours of the Soviet Union by American orchestras included the Boston Symphony under Charles Munch and Pierre Monteux (1956), the Philadelphia Orchestra under Eugene Ormandy (1958), New York Philharmonic under Leonard Bernstein (1959), and the Cleveland Orchestra under George Szell (1965). American composers Aaron Copeland and Lucas Foss toured the country in 1960, and in the autumn of 1962, Yehudi and Hephzibah Menuhin, the New York City Ballet under George Balanchine, Robert Shaw and his Chorale, and Igor Stravinsky all paid visits to the Soviet Union. Tours by British and European orchestras from 1956 to 1967 included the London Philharmonic, Royal Philharmonic, BBC Symphony, Leipzig Gewandhaus, French Radio and TV, Czech Philharmonic, and Vienna Philharmonic. Benjamin Britten and Peter Pears made a celebrated visit to the Soviet Union in 1963. Along with the established repertoire, these performers and ensembles introduced Soviet audiences to a variety of new music that undoubtedly most had never heard before, at least live. Aaron Copeland, Lucas Foss, and Igor Stravinsky performed a broad range of their own music, for example, and the Cleveland Orchestra under George Szell presented an all-American program in the spring of 1965. All of this added up to rich fare indeed, signifying a substantial departure from concert programming in the Stalin era.[49]

As one might expect, exposure to Western ensembles and art forms engendered different reactions among Soviet audiences. On the one hand, it reinforced attitudes of superiority concerning the skills of Soviet artists vis-à-vis their Western counterparts. In the fall of 1971, an American couple shared box seats with some Soviet balletomanes at the Kirov Theater to take in a performance of John Cranko's Stuttgart Ballet. After the performance, which generated a lengthy standing ovation, the Soviet seat mates enthusiastically marveled over the production but then, in classic Soviet fashion, declared, "But ours is better!" Others disagreed. The Soviet ballet star Valerii Panov (b. 1938), describing the Stuttgart Ballet as "representing all that beckoned from the West," attended a performance of the New York City Ballet in October 1962 and declared, "I was in the vanguard of Balanchine's worshippers. Despite Soviet ballet's splendrous staging and execution, I recognized it as heavy, solemn and provincial."[50] In 1972, Panov and his second wife, the Kirov ballerina Galina Ragozina, applied for exit visas to immigrate to Israel. The dancers were expelled from the Kirov, briefly imprisoned, and only in 1974, as a result of appeals by Western artists, including Sir Lawrence Olivier, allowed to depart the country. Earlier, Rudolph Nureyev and Nataliia Makarova had defected to the West (1961 and 1970, respectively) and were followed by Mikhail Baryshnikov (1974), Aleksandr Godunov (1979), and Leonid and Valentina Kozlova (1979). These incidents, though isolated, indicate what was at stake as Soviet authorities opened up their country, if only marginally, to the West, while allowing their own treasured artists to perform abroad. Under the circumstances, they had little option but to accept what was at best a mixed outcome.

Returning to Beethoven by way of conclusion, some commentary on pianism in the late-Soviet period is in order. The piano of course was Beethoven's own instrument. It is therefore appropriate to close this discussion with some thoughts on the significant role the piano played in Beethoven reception history in the post-Stalin era. The careers of the following pianists are especially noteworthy.

Emil Gilels (1916–85) is considered one of the greatest pianists of the twentieth century. He studied at the Odessa Conservatory from 1931 to 1935, undertook advance study with Heinrich Neuhaus at the Moscow Conservatory from 1935 to 1938, and served as a professor at the latter institution from 1952 to 1985. He also served for many years as chair of the jury of the International Tchaikovsky Competition, beginning with the inaugural competition of 1958, where Van Cliburn won first prize. Gilels had perfect pitch; flawless technique; a bold, burnished sound; and a poetic gift for deep expression in the slow movements. He is best known for his performance of the German-Austrian repertoire. At the time of his death, he was recording a complete traversal of the Beethoven piano literature for the Deutsche Gramophone label and had set down Sonatas nos. 2–8, 10–21, 23, and 25–31, along with the *Electoral* Sonatas, WoO 47, nos. 1–2, and the *Eroica Variations*, op. 35. Gilels's recording of the *Hammerklavier* Sonata won the Gramophone award for best instrumental recording in 1984. He died in Moscow in 1985 just shy of his sixty-ninth birthday.[51]

Maria Grinberg (1908–78) was also a graduate of the Odessa and Moscow conservatories, studying under Felix Blumenfeld (teacher of Vladimir Horowitz) and Konstantin Igumnov respectively. A promising career was cut short, however, by the arrest and execution of her father and husband as "enemies of the people" in 1937. She found occasional employment as an accompanist for an amateur dance group and at times played the timpani in a local orchestra. Later regaining the right to perform publicly, she acquired considerable fame as a concert pianist in the Soviet Union and, after the death of Stalin, abroad. Dutch critics thrilled over her recitals in the Netherlands, putting her performances on par with those of Vladimir Horowitz, Artur Rubinstein, and Clara Haskil. "No one communicated better the polyphonic sweetness of late Beethoven," Damian Thompson commented.[52] In 1969 Grinberg became a professor at the Gnessin Russian Academy of Music in Moscow and in 1970 released a thirteen-LP studio traversal of the Beethoven piano sonatas on the Melodiya label, becoming at that point the first Soviet pianist and only the fourth woman worldwide to do so. She also set down the Beethoven piano concertos (1947–70), some lesser Beethoven, and a broad range of music by other composers over the course of her recording career. She died in Tallin, Estonia, in 1978 at sixty-nine.[53]

Tatiana Nikolaeva (1924–93), an exceptional pianist who is highly regarded for her recordings of Bach and Beethoven, was born in the small town of Bezhitsa, halfway between Moscow and Kiev. She began taking piano lessons at age five. In 1937 she entered the Central Secondary School of Music in Moscow, an affiliate of the Moscow Conservatory, where she studied under Aleksandr Gol'denweiser, known for his ability to inculcate in his students note-perfect proficiency in contrapuntal playing. She continued her studies with Gol'denweiser at the Moscow Conservatory and graduated in 1947, quickly acquiring a reputation as a Bach keyboard specialist. In 1950 she won first prize at the inaugural International Johann Sebastian Bach Competition in Leipzig, Germany, bringing her to the attention of Dmitrii Shostakovich, who was on the jury panel. Her playing so impressed Shostakovich that he composed and dedicated to her his Twenty-Four Preludes and Fugues, op. 87, which she premiered in December 1952 and recorded for the Melodiya and Hyperion labels, the latter recording receiving the Gramophone Instrumental Award in 1991. The Shostakovich work remained an important part of her concert repertoire, ranging from Bach to Bartók and beyond. Boris Schwarz observed that Nikolaeva was a "strong advocate of contemporary music."[54] She began teaching at the Moscow Conservatory in 1959 and served as professor of piano from 1965 to 1993. Nikolaeva performed her legendary traversal of the Beethoven piano sonatas at the Great Hall of the Moscow Conservatory from January 10 to April 11, 1984. Melodiya recorded the eleven concerts live, and they continue to occupy a prominent place in the Beethoven discography. She also had set down the *Diabelli Variations* in a studio recording of 1979. In the Gorbachev era and following the collapse of the communist regime, Nikolaeva was in great demand abroad, concertizing especially in Britain and the United States. Tragically, during a recital in San Francisco on November 13, 1993, she suffered a massive stroke while performing the B-flat minor fugue from Shostakovich's Preludes and Fugues and fell into a coma. She died nine days later in Santa Barbara, California, on the cusp of her seventieth birthday.[55]

Sviatoslav Richter (1915–97), like Gilels, studied under Heinrich Neuhaus at the Moscow Conservatory and, again like Gilels, became one of the great pianists of the twentieth century. Born in Zhitomyr, Ukraine, Richter received initial piano instruction from his father but developed largely on his own as a young man. From 1933 to 1937, he served as répétiteur at the Odessa Theater of Opera and Ballet, an experience that led to a lifelong interest in opera.

Figure 7.6. Maria Yudina. Unknown photographer. *The Art of Maria Yudina*, Scribendum CD Collection, SC 813, photo insert.

From 1937 to 1946 (with interruptions), he studied piano under Neuhaus, who described Richter's technique as follows: "His singular ability to grasp the whole and at the same time miss none of the smallest details of a composition suggests a comparison with an eagle who from his great height can see as far as the horizon and yet single out the tiniest detail of the landscape. We have before us an imposing mountain range, but against it we can see the lark, taking wing into the sky."[56] In a career spanning fifty-five years, Richter performed with great success all over the Soviet Union, including a six-month, 150-recital tour of Siberia in 1986. Perhaps he had this tour in mind when he fondly penned the following description of concertizing in Russia's rural areas: "Put a small piano in a truck and drive out on country roads; take time to discover new scenery; stop in a pretty place where there is a good church; unload the piano and tell the residents; give a concert; offer flowers to the people who have been so kind as to attend; leave again."[57] Beginning in 1960, he became a sensation in Europe and America as well. Altogether, Richter gave more than twenty-seven thousand performances at some thirty-six hundred concerts in an untold number of venues. His repertoire ranged from Bach to the moderns. After Shostakovich (4,641 performances), Rachmaninov (2,683 performances), and Debussy (2,444 performances), he performed Beethoven 2,329 times.[58] His discography is vast, with the live recordings winning particular praise from critics. Richter's last recital took place in Lűbeck, Germany, on March 30, 1995, when he played Haydn's Sonatas nos. 55–57 and Max Reger's Variations and Fugue on a Theme of Beethoven for two pianos, op. 86 (Andreas Lucewicz second piano). A little over two years later, while practicing Schubert's *Fűnf Klavierstucke*, D. 459, he suffered a heart attack and died on August 1, 1997, in a Moscow hospital at eighty-two.

Richter described Maria Yudina (1899–1970) as an "eccentric woman and an extraordinary artist."[59] She was both in spades. Yudina was born in the town of Nevel', near Vitebsk, the home of Marc Chagall. At age twelve she entered the St. Petersburg Conservatory to study piano under Anna Esipova and graduated in 1921 with the gold medal. She taught at the St. Petersburg Conservatory (1921–30), the Tbilisi Conservatory (1932–33), the Moscow Conservatory (1936–51), and the Gnessin Russian Academy of Music (1951–60). She was an extremely religious person, having converted from Judaism to the Russian Orthodox faith in 1919. This lent to her playing a deep spiritual character that, combined with exceptional technique, produced unforgettable results. In addition to Beethoven, her repertoire ranged from Bach to Bartók and included excursions into the atonal sound worlds of Pierre Boulez, Ernst Krenek, Karlheinz Stockhausen, and others. A wide range of her recordings is available on disc. From 1943 to the end of World War II, frequently performed the music of Bach, Beethoven, and the Russian masters over the airwaves of Radio Moscow. She also flew over enemy lines to perform Beethoven in Leningrad in 1943—Emil Gilels did as well. Her eccentricities are well known. Her concert attire consisted solely of a floor-length black dress with wide sleeves set off by a white collar. An oversize cross suspended by a heavy chain completed the ensemble. She often angered the authorities by her dress and penchant for reading the poetry of Pasternak and other blacklisted writers as encores. But she persevered and remained undaunted to the end.

There is an oft-told story that in 1944 Stalin heard a radio broadcast of Yudina performing Mozart's Piano Concerto no. 23 in A, K. 488, and was so taken by what he assumed was a recording that he ordered an aide to acquire a copy for him. Unfortunately, the performance had only been transmitted live. Yudina was therefore hauled out of bed in the middle of the night and driven to a recording studio to set down the piece with a hastily assembled orchestra. The recording was presented to Stalin the next morning, prompting him to send the artist a gift of twenty thousand rubles as a measure of his appreciation. Yudina responded, "Thank you, Iosif Vissarionovich, for your aid. I will pray for you day and night and beseech the Lord to forgive your great sins before the people and the country. The Lord is merciful and will forgive you. I have donated the money for repair of the church I attend." It is said that the recording was found on the turntable next to Stalin's bed following his stroke on March 1, 1953. While this story is considered apocryphal by many, it accords well with Yudina's free spirit and deep religious convictions and was considered authentic by Dmitrii Shostakovich, who knew her well, and the German music critic Hans-Heinz Stuckenschmidt.[60] Yudina outlived the dictator by seventeen years, dying on November 19, 1970, at seventy-one. She is buried at Moscow's Vvedenskoe Cemetery, her grave subsequently becoming a popular pilgrimage site for those disaffected by the communist regime.[61]

All of these pianists, and countless others, could trace their lineage back to that moment on Easter Sunday in 1850 when a young Anton Rubinshtein innocently responded to the deacon's query as to his name and rank by declaring, "Rubinshtein, artist." And so began the saga of the founding of the Russian Musical Society, the establishment of the St. Petersburg and Moscow Conservatories, and the emergence over time of the heralded Russian piano school, considered by many to be the greatest in the world. It is appropriate that Beethoven's music, which Rubinshtein had championed in his criticism and playing, should remain at the heart of the school's performing tradition as the history of Russian Beethoven reception drew to a close.

* * *

The St. Petersburg Philharmonic Society, the institution most responsible for promoting Beethoven's music in both the imperial and Soviet periods, celebrated its centennial in 2002.[62] On June 8 of that year, a visitor from abroad sat in the majestic colonnaded space of the Philharmonia's Great Hall awaiting an evening concert. On the program were two of Dvořák's Slavonic Dances, the Violin Concerto by Sibelius, and Beethoven's Third (*Eroica*) Symphony. The visitor observed that the program note's discussion of the Third Symphony was entirely free of the political jargon of earlier times and that it closed with a quote by the Russian critic Aleksandr Serov to the effect that the multifaceted character of the finale's variations conjured up a picture of the "celebration of the earth." How appropriate, thought the visitor, that Serov, the leading Russian Beethoven critic of the nineteenth century, should have the last word in these program notes; that the venue for the evening's concert should once again bear the name of St. Petersburg, the city in whose salons and concert halls Beethoven's music had first been seriously explored; and that the year itself should mark the centennial of the institution most responsible for bringing Beethoven's music to the attention of the concertgoing public. Figuratively speaking, Beethoven had come home, his status as a free artist restored at last.

The bell announced the second half of the program. When the lights dimmed and the conductor swept up his baton to launch the hammer strokes of the *Eroica* Symphony's opening tutti, the unfiltered power and beauty of Beethoven's mighty music filled the hall. It was as if the heavens had suddenly opened up. Everything made sense that evening, pointing in the direction of a promising new era in how Russians heard Beethoven.

Notes

1. Following the death of Stalin on March 5, 1953, a brief period of "collective leadership" ensued that saw Khrushchev elevated to the post of party leader as primus inter pares. The fiction of joint rule came to an end with Khrushchev's defeat of the "Anti-Party Group" in June 1957 and his acquisition of the premiership in March 1958.

2. William Taubman, *Khrushchev: The Man and His Era* (New York: W. W. Norton, 2003), 620.

3. Taubman, *Khrushchev*, xx, 29, 589–90. On Khrushchev's attitudes toward classical music, jazz, and ballet, see also Strobe Talbott, trans., *Khrushchev Remembers: The Last Testament* (Boston: Little, Brown, 1974), 82–83.

4. Taubman, *Khrushchev*, 231, 501. For concertizing during the Cuban Missile Crisis, see ibid., 563, 569, 576.

5. Ibid., 639.

6. The speech did not remain secret for long. Israeli intelligence intercepted a copy posted to the Polish Communist Party and forwarded it to Washington, DC, where it was translated by the US State Department and published by the *New York Times* on June 4, 1956. See also Nikita S. Khrushchev, *The Crimes of the Stalin Era: Special Report to the 20th Congress of the Communist Party of the Soviet Union*, annotated Boris I. Nicolaevsky (New York: New Leader, 1962).

7. Elizaveta Drabkina, *Chernye sukhari: povest' o nenapisannoi knige* (Moscow: Sovetskii pisatel', 1963), 556–57. On Drabkina's early career, arrest, and incarceration, see Orlando Figes, *The Whisperers: Private Life in Stalin's Russia* (New York: Henry Holt, 2007), 1–5, 430–31 and Yuri Slezkine, *The House of Government: A Saga of the Russian Revolution* (Princeton, NJ: Princeton University Press, 2017), 143, 146, 245, 289, 886, 932.

8. Solomon Volkov, *The Magical Chorus: A History of Russian Culture from Tolstoy to Solzhenitsyn*, trans. Antonina W. Bouis (New York: Alfred A. Knopf, 2008), 282.

9. Serge Moreux, *Béla Bartók*, trans. G. S. Fraser and Erik De Mauny (London: Harvill, 1953), 92. Bartók considered the other great innovators in Western music to be Bach, in

demonstrating "the transcendent significance of counterpoint," and Debussy, in reawakening "an awareness of harmony and its possibilities." Ibid.

10. Natalya Reshetovskaya, *Sanya: My Life with Aleksandr Solzhenitsyn*, trans. Elena Ivanoff (New York: Bobbs-Merrill, 1975), 108–9. As an accomplished concert pianist, Reshetovskaya undoubtedly contributed to Solzhenitsyn's increasingly more sophisticated understanding of classical music.

11. Christian Neef and Matthias Schepp, "[*Der Spiegel*] interview with Alexander Solzhenitsyn," *New York Times*, July 23, 2007.

12. Allan Kozinn, "Solzhenitsyn, the Son, in a Spotlight All His Own as Pianist and Conductor," *New York Times*, April 16, 1999. Ignat Solzhenitsyn cites this incident as key to his childhood desire to become an orchestral conductor.

13. Charles Geyer, "Celebrating a Century of Aleksandr Solzhenitsyn with Poetry and Music," *La Scena Musicale*, November 19, 2018. During his incarceration, Solzhenitsyn committed to memory some twelve thousand lines of original poetry. Ignat Solzhenitsyn is currently translating the poems into English and quoted the lines cited above in his interview with Charles Geyer. The phrase "drawn out into" has been enclosed in brackets since it is not part of the original translation. Many thanks to Ignat Solzhenitsyn for clarifying the gulag reminiscence (email of November 29, 2019). See Sophy Roberts, *The Lost Pianos of Siberia* (New York: Grove, 2020), 217–34, for commentary on music making in the gulag. For the manner in which the *Largo e mesto* of op. 10, no. 3 works musically, see William Kinderman, *Beethoven: A Politial Artist in Revolutionary Times* (Chicago: University of Chicago Press, 2020), 46–48.

14. B. A. Kats, comp., *Muzyka v tvorchestve, sud'be i v dome Borisa Pasternaka: sbornik literaturnykh, muzykal'nykh i izobrazitel'nykh materialov* (Leningrad: Sovetskii kompozitor, 1991), 25, 139–40.

15. Christopher Barnes, *Boris Pasternak: A Literary Biography*, I (Cambridge: Cambridge University Press, 1989), 113.

16. Ibid., 318.

17. Anna Lisa Crone and Patricia Suhrcke, "Pasternak's 'Pushkin Variations,'" *Die Welt der Slaven*, XXIV, 2 (1979): 328. The authors argue that Variation 3, initially called *Sakrokomicheskaia*, recalls Sonata no. 29 in B-flat (*Hammerklavier*), op. 106, by its "fugue-like repetitions"; that Variation 4, initially called *Dramaticheskaia*, recalls Sonata no. 14 in C-sharp minor (*Moonlight*), op. 27, no. 2, by its "initial image of the moon and its strong dactylic rhythm"; that Variation 5, initially called *Pateticheskaia*, recalls Sonata no. 8 in C minor (*Pathétique*), op. 13, by its "clear titular reference" and "images of fevered, stormy agitation"; and that Variation 6, initially called *Pastoral'naia*, recalls Sonata no. 15 in D (*Pastoral*), op. 28, by its "reflective, lyrical mood." Ibid., 328n28. For the Russian text of the poems, see Boris Pasternak, *Stikhi i poemy, 1912–1932*, ed. G. P. Struve and B. A. Filippova (Ann Arbor: University of Michigan Press, 1961), 63–69.

18. Munir Sendich, "Boris Pasternak: A Selected Annotated Bibliography of Literary Criticism (1914–1990)," *Russian Language Journal*, XLV, 150 (Winter 1991): 41–259. For extended discussion of the role music played in Pasternak's life and career, see Barnes, *Boris Pasternak*, I, 77–90.

19. Henry Gifford, *Pasternak: A Critical Study* (Cambridge: Cambridge University Press, 1977), 21. For a broader, if highly technical, analysis, see Dale L. Plank, *Pasternak's Lyric: A Study of Sound and Imagery* (The Hague: Mouton, 1966).

20. Burton Bernstein and Barbara B. Haws, *Leonard Bernstein: American Original* (New York: Harper Collins, 2008), 129. See also Jonathan Rosenberg, *Dangerous Melodies: Classical Music in America from the Great War through the Cold War* (New York: W. W. Norton, 2020), 349–51.

21. Boris Pasternak, *I Remember: Sketch for an Autobiography*, trans. David Magarshack (New York: Pantheon Books, 1959), 121–22.

22. Boris Pasternak, *Doctor Zhivago: A Novel*, trans. Richard Pevear and Larissa Volokhonsky (New York: Pantheon Books, 2010), 390.

23. Pasternak, *I Remember*, 122; Mary F. Rowland and Paul Rowland, *Pasternak's Doctor Zhivago* (Carbondale: Southern Illinois University Press, 1967), 58. Most translations present "The Poems of Yuri Zhivago" with no chapter designation on the title page, thus implying that the verses represent a standalone section with no immediate relationship to the work as a whole. See, for example, the translation by Max Hayward and Manya Hahari (New York: Pantheon Books, 1958), 521. The translation by Pevear and Volokhonsky, p. 462, on the other hand, preserves the original chapter 17 designation, a rendering that accords with the text of the original Soviet edition. See B. Pasternak, *Doktor Zhivago: Roman* (Moscow: Knizhnaia palata, 1989), 387.

24. In the Pevear/Volokhonsky translation, the poems and corresponding prose antecedents are as follows: poem 1, "Hamlet"—p. 435; poem 5, "Bad Roads in Spring"—p. 257; poem 6, "A Final Talk"—p. 381; poem 11, "A Wedding"—p. 60; poem 13, "A Tale"—p. 394; poem 15, "A Winter Night"—pp. 72, 444; poem 16, "Separation"—p. 404; poem 23, "Magdalene I,"—p. 369; poem 25, "The Garden of Gethsemane"—p. 3. Correlations based on my reading of the novel.

25. The poems follow the seasons in the following five groups: spring (poems 1–5), summer (poems 6–9), autumn (poems 10–14), winter (poems 15–19), spring (poems 20–25). Rowland and Rowland, *Pasternak's Doctor Zhivago*, 58.

26. Angela Livingstone offers an intriguing parallel mode of analysis in her discussion of the sudden transition from black-and-white to color in Andrei Tarkovsky's film *Andrei Rublev* (1966). Angela Livingstone, *Pasternak: Doctor Zhivago* (Cambridge: Cambridge University Press, 1989), 114.

27. "Novyi Mir Editors' Letter Rejecting 'Doctor Zhivago,'" *Current Digest of the Soviet Press*, X, 43 (December 3, 1958): 6–7, 11. The letter had been published by *Literaturnaia gazeta* (*Literary Gazette*) on October 25, 1956.

28. Lazar Fleishman, *Boris Pasternak: The Poet and His Politics* (Cambridge, MA: Harvard University Press, 1990), 275.

29. Ibid., 288, 290; Richard Pevear, "Introduction," *Doctor Zhivago*, ix–x.

30. Peter Finn and Petra Couvée, *The Zhivago Affair: The Kremlin, the CIA, and the Battle over a Forbidden Book* (New York: Vintage Books, 2015), 240.

31. Pasternak, *Doctor Zhivago*, trans. Pevear and Volokhonsky, 461.

32. Taubman, *Khrushchev*, 628.

33. Luba Brezhneva, *The World I Left Behind: Pieces of a Past*, trans. Geoffrey Polk (New York: Random House, 1995), 3; John Dornberg, *Brezhnev: The Masks of Power* (New York: Basic Books, 1974), 15. Brezhnev did write poetry and loved the Russian classics, especially Pushkin and Esenin, but showed no interest in art or music. Brezhneva, *The World I Left Behind*, 307, 315, 347, 366–67. His interests extended rather to such pursuits as attending soccer games, hunting, yachting, and driving fast and expensive cars—the latter, mostly gifts from foreign heads of state, included a Rolls-Royce, Cadillac, Lincoln Continental, and Mercedes 450-SCL. Dornberg, *Brezhnev*, 18.

34. "Beethoven Memorialized Many Ways," *New York Times*, December 17, 1970, 58.

35. "The Soviet Union CPA 3949 stamp," *Wikimedia Commons; Billboard Magazine*, July 18, 1970, 70.

36. V. S. Fomin, ed., *Liudvig van Betkhoven: estetika, tvorcheskoe nasledie, ispolnitel'stvo. Sbornik statei k 200-letiiu so dnia rozhdeniia* (Leningrad: Muzyka, 1970), 5–254.

37. Larissa Kirillina, "Recent Russian Beethoven Scholars," *Beethoven Newsletter*, VII, 1 (Spring 1992): 10, 14. In 1981, Kirillina became Fishman's assistant and coauthor. She received her doctorate from the Moscow Conservatory in 1989 (dissertation topic: "Betkhoven i teoriia muzyki XVIII-nachala XIX vekov") and has since published *Betkhoven: zhizn' i tvorchestvo*, 2 vol. (Moscow: Nauchno-izdatel'skii tsentr "Moskovskaia konservatoriia," 2009).

38. L. Betkhoven, *Kniga eskizov za 1802–1803 gody* [issledovanie i rasshifrovka N. L. Fishman] (Moscow: Gosudarstvennoe muzykal'noe izdatel'stvo, 1962). Kirillina quote in "Recent Russian Beethoven Scholars," 10. See also Boris Schwarz, *Music and Musical Life in Soviet Russia, 1917–1970* (New York: W. W. Norton, 1972), 409.

39. As of 1992, a final fourth volume of letters had been completed and was due to be issued by the Muzyka publishing house, but there is no record that the volume ever appeared in print. Kirillina, "Recent Russian Beethoven Scholars," 14.

40. N. L. Fishman, ed., *Liudvig van Betkhoven, 1770–1827: zhizn', tvorchestvo, okruzhenie* (Moscow: Muzyka, 1971), 222, 232, 236, 242–43.

41. N. L. Fishman, ed., *Betkhoven: sbornik statei*, 2 vol. (Moscow: Muzyka, 1971–72). The bibliography consisted of 1,120 items drawn largely from journal and newspaper articles until the post-Stalin era when book-length studies began to proliferate. See N. N. Grigorovich, "Bibliografiia literatury o Betkhovene na russkom iazyke," *Betkhoven: sbornik statei*, II, 310–74. For the political note on Beethoven and socialist construction, see N. S. Nikolaeva, "Puti v budushchee ot deviatoi simfonii Betkhovena," *Betkhoven: sbornik statei*, II, 302.

42. N. L. Fishman, ed., *Iz istorii sovetskoi betkhoveniany* (Moscow: Sovetskii kompozitor, 1972).

43. N. Fishman, *Etiudy i ocherki po betkhoveniane* (Moscow: Muzyka, 1982).

44. Kirillina, "Recent Russian Beethoven Scholars," 14.

45. L. Gakkel', *V kontsertnom zale: vpechatleniia 1950–1980-kh godov* (St. Petersburg: Kompozitor, 1997), 72, 221.

46. Ibid., 63.

47. Galina Ustvol'skaia (1919–2006), Shostakovich's favorite pupil, is perhaps best representative of the Soviet modernist school. She is heard to excellent effect in her Duet for Violin and Piano (1964) as performed by Patricia Kopatchinskaja and Markus Hinterhauser on the ECM New Series label, ECM 2329 (2014).

48. Kenzo Amoh, trans. and ed., *Yevgeni Mravinsky: A Concert Listing, 1930–1987* (Tokyo, Japan: Japanese Mravinsky Society, 2000), 1–59. I thank Galina Retrovskaia of the St. Petersburg Philharmonic Archive for gifting me this item. For Mravinsky's diary, see Evgenii Mravinskii, *Zapiski na pamiat': dnevniki, 1918–1987* (St. Petersburg: Iskusstvo, 2004).

49. Gakkel', *V kontsertnom zale*, 50–59, 85, 211; Rosenberg, *Dangerous Melodies*, 320–55, 370–73; Schwarz, *Music and Musical Life in Soviet Russia*, 313–58, 431–34, 464. For concert programming by Igor Stravinsky, see Stephen Walsh, *Stravinsky: The Second Exile: France and America, 1934–1971* (New York: Alfred A. Knopf, 2006), 449–52, 460–71.

50. David Caute, *The Dancer Defects: The Struggle for Cultural Supremacy during the Cold War* (Oxford: Oxford University Press, 2003), 498.

51. Gilels's Beethoven recordings are available in a nine-CD boxed set, DG 28947-76360 (1996).

52. Damian Thompson, "Why Did the Soviets Not Want Us to Know about the Pianist Maria Grinberg?," *Spectator*, September 7, 2019.

53. Grinberg's Beethoven recordings, issued in conjunction with the bicentennial of Beethoven's birth, are available in a thirty-four-CD boxed set, Scribendum SC814 (2019).

54. Schwarz, *Music and Musical Life in Soviet Russia*, 353.

55. Nikolaeva's recordings, including the Beethoven traversal, are available in a thirty-seven-CD boxed set, Scribendum 810 (2018).

56. Alexander Lipovsky, comp., *Soviet Stars in the World of Music: Lenin Prize Winners*, trans. Olga Shartse (Moscow: Progress, 1966), 214–15.

57. Alan Lompech, "A Free Spirit among Artists," liner notes to *Richter Performs Beethoven*, Philips 438624. For Richter's Siberian tour, see Roberts, *The Lost Pianos of Siberia*, 283–85.

58. Bruno Monsaingeon, *Sviatoslav Richter: Notebooks and Conversations*, trans. Stewart Spencer (Princeton, NJ: Princeton University Press, 2001), 379, 385–86.

59. Ibid., 48, 52.

60. Hans-Heinz Stuckenschmidt, "Pal'tsy, kak orlinnye kogti," *Nevel'skii sbornik*, 4, ed. L. M. Maksimovskaia (St. Petersburg: Akropol', 1999), 46. Stuckenschmidt misleadingly identifies the concerto as "No 25 in A, K. 503."

61. For recent discussion (and debunking) of the Yudina-Stalin tale, see Elizabeth Wilson, *Playing with Fire: The Story of Maria Yudina, Pianist in Stalin's Russia* (New Haven, CT: Yale University Press, 2022), 300–5. Yudina's recordings are available in a twenty-six-CD boxed set, Scribendum SC-813 (2018). The Beethoven recordings include the *Eroica* Variations; *Diabelli Variations*; Thirty-Two Variations on an Original Theme; Piano Sonatas nos. 5, 12, 14, 16–17, 22, 27–29, 32; Piano Concertos nos. 4 and 5 (live recordings); Violin Sonata no. 6; and the *Choral Fantasy*. See the *Nevel'skii sbornik* issue cited above for an early diary Yudina kept and additional commentary on her life and career by contemporaries.

62. For historical background, see Boris Berezovskii, *Filarmonicheskoe obshchestvo Sankt-Peterburga: istoriia i sovremennost'* (St. Petersburg: Kul't Inform, 2002), 311–70.

POSTLUDE

Project Gulag 2010

OR HAD IT? PERFORMING BEETHOVEN IN A FORMER gulag labor camp would seem to call such an assurance into question. On July 3, 2010, the Perm' Academic Opera and Ballet Theater, under the baton of the British theater director Michael Hunt, premiered a new production of the opera *Fidelio* in Perm'-36, one of the harshest political camps in the former gulag system. Located in the foothills of the Ural Mountains some sixty miles northeast of Perm', the prison was established in 1946 as a "corrective labor timber-logging camp." In 1972, on the orders of KGB chief Iurii Andropov, a portion of the camp was transformed into a "strict regime" maximum-security prison consisting of minuscule (thirty-three square feet) windowless twenty-four-hour isolation cells designed to house the Soviet Union's most prominent political dissidents.[1] It was not until December 8, 1987, that the camp was finally closed on orders of Mikhail Gorbachev, though the remaining prisoners were not released from custody until Boris Yeltsin's general amnesty of February 1992. In 1994, the prison was converted into a "Museum of the History of Political Repression Perm'-36" by the Russian human rights organization Memorial International. However, due to diminished funds, Vladimir Putin's reactionary policies, and the wave of patriotism generated by the annexation of Crimea on March 18, 2014, the Perm' regional government seized control of the prison and transformed the museum into a facility honoring the gulag system itself rather than its countless victims.[2] Today, Perm'-36 remains the last remnant of the once vast gulag labor camp system, the other prisons, some eight thousand strong, having been demolished or allowed to fall into ruin following the dissolution of the Soviet Union in 1991.

Hunt and his crew intended for their production of *Fidelio* to be an immersive theater experience designed to draw the audience as deeply as possible into the emotional compass of the opera. For some operagoers, the drama began with a twenty-four-hour journey from Moscow to Perm' via the Trans-Siberian Railway, the train's clacking wheels repetitively echoing the old gulag lament, "The farther it is, the worse it will be." A two-hour trip by bus along dusty, potholed roads brought the audience members to the gates of Perm'-36,

Figure 8.1. Perm'-36. https://www.rferl.org/a/russia-gulag-perm/26910251.html.

as if they themselves were new arrivals. The group was met by a throng of women carrying photographs of loved ones (pictures of actual former prisoners, it turned out), wailing and rushing the gate, to be beaten back by armed guards. The audience was herded through the gate—*Bystree! Bystree!* ("Faster! Faster!"), the guards shouted. They came on a field where a small orchestra sat on an upraised stage, the only object to detract from the verisimilitude of the setting. With its microphones wired to loudspeakers throughout the camp, the orchestra soon struck up the overture to *Fidelio*, and Leonore, dressed as an avenging angel, made her initial appearance. Act 1 took place at various points in the camp, including the barracks, mess hall, prison yard, and various workstations, with audience members hustled from one site to the next by armed guards and ferocious barking dogs. Act 2 was staged for optimum effect in the narrow corridor of the maximum-security prison, causing those crammed inside the facility to press up against the dank walls as the dungeon scene unfolded directly in front of them. The finale brought the audience back to the orchestra stage, where a beneficent Don Fernando, liberated Florestan, victorious Leonore, kindhearted Rocco, chastened Don Pizzaro, and other cast members took their respective bows. "In these days," Michael Hunt enthused, "we have brought music, we have brought Beethoven to this place." He called to the stage Michael Mylac, a former prisoner of the camp, and acknowledged him as his main inspiration in bringing the *Fidelio* project to fruition. Mylac, Hunt said, had often spoken to him "about the importance of Beethoven in this place." Mylac confirmed that the production had been cathartic. It had "cleansed the place."[3]

The production of *Fidelio* in such a setting would appear to belie the claim that Russian Beethoven reception had freed itself from the political posturing of earlier times. But there is a world of difference between serving as a vehicle for enhancing the power of a one-party state and serving as a means of enlarging the spirit and promoting the common good. The former breeds propaganda, the latter fosters education. It is important to note that, unlike in South Africa, where a Truth and Reconciliation Commission was established in 1996 to adjudicate abuses suffered under apartheid, no such body was created in Russia after the fall of communism. Consequently, only private organizations such as the Memorial International rights group have provided a means by which the Russian people can come to terms with the brutality of the Stalin era. As a tour guide at the Perm'-36 museum put it, "Our aim is . . . to draw a line [under the past] and show how far we've come—and make it harder for anything like this ever to happen again." Or as Liudmila Alexeeva of Memorial International asserted, "For others, let [Perm'-36] be an education; for Russians, let it be a reminder."[4] It was therefore entirely appropriate for *Fidelio* to be performed in this despotic and wicked place, even if now it is but an abandoned prison at the end of a long, dusty road. Honoring memory is a noble undertaking. Beethoven's integrity as a free artist remains intact.[5]

Notes

1. Among the more notable prisoners were Balys Gajaukas, a Lithuanian nationalist who in 1989 became interior minister of the newly independent state of Lithuania; Sergei Kovalev, a human rights advocate and closest ally of Andrei Sakharov, who in 1994 became an elected member of the State Duma and chairman of Boris Yeltsin's Human Rights Commission; and Natan Shcharanskii, a leader of the Soviet "refusniks," those Russian Jews whose applications for emigration to Israel had been denied, who in 1986 was released from prison as a result of an international campaign waged by his wife, Avital, and allowed to resettle in Israel.

2. For details, see J. Paul Goode, "Patriotism without Patriots? Perm'-36 and Patriotic Legitimation in Russia," *Slavic Review*, LXXIX, 2 (Summer 2020): 390–411. See also Susanne Sternthal, "Let History Be Judged: The Lesson of Perm-36," *oDR Russia and Beyond*, January 6, 2012, 1–9.

3. Quotes come from the final production of July 11, 2010, which can be viewed in its entirety on YouTube at operaonvideo.com/fidelio-perm-2010. For moving commentary by an audience member, see Andrea Wulf, "Cry Freedom," *Opera News*, January–February 2011, 36–39.

4. Jeremy Hildreth, "Gulag a Go-Go," *Wall Street Journal*, November 1, 2010.

5. Tragically, on December 28, 2021, the Russian Supreme Court ordered that Memorial International be shut down; on December 29, it also ordered the closing of the organization's Human Rights Center. Both actions reflected Vladimir Putin's ongoing campaign to stifle dissent in post-Soviet Russia.

APPENDIX

Tables

Table 1. Beethoven Instrumental Performances in the Provinces, 1895–1917[1]

Arkhangel'sk[2]
- 1914: Symphony 2

Astrakhan[3]
- 1899: Symphony 8
- 1900: Symphonies 4–6
- 1901: *Leonore* 3 Overture, Symphony 3
- 1902: *Wellington's Victory*
- 1903: Symphony 4
- 1907: Violin Concerto, Symphony 1
- 1908: *Coriolan* Overture
- 1909: *Ah! perfido*
- 1912: *Egmont* Overture, *Leonore* 3 Overture, Violin Concerto

Baku
- 1897: *Egmont* Overture (eight-hand)
- 1903: *Leonore* 3 Overture, Symphony 3
- 1904: Symphony 5
- 1905: Symphony 4
- 1909: Symphony 5
- 1910: *Egmont* Overture
- 1913: *Leonore* 3 Overture, Symphony 7
- 1917: *Egmont* Overture, Symphonies 3 and 5

Batum
- 1906: Incidental Music to Goethe's *Egmont* (excerpts)

Cheliabinsk[4]
- 1907: Symphony 1

Ekaterinburg
- 1915: Symphony 3
- 1916: Symphony 7

Ekaterinodar
- 1903: *Egmont* Overture, Piano Concerto 2
- 1907: Symphonies 5 and 6
- 1916: Violin Concerto

Ekaterinoslav
- 1910: Symphony 5

Essentuki
- 1909: Symphony 5

(*Continued*)

Table 1. (*Continued*)

Helsinki
- 1908: *Leonore* 3 Overture
- 1910: Symphonies 5 and 8

Irkutsk
- 1904: Symphony 3

Kazan'[5]
- 1898: *Egmont* Overture
- 1900: Symphony 5
- 1903: Symphonies 3 and 5
- 1905: *Coriolan* Overture, Symphonies 3 and 4
- 1907: *Coriolan* Overture, *Egmont* Overture, *Leonore* 3 Overture, Symphonies 5 and 7
- 1908: *Coriolan* Overture, Piano Concerto 4, Violin Concerto, Symphony 6
- 1909: Symphonies 3 and 5
- 1910: Violin Concerto, *Coriolan* Overture, *Leonore* 3 Overture, Symphonies 2 and 4–7
- 1913: Piano Concerto 5, *Egmont* Overture, *Leonore* 3 Overture, *Consecration of the House* Overture, Symphonies 1 and 2

Khar'kov
- 1898: *Leonore* 3 Overture
- 1899: Symphony 4
- 1900: Violin Concerto, Piano Concertos 2 and 5, Symphony 5
- 1901: Symphony 7
- 1902: *Ah! perfido*, Piano Concerto 3, Symphony 8
- 1903: Piano Concerto 3, Symphonies 2 and 6
- 1904: Symphony 3
- 1905: Symphony 4
- 1907: Symphony 7
- 1909: *Ruins of Athens*, Symphony 7
- 1910: Romance for Violin and Orchestra in F, Piano Concerto 5, *Creatures of Prometheus* Overture, *Egmont* Overture, *Leonore* 3 Overture, Symphonies 2 and 6
- 1911: *Leonore* 3 Overture, Symphonies 3 and 4
- 1913: *Fidelio* Overture; Koussevitzky concerts
- 1914: Piano Concerto 5, Symphony 7
- 1916: Symphonies 1 and 5

Kiev
- 1895: Symphonies 3 and 4
- 1896: *Egmont* Overture, Symphony 5
- 1899: Piano Concerto 3, *Creatures of Prometheus* (excerpts), *Ruins of Athens* (excerpts), *Coriolan* Overture, Symphony 6
- 1901: *Consecration of the House* Overture, Symphony 5
- 1902: *Egmont* Overture, Symphonies 3 and 7
- 1903: *Creatures of Prometheus* (excerpts), *Egmont* Overture, Symphony 4
- 1905: Piano Concerto 5, Symphony 2
- 1906: *Fidelio* (excerpts), *Ruins of Athens* (excerpts)

(*Continued*)

Table 1. (*Continued*)

1909: Symphony 7
1910: Symphonies 5 and 6, Mass in C
1912: *Egmont* Overture
1913: Symphonies 3 and 5–8; Koussevitzky concerts

Kishinev
1898: *Fidelio* Overture, Symphony 6 (four-hand)
1901: Symphony 6
1902: Symphonies 1 and 4
1903: Symphony 5
1907: Piano Concerto (unidentified)

Konstantinograd
1903: Symphony 2

Kremenchug
1900: Symphony 8

Kursk
1903: *Creatures of Prometheus* Overture, Symphony 5

Libav
1898: Symphony 9 (without chorus)

Łodz
1909: Symphony 5

Lublin
1911: Piano Concerto 4

Nikolaev
1900: *Fidelio* Overture, Symphony 3
1902: Symphony 6
1903: *Egmont* Overture, Symphonies 3 and 8

Nizhnii-Novgorod
1896: *Ruins of Athens*
1897: *Fidelio* Overture
1898: *Fidelio* Overture, Symphony 8
1899: Piano Concerto 4
1903: *Creatures of Prometheus* Overture, Symphonies 4 and 7
1904: Piano Concerto 5
1906: Piano Concerto (unidentified)
1908: *Egmont* Overture (eight-hand), Symphony 2
1910: *Egmont* Overture, Symphony 7
1912: *Egmont* Overture, Symphony 5

Odessa[6]
1896: Violin Concerto, *Leonore* 3 Overture
1897: Piano Concerto 4, Symphonies 2, 3, 5, and 8 (premiere of Symphony 8)
1898: *Coriolan* Overture, *Egmont* Overture, *Leonore* 3 Overture (performed twice), Symphonies 5 and 7
1899: Symphony 3
1901: *Ruins of Athens* (excerpts), Symphonies 1 and 9 (premiere of Symphony 9 [two performances])

(*Continued*)

Table 1. (*Continued*)

1902: Symphony 8
1904: Violin Concerto, *Leonore 3* Overture (performed twice), Symphony 3 ("Funeral March")
1907: Symphonies 3 and 7
1909: *Ah! perfido*, *Coriolan* Overture, *Leonore* 3 Overture, Symphonies 5 and 6
1910: Symphony 3
1911: *Leonore* 3 Overture, Mass in C
1912: Piano Concerto 4, Violin Concerto, *Coriolan* Overture, *Choral Fantasy*, Symphonies 1, 2, and 7
1913: *Leonore* 3 Overture, Symphony 2; Koussevitzky concerts

Orel
1903: *Creatures of Prometheus* Overture, Symphony 5
1909: Piano Concerto 4, Symphony 1
1910: Piano Concerto 4

Orenburg
1902: Symphony 5

Pavlovsk
1900: Symphony 7

Perm'
1899: *Fidelio* (full dress performance)
1909: *Coriolan* Overture, *Egmont* Overture

Poltava[7]
1898: *Egmont* Overture, Symphony 3
1899: Piano Concerto 3, *Leonore* 2 Overture, Symphonies 6 and 7
1900: *Coriolan* Overture, *Leonore* 3 Overture, Symphonies 1 and 8
1901: Piano Concerto 5, *Dedication of the House* Overture, Symphonies 2 and 5
1902: *Coriolan* Overture, *Leonore* 3 Overture, *Name Day* Overture, *King Stephen* Overture, Symphonies 3 and 7
1903: *King Stephen* Overture, Symphonies 2 and 5
1907: *Wellington's Victory*
1908: Symphony 1
1911: Symphony 2

Riga
1898: *Wellington's Victory*, *Coriolan* Overture, Symphonies 2 and 3
1899: Violin Concerto, Symphony 3
1900: Symphony 9
1901: Symphonies 1 and 3
1902: Symphony 5
1904: *Fidelio* (full dress performance)
1907: *Leonore* Overture (unidentified), Symphonies 4, 5, and 7
1910: Symphonies 1–3 and 5–8
1912: Symphonies 4 and 6

Rostov-on-Don
1900: Symphonies 6 and 7
1903: Violin Concerto, Symphonies 3–5

(*Continued*)

Table 1. (*Continued*)

1905: Piano Concerto 4, Symphony 2
1913: Koussevitzky concerts
1916: *Coriolan* Overture

Sarapul
1910: *Egmont* Overture

Saratov
1897: Symphony 3
1900: *Leonore* 3 Overture, Symphony 8
1903: Symphonies 5 and 7
1904: Symphony 3 ("Funeral March")
1910: *Egmont* Overture
1913: Piano Concerto 4, Symphony 2

Smolensk
1902: Symphony 5

Stavropol'
1901: Symphony 1
1903: Symphonies 3 and 6
1904: Symphony 1
1905: *Creatures of Prometheus* Overture, Symphonies 3 and 5
1906: Symphonies 2, 3, and 7

Taganrog
1902: Symphonies 5 and 6
1910: Symphonies 1, 2, and 6

Tambov[8]
1899: Violin Concerto, *Creatures of Prometheus* Overture
1900: Symphony 6
1902: Symphonies 1 and 5
1903: Symphony 8
1907: Symphony 3
1910: *Leonore* 3 Overture
1912: Symphony 5

Tbilisi (Tiflis)
1896: Piano Concerto 5, Symphony 4
1897: *Leonore* 3 Overture, Symphony 6
1899: Piano Concerto (unidentified), *Egmont* Overture, Symphony 5
1900: Symphony 3
1901: Symphony 3
1904: Symphony 7
1905: Symphony 6
1908: *Leonore* 3 Overture
1910: Piano Concerto 4, Symphony 7, *Fidelio* (*Leonore* aria)
1912: Symphony 7
1913: Symphony 7
1914: Piano Concerto 5, Symphony 7
1916: Piano Concerto 4, Symphony 2

(*Continued*)

Table 1. (*Continued*)

1917: *Egmont* Overture, Symphony 4

Tomsk[9]

1895: Symphonies 3 and 5
1906: *Egmont* Overture
1909: Symphony 1
1914: *Egmont* Overture

Tsaritsyn[10]

1910: Symphony 5

Viatka

1898: Violin Concerto

Vil'na (Vilnius)

1898: Symphony 1
1899: Symphony 5
1913: Symphony 5

Vladikavkaz

1909: Symphony 5

Voronezh

1909: Symphony 5

Warsaw

1902: Romance for Violin and Orchestra in F, Violin Concerto, *Egmont* Overture, Symphonies 2–4, and 9 (premiere of Symphony 9)
1903: Symphonies 1, 3, and 6
1904: *Egmont* Overture
1908: Symphony 6
1909: Symphonies 3 and 5
1910: Piano Concerto 5, *Coriolan* Overture, Symphony 5
1911: *Leonore* 3 Overture, Symphony 9
1912: Symphony 3
1913: *Choral Fantasy*, *Leonore* 1–3 Overtures, Symphonies 5 and 9
1914: Symphonies 8 and 9 (Symphony 9 performed three times)

Yalta

1911: Symphonies 1–3

Yaroslavl'

1904: Symphony 5
1914: Piano Concerto 5

Zhitomir

1909: Romance for Violin and Orchestra in F, Piano Concerto 5, *Coriolan* Overture, Symphony 5
1915: Piano Concerto 3, *Creatures of Prometheus* Overture, Symphony 1
1917: Piano Concerto 1, *Coriolan* Overture, Symphonies 3 and 5

1. *Russkaia muzykal'naia gazeta*, I-XXIV (St. Petersburg/Petrograd, 1895–1917). All data from this source unless otherwise indicated.

2. G. S. Shchurov, *Arkhangel'sk-gorod muzykal'nyi* (Arkhangel'sk: Pravda Severna, 1995–97), 171.

(*Continued*)

Table 1. (*Continued*)

3. M. A. Etunger, *Muzykal'naia kul'tura Astrakhani* (Volgograd: Nizhno-Volzhkoe knizhnoe izdatel'stvo, 1989), 24, 30, 36. For years 1899, 1900, 1903.

4. V. Vol'fovich, *Cheliabinsk muzykal'nyi* (Cheliabinsk: Iuzhno-Uralskoe knizhnoe izdatel'stvo, 1989), 11. The source states that unidentified Beethoven works were also performed in the 1908 concert season.

5. *Iz istorii muzykal'noi kul'tury i obrazovaniia v Kazani* (Kazan': Kazanskaia gosudarstvennaia konservatoriia, 1993), 82–241. For years 1900 (Symphony 5), 1905 (Symphony 3), 1907 (*Leonore 3* Overture), 1908 (Violin Concerto), 1909/10 (*Coriolan* Overture, Symphonies 4/7).

6. V. I. Malishevskii, ed., *Kratkii istoricheskii ocherk deiatel'nosti Odesskogo otdeleniia Imperatorskogo Russkogo muzykal'nogo obshchestva i sostoiashchego pri nem muzykal'nogo uchilishcha za dvadtsat' piat' let (1886–1911)* (Odessa, Ukraine: Tipo-litorg. Shtaba Okr., 1911), 109–36. For years 1896, 1897 (Piano Concerto 4, Symphony 5), 1898 (*Egmont* Overture, *Leonore 3* Overture [two performances], Symphony 7), 1901 (*Ruins of Athens*), 1904 (*Leonore 3* Overture [one performance], 1907 (Symphony 7), 1909 (*Coriolan* Overture, Symphony 5). For the period 1886–1894, the source lists the following Beethoven performances: 1887: Symphonies 3/7; 1888: *Coriolan* Overture, Symphony 5; 1891: Symphony 3; 1893: Violin Concerto, Symphony 7; 1894: Symphony 3.

7. N. Findeizen, ed., *Ocherk deiatel'nosti Poltavskogo otdeleniia Imperatorskogo Russkogo muzykal'nogo obshchestva za 1899–1915* (Poltava, Ukraine: Tovarishchestvo pechatnoe delo, 1915). For year 1898. The source states that the Poltava orchestra performed altogether ten overtures (*Prometheus, Coriolan, Consecration of the House, King Stephen, Egmont, Name Day, Fidelio* and *Leonore 1–3, Wellington's Victory*, and Symphonies 1–8.

8. N. Emel'ianova, *Muzykal'nye vechera: khronika muzykal'noi zhizni tambovskogo kraia za 100 let* (Voronezh, Russia: Tsentral'no-Chernozemnoe knizhnoizdatel'stvo, 1977), 54. For year 1912.

9. T. Kupert, *Muzykal'noe proshloe Tomska* (Tomsk, Russia: T. Kupert, 2006). For years 1895, 1914. For 1878–92, the source lists the following performances: 1878: *Egmont* Overture (four-hand); 1885: Symphony 5; 1888: *Coriolan* Overture, *Egmont* Overture, Symphony 1; 1889: Symphony 8; 1892: Symphony 2.

10. G. N. Andrianova, *Khudozhestvennyi oblik Tsaritsyna-Stalingrada* (Volgograd, Russia: Universal, 1991), 38.

Table 2. Beethoven Performances in Petrograd/Leningrad, 1921–1927[1]

1921–22 Season

- 7/10: Symphony 5
- 7/17: Symphony 5
- 8/10: *Egmont* Overture, Piano Concerto 5, Symphony 3
- 8/12: *Leonore 3* Overture, Violin Concerto, Symphony 5
- 8/13: Symphonies 8 and 9
- 8/17: Symphonies 8 and 9
- 8/20: *Egmont* Overture, Piano Concerto 5, Symphony 3
- 12/4: Symphonies 5 and 9
- 3/22: Piano Concerto 5
- 4/9: *Missa solemnis*
- 5/14: Symphonies 5 and 9
- 5/21: [repeat of 4/9 concert]
- 6/7: [repeat of 5/14 concert]

(*Continued*)

Table 2. (*Continued*)

1922–23 Season
8/22: Piano Concerto 5
12/18: *Egmont* Overture, Piano Concerto 4, Symphony 7
1/31: Symphonies 3 and 5
2/5: [repeat of 1/31 concert]
3/7: *Leonore* 3 Overture
3/12: *Leonore* 3 Overture
3/14: *Missa solemnis*
4/18: *Leonore* 3 Overture, Symphonies 2 and 6
4/22: *Ah! perfido*, Symphonies 4 and 7
4/25: *Coriolan* Overture, Piano Concerto 4, Symphony 9
4/30: *Ah! perfido*, Symphonies 4 and 7
1923–24 Season
11/8: *Egmont* Overture, Piano Concerto 5, Symphony 9
3/2: Piano Concerto 4, Symphonies 1 and 3
3/3: [repeat of 3/2 concert]
3/5: *Ah! perfido*, Symphonies 2 and 5
3/7: [repeat of 3/5 concert]
3/9: Piano Concerto 5, Symphonies 4 and 7
3/10: [repeat of 3/9 concert]
3/12: Violin Concerto, Symphonies 6 and 8
3/14: [repeat of 3/12 concert]
3/16: *Fidelio* arias, *Coriolan* Overture, Symphony 9
3/17: [repeat of 3/16 concert]
4/9: Symphony 7
4/18: Piano Concerto 5
4/20: *Leonore* 3 Overture
1924–25 Season
10/8: *Leonore* 3 Overture, Symphony 5
10/19: *Ah! perfido*, Symphony 5
11/15: Piano Concerto 5
11/26: *Adelaida*
12/3: Violin Concerto
1/7: Symphony 7
1/20: Symphony 3
1/22: *Egmont* Overture, Symphony 3 ("Funeral March")
1/27: Piano Concerto 4, Symphony 2
2/1: *Leonore* 3 Overture
3/17: Symphony 8
3/25: Symphony 5
4/14: Symphony 9
4/26: *Egmont* Overture, Symphony 3
4/27: Violin Concerto
4/30: Violin Concerto
5/6: *Grosse Fuge* for String Quartet (Weingartner orchestration), Symphony 5

(*Continued*)

Table 2. (Continued)

1925–26 Season

10/10: Violin Concerto
11/11: *Coriolan* Overture, Piano Concerto 5, Symphony 5
11/14: [repeat of 11/11 concert]
12/1: Symphonies 6 and 7
12/11: Symphony 5
12/14: Symphony 5
12/15: Symphony 7
12/19: Symphony 9
12/20: [repeat of 12/19 concert]
12/27: Symphony 3
1/16: *Leonore* 3 Overture
1/20: *Leonore* 3 Overture
1/21: Symphony 3
3/27: *Adelaida*, Music to Goethe's Tragedy *Egmont*
3/28: [repeat of 3/27 concert]
4/13: Symphony 5
4/20: *Leonore* 3 Overture

1926–27 Season

11/8: *Egmont* Overture
12/29: Music to Goethe's Tragedy *Egmont*, Symphony 5
3/9: *Coriolan* Overture, Piano Concertos 1 and 4, *Choral Fantasy*
3/12: Symphony 5
3/16: *Leonore* 2 Overture, Piano Concertos 2, 3, and 5
3/23: Symphony 5
3/26: Symphony 3 ("Funeral March"), Symphony 1, Scottish Songs (selections), Music to Goethe's Tragedy *Egmont*
3/27: Three Solemn Songs for Trombone Quartet, Piano Concerto 5, Music to Goethe's Tragedy *Egmont*, Symphony 3
4/8: Symphony 9 (Finale)
4/19: *Missa solemnis*
4/20: [repeat of 4/19 concert]
4/27: Violin Concerto, Symphonies 2 and 5
4/30: Violin Concerto, Symphonies 3 and 4
5/1: *Egmont* Overture
5/4: Symphonies 6 and 7
5/6: Symphonies 5 and 9
5/7: Symphonies 8 and 9
5/8: [repeat of 5/7 concert]

1927–28 Season (to 12/18)

10/18: Symphony 9 (Finale)
11/23: Symphony 3

1. N. A. Mal'ko et al., ed., *Desiat let simfonicheskoi muzyki, 1917–1927* (Leningrad: Gosudarstvennaia akademicheskaia filarmoniia, 1928), 147–73; Arkhiv muykal'noi biblioteki Gosudarstvennoi S.-Petersburgskoi filarmonii im. D. D. Shostakovicha/Papka No. 3 (June–December 1921) / Alfavitnyi katalog: Betkhoven (1921–27).

Table 3. Beethoven Performances by the Leningrad Philharmonia, 1928–1953[1]

CHART A	1928	1929	1930	1931	1932	1933	1934	1935	1936	1937	1938
Symphonies											
	1928	1929	1930	1931	1932	1933	1934	1935	1936	1937	1938
Symphony 1	3x	—	1x	—	—	—	—	—	—	2x	—
Symphony 2	—	—	1x	1x	1x	—	1x	—	—	—	—
Symphony 3	2x	7x	4x	4x	3x	—	2x	2x	3x	3x	—
Symphony 4	1x	—	2x	1x	—	1x	—	—	1x	1x	1x
Symphony 5	6x	3x	5x	4x	2x	—	2x	8x	11x	5x	6x
Symphony 6	—	—	1x	2x	—	2x	1x	—	2x	2x	—
Symphony 7	—	1x	1x	2x	1x	—	5x	1x	4x	1x	1x
Symphony 8	—	2x	1x	5x	—	—	1x	1x	—	2x	1x
Symphony 9	—	3x	2x	5x	2x	2x	3x	2x	4x	4x	3x
Concertos											
	1928	1929	1930	1931	1932	1933	1934	1935	1936	1937	1938
Violin Con.	—	1x	—	2x	—	1x	2x	—	5x	—	2x
Piano Con. 1	—	1x	—	—	—	—	2x	—	—	3x	—
Piano Con. 2	—	—	—	—	—	—	—	—	1x	—	—
Piano Con. 3	—	—	1x	2x	—	1x	—	1x	—	2x	—
Piano Con. 4	—	1x	1x	—	—	5x	—	1x	1x	—	1x
Piano Con. 5	—	—	1x	2x	1x	1x	2x	—	1x	3x	1x
Triple Con.	—	—	1x	—	—	—	—	—	—	—	—
Overtures											
	1928	1929	1930	1931	1932	1933	1934	1935	1936	1937	1938
Consecration of the House	—	—	—	—	—	1x	—	1x	2x	—	—
Coriolan	1x	2x	2x	—	1x	2x	—	2x	1x	2x	3x
Egmont	5x	12x	2x	1x	3x	5x	3x	—	2x	1x	6x
Fidelio	1x	1x	—	—	—	—	2x	—	—	—	—
King Stephen	—	1x	—	—	—	—	—	1x	—	—	—
Leonore 1	—	—	—	—	—	—	—	—	—	—	—
Leonore 2	—	—	—	—	—	—	1x	—	—	—	—
Leonore 3	—	2x	3x	2x	7x	5x	4x	4x	3x	2x	4x
Nameday	—	—	—	—	—	—	—	—	—	—	—
Prometheus	1x	—	—	—	—	—	—	—	—	—	1x

(*Continued*)

Table 3. (*Continued*)

Incidental Music

	1928	1929	1930	1931	1932	1933	1934	1935	1936	1937	1938
Egmont	2x	3x	7x	9x	2x	—	—	—	2x	3x	3x
Egmont/Arias	—	1x	—	—	—	—	—	—	—	1x	1x
Prometheus	—	1x	—	—	1x	—	—	—	—	—	—
Ruins of Athens / "Turkish March"	6x	—	—	—	—	—	—	—	—	—	—

Choral/Opera

	1928	1929	1930	1931	1932	1933	1934	1935	1936	1937	1938
Missa solemnis	—	—	—	—	—	—	—	—	—	—	—
Choral Fantasy	—	—	—	—	—	—	—	—	1x	—	—
Fidelio/Complete	—	—	—	—	—	—	—	—	—	—	—
Fidelio/Arias	—	—	—	—	1x	—	—	1x	—	—	—

Other

	1928	1929	1930	1931	1932	1933	1934	1935	1936	1937	1938
Ah! perfido	—	—	—	1x	—	—	—	—	—	—	—
Adelaida	—	—	—	—	—	—	1x	—	1x	—	—
Calm Sea	—	—	—	—	—	—	—	—	—	—	—
German Dances	—	—	1x	—	—	—	—	—	—	—	—
TOTAL	**28**	**42**	**37**	**43**	**25**	**26**	**32**	**25**	**45**	**37**	**34**

CHART B	**1939**	**1940**	**1941**	**1942**	**1943**	**1944**	**1945**	**1946**	**1947**	**1948**	**1949**

Symphonies

	1939	1940	1941	1942	1943	1944	1945	1946	1947	1948	1949
Symphony 1	—	1x	—	—	—	—	—	1x	—	—	—
Symphony 2	—	2x	—	—	—	—	1x	1x	—	—	2x
Symphony 3	1x	1x	1x	—	—	1x	—	2x	—	2x	1x
Symphony 4	—	—	—	—	—	—	—	1x	—	1x	—
Symphony 5	6x	4x	2x	1x	1x	3x	2x	3x	4x	3x	4x
Symphony 6	—	—	1x	1x	—	1x	1x	1x	1x	—	2x
Symphony 7	2x	—	1x	—	—	—	—	2x	—	1x	1x
Symphony 8	1x	—	3x	1x	2x	—	2x	1x	—	—	2x
Symphony 9	4x	4x	—	—	—	—	—	2x	—	3x	2x

(*Continued*)

Table 3. (*Continued*)

Concertos

	1939	1940	1941	1942	1943	1944	1945	1946	1947	1948	1949
Violin Con.	—	—	1x	1x	—	—	1x	2x	3x	—	—
Piano Con. 1	—	2x	1x	—	—	—	2x	1x	—	1x	—
Piano Con. 2	—	—	—	—	—	—	—	1x	—	—	—
Piano Con. 3	—	1x	1x	1x	1x	—	—	2x	—	—	1x
Piano Con. 4	1x	1x	—	—	1x	1x	1x	1x	—	—	1x
Piano Con. 5	2x	2x	2x	1x	1x	1x	—	1x	—	1x	1x
Triple Con.	—	—	—	—	—	—	—	—	—	1x	—

Overtures

	1939	1940	1941	1942	1943	1944	1945	1946	1947	1948	1949
Consecration of the House	—	—	1x	—	—	—	—	—	—	—	—
Coriolan	2x	2x	1x	—	3x	—	—	3x	—	—	—
Egmont	3x	2x	1x	—	—	2x	1x	1x	—	—	1x
Fidelio	—	—	—	—	—	—	—	1x	—	—	—
King Stephen	—	—	1x	—	—	—	—	1x	—	—	—
Leonore 1	—	—	1x	—	—	—	—	—	—	—	1x
Leonore 2	—	—	1x	—	—	—	—	—	—	—	—
Leonore 3	3x	5x	3x	2x	—	—	2x	3x	—	1x	1x
Nameday	—	—	1x	—	—	—	—	—	—	—	—
Prometheus	1x	1x	—	—	—	—	1x	—	—	—	—

Incidental Music

	1939	1940	1941	1942	1943	1944	1945	1946	1947	1948	1949
Egmont	1x	2x	1x	1x	—	—	1x	1x	—	1x	—
Egmont/Arias	2x	—	—	—	—	—	2x	—	—	—	—
Prometheus	—	—	1x	—	—	—	—	—	—	—	—
Ruins of Athens / "Turkish March"	3x	1x	—	—	1x	1x	—	—	—	4x	2x

Choral/Opera

	1939	1940	1941	1942	1943	1944	1945	1946	1947	1948	1949
Missa solemnis	—	3x	2x	—	—	—	—	—	—	—	—
Choral Fantasy	1x	—	1x	—	—	—	—	1x	—	1x	—
Fidelio/ Complete	—	—	2x	—	—	—	—	—	—	—	—
Fidelio/Arias	—	—	—	—	—	—	—	—	—	—	—

(*Continued*)

Table 3. (*Continued*)

Other	1939	1940	1941	1942	1943	1944	1945	1946	1947	1948	1949
Ah! perfido	—	—	—	—	—	—	—	—	—	—	—
Adelaida	—	—	—	—	—	—	—	—	—	—	—
Calm Sea	—	—	—	—	—	—	—	1x	—	—	—
German Dances	—	—	—	—	—	—	—	—	—	—	—
TOTAL	**33**	**34**	**30**	**9**	**10**	**10**	**17**	**34**	**8**	**20**	**22**

CHART C	**1950**	**1951**	**1952**	**1953**	**TOTAL PERFORMANCES (1928–1953)**
Symphonies					
Symphony 1	3x	1x	1x	1x	**14**
Symphony 2	—	2x	—	—	**12**
Symphony 3	2x	1x	—	3x	**45**
Symphony 4	2x	1x	—	3x	**16**
Symphony 5	5x	3x	6x	2x	**101**
Symphony 6	—	2x	—	—	**20**
Symphony 7	1x	2x	1x	3x	**31**
Symphony 8	2x	—	—	2x	**29**
Symphony 9	2x	—	3x	1x	**51**
Concertos					
Violin Con.	—	—	1x	—	**22**
Piano Con. 1	1x	—	1x	—	**15**
Piano Con. 2	1x	—	—	—	**3**
Piano Con. 3	—	1x	3x	—	**18**
Piano Con. 4	1x	—	—	—	**18**
Piano Con. 5	1x	1x	2x	—	**28**
Triple Con.	—	1x	—	—	**3**
Overtures					
Consecration of the House	—	—	—	—	**5**
Coriolan	2x	—	1x	—	**30**
Egmont	1x	—	3x	3x	**58**
Fidelio	—	1x	—	—	**6**
King Stephen	1x	—	—	—	**5**
Leonore 1	—	—	—	—	**2**

(*Continued*)

Table 3. (*Continued*)

Overtures					
Leonore 2	—	—	—	—	**2**
Leonore 3	—	—	—	—	**56**
Nameday	—	—	—	—	**1**
Prometheus	1x	—	—	1x	**7**
Incidental Music					
Egmont	2x	—	1x	2x	**44**
Egmont/Arias	—	—	—	—	**7**
Prometheus	—	—	—	—	**3**
Ruins of Athens / "Turkish March"	2x	—	—	4x	**24**
Choral/Opera					
Missa solemnis	—	—	—	—	**5**
Choral Fantasy	—	—	1x	2x	**8**
Fidelio/ Complete	—	1x	—	—	**3**
Fidelio/Arias	—	—	—	—	**2**
Other					
Ah! perfido	—	—	—	—	**1**
Adelaida	—	—	—	—	**2**
Calm Sea	—	—	—	—	**1**
German Dances	—	—	—	—	**1**
TOTAL	**30**	**17**	**24**	**27**	**699**

1. Arkhiv muzykal'noi biblioteki Gosudarstvennoi S.-Peterbugskoi filarmonii im. D. D. Shostakovicha/Alfavitnyi katalog: Betkhoven (1928–1953).

Table 4. Beethoven Performances by the Leningrad Radio Symphony Orchestra and Guest Artists, 1941–1944[1]

Date	**Work**
October 1941	Symphony no. 9 in D minor (2x)
November 9, 1941	Symphony no. 9 in D minor
December 7, 1941	Symphony no. 5 in C minor
December 15, 1941	unidentified piano works (Kamenskii)
January 12, 1942	Symphony no. 9 in D minor

(*Continued*)

Table 4. (*Continued*)

July 4, 1942	Symphony no. 5 in C minor
October 10, 1942	Symphony no. 4 in B-flat
October 25, 1942	unidentified piano works (Kamenskii)
December 1, 1942	Symphony no. 5 in C minor
January 23, 1943	unidentified piano works (Kamenskii)
February 19, 1943	unidentified piano works (Kamenskii)
February 27, 1943	Piano Concerto no. 5 in E-flat (Yudina)
June 2, 1943	Symphony no. 4 in B-flat
September 25, 1943	unidentified piano works (Yudina)
November 15, 1943	*Diabelli Variations* (Gilels)
January 15, 1944	Piano Concerto no. 5 in E-flat (Edel'man)

1. V. M. Bogdanov-Berezovskii and I. Gusin, ed., *V gody velikoi otechestvennoi voiny: vospominaniia, materialy* (Leningrad: Sovetskii kompozitor, 1959), 42–48, 94–111; A. N. Kriukov, *Muzyka v dni blokady: khronika* (St. Petersburg: Kompozitor, 2002), 55–492; A. N. Kriukov, *Muzyka v efire voennogo Leningrada* (St. Petersburg: Kompozitor, 2005), 26–260.

Table 5. Beethoven Performances by the Leningrad / St. Petersburg Philharmonia, 1954–2004[1]

Concertos		**Overtures**	
Piano no. 1	69x	*Coriolan*	45x
Piano no. 2	42x	*Fidelio*	7x
Piano no. 3	84x	*Egmont*	63x
Piano no. 4	79x	*King Stephen*	6x
Piano no. 5	88x	*Consecration of the House*	4x
Triple	23x	*Prometheus*	12x
Violin	74x	*Leonore 3*	56x
Total	**459**	**Total**	**193**
Symphonies			
No. 1	29x	No. 6	43x
No. 2	58x	No. 7	105x
No. 3	75x	No. 8	56x
No. 4	59x	No. 9	67x
No. 5	122x	**Total**	**614**
Other			
Adelaida	1x	Minuet no. 9	1x
Ah! perfido	1x	*Missa solemnis*	3x
Calm Sea	2x	Romances no. 1 and 2	14x
Choral Fantasy	24x	"Turkish March"	20x
Christ on the Mount of Olives	2x	Two Contredanses	1x

(*Continued*)

Table 5. (*Continued*)

Egmont	17x	Viennese Dances	1x
German Dances	1x	*Wellington's Victory*	1x
Mass in D	4x	Miscellaneous	11x
		Total	**104**

1. Arkhiv muzykal'noi biblioteki Gosudarstvennoi S.-Petersburgskoi filarmonii im. D. D. Shostakovicha/Alfavitnyi katalog: Betkhoven (1954–2004). This data does not include performances in other parts of the country or abroad, nor guest performances at the Philharmonia Hall by other Soviet/Russian ensembles or ensembles from abroad.

BIBLIOGRAPHY

Archives

Arkhiv Muzykal'noi Biblioteki Gos. S-Peterburgskoi Filarmonii im. D. D. Shostakovicha
Alfavitnyi katalog: Bethoven / catalogue box 1 (Berlioz-Betkhoven), catalogue box 2 (Betkhoven-Bize)
Papka No. 1 (1904–1919)/Paka No. 2 (June–December 1921)
Programmy simfonicheskikh kontsertov S. Kusevitskogo, 1910–1916 gg. / Inventor NN. 18229–18234
Russkaia Gos. Biblioteka im. M. Saltykova-Shchedrina/Rukopisnyi Otdel
F. 41 (Balakirev), op. 1, ed. khr. 1849
F. 124 (Vaksel'), ed. khr. 1220
F. 187 (Glazunov), ed. khr. 657, 658, 703, 790
F. 355 (Kobeliatskaia), ed. khr. 139
F. 406 (Kurbanov), ed. khr. 77, 337
F. 437 (Liszt), ed. khr. 20
F. 451 (Liapunov), op. 1, ed. khr. 364
F. 539 (Odoevskii), ed. khr. 605
F. 773 (Timofeev), ed. khr. 55, 131, 217, 271
F. 816 (Findeizen), op. 1, ed. khr. 186, 321, 441, 444, 581, 689, 3206, 3211; op. 4, ed. khr. 3153
S.-Peterburgskaia Gos. Konservatoriia im. N. A. Rimskogo-Korsakova / Spravochno-Bibliograficheskii Otdel

Beethoven

Albrecht, Theodore, trans. and ed. *Letters to Beethoven and Other Correspondence*, II (1813–1823). Lincoln: University of Nebraska Press, 1996.
Alekseev, M. P. "Beethoven in der russischen schőnen Literatur des 19.Jhr." *Germanoslavica*, II, 2 (1932–33): 163–79; 3, 301–27.
Al'shvang, A. *Bethoven*. Moscow: Gosudarstvennoe muzykal'noe izdatel'stvo, 1952.
Altaev, A. *Betkhoven*. Petrograd-Moscow: Kniga, 1924.
Autexien, Phillipe A. *Beethoven: The Composer as Hero*. Translated by Carey Lovelace. New York: Abrams, 1992.
Bekker, Paul. *Beethoven*. Translated by M. M. Bozman. London: Denet and Sons, 1925.
"Betkhoven," *Bol'shaia sovetskaia entsiklopediia*, VI. Moscow: Sovetskaia entsiklopediia, 1927.
Betkhovenskii biulleten' 1. Moscow: Betkhovenskii komitet pri Narkomprose RSFSR, 1927.
Braudo, E. M. *Betkhoven i ego vremia: opyt muzykal'no-sotsiologicheskogo issledovaniia*. Moscow: Muzykal'nyi sektor gosudarstvennogo izdatel'stva, 1927.
Broyles, Michael. *Beethoven in America*. Bloomington: Indiana University Press, 2011.
Brumberg, E. V. *Betkhoven*. Rostov-na-Donu, Russia: Azovo-Cherenomorskaia filarmoniia, 1935.
Burnham, Scott. *Beethoven Hero*. Princeton, NJ: Princeton University Press, 1995.

Burnham, Scott, and Michael P. Steinberg, ed. *Beethoven and His World*. Princeton, NJ: Princeton University Press, 2000.

Caeyers, Jan. *Beethoven: A Life*. Translated by Brent Annable. Oakland: University of California Press, 2020.

Cheshikhin, V. *Betkhoven*. Riga, Latvia: Rigaer tageblatt, 1892.

Clubbe, John. *Beethoven: The Relentless Revolutionary*. New York: W. W. Norton, 2019.

Comini, Allesandra. *The Changing Image of Beethoven: A Study in Mythmaking*. New York: Rizzoli, 1985.

Cooper, Barry. *Beethoven*. Oxford: Oxford University Press, 2000.

———, ed. *The Beethoven Compendium: A Guide to Beethoven's Life and Music*. London: Thames and Hudson, 1991.

Davidov, I. A. *Betkhoven, ego zhiznn' i muzykal'naia deiatel'nost': biograficheskii ocherk*. St. Petersburg: Obshchestvennaia pol'za, 1893.

Dennis, David B. *Beethoven in German Politics, 1870–1989*. New Haven, CT: Yale University Press, 1996.

DeNora, Tia. *Beethoven and the Construction of Genius: Musical Politics in Vienna, 1792–1803*. Berkeley: University of California Press, 1995.

Engel, Iu. *Ocherki po istorii muzyki*. Moscow: Kliuchkov, 1911.

Engel, Robert. "Beethoven und Russland." *Ősteuropa*, III (1927/28): 276–84.

Errico, Eduard. *Zhizn' Betkhovena*. 4th ed. Translated by A. Edel'man. Moscow: Muzyka, 1975.

Genika, R. *Betkhoven: znachenie ego tvorchestva v oblasti fortepiannoi kompozitsii*. St. Petersburg: Russkaia muzykal'naia gazeta, 1899.

Gingol'd, L. *V poedinke s sudboi: georicheskie dni Liudviga van Betkhovena*. 2nd ed. Moscow: Muzyka, 1973.

Glebov, I. *Betkhoven (1770–1827)*, NRL, Otdel rukopisei, F. 816 (Findeizen), op. 4, ed. khr. 3153, l. 5–9.

Gruber, R. I., et al. *Muzyka frantsuzskoi revoliutsii XVIII veka: Betkhoven*. Moscow: Muzyka, 1967.

Herttrich, Ernest. *Liudwig van Beethoven: An Illustrated Biography*. Bonn, Germany: Beethoven-Haus, 2000.

Il'inskii, A. A. *Betkhoven: zhizn' i tvorchestvo*. Moscow: Mashistov, 1909.

Ivanov-Boretskii, M. V. *Betkhoven (k stoletiiu so dnia smerti, 1827–1927 g.g.): biograficheskii ocherk*. Moscow: Muzykal'nyi sektor gosudarstvennogo izdatel'stva, 1927.

Johnson, James H. "Beethoven and the Birth of Romantic Musical Experience in France." *19th Century Music*, XV, 1 (Summer 1991): 23–35.

Karasevicha, S. *Kartiny iz zhizni Betkhovena*. St. Petersburg: Suvorin, 1901.

Karintsev, N. *Betkhoven (kartiny iz zhizni)*. 4th ed. Moscow: Muzgiz, 1936.

Ken, A. G. [A. Junker]. *Betkhoven: zhizn', lichnost', tvorchestvo*, 3 vol. St. Petersburg: Orlov, 1909–10.

Kerman, Joseph, and Alan Tyson. *The New Grove Beethoven*. New York: W. W. Norton, 1983.

Kerst, Friedrich, and Henry E. Krehbiel, ed. *Beethoven: The Man and the Artist as Revealed in His Own Words*. New York: Dover, 1905/1964.

Khokhlovkina, A. *Betkhoven*. Moscow: Muzgiz, 1955.

———. "Betkhoven i russkaia muzykal'naia kul'tura." *Sovetskaia muzyka*, XVI/3 (March 1952): 43–49.

Kinderman, William. *Beethoven*. 2nd ed. Oxford: Oxford University Press, 2009.

———. *Beethoven: A Political Artist in Revolutionary Times*. Chicago: University of Chicago Press, 2020.

Klimovitskii, A. "Betkhoven." *Muzykal'nyi Peterburg*, I. St. Petersburg: Kompozitor, 2000.

Knight, Frida. *Beethoven and the Age of Revolution*. New York: International, 1973.
Korganov, V. D. *Betkhoven (1770–1827)*. Erivan, Armenia: Gosizdata, 1927.
———. *Betkhoven: biograficheskii etiud*. St. Petersburg-Moscow: Vol'f, 1910.
Kremlev, B. *Betkhoven*. Moscow: Molodaia gvardiia, 1961.
Kuzminskii, I. M. *Stoletie rozhdeniia Betkhovena*. Odessa, Ukraine: Odesskie liubiteli muzyki, 1870.
Liudvig fon-Betkhoven. Moscow: Obshchestvo rasprostraniia poleznykh knig, 1878.
Liudvig van Betkhoven: zhizn', tvorchestvo, okruzhenie. Moscow: Muzyka, 1971.
Lockwood, Lewis. *Beethoven: The Music and the Life*. New York: W. W. Norton, 2003.
———. *Beethoven's Lives: The Biographical Tradition*. Woodbridge, UK: Boydell, 2020.
Mai, François Martin. *Diagnosing Genius: The Life and Death of Beethoven*. Montreal: McGill-Queen's University Press, 2007.
Marek, George R. *Beethoven: Biography of a Genius*. New York: Funk and Wagnalls, 1961.
Martin, Russell. *Beethoven's Hair*. New York: Broadway Books, 2000.
Matthews, Denis. *Beethoven*. New York: Vintage Books, 1988.
Misch, Ludwig. *Beethoven Studies*. Norman: University of Oklahoma Press, 1953.
Morris, Edmund. *Beethoven: The Universal Composer*. New York: Harper Collins, 2005.
Nettle, Paul. *The Beethoven Encyclopedia: His Life and Art from A to Z*. New York: Citadel, 1964.
Newman, Ernest. *The Unconscious Beethoven: An Essay in Musical Psychology*. New York: Alfred A. Knopf, 1927.
Nikolaeva, N. S. *Liudvig van Betkhoven (1770–1970)*. Moscow: Znanie, 1970.
Orga, Ates. *Beethoven*. London: Omnibus, 1983.
Orlova, N. A. *O velikom muzykante Betkhovene*. St. Petersburg: Sokolov, 1873.
Paskhalov, Viacheslav. "Russkaia tematika v proizvedenniakh Betkhovena." *Russkaia kniga o Betkhovene*, edited by K. A. Kuznetsov. Moscow: Muzykal'nyi sektor gosudarstvennoe izdatel'stvo, 1927.
Popova, T. *Liudvig van Betkhoven: zhizn' i tvorchestvo*. Moscow: Komitet po delam iskusstv pri SNK SSSR, 1940.
Pshibyshevskii, B. *Betkhoven: opyt issledovaniia*. Moscow: Gosudarstvennoe muzykal'noe izdatel'stvo, 1932.
Ratskaia, Ts. *Betkhoven (1770–1827): kratkii ocherk*. Moscow: Profizdat, 1938.
Rokotov, A. *Smert' Betkhovena*. Moscow: Mashishtov, 1904.
Rolland, Romain. *Beethoven: The Creator*. Translated by Ernest Newman. New York: Harpers, 1964.
Rostislava [F. M. Tolstoi]. *Liudvig van Betkhoven: biograficheskii otchet*. Moscow: Otdel izdatel'stva i knizhnoi torgovli Moskovskogo Soveta R. i K.D., 1919.
Rozen, D. *Betkhoven*. Odessa, Ukraine: Odes'ka Oblasna derzhavna filarmoniia, 1938.
Russkaia muzykal'naia gazeta, 3–4, January 15, 1918; 5–6, February 15, 1918.
Sachs, Harvey. *The Ninth: Beethoven and the World in 1824*. New York: Random House, 2010.
Schauffler, Robert Haven. *Beethoven: The Man Who Freed Music*. New York: Tudor, 1947.
Schmidt-Gorg, Joseph, and Hans Schmidt, ed. *Ludwig van Beethoven: Bicentennial Edition, 1770–1970*. Hamburg, Germany: Deutsche Gramophon, 1970.
Shor, D. [O Betkhovene]. In *Vospominaniia*, edited by Iulii Matveev. Moscow: Mosty kul'tury, 2001, pp. 277–78.
———. "Pamiati Betkhovena." *Russkie vedomosti*, December 17, 1910.
Siepmann, Jeremy. *Beethoven: His Life and Music*. Norfolk, UK: Naxos Books, 2006.

Siniaver, L. *Betkhoven; lektsiia*. Moscow-Leningrad: Gosudarstvennoe muzykal'noe izdatel'stvo, 1950.
Solomon, Maynard. *Beethoven*. 2nd rev. ed. New York: Schirmer Books, 1998.
———. *Beethoven Essays*. Cambridge, MA: Harvard University Press, 1988.
Stanley, Glenn, ed. *The Cambridge Companion to Beethoven*. Cambridge: Cambridge University Press, 2000.
Strel'nikov, N. *Betkhoven*. Moscow: Gosudarstvennoe izdatel'stvo, 1922.
Suchet, John. *Beethoven: The Man Revealed*. New York: Atlantic Monthly, 2012.
Sullivan, J. W. N. *Beethoven: His Spiritual Development*. New York: Vintage, 1955.
Swafford, Jan. *Beethoven: Anguish and Triumph*. New York: Houghton Mifflin Harcourt, 2014.
Tchaikovsky, P. I. "Betkhoven i ego vremia." *Grazhdanin*, 7 (February 11, 1872): 211–16; 8 (February 19, 1872): 245–49; 11 (March 12, 1872): 356–58; 12 (March 19, 1872): 386–89.
Thayer, Alexander Wheelock. *Thayer's Life of Beethoven*, edited by Elliott Forbes. Princeton: Princeton University Press, 1967.
Tovey, Donald Francis. *Beethoven*. Oxford: Oxford University Press, 1945.
Tunbridge, Laura. *Beethoven: A Life in Nine Pieces*. New York: Penguin Random House, 2020.
U Betkhovena. Ekaterinoslav, Ukraine: Iakovlev, 1902.
Vainkop, Iu. *Betkhoven i ego tvorchestvo*. 2nd rev. ed. Leningrad: Triton, 1934.
———. *L. Betkhoven i ego tvorchestvo*. Leningrad: Volodarskii, 1938.
———. *Pamiatka o Betkhovene (k stoletiiu so dnia smerti), 1827–1927*. Leningrad: Triton, 1927.
Val'ter, V. "Ideinoe soderzhanie Betkhovenskoi muzyki. (Paul Bekker, "Beethoven")." *Russkaia muzykal'naia gazeta*, XX, 8–9 (February 24–March 3, 1913): 210–15; 10 (March 10, 1913): 242–45.
Vetter, Walther. "Beethoven und Russland." In *Mythos-Melos-Musica*. Leipzig: Deutscher verlag fűr Musik, 1957.
Von Breuning, Gerhard. *Memories of Beethoven: From the House of the Black-Robed Spaniards*. Edited by Maynard Solomon and translated Henry Mins and Maynard Solomon. Cambridge: Cambridge University Press, 1992.
Wagner, Richard. *Eine Pilgerfahrt zu Beethoven*. Stuttgart, Germany: Kohlhammer, 1944.
Walden, Edward. *Beethoven's Immortal Beloved: Solving the Mystery*. Lanham, MD: Scarecrow, 2011.
Wallace, Robin. *Beethoven and His Critics: Aestheteic Dilemmas and Resolutions during the Composer's Lifetime*. Cambridge: Cambridge University Press, 1986.
———. *Hearing Beethoven: A Story of Musical Loss and Discovery*. Chicago: University of Chicago Press, 2018.
Zgorzh, Antonin. *Odin protiv sud'by: povest' o zhizni Liudviga van Betkhovena*. Moscow: Pravda, 1987.

Bibliography

Alekseev, M. P., and Ia. Z. Berman. "Kratkii bibliograficheskii ukazatel' vazhneishei literatury o Betkhovene." *Muzyka i revoliutsiia*, 3(15) (March 1927): 41–44.
———. *Betkhoven: materialy dlia bibliograficheskogo ukazatelia russkoi literatury o nem*. Odessa, Ukraine: Odespoligraf, 1927.
Al'shvang, A. "Kratkaia bibliografiia epistoliarnogo nalediia Betkhovena i literatury o Betkhovene." In *Betkhoven: ocherk zhizni i tvorchestva*, 3rd ed. Moscow: Muzyka, 1966.
Bartlett, Rosamund. *Wagner and Russia*. Cambridge: Cambridge University Press, 1995.
Dorfműller, Kurt, ed. *Beiträge Beethoven—Bibliograhie*. Munich: Henle, 1978.

Findeizen, N. "Spisok russkikh knig po muzyke, izdannykh v 1773–1873 gg." In *Muzykal'naia starina: sbornik statei i materialov dlia istorii muzyki v Rossii*, II. St. Petersburg: Kate, 1903.
Gerashko, L. V., et al. *Muzyka i muzykanty. Tvorcheskie i biograficheskie materialy v fondakh i kollektsiiakh rukopisnogo otdela Pushkinskogo Doma. XVIII-XX vv. Ukazatel'*. St. Petersburg: Bulanin, 2003.
Grigorovich, N. N. "Bibliografiia literatury o Betkhovene na russkom iazyke." In *Betkhoven: sbornik statei*, edited by N. L. Fishman, II. Moscow: Muzyka, 1972.
Horecky, Paul L., ed. *Basic Russian Publications: A Selected and Annotated Bibliography on Russia and the Soviet Union*. Chicago: University of Chicago Press, 1962.
Kirillina, Larissa. "A New List of Beethoven Sources in Russia." *Beethoven Journal*, XIV, 1 (Summer 1999): 16–26; 2 (Winter 1999): 65–84.
Livanova, T. N., ed. *Muzykal'naia bibliografiia russkoi periodicheskoi pechati XIX veka*, I–VI. Moscow: Gosudarstvennoe muzykal'noe izdatel'stvo/Sovetskii kompozitor, 1960–74.
Petrovskaia, I. F. *Teatr i muzyka v Rossii XIX-nachala XX veka: obzor bibliograficheskikh i spravochnykh materialov*. Leningrad: LGITMiK, 1984.
Putevoditel' po arkhivnym fondam Leningradskogo gosudarstvennogo instituta teatra, muzyki i kinematografii. Leningrad: LGITMiK, 1984.
Schwarz, Boris. "Beethoveniana in Soviet Russia." *Musical Quarterly*, XLVII, 1 (January 1961): 4–21.
———. "More Beethoveniana in Soviet Russia." *Musical Quarterly*, XLIX, 2 (April 1963): 143–49.

Biography

Aksakov, S. T.

Annenkova, E. "Tvorcheskii put' Sergeia Timofeevicha Aksakova." In *Sobranie sochinenii*, by S. T. Aksakov. Moscow: Khudozhestvennaia literatura, 1986.
Bogdanov, V. A. "Zhizn' i tvorchestvo S. T. Aksakova." In *Izbrannye sochineniia*, edited by S. T. Aksakov. Moscow: Sovremennik, 1985.
Mashinkskii, S. "Sergei Timofeevich Aksakov." In *Sobranie sochinenii*, I, edited by S. T. Aksakov. Moscow: Gosudarstvennoe izdatel'stvo khudozhestvennoi literatury, 1956.

Aliab'ev, A. A.

Shteinpress, B. *Stranitsy iz zhizni A. A. Aliab'eva*. Moscow: Gosudarstevennoe muzykal'noe izdatel'stvo, 1956.

Al'shvang, A.

Bernandt, G. "A. A. Al'shvang." *Sovetskaia muzyka*, IX, 1 (January 1941): 59–65.

Arnol'd, Iu.

L. "Iurii Arnol'd. Ocherk ego muzykal'noi deiatel'nosti." *Russkaia muzykal'naia gazeta*, III, 12 (December 1896): 1564–70.
Vospominaniia Iuriia Arnol'da, 3 vol. Moscow: n.p., 1892–93.

Asaf'ev, B. V.

Bogdanov-Berezovskii, V. "Put' kompozitora i uchenogo (k 25-letiiu tvorcheskoi i nauchnoi deiatel'nosti zasluzhennogo deiatelia iskusstv B. V. Asaf'eva)." *Zvezda*, VI (1935): 166–75.

Bakunin, M. A.

Bakunin, M. A. *The Confession of Michael Bakunin*. Translated by Robert C. Howes. Ithaca, NY: Cornell University Press, 1977.

Berlin, Isaiah. *Russian Thinkers*. New York: Viking, 1978.

Belinskii, V. G.

Annenkov, P. V. *The Extraordinary Decade: Literary Memoirs*, edited by Arthur P. Mandel. Ann Arbor: University of Michigan Press, 1968.

Berlin, Isaiah. *Russian Thinkers*. New York: Viking, 1978.

D'iachenko, M. "Evoliutsiia literaturnykh i obshchestvennykh vzgliadov Belinskogo." *Russkaia starina*, XLII, 5 (May 1911): 291–328.

Benua, A.

Bernandt, G. *Aleksandr Benua i muzyka*. Moscow: Sovetskii kompozitor, 1969.

Blok, A.

Khoprova, T., and M. Dunaevskii, ed. *Blok i muzyka: khronika, notografiia, bibliografiia*. Leningrad: Sovetskii kompozitor, 1980.

Borodin, A. P.

Suvorin, A. S., ed. *Aleksandr Porfir'evich Borodin: ego zhizn', perepiska i muzykal'nye stat'i, 1834–1887*. St. Petersburg: Suvorin, 1889.

Bulgarin, F. V.

Altunian, A. G. *"Politicheskie mneniia" Faddeia Bulgarina: ideino-stilisticheskii analiz zapisok F. V. Bulgarina k Nikolaiu, I*. Moscow: URAO, 1998.

Bulgarin, F. *Vospominaniia*. Moscow: Zakharov, 2001.

Grech, N. I. "Faddei Venediktovich Bul'garin, 1789–1859." *Russkaia starina*, II, 2 (1871): 483–523.

Lemke, M. *Ocherk istorii russkoi tsenzury i zhurnalistiki XIX stoletiia*. St. Petersburg: Trud, 1904.

Reitblat, A. I. *Vidok Figliarin: pis'ma i agenturnye zapiski F. V. Bulgarina v III otdelenie*. Moscow: Novoe literaturnoe obozrenie, 1998.

Chaadayev, P. Ia.

Stasov, V. V. "Petr Iakovlevich Chaadaev; biograficheskii orcherk." *Russkaia starina*, XXXIX, 1 (January 1908): 33–54; XXXIX, 2 (February 1908): 271–97.

Chemberdzhi, V.

V dome muzyka zhila: memuary o muzykantakh. Moscow: Agraf, 2002.

Chernyshevskii, N. G.

Reingardt, N. V. "N. G. Chernyshevskii (po vospominaniiam i rasskazam raznykh lits)." *Russkaia starina*, XXXVI, 2 (February 1905): 447–76.

Cui, Ts. A.

"Ts. A. Kiui (k 50-letiiu muzykal'noi deiatel'nosti)." *Russkaia starina*, XLI, 2 (February 1910): 363–66.

Dostoevsky, F. M.

Belov, S. V. *Peterburg Dostoevskogo: nauchnoe izdanie*. St. Petersburg: Aleteiia, 2002.
———. *Dostoevskii i muzykal'no-teatral'noe iskusstvo: issledovanie*. Leningrad: Sovetskii kompozitor, 1981.
Dostoevsky, Anna. *Dostoevsky Reminiscences*. Translated by Beatrice Stillman. New York: Liveright, 1975.
Frank, Joseph. *Dostoevsky*, 5 vol. Princeton, NJ: Princeton University Press, 1976–2002.
Gozenpud, A. *Dostoevskii i muzyka*. Leningrad: Muzyka, 1971.
Kriukov, P. "F. M. Dostoevskii i muzyka." *Sovetskaia muzyka*, XXXV, 11 (November 1971): 87–94.
Sekirin, Peter. *The Dostoevsky Archive*. Jefferson, NC: McFarland, 1997.

Findeizen, N. F.

Dnevniki, 1892–1901. St. Petersburg: Dmitrii Bulanin, 2004.
Iz moikh vospominanii. St. Petersburg: Rossiiskaia natsional'naia biblioteka, 2004.

Glinka, M. I.

Glinka, M. I. *Sbornik statei*. Moscow: Gosudarstvennoe muzykal'noe izdatel'stvo, 1958.
Literaturnoe nasledie, II. Leningrad: Gosudarstvennoe muzykal'noe izdatel'stvo, 1953.
Martynov, I. "Glinka i Betkhoven." In *O liubimom iskusstve*. Moscow: Sovetskii kompozitor, 1989.
"Poslednie gody zhizni i konchina Mikhaila Ivanovicha Glinki (vospominaniia sestry ego, L. I. Shestakovoi), 1854–1857." In *Zapiski Mikhaila Ivanovicha Glinki i perepiska ego s rodnymi i druz'iami*. St. Petersburg: Duborin, 1887.
Stasov, V. V. *Mikhail Ivanovich Glinka*. Moscow: Gosudarstvennoe muzykal'noe izdatel'stvo, 1953.
Zapiski Mikhaila Ivanovicha Glinki, 1804–1854. St. Petersburg: Russkaia starina, 1871.

Gogol', N. V.

Gippius, V. V. *Gogol*. Translated by Robert A. Maguire. Ann Arbor, MI: Ardis, 1981.
Maguire, Robert A. *Exploring Gogol*. Stanford, CA: Stanford University Press, 1994.
Neelov, P. "Gogol' i muzyka." *Muzykal'nyi truzhenik*, III, 6 (March 15, 1909): 1–2.
Tiumeneva, G. A. *Gogol' i muzyka*. Moscow: Muzyka, 1966.
Troyat, Henri. *Divided Soul: The Life of Gogol*. Translated by Nancy Amphoux. New York: Minerva, 1975.

Golitsyn, N. B.

Alekseev, M. "Russkie vstrechi i sviazi Betkhovena." In *Russkaia kniga o Betkhovene: k stoletiiu so dnia smerti kompozitora (1827–1927)*, edited by K. A. Kuznetsov, 92–100. Moscow: Muzykal'nyi sektor, 1927.
Ginzburg, L. *Istoriia violonchel'nogo iskusstva*, II. Moscow: Muzgiz, 1957.

———. "Liudvig van Betkhoven i N. B. Golitsyn." In *Betkhoven: sbornik statei*, II, edited by N. L. Fishman. Moscow: Muzyka, 1972.
———. "Ludwig van Beethoven und Nikolai Fűrst [*sic*] Golitzyn." *Ősterreichsische Musikzeitschrift*, IX, 10 (October 1964): 523–29.
Goriainov, Iu. S. *Liudvig van Betkhoven i kniaz Nikolai Golitsyn: k 200-letiiu so dnia rozhdeniia N. B. Golitsyna*. Belgorod, Russia: Bezelitsa, 1993.

Gor'kii, M.

Piksanov, N. "Gor'kii i muzyka." *Sovetskaia muzyka*, VII, 6 (June 1939): 61–70.
Shaporin, Iu. "M. Gor'kii i muzyka." *Sovetskaia muzyka*, VI, 6 (June 1938): 13–15.

Griboedov, A. S.

Voinova, A. "Griboedov-Muzykant." *Sovetskaia muzyka*, XLIII, 5 (May 1979): 89, 92.

Grigor'ev, A.

Egorov, B. F. "Apollon Grigor'ev—poet, prozaik, kritik." In *Sochineniia*, I, by A. Grigor'ev. Moscow: Khudozhestvennaia literatura, 1990.

Heifetz, J.

Kopytova, Galina. *Iasha Kheifets v Rossii: iz istorii muzykal'noi kul'tury Serebrianogo veka*. St. Petersburg: Kompozitor, 2004.

Herzen, A. I.

Berlin, Isaiah. *Russian Thinkers*. New York: Viking, 1978.
Bernandt, G. "Gertsen i muzyka." *Sovetskaia muzyka*, XXVI, 5 (May 1962): 77–84.
Ia, El'sberg. *Gertsen: zhizn' i tvorchestvo*. 3rd ed. Moscow: Khudozhestvennaia literatura, 1956.
Herzen, Alexander. *My Past and Thoughts: The Memoirs of Alexander Herzen*. Translated by Constance Garnett. New York: Alfred A. Knopf, 1968.
Malia, Martin. *Alexander Herzen and the Birth of Russian Socialism*. Cambridge, MA: Harvard University Press, 1961.

Iudina, M. V.

"K 100-letiiu so dnia rozhdeniia M. V. Iudinoi." In *Nevel'skii sbornik: stat'i i vospominaniia*, IV, edited by L. M. Maksimovskaia. St. Petersburg: Akropol', 1999.
Wilson, Elizabeth. *Playing with Fire: The Story of Maria Yudina, Pianist in Stalin's Russia*. New Haven, CT: Yale University Press, 2022.

Kashkin, N. D.

"N. D. Kashkin; biograficheskii ocherk." *Muzykal'nyi truzhenik*, III, 4 (February 15, 1909): 3.

Khomiakov, A. S.

Arsen'ev, N. "A. S. Khomiakov (ego lichnost' i mirovozrenie)." In *Izbrannye sochineniia*, by A. Khomiakov, 3–43. New York: Chekhov, 1955.
Egorov, B. F. "Poeziia A. S. Khomiakova." In *Stikhotvoreniia i dramy*, by A. S. Khomiakov, 5–56. Leningrad: Sovetskii pisatel', 1969.

Koshelev, V. A. "Paradoksy Khomiakova." In *Sochineniia*, I, by A. S. Khomiakov, 3–14. Moscow: Medium, 1994.

Kireevskii, I. V.

Dorn, N. *Kireevskii. Opyt kharakteristiki ucheniia i lichnosti*. Paris: [n.p.], 1938.
Kotel'nikov, V. "Literator-filosov." In *Izbrannye stat'i*, by I. V. Kireevskii, 5–28. Moscow: Sovremennik, 1984.
Mann, Iu. "Esteticheskaia evoliutsiia I. Kireevskogo." In *Kritika i estetika*, by I. V. Kireevskii, 7–39. Moscow: Iskusstvo, 1979.

Koussevitzky, S.

Iusefovich, V. A. *Sergei Kusevitskii: russkie gody*, I. Moscow: Iazyki slavianskoi kul'tury, 2004.

Krylov, I.

Iampol'skii, I. *Krylov i muzyka, 1769–1969*. Moscow: Muzyka, 1970.
Korovin, V. *Poet i mudrets: kniga ob Ivane Krylove*. Moscow: Terra, 1996.
N. L. Stepanov. "I. A. Krylov." In *Sochineniia*, I, by I. A. Krylov, 5–35. Moscow: Khudozhestvennaia literatura, 1969.
Stepanov, Nikolay. *Ivan Krylov*. New York: Twayne, 1973.

Lenin, V. I.

Dreiden, S. "Lenin slushaet Betkhovena." *Sovetskaia muzyka*, XXVII, 4 (April 1963): 5–11.
Fotieva, L. A. *Iz zhizni V. I. Lenina*. Moscow: Politicheskaia literatura, 1967.
Gol'denshtein, M. *Muzyka v zhizni Vladimira Il'icha Lenina*. Leningrad: Sovetskii kompozitor, 1959.
Gor'kii, M. *Sobranie sochineniia*, XVII. Moscow: AN SSSR, 1952.
Izvestiia Arkhangel'skogo gubrebkoma i Arkhgubkoma RKP (b), April 23, 1920, 3.
Kedrov, M. *Iz krasnoi tetradi ob Il'iche*. Moscow: Politicheskaia literatura, 1957.
Krupskaia, N. K. *Vospominaniia o Lenine*. 2nd ed. Moscow: Politicheskaia literatura, 1968.
Serebriakova, G. *Svet neugasimyi*. Moscow: Politicheskaia literatura, 1962.
Vinogradskaia, S. *Iskorka: rasskaz o V. I. Lenine*. Moscow: Detskaia literatura, 1965.

Lenz, V.

Findeizen, N. "Vil'gel'm fon Lenz (k 25-letiiu ego smerti)." *Russkaia muzykal'naia gazeta*, XV, 3 (January 20, 1908): 66–71; 6 (February 10, 1908): 157–60.

Lermantov, M. Iu.

Andronikov, I. "Muzykal'nost' Lermontova." *Sovetskaia muzyka*, XXVIII, 10 (October 1964): 52–58.
Glovatskii, B. *Lermontov i muzyka*. Moscow-Leningrad: Muzyka, 1964.

Lunacharskii, A. V.

Dreiden, S. *Muzyka-revoliutsii*. 2nd ed. Moscow: Sovetskii kompozitor, 1970.
Elkin, A. *Lunacharskii*. Moscow: Molodaia gvardiia, 1967.
Fitzpatrick, Sheila. "A. V. Lunacharsky: Recent Soviet Interpretations and Republications." *Soviet Studies*, XVIII, 1 (January 1967): 267–89.
———*Education and Social Mobility in the Soviet Union, 1921–1934*. Cambridge: Cambridge University Press, 1979.

——"Lunacharskii." *Soviet Studies* 20, no. 4 (April 1969): 527–35.
——*The Commissariat of Enlightenment: Soviet Organization of Education and the Arts under Lunacharsky, October 1917–1921.* Cambridge: Cambridge University Press, 1970.
Glagoleva, Nina A. *O Lunacharskom: issledovaniia, vospominaniia.* Moscow: Znanie, 1976.
Gryaznukhina, Tatiana V., and Alexander G. Gryaznukhin. "Triumph and Tragedy of People's Commissar A. V. Lunacharsky." *Byloe gody,* 2014, no. 31 (1): 43–48.
Kairov, I. A. *A. V. Lunacharskii—vydaiushchiisia deiatel' sotsialisticheskogo prosveshcheniia.* Moscow: Prosveshchenie, 1966.
Khalatov, A. B., ed. *Pamiati A. V. Lunacharskogo, 1875–1933.* Moscow: Moskovskii dom, 1935.
Kokhno, Igor P. *Cherty portreta: stranitsy zhizni i deiatel'nosti A. V. Lunacharskogo.* Minsk, Belarus: Izdatel'stvo BGU im. V. I. Lenina, 1972.
Lebedev-Polianskii, Pavel I. *A. V. Lunacharskii: biograficheskii ocherk k piatidesiatiletiiu so dnia rozhdeniia.* Moscow: Rabotnik prosveshcheniia, 1926.
Lunacharskaia, Irina A. "K nauchni biografii A. V. Lunacharskogo." *Russkaia literatura,* XX, 4 (April 1979): 110–27.
Lunacharskii, A. V. *Vospominaniia i vpechatleniia.* Moscow: Sovetskaia Rossiia, 1968.
O'Connor, Timothy E. *The Politics of Soviet Culture: Anatolii Lunacharskii.* Ann Arbor, MI: UMI Research, 1983.
Pel'she, R. A. "A. V. Lunacharskii." *Sovetskoe iskusstvo,* V, 5 (May 1926): 5–17.
Tait, A. I. *Lunacharsky: Poet of the Revolution (1875–1907).* Birmingham, UK: University of Birmingham, 1984.
Trifonov, Nikolai A. *Lunacharskii i sovetskaia literatura.* Moscow: Khudozhestvennaia literatura, 1974.
Trifonov, Nikolai A., and L. M. Khlebnikov, ed. *Anatolii Vasil'evich Lunacharskii: zhizn' i deiatel'nost' v fotografiiakh i dokumentakh.* Moscow: Plakat, 1975.

Mravinskii, E.

Amoh, Kenzo, ed. *Yevgeni Mravinsky: A Concert Listing, 1930–1987.* Tokyo: Japanese Mravinsky Society, 2000.
Amoh, Kenzo, and Frank Forman, comp. *Yevgeni Mravinsky Legacy: A Recording Listing, 1938–1984.* Tokyo: Japanese Mravinsky Society, 2000.
Zapiski na pamiat': dnevniki, 1918–1987. St. Petersburg: Iskusstvo-SPB, 2004.

Mussorgsky, M. P.

Emerson, Caryl. *The Life of Mussorgsky.* Cambridge: Cambridge University Press, 1999.
Orlova, A., ed. *Musorgsky Remembered.* Bloomington: Indiana University Press, 1991.

Napravnik, E. F.

E. F. Napravnik i ego sovremenniki. Leningrad: Muzyka, 1991.
Findeizen, N. L. "K biografii E. F. Napravnika." *Russkaia muzykal'naia gazeta,* XX, 37 (September 15, 1913): 782–87.
Stanislavskii, M. V. "Eduard Frantsevich Napravnik; monograficheskii etiud po povodu ego poluvekovogo sluzheniia russkomu muzykal'nomu iskusstvu, 1863–1913." *Russkaia starina,* XLV, 1 (January 1914): 114–31.

Nekrasov, N. A.

Ivanov, G. K., ed. *N. A. Nekrasov v muzyke.* Moscow: Sovetskii kompozitor, 1972.

Odoevskii, A. F.

Sirotin, A. N. "Kniaz A. F. Odoevskii; biograficheskii ocherk." *Istoricheskii vestnik*, IV, 5 (May 1883): 398–414.

Odoevskii, V. F.

Bernandt, G. B. "Ideia narodnosti v rabotakh V. F. Odoevskogo." *Sovetskaia muzyka*, XII, 3 (May 1948): 44–52.

———. "Iz istorii russkoi betkhoveniany." *Sovetskaia muzyka*, XXXIV, 12 (December 1970): 47–58.

———. *V. F. Odoevskii i Betkhoven; stranitsa iz istorii russkoi betkhoveniany*. Moscow: Sovetskii kompozitor, 1971.

———. "V. F. Odoevskii—muzykal'nyi pisatel'." *Sovetskaia muzyka*, VII, 8 (August 1939): 49–54.

———, ed. *V. F. Odoevskii: muzykal'no-literaturnoe nasledie*. Moscow: Gosudarstvennoe muzykal'noe izdatel'stvo, 1956.

Campbell, James Stuart. *V. F. Odoevsky and the Formation of Russian Musical Taste in the Nineteenth Century*. New York: Garland, 1989.

Cornwell, Neil. *The Life, Times and Milieu of V. F. Odoevsky, 1804–1869*. London: Athlone, 1986.

Findeizen, N. F. "Kniaz V. F. Odoevskii (k 100-letiiu so dnia ego rozhdeniia: 1803–1903)." *Russkaia muzykal'naia gazeta*, X, 33–34 (August 17–24, 1903): 722–29.

Golubeva, O. D. *V. F. Odoevskii*. St. Petersburg: Rossiiskaia natsional'naia biblioteka, 1995.

Iagolim, B. "Biblioteka Odoevskogo." *Sovetskaia muzyka*, XXXIII, 6 (June 1969): 96–99.

Ivanov-Korsunskii, V. "Drug russkoi muzyki (kn. V. F. Odoevskii)." *Ezhegodnik Imperatorskikh teatrov*, IV (1910): 48–74.

Murav'ev, V., ed. *V. F. Odoevskii: Poslednii kvartet Betkhovena; povesti, rasskazy, ocherki; Odoevskii v zhizni*. Moscow: Rabochii, 1982.

Odoevskii, Vladimir. *Dnevnik, Perepiska, Materialy*, edited by M. P. Rakhmanova. Moscow: Deka-VS, 2005.

Odoevsky, V. F. *Russian Nights*. Translated by Olga Koshansky-Olienikov and Robert E. Matlaw. New York: Dutton, 1965.

Piatkovskii, A. "Kniaz V. F. Odoevskii; literaturno-biograficheskii ocherk v sviazi s lichnymi vospominaniiami." *Istoricheskii vestnik*, I, 3 (March 1880): 505–31; 4 (April 1880): 681–712.

Protopopov, V. "V. F. Odoevskii kak muzykal'nyi kritik." In *Izbrannye muzykal'no-kriticheskie stat'i*, by V. F. Odoevskii, 3–18. Moscow-Leningrad: Gosudarstvennoe muzykal'noe izdatel'stvo, 1951.

Savelova, Z. "Betkhoven i Odoevskii." *Muzykal'noe obrazovanie*, I–II (1927): 115–17.

Ogarev, N. P.

N. P. Ogarev v vospominaniiakh sovremennikov. Moscow: Khudozhestvennaia literatura, 1989.

Voronina, N. I. *Ogarev i muzyka*. Saransk, Russia: Mordovskoe knizhnoe izdatel'stvo, 1981.

Pasternak, B.

Kats, B. A., ed. *Muzyka v tvorchestve, sud'be i v dome Borisa Pasternaka*. Leningrad: Sovetskii kompozitor, 1991.

Prokofiev, S.

Dnevnik, 1907–1918. Paris: DIAKOM, 2002.

Vospominaniia, pis'ma, stat'i: k 50-letiiu so dniia smerti. Moscow: Deka-VS, 2004.

Pushkin, A.

Eiges, I. *Muzyka v zhizni i tvorchestve Pushkina*. Moscow: Muzgiz, 1937.
Glumov, A. *Muzykal'nyi mir Pushkina*. Moscow-Leningrad: Gosudarstvennoe muzykal'noe izdatel'stvo, 1950.
Iakovlev, V. *Pushkin i muzyka*. 2nd ed. Moscow: Gosudarstvennoe muzykal'noe izdatel'stvo, 1957.
Katz, Boris, and Caryl Emerson, "Pushkin and Music." In *The Pushkin Handbook*, edited by David M. Bethea. Madison: University of Wisconsin Press, 2005.
Serapin, S. *Pushkin i muzyka*. Sofiia, Bulgaria: Iugo-vostok, 1926.
Simons, Ernst J. *Pushkin*. Cambridge, MA: Harvard University Press, 1937.
Troyat, Henri. *Pushkin*. Translated by Nancy Amphoux. New York: Doubleday, 1970.
Turygina, L. M. *A. S. Pushkin v oblasti muzyki*. St. Petersburg: Izdanie Pervorazriadnogo zhenskogo uchebnogo zavedeniia L. M. Turyginoi, 1899.
Vitale, Serena. *Pushkin's Button*. Translated by Ann Goldstein and Jon Rothschild. London: Fourth Estate, 1999.

Razumovskii, A. K.

J. S. S., "Andreas Rasoumowsky." *Monthly Musical Record*, XLVII (September 1917): 196–97.
Razumovskaia, Mariia. *Razumovskie pri tsarskom dvore: glavy iz rossiiskoi istorii, 1740–1815 g.g.* St. Petersburg: XXI Vek, 2004.
Vasil'chikov, A. A. *Semeistvo Razumovskikh*, III–IV, 1–2. St. Petersburg: Stasiulevich, 1882–87.

Rimsky-Korsakov, N. A.

Findeizen, N. *Nikolai Andreevich Rimskii-Korsakov: ocherk po muzykal'noi deiatel'nosti*. St. Petersburg-Moscow: Bessel', 1908.
Iastrebtsev, V. V. *Moi vospominaniia o Nikolae Andreeviche Rimskom-Korsakove*, 2 vol. St. Petersburg: Russkaia muzykal'naia gazeta, 1915.
Rimsky-Korsakoff, N. A. *My Musical Life*. Translated by Judah A. Joffe. New York: Tudor, 1923.

Rostropovich, M. L.

Akin'shii, Aleksandr. *Voronezhskie Rostropovichi: semeinyi portret na fone istorii*. Voronezh, Russia: Tsentr dukhovnogo vozrozhdeniia Chernozemnogo kraia, 2006.

Rozen, A. E.

Rozen, A. E. *Zapiski dekabrista*. Irkutsk, Russia: Vostochno-Sibirskoe izdatel'stvo, 1984.

Rubinshtein, A. G.

"Anton Grigor'evich Rubinshtein; iubilei ego poluvekovoi muzykal'no-artisticheskoi deiatel'nosti." *Russkaia starina*, XX, 11 (November 1889): 513–632.
Bessel', V. "Moi vospominaniia ob Antone Grigor'eviche Rubinshteine (1829–1894)." *Russkaia starina*, XXIX, 5 (May 1898): 351–74.
Davidova, M. "Vospominaniia ob A. G. Rubinshteine." *Istoricheskii vestnik*, XX, 4 (April 1899): 76–95.

Findeizen, N. *Anton Grigor'evich Rubinshtein: ocherk ego zhizni i muzykal'noi deiatel'nosti*. St. Petersburg: Iurgenson, 1907.

———. "Pamiati A. G. Rubinshteina." *Russkaia muzykal'naia gazeta*, XXI, 45 (November 9, 1914): 802–7.

Kavos-Dekhtereva, S. *A. G. Rubinshtein: biograficheskii ocherk 1829–1894 g. i muzykal'nye lektsii (kurs fort'epiannoi literatury, 1888–1889)*. St. Petersburg: Stasiulevich, 1895.

Larosh, G. A. "Pamiati Antona Rubinshteina." *Ezhegodnik Imperatorskikh teatrov*, IV (1893–1894 Season): 436–46.

Lott, R. Allen. *From Paris to Peoria: How European Piano Virtuosos Brought Classical Music to the American Heartland*. Oxford: Oxford University Press, 2003.

Rubinshtein, A. G. *Avtobiograficheskie vospominaniia, 1829–1889 gg*. 2nd ed. St. Petersburg: Russkaia starina, 1889.

Taylor, Philip. *Anton Rubinstein: A Life in Music*. Bloomington: Indiana University Press, 2007.

Val'ter, V. "Anton Grigor'evich Rubinshtein; k dvadtsatiletiiu so dnia ego smerti." *Vestnik Evropy*, XLIX, 12 (December 1914): 294–304.

———. "A. G. Rubinshtein o muzyke." *Russkaia muzykal'naia gazeta*, XI, 43 (October 24, 1904): 976–81.

Rubinshtein, N. G.

"Pamiati N. G. Rubinshteina." *Muzyka i zhizn'*, V, 3 (March 1912).

Samarin, Iu. F.

Izbrannye proizvedeniia. Moscow: Rossiiskaia politicheskaia entsiklopediia, 1996.

Stat'i, vospominaniia, pis'ma, 1840–1876. Moscow: Terra, 1997.

Scriabin, A. N.

Bowers, Faubion. *Scriabin: A Biography*. 2nd rev. ed. Mineola, NY: Dover, 1996.

Serov, A. N.

Baskin, V. S. "A. N. Serov: biograficheskii ocherk." In *Russkie kompozitory*, III. Moscow: Iurgenson, 1890.

Bazunov, S. A. *A. N. Serov, ego zhizn' i muzykal'naia deiatel'nost': biograficheskii ocherk*. St. Petersburg: Obshchestvo pol'za, 1893.

Cherkashina, M. R. *Aleksandr Nikolaevich Serov*. Moscow: Muzyka, 1985.

Findeizen, N. *Aleksandr Serov: ego zhizn' i muzykal'naia deiatel'nost'*. 2nd rev. ed. Moscow: Iurgenson, 1904.

———. "Aleksandr Nikolaevich Serov; ocherk ego zhizni i muzykal'noi deiatel'nosti'." *Ezhegodnik Imperatorskikh teatrov*, VII (1897–1898 Season): 75–115.

———. "Muzykal'no-kriticheskaia deiatel'nost' Serova." *Russkaia muzykal'naia gazeta*, XIII, 4–5 (January 22–29, 1906): 106–20.

Khubov, G. "A. Serov—klassik russkoi muzykal'noi kritiki." *Sovetskaia muzyka*, VI, 9 (September 1938): 23–47; 10–11 (October–November 1938): 128–43.

———. *Zhizn' A. Serova*. Moscow-Leningrad: Gosudarstvennoe muzykal'noe izdatel'stvo, 1950.

Molchanov, M. M. "Aleksandr Nikolaevich Serov v vospominaniiakh starogo pravoveda." *Russkaia starina*, XIV, 8 (August 1883): 331–60.

Stasov, V. V. "Aleksandr Nikolaevich Serov; materialy dlia ego biografii, 1820–1871." *Russkaia starina*, VI, 8 (August 1875): 581–87.

Tolstoi, F. M. [Rostislav]. "Aleksandr Nikolaevich Serov, 1820–1871." *Russkaia starina*, V, 2 (February 1874): 339–80.
Zvantsev, K. "Aleksandr Nikolaevich Serov v 1857–1871 gg.; vospominaniia o nem i ego pis'ma." *Russkaia starina*, XIX, 8 (August 1888): 343–84; 9 (September 1888): 647–82.

Serov, A. N., and Serov, V. A.

Serova, V. S. *Kak ros moi syn*. Leningrad: Khudozhnik RSFSR, 1968.
———. *Serovy, Aleksandr Nikolaevich i Valentin Aleksandrovich: vospominaniia V. S. Serovoi*. St. Petersburg: Shipovnik, 1914.

Shaliapin, F. I.

Fedor Ivanovich Shaliapin: Al'bom-katalog iz fondov GTsTM im. A. A. Bakhrushina. Moscow: Gosudarstvennyi tsentral'nyi teatral'nyi muzei imeni A. A. Bakhrushina, 2012.

Shostakovich, D. D.

Fay, Laurel E. *Shostakovich: A Life*. Oxford: Oxford University Press, 2000.
Lesser, Wendy. *Music for Silenced Voices: Shostakovich and His Fifteen Quartets*. New Haven, CT: Yale University Press, 2011.
Wilson, Elizabeth. *Shostakovich: A Life Remembered*. Princeton, NJ: Princeton University Press, 1994.

Shteibel't, D.

Zolonitskaia, L. *Daniel Shteibel't v Rossii*. St. Petersburg: Rossiiskii institut istorii iskusstv, 2000.

Sollertinskii, I. I.

Mikheev, L., ed. *Pamiati I. I. Sollertinskogo: vospominaniia, materialy, issledovaniia*. Leningrad-Moscow: Sovetskii kompozitor, 1974.

Stalin, J. V.

Antonov-Ovseyenko, Anton. *The Time of Stalin: Portrait of a Tyranny*. New York: Harper and Row, 1981.
Deutscher, Isaac. *Stalin: A Political Biography*. Oxford: Oxford University Press, 1960.
Hingley, Ronald. *Joseph Stalin: Man and Legend*. New York: McGraw-Hill, 1974.
Montefiore, Simon Sebag. *Stalin: The Court of the Red Tsar*. New York: Alfred A. Knopf, 2004.
Randall, Francis B. *Stalin's Russia: An Historical Reconsideration*. New York: Free Press, 1965.
Service, Robert. *Stalin: A Biography*. Cambridge, MA: Harvard University Press, 2005.
Trotsky, Leon. *Stalin: An Appraisal of the Man and His Influence*. Translated and edited by Charles Malamuth. New York: Stein and Day, 1967.
Tucker, Robert. *Stalin as Revolutionary: A Study in History and Personality*. New York: W. W. Norton, 1973.
———. *Stalin in Power: The Revolution from Above, 1928–1941*. New York: W. W. Norton, 1990.
Ulam, Adam B. *Stalin: The Man and His Era*. New York: Viking, 1973.

Stasov, V. V.

Golubeva, O. D., ed. *V. V. Stasov*. St. Petersburg: Rossiiskaia natsional'naia biblioteka, 1995.

Hoops, Richard. "Vladimir Vasil'evich Stasov: The Social and Ethical Foundations of His Relation to Russian Music." *Canadian American Slavic Studies*, XXXIV, 1 (Spring 2000): 63–97.
Lebedev, A. K., and A. V. Solodovnikov. *Vladimir Vasil'evich Stasov: zhizn' i tvorchestvo.* Moscow: Iskusstvo, 1976.
Olkhovsky, Yuri. *Vladimir Stasov and Russian National Culture.* Ann Arbor, MI: UMI Research, 1983.
Rimskii-Korsakov, A. N. "Stasov i muzyka." In *Vladimir Vasil'evich Stasov, 1824–1906: k 125 letiiu so dnia rozhdeniia.* Moscow-Leningrad: Gosudarstvennoe muzykal'noe izdatel'stvo, 1949.
Rostislavov, A. "Stasov." *Teatr i iskusstvo*, 43 (1906): 659–70.
Salita, E. G. *Stasovy v Peterburge-Petrograde.* Leningrad: Lenizdat, 1982.
Stupel', A. *Russkaia mysl' o muzyke, 1895–1917: ocherk istorii russkoi muzykal'noi kritiki.* Leningrad: Muzyka, 1980.
Vladimir Vasil'evich Stasov, 1824–1906: k 125-letiiu so dnia rozhdeniia. Moscow-Leningrad: Gosudarstvennoe muzykal'noe izdatel'stvo, 1949.

Stravinsky, I. F.

Stravinsky, Igor. *An Autobiography.* New York: W. W. Norton, 1936.
Walsh, Stephen. *Stravinsky: A Creative Spring: Russia and France, 1882–1934.* New York: Alfred A. Knopf, 1999.
———. *Stravinsky: The Second Exile: France and America, 1934–1971.* New York: Alfred A. Knopf, 2006.

Svistunov, P. N.

Ginzburg, L. *Istoriia violonchel'nogo iskusstva*, II. Moscow: Muzgiz, 1957.

Tchaikovsky, P. I.

Bowen, Catherine D., and Barbara von Meck. *"Beloved Friend:" The Story of Tchaikowsky and Nadejda von Meck.* New York: Random House, 1937.
Brown, David. *Tchaikovsky: A Biographical and Critical Study*, 4 vol. New York: W. W. Norton, 1991.
Kashkin, N. *Vospominaniia o P. I. Chaikovskom.* Moscow: Iurgenson, 1896.
Khokhlov, Iu. "Betkhoven i Chaikovskii." In *Russko-nemetskie muzykal'nye sviazi.* Moscow: Gosudarstvennyi institut iskusstvoznaniia, 1996.
Klimenko, I. A. *Moi vospominaniia o Petre Il'iche Chaikovskom.* Riazan, Russia: Liubomudrov, 1908.
Nikitin, B. S. *Chaikovskii: staroe i novoe.* Moscow: Znanie, 1990.
Poberezhnaia, G. *Petr Il'ich Chaikovskii.* Kiev, Ukraine: Vipol, 1994.
Poznansky, Alexander. *Tchaikovsky: The Quest for the Inner Man.* New York: Schirmer Books, 1991.

Tolstoy, L, N.

Bartlett, Rosamund. *Tolstoy: A Russian Life.* New York: Houghton Mifflin Harcourt, 2011.
Bendavid-Val, Leah. *Songs without Words: The Photographs and Diaries of Countess Sophia Tolstoy.* Washington, DC: National Geographic, 2007.
Berlin, Isaiah, "The Hedgehog and the Fox" and "Tolstoy and Enlightenment." In *Russian Thinkers*, edited by Henry Hardy and Aileen Kelly, 22–81, 238–60. New York: Viking, 1978.

Gifford, Henry. *Tolstoy*. Oxford: Oxford University Press, 1982.
N., V. "L. N. Tolstoi i muzyka." *Russkaia muzykal'naia gazeta*, XVII, 51–52 (December 19–26, 1910): 1150–55.
Nazaroff, Alexander I. *Tolstoy: The Inconstant Genius*. New York: Frederick A. Stokes Co., 1929.
Noyes, Rapall. *Tolstoy*. New York: Duffield, 1918.
P—v, G. "Lev Tolstoi i muzyka." *Russkaia muzykal'naia gazeta*, XV, 34–35 (August 24–30, 1908): 674–76.
Rancour-Laferriere, Daniel. *Tolstoy on the Couch: Misogyny, Masochism and the Absent Mother*. New York: New York University Press, 1998.
Rischin, Ruth. "*Allegro Tumultuosissimamente*: Beethoven in Tolstoy's Fiction." In *In the Shade of the Giant: Essays on Tolstoy*, edited by Huge McLean, 12–60. Berkeley: University of California Press, 1989.
Rolland, Romain. *Tolstoy*. Translated by Bernard Miall. Port Washington, NY: Kennikat, 1972.
Rowe, William W. *Leo Tolstoy*. Boston: Twayne, 1986.
Simmons, Ernest J. *Leo Tolstoy*. Boston: Little, Brown, 1946.
Steiner, George. *Tolstoy or Dostoevsky: An Essay in the Old Criticism*. New York: Alfred A. Knopf, 1959.
Tolstoi, S. L. "Muzyka v zhizni L. N. Tolstogo." *Muzyka* 50 (November 12, 1911): 1100–8; 51 (November 19, 1911): 1130–36.
Tolstoy, Alexandra. *Tolstoy: A Life of My Father*. Translated by Elizabeth Reynolds Hapgood. New York: Harper and Brothers, 1953.
Troyat, Henri. *Tolstoy*. Translated by Nancy Amphoux. Garden City, NY: Doubleday, 1967.
Wilson, A. N. *Tolstoy*. New York: Fawcett Columbine, 1988.

Turgenev, I. S.

Kruikov, A. *Turgenev i muzyka: muzykal'nye stranitsy zhizni i tvorchestva pisatelia*. Leningrad: Gosudarstvennoe muzykal'noe izdatel'stvo, 1963.
Lehrman, Edgar H., ed. and trans. *Turgenev's Letters: A Selection*. New York: Alfred A. Knopf, 1961.
Magarschack, David. *Turgenev: A Life*. London: Faber and Faber, 1954.
———, trans. *Turgenev's Literary Reminiscences and Autobiographical Fragments*. New York: Farrar, Straus and Giroux, 1958.
I. S. Turgenev v vospominaniiakh sovremennikov, 2 vol. Moscow: Khudozhestvennaia literatura, 1969.
Turgenev, Ivan, Pauline Viardot, et al. *The Portrait Game*. Translated and edited by Marion Mainwaring. New York: Horizon, 1973.
Turgenevskii sbornik: materialy k polnomu sobraniiu sochinenii i pisem I. S. Turgeneva, I, 3–4. Moscow-Leningrad: Nauka, 1964–68.

Ulybyshev, A. D.

"Aleksandr Dmitrievich Ulybyshev." *Nuvellist* XIX, 3 (March 1858): 17–18.
Aronson, M. "Zapiski A. D. Ulybysheva." *Zvezda* 3 (1935): 174–77.
Savvin, N. "V zabytoi usad'be (pamiati A. D. Ulybysheva)." *Russkaia muzykal'naia gazeta*, XVII, 41 (October 9, 1910): 882–86.

Viel'gorskie

Faber, Toby. *Stradivari's Genius: Five Violins, One Cello, and Three Centuries of Enduring Perfection*. New York: Random House, 2006.

Findeizen, N. "Graf Mikhail Iur. Viel'gorskii (k 50-letiiu ego smerti)." *Russkaia muzykal'naia gazeta* XIII, 35–36 (August 27–September 3, 1906): 749–52; 37 (September 11, 1906): 783–88.
Ginzburg, L. *Istoriia violonchel'nogo iskusstva*, II. Moscow: Muzgiz, 1957.
Liamina, E. E., and N. V. Samover. *"Bednyi Zhosef": zhizn' i smert' Iosifa Viel'gorskogo i opyt biografii cheloveka 1830-kh godov*. Moscow: Iazyki russkoi kul'tury, 1999.
Markevitch, Dimitry. *Cello Story*. Translated by Florence W. Seder. Van Nuys, CA: Summy-Birchard Inc., 1984.
Serov, A. "Graf Mikhail Iur'evich Viel'gorskii. Stat'ia V. Lentsa (perevod s nemetskogo)." *Muzykal'nyi i teatral'nyi vestnik* I, 49 (December 9, 1856): 881–84; 51 (December 23, 1856): 917–19.
Shcherbakova, T. *Mikhail i Matvei Viel'gorskie: ispolniteli, prosvetiteli, metsenaty*. Moscow: Muzyka, 1990.
Shteinpress, B. "Mikhail Iur'evich Viel'gorskii, blagozhelatel' Glinki." In *M. I. Glinka: sbornik statei*, edited by E. Gordeeva. Moscow: Gosudarstvennoe muzykal'noe izdatel'stvo, 1958.
Skonechnaia, A. D. *Torzhestvo muz*. Moscow: Sovetskaia Rossiia, 1989.
Trofimova, T. "M. Iu. Viel'gorskii." *Sovetskaia muzyka* VII, 5 (May 1937): 61–70.
Venevitinov, M. A. "Frants List i graf Mikh. Iur'evich Viel'gorskii v 1839 g." *Russkaia starina* XVII (November 1886): 485–90.

Volkonskaia, Mariia Nikolaevna

Shchegolev, P. E. "Podvig kniagini M. N. Volkonskoi." In *Zapiski kniagini Marii Nikolaevny Volkonskoi*, translated by A. N. Kudriavtseva, 11–49. St. Petersburg: Prometei, 1914.

Von der Briggen, A. F.

Brailovskii, S. N. "Iz zhizni odnogo dekabrista." *Russkaia starina* XXXIV, 3 (March 1903): 541–65.

Zavalishin, D.

Zavalishin, D. *Vospominaniia*. Moscow: Zakharov, 2003.

Ziloti, A. I.

Kutateladze, L. M., ed. *Aleksandr Il'ich Ziloti 1863–1945: vospominaniia i pis'ma*. Leningrad: Gosudarstvennoe muzykal'noe izdatel'stvo, 1960.

Compositions

Sonatas

Feinberg, S. E. *32 sonaty Betkhovena*. Moscow: Moskovskaia gosudarstvennaia filarmoniia, 1945.
Genika, R. "Betkhoven. Znachenie ego tvorchestva v oblasti fortepiannoi kompozitsii." *Russkaia muzykal'naia gazeta*, VI, 1 (January 1, 1899): 4–8; 2 (January 9, 1899): 44–48; 3 (January 16, 1899): 74–78.
Gol'denveizer, A. B. *Tridtsat' dve sonaty Betkhovena: ispolnitel'skie kommentarii*. Moscow: Muzyka, 1966.
Khentova, S. *"Lunnaia Sonata" Betkhovena*. Moscow: Muzyka, 1975.
———. *Rasskaz o "Lunnoi Sonate": sonata L. Betkhovena soch. 27 No. 2 i ee ispolniteli*. Leningrad: Gosudarstvennoe muzykal'noe izdatel'stvo, 1961.

Kremlev, Iu. A. *Fortepiannye sonaty Betkhovena*. Moscow: Gosudarstvennoe muzykal'noe izdatel'stvo, 1953.
Timusheva, O. *"Mavzolei," ritmicheskoe shestvie: muzyka Betkhovena*. Moscow: Muztorga, 1930.
Ulybyshev, A. D. "Sonata 'Quasi Fantasia.' 27-e sochinenie Betkhovena. Otryvok iz novogo sochineniia A. D. Ulybysheva," translated by A. N. Serov. *Muzykal'nyi i teatral'nyi vestnik*, I, 1 (January 1, 1856): 10–11.
———. "Sonata Betkhovena. D-moll (Op. 31). 2-i otryvok iz novogo sochineniia A. D. Ulybysheva o Betkhovene," translated by A. N. Serov. *Muzykal'nyi i teatral'nyi vestnik*, I, 7 (February 12, 1856): 120–22.

Chamber

Kvartet im. Ego Vysochestva Gertsoga g.g. Meklenburg-Strelitskogo. *12 abonemetnykh kontsertov iz proizvedenii Betkhovena (k XX-letiiu deiatel'nosti kvarteta); Kontsert No. 8 (15 ianvariia 1917 g.), No. 11 (5 fevralia 1917 g.).*

Quartets

Dolgov, P. *Smychkovye kvartety Betkhovena*. Moscow: Muzyka, 1980.
Dusinberre, Edward. *Beethoven for a Later Age: Living with the String Quartets*. Chicago: University of Chicago Press, 2016.
Ferraguto, Mark. "Beethoven *a la moujik*: Russianness and Learned Style in the 'Razumovsky' String Quartets." *Journal of the American Musicological Society*, LXVII, 1 (Spring 2014).
Ginzburg, L. *Issledovaniia, stat'i, ocherki*. Moscow: Sovetskii kompozitor, 1971.
Kerman, Joseph. *The Beethoven Quartets*. New York: W. W. Norton, 1966.
Khokhlovkina, A. *Kvartety Betkhovena: annotatsii k kontsertam*. Moscow: Moskovskaia gosudarstvennaia filarmoniia, 1954.
Mahaim, Ivan. *Beethoven: naissance et renaissance des dernièrs quatours*, II. Paris: Declée De Brouwer, 1964.
Steinberg, Michael. "Notes on the Quartets." In *The Beethoven Quartet Companion*, edited by Robert Winter and Robert Martin. Berkeley: University of California Press, 1994.
Val'ter, V. G. *Smychkovye kvartety Betkhovena*. St. Petersburg: Glavnoe upravlenie udelov, 1912.
Winter, Robert, and Robert Martin, ed. *The Beethoven Quartet Companion*. Berkeley: University of California Press, 1994.

3rd Symphony

Hamilton-Paterson, James. *Beethoven's Eroica: The First Great Romantic Symphony*. New York: Basic Books, 2017.
Sipe, Thomas. *Beethoven: Eroica Symphony*. Cambridge: Cambridge University Press, 1998.

4th Symphony

Lopukhov, F. *Velichie mirozdaniia: tantssimfoniia Fedora Lopukhova muz. L. Betkhovena; 4-aia simfoniia s avtolitosiluetami Pavla Goncharova*. Petrograd: Liubarskii, 1922.
Shol'p, A. E. *Chetvertaia simfoniia Betkhovena*. 2nd ed. Leningrad: Leningradskaia gosudarstvennaia filarmoniia, 1946.

5th Symphony

Guerrieri, Matthew. *The First Four Notes: Beethoven's Fifth and the Human Imagination*. New York: Random House, 2012.

Shlifshtein, S. *Piataia simfoniia Betkhovena: poiasnenie*. Moscow-Leningrad: Gosudarstvennoe muzykal'noe izdatel'stvo, 1950.

6th Symphony

Druskin, M. S. *Shestaia simfoniia Betkhovena*. 3rd rev. ed. Leningrad: Leningradskaia gosudarstvennaia filarmoniia, 1946.
Jones, David W. *Beethoven: Pastoral Symphony*. Cambridge: Cambridge University Press, 1995.
Pokrovskii, N. *Muzykal'naia drama: ee nedavnee proshloe, sovremennoe polozhenie i nadezhdy na budushchee*. St. Petersburg: Porokhovshchikov, 1900.

7th Symphony

Beliaev, V. "Po povodu stat'i A. Ziloti." *Muzyka*, 149 (September 28, 1913): 609–13.
Ziloti, A. "Ne dolzhno-li skertso iz 7-oi simfonii Betkhovena byt' v takte 6/4 vmesto 3/4?." *Russkaia muzykal'naia gazeta*, XX, 36 (August 31, 1913): 730–34.

8th Symphony

Strel'nikov, N. [Performance], *Zhizn' iskusstva* (August 28–29, 1919).

9th Symphony

Al'shvang, A. "Deviataia simfoniia Betkhovena." *Sovetskaia muzyka*, V, 3 (March 1937): 57–64.
———. "Deviataia simfoniia Betkhovena." *Sovetskaia muzyka*, XIII, 5 (May 1949): 66–71.
Buch, Estban. *Beethoven's Ninth: A Political History*. Translated by Richard Miller. Chicago: University of Chicago Press, 2003.
Cook, Nicholas. *Beethoven: Symphony No. 9*. Cambridge: Cambridge University Press, 1993.
Deviataia simfoniia Betkhovena. Moscow: GABT SSSR, 1936.
Fouque, Octave. "La Neuvième Symphonie de Beethoven." In *Les révolutionnaires de la musique*. Paris: Ancienne Maison Michel Lévy Frères, 1882.
Larosh, G. A. *Deviataia simfoniia Betkhovena: muzyka budushchnosti i Pavlovskii vokzal*. St. Petersburg: Novosti, 1895.
Levy, David Benjamin. *The Ninth Symphony*, rev. ed. New Haven, CT: Yale University Press, 2005.
Linitskii, A. "9-ia simfoniia Betkhovena i ee poeticheskaia ideia (k ispolneniiu ee v kontsert S. Kusevitskogo)." *Russkaia muzykal'naia gazeta*, XX, 8 (February 22, 1915): 154–58.
Nadstrochnyi perevod khora 9-i simfonii Betgovena na odu Shillera "K radosti" ("An Die Freude"). St. Petersburg: St. Peterburgskoe filarmonicheskoe obshchestvo, 1836.
Nikolaeva, N. "Deviataia simfoniia Betkhovena—puti v budushchee." *Sovetskaia muzyka*, XXXV, 8 (August 1971): 116–19.
"Posle Deviatoi." *Russkaia muzykal'naia gazeta*, XV, 46 (November 16, 1908): 1026–28.
Rabinovich, A. *Deviataia simfoniia Betkhovena: putevoditel' po kontsertam*. Leningrad: Leningradskaia filarmoniia, 1936.
Sachs, Harvey. *The Ninth: Beethoven and the World in 1824*. New York: Random House, 2010.
Serov, A. N. *Deviataia simfoniia Betkhovena: ee sklad i smysl*. Moscow: Gosudarstvennoe muzykal'noe izdatel'stvo, 1952.
Solie, Ruth A. "Beethoven as Secular Humanist: Ideology and the Ninth Symphony in Nineteenth-Century Criticism." In *Explorations in Music, the Arts, and Ideas: Essays in Honor of Leonard B. Meyer*, edited by Eugene Narmour and Ruth A. Solie. Stuyvesant, UK: Pendragon, 1988.

Wagner, Richard. "Vospominaniia ob ispolnenii deviatoi simfonii Betkhovena v 1846 g. v Dresdene i programma k nei." *Muzyka*, 77 (May 16, 1912): 440–55.

Symphonies/Various

Grove, George. *Beethoven and His Nine Symphonies*. 3rd ed. New York: Dover, 1962.
Lockwood, Lewis. *Beethoven's Symphonies: An Artistic Vision*. New York: W. W. Norton, 2015.
Ogolevets, V. *Simfoniia Betkhovena: populiarno-kriticheskii ocherk*. Kiev, Ukraine: Samonenko, 1913.
Rabinovich, A. S. *Pervaia i vtoraia simfonii Betkhovena*. Moscow: Gosudarstvennoe muzykal'noe izdatel'stvo, 1954.
Shantyr, G. *Betkhoven: pervaia i sed'maia simfoniia*. Moscow: Moskovskaia gosudarstvennaia filarmoniia, 1954.
Shaverdian, A. *Simfonii Betkhovena (putevoditel')*. Moscow: Moskovskaia gosudarstvennaia filarmoniia, 1936.
Tupitsyn, O. V. *Chaikovskii, Betkhoven, Vagner: khristianskoe vospriiatie i istolkovanie muzykal'nykh proizvedenii*. Moscow: Lestvitsa, 2000. [5th and 9th Symphonies]

Overtures

Aksenov, V. *Literaturno-muzykal'nyi spektakl' 'Egmont'*. Moscow: Moskovskaia gosudarstvennaia filarmoniia, 1957.
Grachev, P. *Uvertiury Betkhovena*. Leningrad: Leningradskaia filarmoniia, 1937.
Serov, A. N. *Tematizm uvertiury "Leonore": etiud o Betkhovene*. Moscow: Gosudarstvennoe muzykal'noe izdatel'stvo, 1954.
Strel'nikov, N. [*Leonore No. 1*], *Prilozhenie k No. 227–228 gaz. Zhizn' iskusstva* (August 28–29, 1919).
——. [*Leonore No. 3*], *Prilozhenie k No. 207 gaz. Zhizn' iskusstva* (August 5, 1919).

Fidelio/Leonore

Khokhlovkina, A. *Fidelio L. Betkhovena*. Moscow: Gosudarstvennoe muzykal'noe izdatel'stvo, 1961.
Khokhlovkina, A., and N. Biriukov. *L. Betkhoven: Fidelio (Leonore)*. Moscow: Gosudarstvennyi Bol'shoi Teatr SSSR, 1954.
"Khronika. S-Peterburg. Mariinskii teatr. *Fidelio*." [Performance]. *Russkaia muzykal'naia gazeta*, XII, 41 (October 9, 1905): 980–83.
Kn–skii, I. "Marinskii teatr; 'Fidelio' Betkhovena." *Teatral'naia Rossiia*, 40 (October 1, 1905): 1201.
L. "K 100-letiiu 'Fidelio' Betkhovena (1805–1905)." *Russkaia muzykal'naia gazeta*, XII, 38 (September 17, 1905): 866–71.
Ossovskii, A. "'Fidelio' Betkhovena." *Muzyka*, 27 (June 3, 1911): 582–84.
Poliakova, L. "Vozrozhdenie 'Leonory'." *Sovetskaia muzyka*, XVIII, 7 (July 1954): 81–86.
Shaverdian, A. *Fidelio: opera Betkhovena*. Moscow: Moskovskaia gosudarstvennaia filarmoniia, 1937.
Sollertinskii, I. "Fidelio Betkhovena." In *Muzykal'no-istoricheskie etiudy*. Leningrad: Gosudarstvennoe muzykal'noe izdatel'stvo, 1956.

Missa solemnis

Adorno, Theodor W. "Alienated Masterpiece: The *Missa Solemnis* (1959)." *Telos*, XXVIII (1976): 113–24.
Dalhaus, Carl. *Ludwig van Beethoven: Approaches to His Music*. Translated by M. Whittal. Oxford: Clarendon, 1991.

Drabkin, William. *Beethoven: Missa Solemnis*. Cambridge: Cambridge University Press, 1991.
Fiske, Roger. *Beethoven's Missa Solemnis*. London: Paul Elek, 1979.
Fishman, N. "Die Uraufführung der Missa solemnis." *Beiträge zur Musikwissenschaft Ludwig van Beethoven, 1770–1970*, 3/4 (1970).
———. "Istoricheskaia peterburgskaia prem'era 'Torzhestvennoi messy'." In *Etiudy i ocherki po betkhoveniany*. Moscow: Muzyka, 1982.
———. "Istoricheskaia prem'era." *Sovetskaia muzyka*, XXXIV, 6 (June 1970): 96–103.
Marek, George R. *Beethoven: Biography of a Genius*. New York: Funk and Wagnalls, 1969.
Schwarz, Boris. "Zur Uraufführung von Beethovens 'Missa Solemnis' in St. Petersburg." In *Bericht über den Internationalen Beethoven-Kongress 10.12.Dezember 1970*, 559–61. Berlin: Neue Musik, 1971.
Tovey, Donald F. *Essays in Musical Analysis*, V. London: Oxford University Press, 1937.

Various Genres

Danilevich, L. *Liudvig van Betkhoven (1770–1827)*. Moscow: Moskovskaia gosudarstvennaia filarmoniia, 1938. [Piano Concerto No. 5 and Symphony No. 5]
Dlia slushatelei simfonicheskikh kontsertov: kratkii putevoditel'. Moscow-Leningrad: Muzyka, 1965.
Findeizen, N. "Ein neues 'Shotlischer Lied.'" RNL, Otdel rukopisei, F. 816 (Findeizen), op. 1, ed. khr. 689, l. 1–6.
———. *Muzykal'nye ocherki i eskizy*. St. Petersburg: Shtauf, 1891.
Glebov, I. *Betkhoven (1827–1927). K ispolneniiu v Gosudarstvennoi Akademicheskoi filarmonii tsikla kontsertov iz proizvedenii Betkhovena v oznamenovanie stoletiei godovshchiny ego smerti*. Leningrad: Gosudarstvennaia Akademicheskaia Filarmoniia, 1927.
Herttrich, Ernst. *Beethoven to the Distant Beloved: A Reader and Picture Book for Beethoven Lovers and Connoisseurs*. Bonn, Germany: Beethoven-Haus, 1999.
Korganov, V. D., ed. *Zhizn' i sochineniia Liudviga van Betkhovena*. Tiflis, Georgia: Rotinianets, 1888.
Levenson, O. *Iz oblasti muzyki*. Moscow: Mamontov, 1885.
Lodes, Birgit. "'*Le congress danse:*' Set Form and Improvisation in Beethoven's Polonaise for Piano, Op. 89." Translated by Sabine Ladislav. *Musical Quarterly*, XCIII, 3–4 (Fall/Winter 2010): 414–49.
Rich, Alan. *Ludwig van Beethoven: Symphony No. 3 "Eroica"; the Egmont Overture*. San Francisco: Harper Collins, 1995.
Sakketti, L. *Iz oblasti estetiki i muzyki*. St. Petersburg: Turgina, 1896.
Strel'nikov, N. *Zhizn' iskusstva* (August 1919), NRL, Otdel rukopisei, F. 729 (Strel'nikov), op. 1, ed. khr. 63, l. 1–2, 3, 6, 7–8, 9–10.

Viel'gorskii Sketchbook

Ivanow-Boretzky, M. "Ein Moskauere Skizzenbuch von Beethoven." In *Beethoven Zentenarfeier*. Vienna: Universal, 1927.
Schwarz, Boris. "Beethoveniana in Soviet Russia." *Musical Quarterly*, XLVII, 1 (January 1961): 4–21.

Correspondence

Aksakov to Family

Aksakov, I. S. *Pis'ma k rodnym, 1844–1849*. Moscow: Nauka, 1988.

Aliab'ev to Verstovskii

Shteinpress, B. *Stranitsy iz zhizni A. A. Aliab'eva*. Moscow: Gosudarstvennoe muzykal'noe izdatel'stvo, 1956.

Bakunin to Family

Bakunin, M. A. *Sobranie sochinenii i pisem, 1828–1876*, I–IV. Moscow: Izdatel'stvo vsesoiuzhnogo obshchestva polit-katorzhan i ssyl'no-poselentsev, 1934–35.

Bakunin to Herzen and Ogarev

Dragomanov, M. P., ed. *Pis'ma M. A. Bakunina k A. I. Gertsenu i N. P. Ogarevu*. St. Petersburg: Vrulebskii, 1906.

Balakirev to/from Stasov

M. A. Balakirev i V. V. Stasov: perepiska, I. Moscow: Muzyka, 1970.

Balakirev to/from Tchaikovsky

Liapunov, S. *Perepiska M. A. Balakireva s P. I. Chaikovskim*. St. Petersburg: Tsimmerman, 1912.

Belinskii to Bakunin

Belinskii, V. G. *Izbrannye pis'ma*, I. Moscow: Gosudarstvenoe izdatel'stvo khudozhestvennoi literatury, 1951.

Belinskii, V. G. *Polnoe sobranie sochinenii*, XI. Moscow: AN SSSR, 1956.

Chernyshevskii to A. N. Chernyshevskii

Chernyshevskii, N. G. *Polnoe sobranie sochinenii*, XV. Moscow: Gosudarstvennoe izdatel'stvo khudozhestvennoi literatury, 1950.

Glinka to Various

Glinka, M. I. *Literaturnoe nasledie*, II. Leningrad: Gosudarstvennoe muzykal'noe izdatel'stvo, 1953.

Polnoe sobranie pisem Mikhaila Ivanovicha Glinki, I. St. Petersburg: Russkaia muzykal'naia gazeta, 1907.

Herzen to Various

Gertsen, A. I. *Sobranie sochinenii*, V, XXII, XXV, XXVI. Moscow: AN SSSR, 1955–62.

Mussorgsky to Balakirev

Musorgskii, M. P. *Pis'ma k M. A. Balakirevu (1857–1872 g.)*. Petrograd: Russkaia muzykal'naia gazeta, 1915.

Mussorgsky to Stasov

Musorgskii, M. P. *Pis'ma k V. V. Stasovu*. St. Petersburg: Russkaia muzykal'naia gazeta, 1911.

Mussorgsky to Various

Musorgskii, M. P. *Pis'ma i dokumenty*. Moscow-Leningrad: Gosudarstvennoe muzykal'noe izdatel'stvo, 1932.

Rachmaninov to Various

Rakhmaninov, S. V. *Pis'ma*. Moscow: Gosudarstvennoe muzykal'noe izdatel'stvo, 1955.

Rimsky-Korsakov to/from Iastrebtsev and Bel'skii

Goriachii, V. V., ed. *N. A. Rimskii-Korsakov: perepiska s V. V. Iastrebtsevym i V. I. Bel'skim*. St. Petersburg: Russkaia kul'tura, 2004.

Rubinshtein to Various

Rubinshtein, A. G. *Izbrannye pis'ma*. Moscow: Gosudarstvennoe muzykal'noe izdatel'stvo, 1954.

Serov to A. A. Bakunin

Findeizen, N. "Novye materialy dlia biografii A. N. Serova; pis'ma ego k Aleksandrovichu Bakuninu (1850–1853 gg.)." *Ezhegodnik Imperatorskikh teatrov*, IV (1893–1894 Season): 110–29.

Serov to Diu-Tur

Findeizen, N., ed. "Novye materialy dlia biografii Aleksandra Nikolaevicha Serova (pis'ma 1845–1849 gg.)." *Russkaia starina*, XXIV, 3 (March 1893): 616–24.

———. *Pis'ma Aleksandra Nikolaevicha Serova k ego sestre S. N. DiuTur (1845–1861 gg.)*. St. Petersburg: Findeizen, 1896.

Serov to D. V. and V. V. Stasov

Muzykal'noe nasledstvo, II, 1; III, 3. Moscow: Muzyka, 1966–70.

Stasov to/from Balakirev

Balakirev, M. A. i V. V. Stasov: perepiska, I. Moscow: Muzyka, 1979.

Stasov to Turgenev

Turgenevskii sbornik, I. Moscow-Leningrad: AN SSSR, 1964.

Stravinsky to/from Stravinsky

Craft, Robert, ed. *Dearest Babushkin: The Correspondence of Vera and Igor Stravinsky, 1921–1954, with Excerpts from Vera Stravinsky's Diaries, 1922–1971*. Translated by Lucia Davidova. London: Thames and Hudson, 1985.

Tchaikovsky to Family

Tchaikovsky, Piotr. *Letters to His Family: An Autobiography*. Translated by Galina von Meck. New York: Stein and Day, 1973.

Tchaikovsky to Von Meck

Tchaikovsky, P. I. *To My Best Friend: Correspondence between Tchaikovsky and Nadezhda von Meck, 1876–1878*. Translated by Galina von Meck. Oxford: Oxford University Press, 1993.

Tchaikovsky to/from Taneev

Pis'ma P. I. Chaikovskogo i S. I. Taneeva. Moscow: Iurgenson, 1916.

Tolstoy, Lev N.

Christian, R. F., ed. and trans. *Tolstoy's Letters*. New York: Charles Scribner's Sons, 1978.

Ulybyshev to Odoevskii and Balakirev

Findeizen, N., ed. *Muzykal'naia starina: sbornik statei i materialov dlia istorii muzyki v Rossii*, V–VI. St. Petersburg: Glavnoe upravlenie udelov, 1911.

Various to Beethoven

Albrecht, Theodore, ed. and trans. *Letters to Beethoven and Other Correspondence*, II–III. Lincoln: University of Nebraska Press, 1996.

Viardot to Matvei Viel'gorskii

Muzykal'noe nasledstvo, II, 2. Moscow: Muzyka, 1968.

Criticism and Theory

Anonymous

"Betkhoven." *Biblioteka dlia chteniia*, 102 (July–August 1850): 53–58; 104 (November–December 1850): 1–18.

Aksakov, I. S.

Sochineniia, II/VIII. Moscow: Volchaninov, 1886–87.

Aksakov, K. S.

Polnoe sobranie sochinenii, I. Moscow: Bakhmetov, 1861.

Aksakov, S. T.

Sobranie sochinenii, I. Moscow: Gosudarstvennoe izdatel'stvo khudozhestvennoi literatury, 1956; IV. Moscow: Pravda, 1966.

Al'shvang, A.

"Novaia kniga Romen Rollana o Betkhovene." *Sovetskaia muzyka*, VII, 5 (May 1939): 90–96.

"Sinfonizm Betkhovena." *Sovetskaia muzyka*, XVI, 3 (March 1952): 50–54.

Arnol'd, Iu.

"Betkhoven, ego kritiki i tolkovateli." *Muzykal'nyi i teatral'nyi vestnik*, II, 21 (June 2, 1857): 341–45.

"Neskol'ko slov o muzykal'nom tvorchestve i o muzykal'noi kritike." *Muzykal'nyi i teatral'nyi vestnik*, II, 16 (April 28, 1857): 264–66.

Ashkinadzi, Z.

"Muzyka i metafizika." *Muzyka*, 75 (May 5, 1912): 396–402; 76 (May 12, 1912): 412–16.

Belinskii, V. G.

D'iachenko, M. "Evoliutsiia literaturnykh i obshchestvennykh vzdgliadov Belinskogo." *Russkaia starina*, XLII, 5 (May 1911): 291–328.
Stat'i i retsenzii, I–VI, VIII–IX. Moscow: AN SSSR, 1953–55.

Berlioz, Hector

Berlioz, Gektor. "Simfonii Betkhovena; kriticheskii ocherk." *Artist*, IV, 9 (September 1892): 55–69.

Bernikov, V. E.

Mirovozrenie Betkhovena i filosovsko-esteticheskie problemy ego tvorchestva. Moscow: Moskovskii gosudarstvennyi universitet im. M. V. Lomonosova, 1982.

Bogdanov-Berezovskii, B.

"Problema realizma v muzyke." *Zvezda*, 11 (1935): 182–94.
Stat'i, vospominaniia, pis'ma. Leningrad-Moscow: Sovetskii kompozitor, 1978.

Braudo, E.

"Betkhoven—grazhdanin." *Muzyka i revoliutsiia*, 3 (15) (March 1927): 3–8.
"Romen Rollan i muzyka." *Sovetskaia muzyka*, III, 9 (September 1935): 27–29.

Bugoslavskii, S.

Dva etiuda o Betkhovene. Moscow-Leningrad: Moskovskoe obshchestvo dramaticheskikh pisatelei i kompozitorov, 1927.

Bulich, S.

"Muzyka i osvoboditel'nye idei." *Vestnik Evropy*, XLIV, 2 (1909): 5–26.

Chemodanov, S.

"Marksizm i muzyka." *Zvezda*, 2 (1924): 286–98.

Chernyshevskii, N. G.

Polnoe sobranie sochinenii, II, III, X, XVI. Moscow: Gosudarstvennoe izdatel'stvo khudozhestvennoi literatury, 1949–53.

Cui, Ts. A.

Izbrannye stat'i. Leningrad: Gosudarstvennoe muzykal'noe izdatel'stvo, 1952.

Dogel, I. M.

Vliianie muzyki na cheloveka i zhivotnykh. Kazan', Russia: Imperatorskii Kazanskii universitet, 1898.

Fétis, G.

"O fizicheskom deistvii muzyki." *Literaturnaia gazeta*, I, 12 (February 25, 1830): 94–96; 13 (March 2, 1830): 101–4.

Findeizen, N.

Kosmovskaia, M. L. *Nasledie N. F. Findeizena*. Kursk, Russia: Izdatel'stvo Kurskogo gospeduniversiteta, 1997.

Fishman, N. L.

Etiudy i ocherki po betkhoveniane. Moscow: Muzyka, 1982.
"Novye betkhovenskie materialy." *Sovetskaia muzyka*, XXIV, 9 (September 1960): 72–78.
"O nekotorykh literaturno-filosofskikh interesakh kompozitora." *Sovetskaia muzyka*, XXXIV, 12 (December 1970): 11–25.

Glebov, I. (B. Asaf'ev)

"Cherez proshloe k budushchemu (iz epokhi obshchestvennogo pod"ema russkoi muzyki 50–60kh godov proshlogo stoletiia)." In *Sovetskaia muzyka, vtoroi sbornik statei*. Moscow: Muzgiz, 1944.

Gogol', N. V.

Sobranie sochinenii, IV. Moscow: Pravda, 1968.

Grigor'ev, A. A.

A. A. Grigor'ev: iskusstvo i nravstvennost'. Moscow: Sovremennik, 1986.
Sochineniia, II. Moscow: Khudozhestvennaia literatura, 1990.
Vospominaniia. Leningrad: Nauka, 1980.

Gutor, V.

"O liubitel'stve v muzyke." *Artist*, VI, 11 (November 1894): 32–38; 12 (December 1894): 6–12.

Herzen, A. I.

Sobranie sochinenii, I, II, IV, VI, X, XVI, XIX. Moscow: AN SSSR, 1954–60.

Hughes, Carol B.

"'Beethoven's Last Quartet:' A 'Hoffmanesque' Tale by Russian Critic Prince Vladimir Odoevskii (1804–1869)." *Beethoven Newsletter*, IV, 2 (Summer 1989): 25–30.

Iudenich, N.

"O slavianskikh elementakh v tvorchestve Betkhovena." *Sovetskaia muzyka*, XXXVIII, 4 (April 1974): 90–92.

Ivanov, M.

"Serov—byl li on meierberistom, vagneriantsem ili samostoiatel'nym tvortsom?." In *Ezhegodnik Imperatorskikh teatrov*, III, 121–36 (1894–1895 Season).

Karatygin, V. G.

Izbrannye stat'i. Moscow-Leningrad: Muzyka, 1965.

Keldysh, Iu.

Betkhoven. Moscow: Gosudarstvennoe izdatel'stvo po voprosam radio, 1936.

Khokhlovkina, A.

"Iz betkhovenskoi literatury v Rossii." *Muzykal'noe obrazovanie*, 1–2 (1927): 122–30.

Khomiakov, A. S.

Izbrannye sochineniia. New York: Chekhov, 1955.

Khubov, G.

Muzykal'naia publitsistika raznykh let: stat'i, ocherki, retsenzii. Moscow: Sovetskii kompozitor, 1976.

Kireevskii, I. V.

Kritika i estetika. Moscow: Iskusstvo, 1998.
Polnoe sobranie sochinenii, I. Moscow: Put', 1911.

Kirillina, L. V.

Betkhoven i teoriia muzyki XVIII-nachala XIX vekov. Moscow: Moskovskaia gosudarstvennaia konservatoriia im. P. I. Chaikovskogo, 1989.
"Recent Russian Beethoven Scholars." *Beethoven Newsletter*, VII, 1 (Spring 1992): 9, 11–16.

Klimovitskii, A.

O tvorcheskom protsesse Betkhovena: issledovanie. Leningrad: Muzyka, 1979.

Knittel, K. M.

"Divining the Enigmas of the Sphinx: Alexander Oulibicheff as a Critic of Beethoven's Late Style." *Beethoven Newsletter*, VIII, 2 (Summer 1993): 34–37.

Kolomitsov, V.

Stat'i i pis'ma. Leningrad: Muzyka, 1971.

Koptiaev, A.

"Evterpe," vtoroi sbornik muzykal'no-kriticheskikh statei. St. Petersburg: Glavnoe upravlenie udelov, 1908.
"K muzykal'nomu idealu"; tretii sbornik muzykal'no-istoricheskikh i kriticheskikh statei. Petrograd: Iurgenson, 1916.
Muzyka i kul'tura: sbornik muzykal'no-istoricheskikh i muzykal'no-kriticheskikh statei. Moscow: Iurgenson, 1903.

Kremlev, Iu.

"Bor'ba za narodnost' i realizm v russkoi muzyke." *Zvezda*, 5 (May 1948): 157–67.

Russkaia mysl' o muzyke: ocherki istorii russkoi muzykal'noi kritiki i estetiki v XIX veke, I-III. Leningrad: Gosudarstvennoe muzykal'noe izdatel'stvo, 1954–60.
"Voprosy sovetskoi muzykal'noi estetiki." *Zvezda*, 2 (February 1949): 138–46.

Kuznetsov, K.

"Tri etiudi o Betkhovene." *Muzyka i revoliutsiia*, 3 (15) (March 1927): 9–20.

Larosh, G. A.

Izbrannye stat'i, I–V. Leningrad: Muzyka, 1974–78.
Muzykal'no-kriticheskie stat'i. St. Petersburg: Brat Panteleevye, 1894.
Sobranie muzykal'no-kriticheskikh statei, I. Moscow: Kushnerev, 1913.

Lenz, W. von

Beethoven: eine kunststudie. Berlin: Schuster and Loeffler, 1908.
Beethoven et ses trois styles. New York: De Capo, 1980.
"Filosofiia muzyki." In *Muzykal'nyi almanakh*, edited by G. Angert and E. Shor, 50–57. Moscow: Betkhovenskaia studiia, 1914.

Lermontov, M. Iu.

Polnoe sobranie sochinenii, IV. Moscow-Leningrad: AN SSSR, 1959.

Levin, Simon

"Beethoven in Soviet Musicology from 1917 to 1970." *Beethoven Newsletter*, V, 1 (Spring 1990): 1, 10–18.

Lunacharskii, A.

Bogdanov-Berezovskii, V. M. "Iz vospominanii o muzykal'noi zhizni revoliutsionnogo Petrograda." In *Muzykal'noe nasledstvo*, III. Moscow: Muzyka, 1970.
"Chto zhivo dlia nas v Betkhovene." *Muzyka i revoliutsiia*, 3 (15) (March 1927): 3–8.
Sobranie sochinenii, VII. Moscow: Khudozhestvennaia literatura, 1967.
V mire muzyki: stat'i i rechi. Moscow: Sovetskii kompozitor, 1958.

Maikapar, S. M.

Znachenie tvorchestva Betkhovena dlia nashei sovremennosti. Moscow: Muzykal'nyi sektor gosudarstvennogo izdatel'stva, 1927.

Miaskovskii, N.

Chaikovskii i Betkhoven. Moscow: Muzyka, 1912.

Mikhailovskii, N. K.

Sochineniia, II. St. Petersburg: Vol'f, 1896.
Literaturnaia kritika: stat'i o russkoi literature XIX-nachala XX veka. Leningrad: Khudozhestvennaia literatura, 1989.
Literaturnaia kritika i vospominaniia. Moscow: Iskusstvo, 1995.
Literaturno-kriticheskie stat'i. Moscow: Gosudarstvenoe izdatel'stvo khudozhestvennoi literatury, 1957.

Misch, Ludwig

Beethoven Studies. Norman: University of Oklahoma Press, 1953.

Neustroev, A. A.

Muzyka i chuvstvo: materialy dlia psikhologicheskogo osnovaniia estetiki muzyki. St. Petersburg: Kirshbaum, 1890.

O proiskhozhdenii muzyki: estetiko-psikhologicheskii ocherk. St. Petersburg: Kirshbaum, 1892.

Odoevskii, V. F.

Bernandt, G. B., ed. *Muzykal'no-literaturnoe nasledie*. Moscow: Gosudarstvennoe muzykal'noe izdatel'stvo, 1956.

Ogarev, N. P.

Izbrannye proizvedeniia, I–II. Moscow: Gosudarstvennoe izdatel'stvo khudozhestvennoi literatury, 1956.

Polevoi, N. A.

Kondrat'ev, B. "Tri 'zhizni' Nikolaia Polevogo." In *Mechty i zhizn'*, edited by N. Polevoi. Moscow: Sovetskaia Rossiia, 1988.

Literaturnaia kritika, stat'i i retsenzii. Leningrad: Shelaev, 1990.

Pshibyshevskii, B.

Betkhoven: opyt issledovaniia. Moscow: Gosudarstvennoe muzykal'noe izdatel'stvo, 1932.

Rostislav [F. M. Tolstoi]

Betkhoven: kritiki i tolkovateli ego proizvedenii; soch. A. D. Ulybysheva. St. Petersburg: Grech, 1857.

Rozenov, E. K.

"Tvorcheskie dostizheniia Betkhovena v oblasti muzykal'noi formy." *Muzyka i revoliutsiia*, 3 (15) (March 1927): 224–27.

Rubinshtein, A. G.

Muzyka i ee predstaviteli: razgovor o muzyke. Moscow: Iurgenson, 1892.

Ryzhkin, I.

Betkhoven i klassicheskii symfonizm. Moscow: Moskovskaia filarmoniia, 1938.

Samarin, Iu. F.

Stat'i, vospominaniia, pis'ma. Moscow: Terra, 1997.

Schumann, Robert

"Kriticheskie stat'i R. Shumana o Betkhovene." *Sovetskaia muzyka*, III, 9 (September 1935): 30–37.

Serov, A. N.

Izbrannye stat'i, I–II. Moscow: Gosudarstvennoe muzykal'noe izdatel'stvo, 1950.
"Nechto o protivopolozhnosti 'glubokomysliiu' na poprishche muzykal'noi polemiki." *Muzykal'nyi i teatral'nyi vestnik*, I, 52 (December 30, 1856): 945–48.
"Novaia kniga G-na Lentsa o Betkhovene." *Muzykal'nyi i teatral'nyi vestnik*, I, 29 (July 22, 1856): 517–20; 30 (July 29, 1856): 533–38.
"Pis'ma o muzyke; k A. D. Ulybyshevu po sluchaiu tolkov o Motsarte i Betkhovene." *Panteon*, III, 6 (June 1852): 1–20; IV, 7 (July 1852): 3–52.
Stat'i o muzyke, I–VI. Moscow: Muzyka, 1984–90.
"Zamechanie na pis'mo A. D. Ulybysheva." *Muzykal'nyi i teatral'nyi vestnik*, I, 14 (April 1, 1856): 261–64; 19 (May 13, 1856): 355–57.

Serova, V.

"Rossini." *Russkaia tsena*, 1 (January 1865): 17; 2 (February 1865): 150–65.
"Vinchentso Bellini i Gaetano Donitsetti." *Russkaia tsena*, 6–7 (June–July 1865): 55–70.

Shapir, N.

"O tipakh muzykal'nogo tvorchestva (Motsart—Betkhoven—Vagner)." *Muzykal'nyi sovremennik*, 3 (November 1916): 5–25.

Stasov, V. V.

Izbrannye sochineniia, II–III. Moscow: Iskusstvo, 1952.
Izbrannye stat'i o muzyke. Leningrad-Moscow: Gosudarstvennoe muzykal'noe izdatel'stvo, 1949.
Selected Essays. Translated by Florence Jonas. London: Barrie and Rockliff, 1968.
Sobranie sochinenii, I, III. St. Petersburg: Stasiulevich, 1894.
Stat'i o muzyke, V-B (1901). Moscow: Muzyka, 1980.

Stravinsky, I.

Fiechtner, H. A. "Strawinsky űber Beethoven." *Ősterreichische Musikzeitschrift*, VII (1952): 156–59.

Tkachev, P. N.

Izbrannye sochineniia na sotsial'no-politicheskie temy, V–VI. Moscow: Vsesoiuznoe obshchestvo politkatorzhan i ssyl'no-poselentsev, 1935–37.
Liudi budushchego i geroi meshchanstva. Moscow: Sovremennik, 1986.
Petr Nikitich Tkachev, I. Moscow: Mysl', 1975.

Ulybyshev, A.

Oulibicheff, Aleksandre. *Beethoven: ses critiques et ses glossateurs*. Leipzig: Brockhaus-Gavelot, 1857.

Val'ter, V. G.

Muzykal'noe obrazovanie liubitelia. 2nd rev. ed. St. Petersburg: Prosveshchenie, 1911.

Vol'fing [E. K. Metner]

Modernism i muzyka: stat'i kriticheskie i polemicheskie (1907–10); prilozheniia (1911). Moscow: Musaget, 1912.

Zaslavskii, D.

"Betkhoven nashikh dnei." *Sovetskaia muzyka*, XVI, 3 (March 1952): 28–32.

History

Aldanov, Mark. *The Tenth Symphony*. Translated by Gregory Golubeff. New York: Scribner's Sons, 1948.

Alekseev, M. "Russkie vstrech i sviazi Betkhovena,' *Russkaia kniga o Betkhovene: k stoletiiu so dnia smerti kompozitora (1827–1927)*, edited by K. A. Kuznetsov, 79–85. Moscow: Muzykal'nyi sektor, 1927.

Barratt, Glynn. *Voices in Exile: The Decembrist Memoirs*. Montreal: McGill-Queens University Press, 1974.

Brailovskii, S. N. "Iz zhizni odnogo dekabrista." *Russkaia starina*, XXXIV, 3 (March 1903): 541–65.

Chernovskii, A., and M. Gavrilov, eds. *Chetyrnadtsatoe dekabriia: sbornik k stoletiiu vosstaniia dekabristov*. Leningrad: Gosudarstvennoe izdatel'stvo, 1925.

Eidelman, N. *Conspiracy against the Tsar*. Translated by Cynthia Carlile. Moscow: Progress, 1985.

Ferrugato, Mark. "Representing Russia: Luxury and Diplomacy at the Razumovsky Palace in Vienna, 1803–1815." *Music and Arts*, XCVII, 3 (2026): 383–408.

Figes, Orlando. *Natasha's Dance: A Culutral History of Russia*. New York: Metropolitan Books, 2002.

Grimstead, Patricia Kennedy. *The Foreign Ministers of Alexander I: Political Attitudes and the Conduct of Russian Diplomacy, 1801–1825*. Berkeley: University of California Press, 1969.

Kandinskii, A. I., ed. *Istoriia russkoi muzyki*, IV. Moscow: Muzyka, 1986.

Kildea, Paul. *Chopin's Piano: In Search of the Instrument That Transformed Music*. New York: W. W. Norton, 2018.

King, David. *Vienna 1814: How the Conquerors of Napoleon Made Love, War, and Peace at the Congress of Vienna*. New York: Harmony Books, 2008.

Lincoln, W. Bruce. *Between Heaven and Hell: The Story of a Thousand Years of Artistic Life in Russia*. New York: Viking, 1998,

———. *Sunlight at Midnight: St. Petersburg and the Rise of Modern Russia*. New York: Basic Books, 2000.

Maes, Francis. *A History of Russian Music: From Kamarinskaya to Babi Yar*. Translated by Arnold J. and Erica Pomerans. Berkeley: University of California Press, 2002.

Mazour, Anatole. G. *The First Russian Revolution, 1825*. Stanford, CA: Stanford University Press, 1975.

———. *Women in Exile: Wives of the Decembrists*. Tallahassee, FL: Diplomatic, 1975.

Mirsky, D. S. *A History of Russian Literature*, edited by Francis J. Whitfield. New York: Vintage Books, 1958.

Nechkina, V. *Dekabristy*. Moscow: Mysl', 1975.

Nekrasov, N. "Russkie zhenshchini." In *Izbrannye stikhotvorenii*, II, edited by K. I. Chukovskii. Leningrad: Sovetskii pisatel', 1967.

Raeff, Marc. *The Decembrist Movement*. Englewood Cliffs, NJ: Prentice-Hall, 1960.

Roberts, Sophy. *The Lost Pianos of Siberia*. New York: Grove, 2020.

Slezkine, Yuri. *The House of Government: A Saga of the Russian Revolution*. Princeton, NJ: Princeton University Press, 2017.

Stites, Richard. *Revolutionary Dreams: Utopian Vision and Experimental Life in the Russian Revolution*. Oxford: Oxford University Press, 1989.

——. *Serfdom, Society, and the Arts in Imperial Russia: The Pleasure and the Power.* New Haven, CT: Yale University Press, 2005.
Taruskin, Richard. *Defining Russia Musically: Historical and Hermeneutical Essays.* Princeton, NJ: Princeton University Press, 2005.
——. *On Russian Music.* Berkeley: University of California Press, 2009.
Tikhvinskaia, Liudmila. *Povsednevnaia zhizn' teatral'noi bogemy Serebrianogo veka: kabare i teatry miniatiur v Rossii, 1908–1917.* Moscow: Molodaia gvardiia, 2005.
Volkov, Solomon. *St. Petersburg: A Cultural History.* Translated by Antonina W. Bouis. New York: Free Press, 1995.
Ward, Charles A. *Moscow and Leningrad: A Topographical Guide to Russian Cultural History,* II. Munich: K. G. Saur, 1992.
Wilson, Elizabeth. *Jacqueline du Pré: Her Life, Her Music, Her Legend.* New York: Arcade, 1999.
Zamoyski, Adam. *Moscow1812: Napoleon's Fatal March.* New York: Harper Collins, 2004.

Moscow

Danilevich, L. *Liudvig van Betkhoven (1770–1827)—Rikhard Vagner (1813–1883)—Berlioz (1803–1869): poiasnenie k kontsertu.* Moscow: Moskovskaia gosudarstvennaia filarmoniia, 1938.
Diubiuk, A. "Iz vospominanii o muzykal'noi zhizni staroi Moskvy." *Russkaia muzykal'naia gazeta,* XXIII, 34–35 (August 21–28, 1916): 618–20; 38–39 (September 18–25, 1916): 671–75; 40 (October 2, 1916): 706–10.
Kashkin, N. D. *Pervoe dvadtsatipiatiletie Moskovskoi konservatorii: istoricheskii ocherk.* Moscow: Iakovlev, 1891.
——, ed. *Moskovskoe otdelenie Imperatorskogo russkogo muzykal'nogo obshchestva: ocherk deiatel'nosti za piatidesiatiletie, 1860–1910 g.* Moscow: n.p., 1910.
Lipaev, I. "Moskovskoe filarmonicheskoe obshchestvo (iubileinaia spravka)." *Russkaia muzykal'naia gazeta,* X, 44 (November 2, 1903): 1048–50.
McQuere, Gordon D. "The Moscow Conservatory 1866–1889: Nikolai Rubinshtein and Sergei Taneev." *Canadian American Slavic Studies,* XXXIV, 1 (Spring 2000): 33–61.
Manykin-Nevstriev, N. A. *Simfonicheskie sobraniia 1–500: statisticheskii pravitel'.* Moscow: Iakovlev, 1899.
Morov, A. *Moskva muzykal'naia.* Moscow: Moskovskii rabochii, 1964.
Moskovskaia gosudarstvennaia filarmoniia. Moscow: Sovetskii kompozitor, 1973.
Moskovskaia gosudarstvennaia filarmoniia: XX let. Moscow: Moskovskaia gosudarstvennia filarmoniia, 1941.
Moskovskaia konservatoriia, 1866–1966. Moscow: Muzyka, 1966.
Muzykal'naia zhizn' Moskvy v pervye gody posle oktiabria. Moscow: Sovetskii kompositor, 1972.
Palii, E. N. *Literaturno-muzykal'nye stranitsy Moskvy pervoi treti XIX veka.* Moscow: Moskovskii gosudarstvennyi otkrytyi pedagogicheskii universitet, 1996.
Pribegina, G. A. *Moskovskaia konservatoriia, 1866–1991: k 125-letiiu so dnia osnovaniia.* Moscow: Muzyka, 1991.
XX let Moskovskoi gosudarstvennoi filarmonii. Moscow: Moskovskaia gosudarstvennaia filarmoniia, 1940.

Musical Life

Russian

Al'brekht, E., ed. *Proshloe i nastoiashchee orchestra (ocherk sotsial'nogo polozheniia muzykantov).* St. Petersburg: Goppe, 1886.

AN SSSR. *Kratkii orcherk istorii russkoi kul'tury s drevneishikh vremen do 1917 goda*. Leningrad: Nauka, 1967.
Arsen'ev, I. A. "Vospominanie o Liste." *Istoricheskii vestnik*, VII (September 1886): 576–79.
Bartlett, Rosamund. *Wagner and Russia*. Cambridge: Cambridge University Press, 1995.
Berezovskii, V. V. *Russkaia muzyka*. St. Petersburg: Erlikh, 1898.
Bessel', V. V. *Kratkii ocherk muzyki v Rossii*. St. Petersburg-Moscow: Bessel', 1905.
"Betkhovenskaia akademiia." *Muzykal'nyi truzhenik*, IV, 7 (April 1, 1910): 16–18.
Blaramberg, P. "Tsenzura v muzyke: iz lichnykh vospominaniia." In *V zashchitu slova*. St. Petersburg: Kliubov, 1905.
Calvocoressi, M. D., and Gerald Abraham. *Masters of Russian Music*. New York: Tudor, 1944.
Cheshikhin, V. "Istoriia russkogo smychkovogo kvarteta." *Russkaia muzykal'naia gazeta*, XXIV, 24, 27–28 (August 1, 1917): 449–54.
———. "Kompozitory i revoliutsii." *Russkaia muzykal'naia gazeta*, XXIV, 13–18 (April 1–8 / April 16–23 / April 30–May 7, 1917): 282–92, 314–21, 338–46.
Cui, Ts, ed. *Istoriia literatury fortepiannoi muzyki: kurs' A. G. Rubinshteina, 1888–89*. St. Petersburg: Golike, 1889.
Denisova, Iu., et al. *Zaly i zdaniia gosudarstvennogo Ermitazha: Ermitazhnyi teatr*. St. Petersburg: Gosudarstvennyi Ermitazh, 2004.
Druskin, M. S., and Iu. V. Keldysh, ed. *Ocherki po istorii russkoi muzyki, 1790–1825*. Leningrad: Gosudarstvennoe muzykal'noe izdatel'stvo, 1956.
Dunlop, Carolyn C. *The Russian Court Chapel Choir, 1796–1917*. Amsterdam: Harwood Academic, 2000.
Fatov, N. "Iskusstvo vragov." *Russkaia muzykal'naia gazeta*, XXI, 38–39 (September 21–28, 1914): 728–29; 44 (November 2, 1914): 782–85; 46 (November 16, 1914): 843–45.
Findeizen, N. F. "Motsart v Rossii." *Russkaia muzykal'naia gazeta*, XIII, 3 (January 15, 1906): 66–81; 4–5 (January 22–29, 1906): 120–21; 16 (April 16, 1906).
———. "Muzyka i teatr v epokhu otechestvennoi voiny." *Russkaia muzykal'naia gazeta*, XIX, 33–34 (August 12–19, 1912): 642–71.
———. "Nash muzykal'nyi biurokratizm." *Russkaia muzykal'naia gazeta*, XII, 7 (February 13, 1905): 186–89; 8 (February 20, 1905): 223–30.
———. *Ocherki po istorii muzyki v Rossii*. Moscow: Novyi khronograf, 2002.
———. "Shuman v Rossii." *Russkaia muzykal'naia gazeta*, XIII, 27–28 (July 2–9, 1906): 622–29.
———. "Vagner v Rossii." *Russkaia muzykal'naia gazeta*, X, 35 (August 30, 1903): 755–69.
Fon Tidebel', E. "Simfoniia na Volge." *Russkaia muzykal'naia gazeta*, XVII, 30–31 (July 25–August 1, 1910): 637–39.
Ginzburg, L. *Istoriia violonchel'nogo iskusstva*, II. Moscow: Muzgiz, 1957.
Girchenko, V. "Muzyka v kazemate dekabristov v gody sibirskoi katorgi." *Sovetskaia muzyka*, XIV, 3 (March 1950): 62–76.
Gordeeva, E. *Iz istorii russkoi muzykal'noi kritiki XIX veka*. Moscow: Gosudarstvennoe muzykal'noe izdatel'stvo, 1950.
Gozenpud, A. "Rikhard Wagner i russkaia kul'tura." *Sovetskaia muzyka*, XLVII, 4 (April 1983): 78–87.
———. *Russkii opernyi teatr XIX veka (1836–1856)*. Leningrad: Muzyka, 1969.
———. *Russkii opernyi teatr XIX veka (1857–1872)*. Leningrad: Muzyka, 1971.
———. *Russkii opernyi teatr na rubezhe XIX-XX vekov i F. I. Shaliapin, 1890–1904*. Leningrad: Muzyka, 1974.
———. *Russkii opernyi teatr mezhdu dvukh revoliutsii, 1905–1917*. Leningrad: Muzyka, 1975.
I., I. "K voprosu o polozhenii orkestrovykh muzykantov." *Muzykal'nyi truzhenik*, IV, 12–13 (July 1, 1910): 13–17; 18 (September 15, 1910): 29–34.
Iablonskii, A. "List v Rossii." *Sovetskaia muzyka*, L, 12 (December 1986): 97–103.

Ippolitov-Ivanov, M. M. *50 let russkoi muzyki v moikh vospominaniiakh*. Moscow: Gosudarstvennoe muzykal'noe izdatel'stvo, 1934.
Ivanov, M. M. *Istoriia muzykal'nogo razvitiia Rossii*, 2 vol. St. Petersburg: Gosudarstvennoe muzykal'noe izdatel'stvo, 1910/1912.
Kandinskii, A. I., ed. *Istoriia russkoi muzyki*. Moscow: Muzyka, 1980.
Kashkin, N. *Ocherk istorii russkoi muzyki*. Moscow: Iurgenson, 1908.
———. "Piatidesiatiletie russkogo muzykal'nogo obshchestva." *Muzykal'nyi truzhenik*, III, 10/11 (June 1, 1909): 5–10; 14/15 (August 1, 1909): 4–6; 16/17 (September 1, 1909): 8–11.
Katalog dvukhstoronnikh plastinok Metropol' Rekord. Moscow: n.p., n.d.
Keldysh, Iu. V., et al. *Istoriia russkoi muzyki*, 10 vol. Moscow: Muzyka, 1983–2011.
Khotuntsov, N. *Dekabristy i muzyka*. Leningrad: Muzyka, 1975.
Khvostenko, V., and T. Trofimova, comp., "List v Rossii." *Sovetskaia muzyka*, IV, 11 (November 1936): 30–48; V, 8 (August 1937): 55–56.
Kleinbort, L. "Rabochaia intelligentsiia i iskusstvo." *Vestnik Evropy*, XLVII (August 1913): 215–26.
Kochetov, N. *Ocherk istorii muzyki*. Moscow: Iurgenson, 1909.
Kratkii ocherk istorii russkoi kul'tury s drevneishikh vremen do 1917 goda. Leningrad: Nauka, 1967.
Lipaev, I. "Brodiachie muzykanty." *Russkaia muzykal'naia gazeta*, XIX, 27–28 (July 1–8, 1912): 571– 76; 29–30 (July 15–22, 1912): 609–14.
———. "Muzykal'nye kritiki, retsenzenty i reportery (ocherk)." *Russkaia muzykal'naia gazeta*, XVIII, 14 (April 3, 1911): 358–60; 17 (April 24, 1911): 420-[end page/s missing]; 18–19 (May 1–8, 1911): 454–56; 20–21 (May 15–22, 1911): 479–81.
———. *Orkestrovye muzykanty (istoricheskie i bytovye ocherki)*. St. Petersburg: Russkaia muzykal'naia gazeta, 1904.
Liricheskii muzeum. St. Petersburg: Departament narodnogo prosveshcheniia, 1851.
Lisovskii, N. M. *Muzykal'nye al'manakhi XVIII stoletiia*. St. Petersburg: Gaberman, 1882.
Livanova, T. *Russkaia muzykal'naia kul'tura XVIII veka v ee sviaziakh s literaturoi, teatrom i bytom*, 2 vol. Moscow: Gosudarstvennoe muzykal'noe izdatel'stvo, 1952–53.
Mikhnevich, V. *Ocherk istorii muzyki v Rossii v kul'turno-obshchestvennom otnoshenii*. St. Petersburg: n.p., 1879.
Miliukov, Paul. *Outlines of Russian Culture*. Translated by Valentine Ughet and Eleanor Davis. Philadelphia: University of Pennsylvania Press, 1948.
Mollengauer, N. *O muzykal'nom obrazovanii*. Moscow: Levenson, 1909.
Muzalevskii, V. *Russkoe fortep'iannoe iskusstvo, XVIII-pervaia polovina XIX veka*. Leningrad: Gosudarstvennoe muzykal'noe izdatel'stvo, 1961.
Muzyka i muzykal'nyi byt staroi Rossii: materialy i issledovaniia, I. Leningrad: Akademia, 1927.
"Muzyka i tsenzura." *Teatr i iskusstvo*, 25 (1906): 391–93.
"Napoleon i muzyka." *Russkaia muzykal'naia gazeta*, XIX, 35 (August 26, 1912): 676–84.
Natanson, V. *Proshloe russkogo pianizma (XVIII-nachalo XIX veka): ocherki i materialy*. Moscow: Gosudarstvennoe muzykal'noe izdatel'stvo, 1960.
Notnye izdaniia v muzykal'noi zhizni Rossii, 3 vols. St. Petersburg: Rosskiiskaia natsional'naia biblioteka, 1999, 2003, 2007.
Novosti muzykal'nye prodaiushchiiasia u Pavla Lengol'da . . . 1849–1852. Moscow: Semen, 1849–52.
Onnore, I. "Odinnadtsat' let v teatre." *Russkaia starina*, XLI, 1 (January 1910): 95–108; 3 (March 1910): 543–55; XLIII, 1 (January 1912): 160–72; 2 (February 1912): 316–26.

Opochinin, E. "Za kulisami starogo teatra; krepostnye muzykanty na sluzhbe direktsii teatrov." *Istoricheskii vestnik*, X, 6 (June 1889): 597–623.
Pekelis, M. S. *Istoriia russkoi muzyki*, 2 vol. Moscow-Leningrad: Muzgiz, 1940.
Perepelitsyn, P. D. *Istoriia muzyki v Rossii s drevneishikh vremen i do nashikh dnei*. St. Petersburg: Vol'f, 1888.
Petronii. "Muzykal'nyi 1916 god." *Russkaia muzykal'naia gazeta*, XXIV, 1 (January 1, 1917): 14–17.
Popov, I. E. "K reforme Imperatorskogo russkogo muzykal'nogo obshchestva." *Russkaia muzykal'naia gazeta*, XIV, 16–17 (April 22–29, 1907): 462–64.
———. "K voprosu o preobrazovanii uchebnykh zavedenii Imperatorskogo russkogo muzykal'nogo obshchestva." *Muzykal'nyi truzhenkik*, III, 20 (October 15, 1909): 1–4.
Presman, M. "O neobkhodimykh reformakh v Ustave Imperatorskogo russkogo muzykal'nogo obshchestva." *Russkaia muzykal'naia gazeta*, XXIII, 4 (January 24, 1916): 82–88.
Problema muzykal'nogo vospriiatiia: anketa. Moscow: Betkhovenskaia studiia, 1913.
Puzyrevskii, A. I., ed. *Imperatorskoe russkoe muzykal'noe obshchestvo: v pervye 50 let ego deiatel'nosti (1859–1909 g.)*. St. Petersburg: Milshtein, 1909.
Sabaneev, L. "Iubilei muzykal'nogo obshchestva (1860–1910g.)." *Muzyka*, 1 (November 27, 1910): 10–18.
———. "Obzor muzykal'noi zhizni 1913 g." In *Muzykal'nyi alamanakh*, edited by G. Angert and E. Shor. Moscow: Izdatel'stvo Beetkhovenskoi studii, 1914.
Sakketti, L. "Muzykal'noe obrazovanie v shkole i zhizni." *Vestnik Evropy*, XIV, 4 (April 1879): 737–62.
Sargeant, Lynn M. *Harmony and Discord: Music and the Transformation of Russian Cultural Life*. Oxford: Oxford University Press, 2010.
Seaman, Gerald R. *History of Russian Music*, I. Oxford: Blackwell, 1967.
Serov, A. N. "K chitateliam." *Muzyka i teatra*, 1 (January 1867): 1–5.
———. "Sud'by opery v Rossii." *Russkaia tsena*, 2 (February 1864): 119–28; 7 (July 1864): 1–11.
Serova, V. "Nashi idealy muzykal'nogo obrazovaniia." *Muzyka i teatr*, 2 (February 1867): 25–29.
———. "Pravda-li chto v nashe vremia net potrebnosti v muzyke?." *Muzyka i teatr*, 11 (November 1867): 161–65.
Shteinberg, A. "U istokov russkoi mysli o muzyke." *Sovetskaia muzyka*, XXXI, 10 (October 1967): 73–82.
Stasov, V. V. "Avtografy muzykantov v Imperatorskoi publichnoi biblioteke." *Otechestvennye zapiski*, CIX (1856): 105–14.
———. "Dvadtsatipiatiletie bezplatnoi muzykal'noi shkoly." *Istoricheskii vestnik*, VIII, 3 (March 1887): 599–642.
———. *List, Shuman i Berlioz v Rossii*. St. Petersburg: Russkaia muzykal'naia gazeta, 1896.
———. "Nasha muzyka za poslednye 25 let." *Vestnik Evropy*, XVIII, 10 (October 1883): 561–623.
Tikhvinskaia, Liudmila. *Povsednevnaia zhizn' teatral'noi bogemy serebrianogo veka: kabare i teatry miniatiur v Rossii, 1908–1917*. Moscow: Molodaia gvardiia, 2005.
Tret'iakova, L. *Molodaia muzykal'naia Rossiia*. Moscow: Sovetskaia Rossiia, 1985.
Trofimova, T., "List v Rossii." *Sovetskaia muzyka*, V, 8 (August 1937).
Turgina, L., ed. *Mysli o muzyke pisatelei drevnikh i novykh*. St. Petersburg: Gliasser, 1890.
Ukolova, Elena, i Valerii Ukolov. *Gastroli Lista v Rossii: illiustrirovannaia khronika*. Moscow: Mezhdunarodnyi fond gumanitarnykh initsiativ, 2012.
Vladishevskaia, T. F. *Istoriia russkoi muzyki*, I. Moscow: Muzyka, 1999.
Vol'man, B. *Russkie notnye izdaniia XIX-nachala XX veka*. Leningrad: Muzyka, 1970.
Zhitomirskii, D. *Robert i Klara Shuman v Rossii*. Moscow: Gosudarstvennoe muzykal'noe izdatel'stvo, 1962.

Soviet

Cherednichenko, T. *Muzykal'nyi zapas 70-e: problemy, portrety, sluchai.* Moscow: Novoe literaturnoe obozrenie, 2002.
D., A. "Simfonicheskie kontserty Gosfila pod upravleniem direizhera Eugena Senkara, (Mart 1935 g.)." *Sovetskaia muzyka*, III, 4 (April 1935): 79–81.
Dreiden, S. *Muzyka—revoliutsii.* 2nd rev. ed. Moscow: Sovetskii kompozitor, 1970.
Druzhina, E. "Muzykal'naia zhizn'." *Sovetskaia muzyka*, III, 4 (April 1935): 90–91.
Fairclough, Pauline. *Classics for the Masses: Shaping Soviet Musical Identity under Lenin and Stalin.* New Haven, CT: Yale University Press, 2016.
Frolova-Walker, Marina. *Stalin's Music Prize: Soviet Culture and Politics.* New Haven, CT: Yale University Press, 2016.
Frolova-Walker, Marina, and Jonathan Walker. *Music and Soviet Power, 1917–1932.* Woodbridge, UK: Boydell, 2012.
Goncharova, N. "Betkhoven v Krasnoi Armii." *Sovetskaia muzyka*, III, 7–8 (July–August 1935): 150–55.
Iampol'skii, I. "Kvartetnye sobraniia (Fevral'-Mart 1937 g.)." *Sovetskaia muzyka*, V, 4 (April 1937): 88–89.
Kabalevskii, D. "O muzykal'noi kritike." *Sovetskaia muzyka*, IX, 1 (January 1941): 4–17.
Khubov, G. "Prazdnik simfonicheskoi muzyki (pervyi kontsert Gosudarstvennogo simfonicheskogo orkestra pod upr. E. Kleibera." *Sovetskaia muzyka*, IV, 11 (November 1936): 77–78.
———, ed. *Muzykal'naia publitsistika raznykh let: stat'i, ocherki, retsenzii.* Moscow: Sovetskii kompozitor, 1976.
Kuznetsov, K. "Smotr raboty trekh konservatorii." *Sovetskaia muzyka*, IV, 8 (August 1936): 51–54.
Lemaire, Frans. C. *Musique du XXe siècle* en *Russie et dans les anciennes republiques sovietiques.* St. Petersburg: Giperion, 2003.
Lipovsky, Alexander, comp. *Soviet Stars: Lenin Prize Winners in the World of Music.* Translated by Olga Shartse. Moscow: Progress, 1966.
Maksimenkov, Leonid, ed. *Muzyka vmesto sumbura: kompozitory i muzykanty v strane sovetov, 1917–1991.* Moscow: Mezhdunarodnyi fond demokratiia, 2013.
Mar, A. "Pervyi vsesoiuznyi radiofestival'." *Sovetskaia muzyka*, IV, 7 (July 1936): 33–44.
Martynov, I. "O rabote Moskovskoi filarmonii." *Sovetskaia muzyka*, VI, 6 (June 1938): 78–85.
"Muzykal'naia zhizn' v SSSR. V komitete po podgotovke betkhovenskikh torzhestv." *Muzykal'noe obrazovanie*, 1–2 (1927): 67–69.
Nelson, Amy. *Music for the Revolution: Musicians and Power in Early Soviet Russia.* University Park: Pennsylvania State University Press, 2004.
Rabinovich, D. "Tsikl konstertov—Betkhoven, Berlioz, Vagner." *Sovetskaia muzyka*, VI, 7 (July 1938): 71–73.
Raku, Marina. *Muzykal'naia klassika v mifotvorchestve Sovetskoi epokhi.* Moscow: Novoe literaturnoe obozrenie, 2014.
Sabaneev, L. *Muzyka posle oktiabria.* Moscow: Rabotnik prosveshcheniia, 1926.
Schwarz, Boris. *Music and Musical Life in Soviet Russia, 1917–1970.* New York: W. W. Norton, 1972.
"Sumbur vmesto muzyki (op opere 'Ledi Makbet Mtsenskogo Uezda')." *Sovetskaia muzyka*, IV, 1 (January 1936): 4–5. [Reprinted from *Pravda*, January 28, 1936.]
Teatral'no-muzykal'nyi spravochnik SSSR na 1928 g. na CD. St. Petersburg: Peterburgskii genealogicheskii portal, 2007. [DVD of *Teatral'no-muzykal'nyi spravochnik na 1928 g.* Moscow-Leningrad: Tea-Kino-Pechat', 1928.]

V pervye gody sovetskogo muzykal'nogo stroitel'stva: stat'i, vospominaniia, materialy. Leningrad: Sovetskii kompozitor, 1959.

Vishnevetskii, I. G. *"Evraziiskoe uklonenie" v muzyke 1920–1930kh godov. Istoriia voprosa. Stat'i i materialy*. Moscow: Novoe literaturnoe obozrenie, 2005.

Provinces

General

"Muzyka v provintsii." *Russkaia muzykal'naia gazeta*, XII, 35–36 (August 28–September 4, 1905); 41 (October 9, 1905).

"Betkhovenskie torzhestva." *Russkaia muzykal'naia gazeta*, XX, 220–21 (May 19–26, 1913).

Poluianov, P. "V plenu." *Russkaia muzykal'naia gazeta*, XX, 14 (April 5, 1915): 248–52.

Arkhangel'sk

Shchurov, G. S. *Arkhangel'sk*, 3 vol. Arkhangel'sk, Russia: Pravda Severna, 1995–97.

Astrakhan

Etinger, M. A. *Muzykal'naia kul'tura Astrakhani*. Volgograd, Russia: Nizhno-Volzhskoe knizhnoe izdatel'stvo, 1987.

Cheliabinsk

Vol'fovich, V. *Cheliabinsk muzykal'nyi*. Cheliabinsk, Russia: Iuzhno-Uralskoe knizhnoe izdatel'stvo, 1989.

Irkutsk

Kharkeevich, I. Iu. *Muzykal'naia kul'tura g. Irkutska dooktiabr'skogo perioda*. Moscow: Irkutskii gosudarstvennyi pedagogicheskii institut, 1976.

———. *Muzykal'naia kul'tura Irkutska*. Irkutsk, Russia: Irkutskii universitet, 1987.

Ivanov

Efimov, Iu. L. *Ivanovskoe muzyykal'noe uchilishche*. Iaroslavl', Russia: Verkhno-Volzhskoe knizhnoe izdatel'stvo, 1979.

Kazan'

Iz istorii muzykal'noi kul'tury i obrazovaniia v Kazani: sbornik nauchnykh trudov. Kazan', Russia: Kazanskaia gosudarstvennaia konservatoriia, 1993.

Khar'kov

Konova, E. V. *Pianisticheskaia kul'tura Khar'kova poslednei treti XIX-nachala XX stoletii*. Kiev, Ukraine: Institut iskusstvovedeniia, fol'klora i etnografii im. M. F. Ryl'skogo, 1984.

Kiev

Chechott, V. "Muzyka i publika v provintsii (itogi muzykal'nogo sezona v Kieve 1888–89 gg.)." *Artist*, II, 1 (September 1889): 86–91.

——. "Kievskaia opera." *Artist*, II, 2 (October 1889): 118–20.
K–k, L. "Geroicheskaia simfoniia Betkhovena." *Kievlianin*, XVI, 7 (January 9, 1880).
Miklashevskii, I., ed. *Ocherk deiatel'nosti Kievskogo otdeleniia Imperatorskogo russkogo muzykal'nogo obshchestva (1863–1913)*. Kiev: Kul'zhenko, 1913.

Krasnoiarsk

Krivosheia, B. G., et al. *Muzykal'naia zhizn' Krasnoiarska*. Krasnoiarsk, Russia: Krasnoiarskoe knizhnoe izdatel'stvo, 1983.

Kronshtadt

Nemo. "Fel'eton. Chto takoe provintsialism. Provintsial'ny-li gorod Kronshtadt. Kronshtadskii teatr," *Kronshtadtskii vestnik*, November 2, 1861.

Nizhnii-Novgorod

Beliakov, B. N., et al. *Opernaia i kontsertnaia deiatel'nost' v Nizhnem Novgorode-gorode Gor'kom (1798–1980)*. Gor'kii, Russia: Volgo-Viatskoe knizhnoe izdatel'stvo, 1980.
Kollar, V. A. *Muzykal'naia zhizn' Nizhnego Novgoroda-goroda Gor'kogo*. Gor'kii, Russia: Volgo-Viatskoe knizhnoe izdatel'stvo, 1976.

Odessa

Anisimov, V. "Otkrytie Odesskoi konservatorii." *Russkaia muzykal'naia gazeta*, XX, 43 (October 7, 1913).
Dagilaiskaia, E. R. *Muzykal'naia zhizn' Odessy XIX-nachala XX v.v.: kontsertnaia i pedagogicheskaia deiatel'nost' pianistov*. Moscow: avtoref. dis., Moskovskaia gosudarstvennaia konservatoriia, 1977.
Engel', R. "25-letie Odesskogo otdeleniia IRMO." *Russkaia muzykal'naia gazeta*, XIX, 27–28 (July 1–8, 1912).
"Iubilei Betkhovena." *Odesski vestnik*, December 15, 1870.
Malishevskii, V. I., ed. *Kratkii istoricheskii ocherk deiatel'nosti Odesskogo otdeleniia Imperatorskogo russkogo muzykal'nogo obshchestva i sostoiashchego pri nem myzykal'nogo uchilishcha za dvadtsat' piat' let (1886–1911)*. Odessa, Ukraine: Shtab okr., 1911.

Orel'

Sizov, P. *Muzykal'naia Orlovshchina*. Tula, Russia: Priokskoe knizhnoe izdatel'stvo, 1980.
——. *Muzykal'nye byli Orla*. Tula, Russia: Priokskoe knizhnoe izdatel'stvo, 1985.

Orenburg

Khavtorin, B. *Muzykal'naia kul'tura Orenburga XX stoletiia*. Orenburg, Russia: Orenburgskoe knizhnoe izdatel'stvo, 1999.

Penza

Sabin, O. M. *Penza muzykal'naia*. Penza, Russia: Departament kul'tury Penzkoi oblasti, 1994.

Poltava

Findeizen, N. *Ocherk deiatel'nosti Poltavskogo otdeleniia Imperatorskogo russkogo muzykal'nogo obshchestva za 1899–1915 g.g.* Poltava, Ukraine: Tovarishchestvo pechatnogo dela, 1916.

Rostov-na-Donu

Chernykh, M. P. *Muzykal'naia zhizn' Rostova-na-Donu ot serediny XVIII do 20-kh godov XX stoletii (puti razvitiia, osobennosti muzykal'nogo uklada)*. Moscow: Kafedr istorii muzyki rossiiskoi muzykal'noi akademii, 1993.

Saratov

Inkognito. "35-letie Saratovskogo otdeleniia IRMO i 25-letie muzykal'noi deiatel'nosti S. K. Eksnera." *Russkaia muzykal'naia gazeta*, XV, 41 (October 11, 1908).

Siberia

Kupert, T. Iu. *Muzykal'naia kul'tura gorodov zapadnoi Sibiri v kontse XIX-nachala XX veka*. Moscow: Sektor istorii muzyki narodov SSSR Vsesoiuznogo nauchno-issledovatel'skogo instituta iskusstvoznaniia, 1986.

Romenskaia, T. A. *Istoriia muzykal'noi kul'tury Sibiri ot pokhodov Ermaka do krest'ianskoi reformy 1861 goda*. Tomsk, Russia: Tomskii universitet, 1992.

Simferopol'

S., O. "Simferopol' (korrespondentsiia)." *Russkaia muzykal'naia gazeta*, XX, 30–31 (July 28–August 4, 1913).

Smolensk

Wz. "Muzykal'noe torzhestvo v Smolenske." *Vestnik Evropy*, XX, 4 (April 1884): 390–400.

Stavropol'

"Stavropol'-Kavkazskii (korrespondentsiia)." *Russkaia muzykal'naia gazeta*, X, 14–15 (April 6–13, 1903); XIII, 13 (March 26, 1906); 46 (November 12, 1906).

Sverdlovsk

Sverdlovskaia gosudarstvennaia filarmoniia: k predstoiashchemu sezonu, 1937–38 g.g. Sverdlovsk, Russia: Sverdlovskaia gosudarstvennaia filarmoniia, 1937.

Taganrog

Kukushin, V. S., and Z. A. Boiko. *Muzykal'naia kul'tura goroda Taganroga*. Rostov-na-Donu, Russia: GinGo, 1999.

Tambov

Emel'ianova, N. *Muzykal'nye vechera: khronika muzykal'noi zhizni tambovskogo kraia za 100 let*. Voronezh, Russia: Tsentral'no-Chernozemnoe knizhnoe izdatel'stvo, 1977.

Tbilisi

Bebutov, P. "Tiflis (korrespondentsiia)." *Russkaia muzykal'naia gazeta*, XXIV, 21–22 (May 30, 1917); XXV, 1 (January 15, 1918).

Gar–skii, L. "Betkhoven i ego simfoniia C-moll." *Kavkaz: gazeta politicheskaia i literaturnaia*, XXVII, 145 (December 10 [22], 1872).

Tomsk

Kupert, Tat'iana. *Muzykal'noe proshloe Tomska*. Tomsk, Russia: n.p., 2006.

Viadro, B. M. "O deiatel'nosti direktsii Tomskogo obshchestva IRMO." *Russkaia muzykal'naia gazeta*, XV, 36 (September 7, 1908): 715–19.

Tsaritsyn

Andrianova, G. N. *Khudozhestvennyi oblik Tsaritsyna-Stalingrada*. Volgograd, Russia: Universal, 1991.

Tver

Tverskaia oblastnaia filarmoniia: vechnaia muzyka. Tver, Russia: Tverskaia oblastnaia filarmoniia, 1996.

Upper Volga

Shikov, V. *Muzykanty verkhne-volzh'ia*. Moscow: Moskovskii rabochii, 1984.

Viatka

Presnetsov R. M. *Muzyka i muzykanty Viatki: ocherki, portrety, dokumenty, vospominaniia*. Gor'kii, Russia: Volgo-Viatskoe knizhnoe izdatel'stvo, 1982.

Vladivostok

Koroleva, V. A. *Khronika kul'turnoi zhizni Vladivostoka, 1917–1922: muzyka, teatr, kino*. Vladivostok, Russia: DVGU, 1998.

Vologda

Kirillova, E. A. *Ocherki muzykal'noi zhizni*. Vologda, Russia: B. izdatel'stvo, 1997.

Warsaw

"Konservatoriia v Varshave." *Literaturnoe pribavlenie k Nuvellistu*, XX, 12 (December 1859).

Varshavskii dnevnik, VII, 262 (December 7 [19], 1870).

Various

Findeizen, N. "Teatr i muzyka v provintsii v nachale XIX v. (1809–1812 gg.)." In *Muzykal'naia starina: sbornik statei i materialov dlia istorii muzyki v Rossii*, III–IV. St. Petersburg: Glavnoe upravlenie udelov, 1907.

Golitsyn, Iu. "Muzykal'naia deiatel'nost' v provintsii." *Russkaia tsena*, 4–5 (April–May 1865): 35–52.

"Iz deiatel'nosti otdelenii IRMO za 1905–06." *Russkaia muzykal'naia gazeta*, XIV, 22–23 (June 3–10, 1907).

"Muzyka v provintsii. Imp. Russkoe muz. obshch. v 1901–1902 akademicheskom godu." *Russkaia muzykal'naia gazeta*, X, 36 (September 7, 1903); 37 (September 14, 1903); 39 (September 28, 1903); 41 (October 12, 1903); XI, 15 (April 11, 1904); 16 (April 18, 1904); 17–18 (April 25–May 2, 1904); 19–20 (May 9, 1904); 21–22 (May 23–30, 1904); 25–26 (June 20–27, 1904); 31–32 (August 1–8, 1904).

"Muzykal'no-pedagogicheskaia deiatel'nost' IRMO po otchetam 1913–14 gg." *Russkaia muzykal'naia gazeta*, XXII, 21–22 (May 24–31, 1915); 25–26 (June 21–28, 1915); 27–28 (July 5–12, 1915); 37–38 (September 13–20, 1915); 46 (November 15, 1915).
Maksimovskaia, L. M., ed. *Nevel'skii sbornik: stat'i i vospominaniia*, IV. St. Petersburg: Akropol', 1999.
Shteinpress, B. S. *Iz muzykal'nogo proshlogo: sbornik ocherkov*. Moscow: Gosudarstvennoe muzykal'noe izdatel'stvo, 1960. [Re: Ekaterinburg/Sverdlovsk, Perm', Orenburg, Saratov, Kazan', Nizhnii Novgorod/Gor'kii, Rostov-na-Donu, Odessa.]

St. Petersburg/Petrograd/Leningrad

Al'brekht, E. *S.-Peterburgskaia konservatoriia*. St. Petersburg: Goppe, 1891.
———, ed. *Obshchii obzor deiatel'nosti Vysochaishe utverzhdennogo S.-Peterburgskogo filarmonicheskogo obshchestva*. St. Petersburg: Goppe. 1884.
Al'ianskii, Iu. *Teatr v kvadrate obstrela*. Leningrad: Iskusstvo, 1985.
Beliakaeva-Kazanskaia, L. V. *Ekho serebrianogo veka: maloizvestnye stranitsy Peterburgskoi kul'tury pervoi treti XX veka*. St. Petersburg: Kanon, 1998.
———. *Siluety muzykal'nogo Peterburga: putevoditel' po muzykal'nym teatram, muzeiam, kontsertnym zalam proshlogo i nastoiashchego*. St. Petersburg: Lenizdat, 2001.
Berezovskii, B. *Filarmonicheskoe obshchestvo Sankt-Peterburga; istoriia i sovremennost'*. St. Petersburg: Kul't Inform, 2002.
Bernatskii, V. A. "Iz zolotogo veka ital'ianskoi opery v Peterburge." *Russkaia starina*, XLVII, 9 (September 1916): 17–24; 12 (December 1916): 434–56.
Bogdan-Berezovskii, V. *Stranitsy muzykal'noi publitsistiki: ocherki, stat'i, retsenzii*. Leningrad: Gosudarstvennoe muzykal'noe izdatel'stvo, 1963.
Bronfin, E. *Muzykal'naia kul'tura Petrograda pervogo poslerevoliutsionnogo piatiletiia: issledovanie, 1917–1922*. Leningrad: Sovetskii kompozitor, 1984.
Dan'ko, L. G., ed. *Peterburgskie stranitsy russkoi muzykal'noi kul'tury: sbornik statei i materialov*. St. Petersburg: Sankt-Peterburgskaia gosudarstvennaia konservatoriia im. N. A. Rimskogo-Korsakova, 2001.
Druskin, M. "Peterburg-Petrograd-Leningrad." *Sovetskaia muzyka*, XXI, 7 (July 1957): 17–25.
Filarmonicheskoe obshchestvo Sankt-Peterburga, 1802–1915, 1992–1997: k 195-letiiu so dnia osnovaniia i 5-letiiu so dnia vozrozhdeniia. St. Petersburg: Kult Inform, 1997.
Findeizen, N., ed. *Ocherk deiatel'nosti S.-Peterburgskogo otdeleniia Imperatorskogo russkogo muzykal'nogo obshchestva (1859–1909)*. St. Petersburg: Glavnoe upravlenie udelov, 1909.
Fomin, V. S. *Stareishii russkii simfonicheskii orkestr, 1882–1982*. Leningrad: Muzyka, 1982.
———, ed. *Leningradskaia gosudarstvennaia ordena trudovogo krasnogo znameni filarmoniia: stat'i, vospominaniia, materialy*. Leningrad: Muzyka, 1972.
Fradkina, E. *Zal dvor'ianskogo sobraniia: zametki o kontsertnoi zhizni Sankt-Peterburga*. St. Petersburg: Kompozitor, 1994.
Gakkel', L. *Teatral'naia ploshchad'*. Leningrad: Kompozitor, 1990.
———. *V kontsertnom zale: vpechatleniia 1950–1980-kh godov*. St. Petersburg: Kompozitor, 1997.
Gozenpud, A. A. *Dom Engel'gardta*. St. Petersburg: Sovetskii kompozitor, 1992.
Gubkina, N. V. *Nemetskii muzykal'nyi teatr v Peterburge v pervoi treti XIX veka*. St. Petersburg: Dmitrii Bulanin, 2003.
Guenther, Roy J. "Evenings in Old St. Petersburg: The Balakirev Circle and Its Origins." *Canadian American Slavic Studies*, XXXIV, 1 (Spring 2000): 5–31.

Kats, B., and R. Timenchik. *Anna Akhmatova i muzyka: issledovatel'skie ocherki*. Leningrad: Sovetskii kompozitor, 1989.
Khotuntsov, N. *Zdes' tozhe muzyka zvuchala*. St. Petersburg: Soiuz khudozhnikov, 2003.
Khronika Peterburgskikh teatrov s kontsa 1826 do nachala 1855 goda, 2 vol. St. Petersburg: Golike, 1877.
Kontserty A. Ziloti; programmy kontsertov za desiat' sezonov (1903/1904—1912/1913). St. Petersburg: Kind, 1913.
Kremlev, Iu. *Leningradskaia gosudarstvennaia konservatoriia, 1862–1937*. Moscow: Muzgiz, 1938.
Kriukov, A. N. *Muzyka v dni blokadi*. St. Petersburg: Kompozitor, 2002.
——. *Muzyka v efire voennogo Leningrada*. Leningrad: Kompozitor, 2005.
——. *Muzyka v gorode-fronte*. Leningrad: Muzyka, 1975.
——. *Muzyka v kol'tse blokady: ocherki*. Moscow: Muzyka, 1973.
——. *Muzykal'naia zhizn' srazhaiushchegosia Leningrada*. Leningrad: Sovetskii kompozitor, 1985.
Leningradskaia filarmoniia, sezon 1934–1935/1935-1936. Leningrad: Leningradskaia gosudarstvennaia filarmoniia, 1935.
Muzyka prodolzhala zvuchat': Leningrad, 1941–1944. Leningrad: Muzyka 1989.
Pamiati Betkhovena (1770–1920). Petrograd: Gosudarstvennyi akademicheskii teatr opery i baleta (byvsh. Marinskii), 1920.
Pavlovskii muzykal'nyi vokzal: istoricheskii ocherk, 1838–1912 g.g. St. Petersburg: Upravlenie Peterburgskoi seti M-V.-R. zh.d., 1912.
Peterburg: muzyka, 1703–2003; k 300-letiiu so dnia osnovaniia Sankt-Peterburga. St. Petersburg: Kompozitor, 2001.
Petrovskaia, I. F. *Kontsertnaia zhizn' Peterburga: muzyka v obshchestvennom i domashnem bytu 1801–1859 gody; materialy dlia entsiklopedii "Muzykal'nyi Petrograd."* St. Petersburg: Petrovskii fond, 2000.
——. *Muzykal'noe obrazovanie i muzykal'nye obshchestvennye organizatsii v Peterburge 1801–1917: Entsiklopediia*. St. Petersburg: Petrovskii fond, 1999.
Popova, N. I., and O. E. Rubinchik. *Anna Akhmatova i fontannyi dom*. St. Petersburg: Nevskii dialekt, 2000.
Porfier'eva, A. L., ed. *Muzykal'nyi Peterburg: entsiklopedicheskii slovar' XVIII vek*, 3 vol. St. Petersburg: Kompozitor, 2000.
Purtov, F. E. "Nemetskie notoizdateli Sankt-Peterburga 1-i poloviny XIX v." In *Notnye izdaniia v muzykal'noi zhizni Rossii*. St. Petersburg: Rossiiskaia natsional'naia biblioteka, 1999.
——. "Peterburgskie notoprodavcheskie katalogi pervoi chetverti XIX v." In *Notnye izdaniia v muzykal'noi zhizni Rossii: sbornik statei*, III. St. Petersburg: Rossiiskaia natsional'naia biblioteka, 2007.
Puzyrevskii, A. I., and L. A. Sakketti, ed. *Ocherk piatidesiatiletiia deiatel'nosti S.-Peterburgskoi konservatorii*. St. Petersburg: Glazunov, 1912.
Rozanov, A. S. *Muzykal'nyi Pavlovsk*. Leningrad: Muzyka, 1978.
Rubtsov, F. A. *Rabota kompozitorov i muzykovedov Leningrada v gody velikoi otechestvennoi voiny*. Leningrad: Iskusstvo, 1946.
Stark, E. *Peterburgskaia opera i ee mastera, 1890–1910*. Leningrad-Moscow: Gosudarstvennoe muzykal'noe izdatel'stvo, 1940.
Stoletnii iubilei S.-Peterburgskogo filarmonicheskogo obshchestva, 1802–1902. St. Petersburg: St. Peterburgskaia filarmoniia, 1902.
Stolpianskii, P. N. *Muzyka i muzitsirovanie v starom Peterburge*. Leningrad: Muzyka, 1989.
Sukharnikova, E. A. *Muzykal'nyi Sankt-Peterburg*. St. Petersburg: Spetslit, 2000.

V gody velikoi otechestvennoi voiny: vospominaniia, materialy. Leningrad: Sovetskii kompozitor, 1959.

Vanderflaas, L. *Simfonicheskaia muzyka v Leningrade.* Leningrad: Gosudarstvennoe muzykal'noe izdatel'stvo, 1963.

Various Subjects

Bericht über den Internationalen Beethoven-Kongress, 10.-12. Dezember 1970 in Berlin. Berlin: Neue Musik, 1971.

Bericht über den Internationalen Musikwissenschaftlichen Kongress, Bonn 1970. Kassel, Germany: Barenreiter, 1970.

Fishman, N. L., ed. *Betkhoven: sbornik statei,* 2 vol. Moscow: Muzyka, 1971–72.

———. *Iz istorii sovetskoi betkhoveniany: sbornik statei i fragmentov iz rabot.* Moscow: Sovetskii kompozitor, 1972.

"Iz istorii muzykal'noi kul'tury." In *Rukopisnye pamiatniki,* 5, edited by N. R. Bochkareva. St. Petersburg: Rossiiskaia natsional'naia biblioteka, 1999.

Iz istorii sovetskoi betkhoveniany: sbornik statei i fragmentov iz rabot. Moscow: Sovetskii kompozitor, 1972.

Fomin, V. S., ed. *Liudvig van Betkhoven: estetika, tvorcheskoe nasledie, ispolnitel'stvo; sbornik statei k 200-letiiu so dnia rozhdeniia.* Leningrad: Muzyka, 1970.

Kruzhnov, Iu. N., ed. *Notnye izdaniia v muzykal'noi zhizni Rossii,* I–II. St. Petersburg: Rossiiskaia natsional'naia biblioteka, 1999, 2003.

Kuznetsov, K. A., ed. *Russkaia kniga o Betkhovene.* Moscow: Muzykal'nyi sector gosudarstvennogo izdatel'stva, 1927.

Livanova, T. N. *Stat'i i vospominaniia.* Moscow: Muzyka, 1989.

Romazanova, N. V., ed. *Mirovaia muzykal'naia kul'tura v fondakh Otdela rukopisei Rossiiskoi natsional'noi biblioteki.* St. Petersburg: Rossiiskaia natsional'naia biblioteka, 2006.

Skonechnaia, A. *Moskovskii Parnas.* Moscow: Moskovskii rabochii, 1983.

INDEX

Note: Unless otherwise identified, all musical works are composed by Beethoven. Italicized page numbers followed by *f* indicate illustrations.

Abendroth, Hermann, 186
Acmeist anti-Symbolist school, 203
Adam, Adolph, 17
Adzhubei, Aleksei, 217
Afanas'ev, Nikolai, 36
Akhmatova, Anna: about, 203; discussion with Berlin, 201, 203; importance of music to, 203–5; "Music," 203; photograph of, *204f*; poems of, 204–7; *Poem without a Hero*, 203, 207; *Requiem*, 203; Zhdanov's harangue on, 207–8
Akron, Iosif, 167
Aksakov, Ivan, 67
Aksakov, Konstantin, 67
Aksakov, Sergei, 16, 67
Aksel'rod, Pavel, 155
Alekseev, Vasilii, 107
Alexander I, 14, 21, 25
Alexander II, 42, 96, 125–26
Alexander III, 126
Alexeeva, Liudmila, 248
Al'shvang, Arnol'd, 98; *Great Soviet Encyclopedia* article on Beethoven, 190–91
Al'tman, Natan, 157
American orchestras, USSR tours by, 234
Andropov, Iurii, 246
anti-Semitism, 209–10
Apraxin, Stepan, 43
Armand, Inessa, 175n10
Arnim, Bettina Brentano von, 70
Arnol'd, Iurii, 18, 35–36, 38, 39, 134
Arrau, Claudio, 233
Asaf'ev, Boris (pseud. Igor Glebov), 160, 167, 183, 231
Ashkenazy, Vladimir, 233
Asmus, Valentin, 227
audiences: attitudes toward Western ensembles and compositions, 235; and Berlioz's music, 41; difficulty with late Beethoven, 78; response to Beethoven string quartets, 23–24; response to Shostakovich's Seventh Symphony, 198; response to wartime concert of Beethoven's Ninth, 195–96
Auer, Leopold, 133

Badura-Shkoda, Paul, 233
Bakhtin, Mikhail, 98, 118n1
Bakunin, Mikhail, 68, 70–71, 93
Barber, Samuel, *Knoxville: Summer of 1915*, 139
Barenboim, Daniel, 140, 233
Barteneva, Polina, 38, 41, 53
Bartók, Béla, 221, 241n9; Concerto for Orchestra, 139; Music for Strings, Percussion, and Celesta, 234
Baryshnikov, Mikhail, 235
Bax, Arnold, Symphony no. 2, 139
Beethoven, Ludwig van: Berlioz on, 41; celebrations of, 133–34, 138, 168, 169–70, 228; compared to Shakespeare, 68, 110, 123n79; critiques of the West through, 190–91; dedications by, 14–15, 21, 24, 25, 47n37; as depicted by Lunacharskii, 161–63; in early nineteenth-century Russian concerts, 15; effect on German soldiers, 198, 200; erotic iconography of, *115f*, 116; kinship with Russia, 137; letters of, 21, 23, 25, 244n39; as metaphor for Moscow and Russian culture, 52, 53–54; moral compass in music of, 117; musical techniques used by, 164; and music's freedom from political biases, 216; Odoevskii's novella about, 62–64; popularity of politically sensitive works of, 133; portrait of, *162f*, 163; power of music of, 2, 100; primacy of struggle in works of, 163–64; Richter's performances of, 239; on the science and art of music, 47n33; Viennese connections with the Russian elite, 11–15; wartime broadcasts of music of, 193, 195, 213n31

——*chamber music:* Clarinet Trio in B-flat, op. 11, 16; Contredanse no. 7 in E-flat, WoO 14, 22; Piano Trio in B-flat (*Archduke*), op. 97, 35; Piano Trio in D (*Ghost*), op. 70, no. 1, 102, 103, 113; Piano Trio in E-flat, op. 70, no. 2, 102, 103; Piano Trios, op. 1, 13, 14, 15; Romances for Violin and Orchestra, 134; Septet in E-flat, op. 20, 16, 34, 103; Three String Trios, op. 9, 14; Violin Sonata no. 6, 245n61; Violin Sonata no. 9 in A (*Kreutzer*), op. 47, 13, 104, 105, 106, 108, 121n59, 151; Violin sonatas, op. 12, 228; Violin sonatas, op. 30, 14. *See also* Beethoven, Ludwig van—piano music; Beethoven, Ludwig van—string quartets; Beethoven, Ludwig van—vocal works

——*large works: Christus am Ölberge (Christ on the Mount of Olives)*, op. 85, 16, 33, 45n15, 134; Concerto for Violin, Cello, and Piano in C, op. 56 (Triple Concerto), 187; *Consecration of the House*, 167; *Die Geschöpfe des Prometheus (The Creatures of Prometheus)*, op. 43, 22; *Die Ruinen von Athen (The Ruins of Athens)*, op. 113, 129, 134, 167; *Die Weihe des Hauses (The Consecration of the House)* in C, op. 124, 24, 25, 133, 167; Fantasia for Piano, Chorus, and Orchestra in C minor (*Choral Fantasy*), op. 80, 16, 45n15, 171, 187, 234, 245n61; *King Stephen*, op. 117, 132; Mass in C, op. 86, 134; *Prometheus* Overture, 188. See also *Coriolan* overture in C minor, op. 62; *Egmont* (Goethe), Beethoven's overture (op. 84) and incidental music to; *Fidelio (Leonore)* (opera), op. 72; *Fidelio (Leonore)* overtures; *Missa solemnis* in D, op.; Violin Concerto in D, op. 61; specific symphonies

——*piano music:* Akhmatova's love for Beethoven's late piano sonatas, 205; analysis of the sonatas, 74, 76; Gilels's recordings of, 236; Grinberg's recordings of, 236; in Beethoven celebrations, 134, 138; Nikolaeva's recorded performances of, 237; sonata performances in Stalin era, 187, 212n15; Yudina's recordings of, 245n61; Concerto no. 1 in C, op. 15, 171; Concerto no. 2 in B-flat, op. 19, 171; Concerto no. 3 in C minor, op. 37, 98, 131, 137, 171; Concerto no. 4 in G, op. 58, 113, 136, 137, 152, 170, 171, 245n61; *Diabelli Variations (33 Variations on a waltz by Anton Diabelli)*, op. 120, 25, 27, 195, 237, 245n61; *Electoral* Sonatas, WoO 47, nos. 1–2, 236; Fifteen Variations and a Fugue on an Original Theme in E-flat (*Eroica* Variations), op. 35, 22, 236, 245n61; Polonaise for Piano in C, op. 89, 14; Seven Variations for Piano and Cello on "Bei Mannern, welche Liebe fühlen" from Mozart's *The Magic Flute*, WoO 46, 14; Six Variations for Piano on "Tandeln und Scherzen" from Süssmayr's Soliman II, WoO 76, 15; Sonata no. 1 in F minor, op. 2, 113; Sonata nos. 5–7, op. 10, 15, 222; Sonata no. 11 in B-flat, op. 22, 14; Sonata no. 12 in A-flat ("Funeral March"), op. 26, 36, 76, 78, 95, 119n7, 183, *185f*; Sonata no. 13 in E-flat, op. 27, no. 1, 40; Sonata no. 15 in D (*Pastoral*), op. 28, 242n17; Sonata no. 17 in D minor (*The Tempest*), op. 31, no. 2, 40, 174n7, 221; Sonata no. 28 in A, op. 101, 94, 103–4; Sonata no. 29 in B-flat (*Hammerklavier*), op. 106, 36, 236, 242n17; Sonata no. 31 in A-flat, op. 110, 205–6; Sonata no. 32 in C minor, op. 111, 74; Thirty-Two Variations on an Original Theme, 245n61; Three Marches for Piano Four-Hands, op. 45, 15; Twelve Variations for Piano on a Russian Dance from Pavel Wranitzky's *Das Waldmädchen*, WoO 71, 15. *See also* Piano Concerto no. 5 in E-flat (*Emperor*), op. 73; Piano Sonata no. 8 in C minor (*Pathétique*), op. 13; Piano Sonata no. 14 in C-Sharp minor (*Moonlight*), op. 27, no. 2; Piano Sonata no. 23 in F minor (*Appassionata*), op. 57

——*string quartets:* A. N. Serov on, 77; Berlin's love for, 202; centenary performances of, 171; criticism of the late quartets, 74; Koussevitzky's programming of, 139; L'vov quartet performances of, 36; performances in the Stalin era of, 187; performed by the Stradivarius Quartet, 167; no. 2 in G, op. 18, no.2, 171; no. 8 in E minor, op. 59, no. 2, 34, 171; no. 9 in C, op. 59, no. 3, 56, 171; no. 10 in E-flat (Harp), op. 74, 34, 78, 171; no. 11 in F minor (*Serioso*), op. 95, 36, 171; no. 12 in E-flat, op. 127, 21, 23–24, 36, 46n26, 47n30, 64; no. 13 in B-flat,

op. 130, 21, 23–24, 46n26, 64, 100; no. 14 in C# minor, op. 131, 21, 64, 173–74; no. 15 in A minor, op. 132, 21, 23–24, 46n26, 64; no. 16 in F, op. 135, 21, 64; Opus 18, 21, 31, 47n37, 78; Opus 59 (Razumovsky Quartets), 13, 16, 21, 45n5, 47n30, 78
——*symphonies:* A. N. Serov on, 77–82; Anton Rubinshtein's reordering of, 113; in Beethoven celebrations, 133–34, 136, 138, 139, 170, 171; extramusical uses of, 211n8; performances at Viel'gorskii Salon, 33; performances by the Bol'shoi Theater Orchestra, 167; on the radio, 188; by the Symphonic Orchestra of the USSR, 186; *Wellingtons Sieg (Battle Symphony)*, op. 91, 16, 33, 63. *See also* specific symphonies
——*vocal works: Adelaide*, op. 46, 38; "Der Wachtelschlag," WoO 129, 14; "Ich bitt' dich, schreib mir die Es-Skala auf," WoO172, 162; Scena and Aria *Ah! perfido*, op. 65, 134; Scottish songs, op. 108, 171; Six Gellert Lieder, op. 48, 14, 15, 129
Beethoven Committee, 169–70, 171
Beethoven Quartet, 187, 213n31
Beethoven studies: reception history in, xii; scholarship under Brezhnev, 227–28; Soviet Beethoven studies, 166, 231. *See also* Fishman, Natan
Bekker, Paul, *Beethoven*, 116–17
Beliaev, Aleksandr, 3
Belinskii, Vissarion, 68–69, 70
Benedetti-Michelangeli, Arturo, 233
Berkshire Music Festival (now Tanglewood), 139, 143n28
Berlin, Isaiah, 202–3, *202f*, 205, 206–7; "The Hedgehog and the Fox," 203
Berlioz, Hector: on Beethoven, 22, 51n81, 79; on the Kapella, 17; musical innovations of, 77; Russian tours of, 40–41, 51n82, 96; Tolstoy on, 103; in the Viel'gorskii salon, 29, 36
Bernhard, Frau, 15, 45n10
Bernstein, Leonard: homage to Koussevitzky by, 139–40; on the manuscript of Beethoven's Fifth, 100; on Pasternak, 224–25; performance of *Ode to Joy* in Berlin, 123n82; Symphony no. 2 (*The Age of Anxiety*), 139; USSR tours of, 234, 235
Bers, Stepan, 107
Bestuzhev, Nikolai, 3, 7n2
Bie, Oskar, 136
Biron-Kurliandskaia, Ekaterina Karlovna, 32, 49n58
Biron-Kurliandskaia, Luiza Karlovna, 32–33
Blagodatov, Georgii, 228
Blazhkov, Igor, 234
Blok, Alexandr, 165, 177n41
Blumenfeld, Felix, 236
Bolshevik Revolution, 169
Bol'shoi Ballet, 154
Bol'shoi Opera, 154
Bol'shoi Theater: celebratory concert at, 184; conference at, 170; *Fidelio*, 187; performance of *Fidelio*, 175n13; performance of *Fidelio* at, 212n20
Bol'shoi Theater Orchestra, 167, 170, 186, 197
Borodin, Aleksandr, 84; Quartet no. 2 in D, 151
Bortnianskii, Dmitrii, 21
Boston Symphony Orchestra, 135, 138–39, 140, 234
Boyer, Paul, 107
Brahms, Johannes, 103, 224; Symphony no. 4 in E minor, 234
Braudo, Evgenii, 172
Brendel, Alfred, 233
Brezhnev, Leonid, 227–28, 243n33
Brezhneva, Luba, 227
Bridgetower, George, 13
Briggen, Aleksandr von der, 5
Britten, Benjamin, *Peter Grimes*, 139, 235
Bronfman, Yefim, 233
Browne-Camus, Anna Margaret, 15
Browne-Camus, Johann Georg von, 14–15
Broyles, Michael, 46n15
Bulgakov, Aleksandr, 40
Bulgarin, Faddei, 40, 68–69
Bulich, Sergei, "Music and Ideas of Liberation," 114–15
Burlak-Andreev, Vasilii, 106

Capet, Lucien, 173, 174
Capet Quartet, 173, 178n58
Cassirer, Feritz, 83
Catherine the Great, 17
Chagall, Marc, 157, 160
Chaliapin, Fedor, 160, 167
Chernyshevskii, Nikolai, 109, 122n70

Cheshikhin, Vsevolod, 118; "Composers and Revolutions," 117
Chita Zavod (prison), 1, 2–3
Chopin, Frédéric: Boris Pasternak and, 223; Golitsyn and, 18; Lenin and, 174n7, 175n16; musical innovations of, 77; music in Khrushchev's funeral, 217; Piano Sonata no. 2 in B-flat minor, op. 35, 227; Tolstoy and, 103, 107
Claudel, Paul, 98
Cleveland Orchestra (Szell), 234, 235
Cliburn, Van, 233, 236
Coates, Albert, 160
Commissariat of Enlightenment (Narkompros), 156, 157
concerts during the Soviet era: all-Beethoven concerts, 170–71; Beethoven anniversary concerts, 167, 168, 228; to celebrate the adoption of the Stalin Constitution, 181, 183–84; Koussevitzky-led concerts, 135, 167; during Leningrad's Nine Hundred Days, 193, 195–96, *196–97f*; in Lenin's apartment, 149; by the Petrograd/ Leningrad orchestras, 167–68; in the post-Stalin era, 228, 232–35; programming of Beethoven in Moscow and Leningrad, 184–90; Russian music featured in, 151; of Shostakovich's Seventh Symphony, 196–98; wartime and new hearings of Beethoven's Ninth, 195, *196f*
concerts in Decembrist prisons and settlements, 3, 4–5
concerts in pre-1917 Russia: across the Russian Empire, 132–34, 142n13; Beethoven as fixture in, 134; conducted by Koussevitzky, 136–38, *137f*; at the Fateevka estate, 33; Russian Musical Society concerts, 129–30, 131–32; variety of repertoire in, 34. See also *Egmont* (Goethe), Beethoven's overture (op. 84) and incidental music to; *Fidelio (Leonore)* (opera), op. 72; *Fidelio (Leonore)* overtures; Imperial Court Chapel Choir (Kapella); Liszt, Franz; *Missa solemnis* in D, op. 123; Russian Musical Society; salons; St. Petersburg Philharmonic Society (Philharmonia)
Concerts Koussevitzky, 135
conservatories, 130, 132, 157–58. *See also* Moscow Conservatory; St. Petersburg Conservatory
Cooper, Barry, 25
Copeland, Aaron, 234, 235; Appalachian Spring Suite, 139; Symphony no. 3, 139
Coriolan overture in C minor, op. 62: A. N. Serov transcription of, 73; Gogol and, 94; Koussevitzky-led performances of, 137, 138; Lenin and, 150, 152; popularity of, 187; radio performances of, 188; Rubinshtein on, 113; in Soviet era concerts, 170, 171; struggle against tyranny in, 190
Cortot, Alfred, 160
Cui, César, 84
cult of Beethoven: and celebration of the Stalin Constitution, 181, 184; in extramusical programming of Beethoven's music, 183–84; in literature of the Stalin era, 190–93; political processes behind, 169; in Stalinist Russia's canon, 179, 186–90

Dalos, György, 208
Dargomyzhskii, Aleksandr, 18, 29, 61
Davydov, Karl, 43
Davydov, Vasilii, 5
Decembrists: Beethoven's music in prisons and exile, 1–2, 5, 7n4; death of, 6; imprisonment of, 2, 3–4, 7n5, 8n9; musical activities of, 2–6, 7n2, 8n6; resettlement of, 5. *See also* Westernizers
defections of artists, 235
Del'vig, Anton, *Severnye tsvety*, 62
Denisov, Edison, 234
de-Stalinization campaign, 210n1, 218–21
Diaghilev, Sergei, 160
Dobroliubov, Nikolai, 109
Dobrovein, Isai, 147, *148f*, 151, 152, 160, 174n1
Doctors' Plot, 209–10
Dolzhanskii, Aleksandr, 191
Dostoevskaia, Anna Grigoreevna (née Snitkina), 96, 97
Dostoevsky, Fedor, 96–100; *The Brothers Karamazov*, 98, *99f*, 100, 120n28; *Crime and Punishment*, 97, 98, 100; *The Idiot*, 97, 98; *The Insulted and Injured*, 98; *Netochka Nezvanova*, 96; *Poor Folk*, 96; *The Possessed*, 100
Douglas, Barry, 233
Downes, Olin, 139
Drabkina, Elizaveta, 152–53, 218–19, *219f*
du Pré, Jacqueline, 43, 44, 51n91

Egmont (Goethe), Beethoven's overture (op. 84) and incidental music to: in all-Beethoven concerts, 136, 138, 167; in anniversary concerts, 134, 170, 171; Lenin and, 150, 152; popularity in late imperial Russia of, xii, 125, 129, 132, 133; popularity in the Soviet era, 168; pre-1917 performances of, 40, 97; on the radio, 188; socialist ideas in, 192; Stalin era performances of, 186, 187; struggle against tyranny in, 190; and struggle for liberty, 110, 114
Ehrenburg, Ilya, *The Thaw*, 218
Eisenstein, Sergei, 157
Elena Pavlovna (Grand Duchess), 38, 127–28, *128f*, 129, 130, 131
Eliasberg, Karl, 193, 195, 197
Elizaveta Alekseevna (Empress), 14
Emancipation of Labor Group, 155
Engel', Iurii, 113
Engel'gardt House, 18, 39, 46n21, 50n75
Engels, Friedrich, 191
Engelsmann, Walter, 83
Ermolenko-Iuzhina, Nataliia, 167
Ershov, Ivan, 167
Esipova, Anna, 239
Esterházy, Maria Josepha, 15
European canon: availability of sheet music and, 15; Decembrists' knowledge of, 3, 4–5; Golitsyn's training in, 20; in the Viel'gorskii salon, 31, 33. *See also* Chopin, Frédéric; Haydn, Franz Josef; Mozart, Wolfgang Amadeus; Wagner, Richard; Westernizers
European orchestras, tours by, 235
exile communities, 1–2, 7n5
Extraordinary 8th All-Union Congress of Soviets of the USSR, 184

Fairclough, Pauline, 186; *Classics for the Masses*, xii
Fateevka estate, 32, 33
Feinberg, Samuil, 231
Feltsman, Vladimir, 233
Ferraguto, Mark, 45n5
Fétis, François-Joseph, 22, 74; *Biographie universelle des musiciens*, 42
Fidelio (Leonore) (opera), op. 72: A. N. Serov on, 77; Berlin's love for, 202; Bol'shoi revival of, 212n20; Bulgarin on, 69; Bulich on, 114; essays on, 230; led by Koussevitzky, 167; Lenin at performance of, 175n13; Leningrad performances of, 212n19; performance in a Gulag labor camp, 246; performances in late imperial Russia of, 140, 142n13; in permanent repertory of the Bol'shoi Theater, 170; popularity of, xii, 125, 132, 133, 134; premiere of, 16, 20; on the radio, 188; republican ideals expressed in, 117; Rubinshtein on, 113; socialist ideas in, 192; Soviet era performances of, 167; Stalin era performances of, 186, 187–88, 212n17; story of, 110; transcriptions of, 73; Turgenev's response to, 94; versions of, 100; writing of, 24
Fidelio (Leonore) overtures: Dostoevsky and, 96, 97; dramatic nature of, 110, 114; Koussevitzky-led performances of, 138; *Leonore 1*, 35; *Leonore 2*, 114, 171; *Leonore 3*, 77, 110, 114, 131, 138, 152, 167, 187, 188; op. 72, 40; popularity in late imperial Russia of, xii, 16, 40, 125, 130, 132, 133, 134, 168; on the radio, 188; Soviet era performances of, 140, 152, 167, 168, 171, 187, 188; struggle against tyranny in, 190
Fischer, Annie, 233
Fishman, Natan, 229–31, *229f*, 244n39, 244n41
Fitelberg, Grzegorz, 167
Fitzpatrick, Sheila, 215n61
Foss, Lucas, 234, 235
Fotieva, Lydiia, 151
free artist, rank of, 130, 131
French Revolution: A. N. Serov's association of Beethoven with, 110; Beethoven and the ideals of, 111–12, 115, 118, 172, 228; Beethoven as exemplar of the "new man" of, 113; Lunacharskii's association of Beethoven with, 154, 165–66, 171; "rescue operas" in, 110
Fried, Oskar, 160, 186
Friedrich Wilhelm III of Prussia, 14
Fröhlich, Franz, 79
Frolova-Walker, Marina, 186; *Music and Soviet Power, 1917–1932*, xii; *Stalin's Music Prize*, xii
Furtwängler, Wilhelm, 160

Gakkel', Leonid, 231, 232
Galitsyn, Nikolai. *See* Golitsyn, Nikolai

García-Viardot, Pauline, 29, 40, 57, 93, 94
Gauk, Aleksandr, 171, 183, 184, 186
Gentry Club (Noble Assembly) building, 18, 39
German Romanticism, 66, 68, 74, 115–16, 118
Gershwin, George, Second Rhapsody, 139
Giangiacomo Feltrinelli publishing house, 226
Gifford, Henry, 224
Gilels, Emil, 181, 233, 236, 239
Ginzburg, Lev, 27, 230
Glazunov, Aleksandr, 186, 231
Glebov, Igor. *See* Asaf'ev, Boris
Glinka, Mikhail: on *Fidelio*, 77; on Griboedov, 54; *A Life for the Tsar (Ivan Susanin)*, 41; on the Ninth Symphony, 65; and Odoevskii, 18, 61; *Ruslan and Lyudmila*, 41–42; *Russlan and Liudmila* overture, 129; Stalin and, 181; Viel'gorski and, 29, 41–42
Gnesina, Elena Fabianovna, 159
Godunov, Aleksandr, 235
Gogol, Nikolai: exposure to Beethoven, 57; *The Inspector General*, 42; and Iosif Viel'gorski, 36; necrology of, 94; in Odoevskii's salon, 61; "Sculpture, Painting, and Music," 57; song in *Dead Souls*, 57–58; in the Viel'gorski salon, 29
Gol'denweiser, Aleksandr, 231, 237
Golitsyn, Nikolai: Beethoven library of, 27; biographical information about, 19–20, 46n22; importance of, 18–19, 27; love and understanding of Beethoven's music, 20–22, 23; and the *Missa Solemnis*, 25–27, 48n46, 48nn42–43; portrait of, *19f*; promotion of Beethoven by, 18, 27; and Russia's introduction to Beethoven, 11; string quartets commissioned by, 21–24, 46n26, 47n32, 47n37; and the Viel'gorskiis, 51n86
Golitsyna, Elena Aleksandrovna (née Saltykova), 20–21
Golitsyn Quartet, 21
Golland, Konstantin, 53
Goncharov, Dmitrii Dmitrievich, 158
Goncharova, Nataliia Nikolaevna, 158
Goncharova, Vera Konstantinovna, 158
Gorbachev, Mikhail, 231, 246
Gorenko, Anna Andreevna. *See* Akhmatova, Anna
Gorky, Maxim, 147–48, 150
Gould, Glen, 233
Gozenpud, Abram, 97, 98
Gramophone Instrumental Awards, 236, 237
Great Purge of 1936–38, 180
Great Reforms of Alexander II, 125–26
Green, Dorothy, 103
Griboedov, Aleksandr, 54–55, 85n10; *Woe from Wit*, 42, 54, 85nn8–9
Grinberg, Maria, 236–37
Grosse Fuge finale of Opus 130, 24, 64
Grove, George, 83
Gubaidulina, Sophia, 234
Gulag concerts, 246

Haydn, Franz Josef: *Die Schöpfung (The Creation)*, 17, 58; Golitsyn and, 15; Griboedov and, 54; Krylov and, 54; political aloofness of, 117; Razumovskii and, 11; sheet music and Russian performances of, 15; Sonatas nos. 55–57, 239; symphonies of, 81; Tolstoy and, 101, 103
Henselt, Adolf von, 35, 94
Herzen, Aleksandr, 68, 69–70, 71
Hitler, Adolf, 194, 196
Hoffman, E. T. A., 118
Honegger, Arthur: Symphony no. 1, 139; Symphony no. 3 (*Liturgique*), 234
Horowitz, Vladimir, 161, 236
Huberman, Bronisław, 160
Hunt, Michael, 246, 248

Iavorskii, Boleslav, 160, 231
Igel'shtrom, Konstantin, 3
Igumnov, Konstantin, 236
Imperial Court Chapel Choir (Kapella), 16, 17, 24, 65. See also *Missa solemnis* in D, op. 123
instruments: Clara Schumann's Russian piano, 40; Guarneri instruments, 6, 36; harpsichords in resettlement communities, 5–6; Koussevitzky's promotion of the double bass, 135; Stradivari instruments, 6, 43–44, 51n91
Internationale (de Geyter), 184, 186
International Tchaikovsky Competition, 236
Ippolitov-Ivanov, Mikhail, 186
Iudenich, Nina, 228

Iushnevskaia, Mariia, 3
Iushnevskii, Aleksei, 3, 6, 7n2, 8n6
Ivan III, 17
Ivanov-Boretski, Mikhail, 231
Ivashev, Vasilii, 3

Jochum, Eugen, 186
Johann Sebastian Bach Competition, 237
July Revolution in Paris, Decembrists response to, 3

Kamenskii, Aleksandr, 198
Kancheli, Giya, 234
Kanne, Friedrich, 79
Kanshin, Dmitrii, 128
Kapella. *See* Imperial Court Chapel Choir (Kapella)
Karatygin, Petr, 54
Karintsev, Nikolai, 191
Katz, Michael, 98
Kaufman, Roza, 223
Kedrov, Mikhail S., 174n7; "Lenin and Beethoven," 150
Keller, Johann, 65
Khachaturian, Aram, 209
Khokhlovkina, Anna, 188, 212n20
Khomiakov, Aleksei, 67
Khrushchev, Nikita, 210, 216–18, 220, 227, 241n1, 241n6
Kireevskii, Ivan, 67
Kireevskii, Petr, 59, 67
Kirillina, Larissa, 230–31, 244n37
Kleiber, Erich, 186
Klemperer, Otto, 160, 170, 171, 186
Klimovitskii, Arkadii, 228, 230
Klüpfeld (Klüpfell), Filipp von, 15
Knappertsbusch, Hans, 171
Kogan, Leonid, 232
Kologrivov, Vasilii, 128
Konstantin Nikolaevich (Grand Duke), 129
Korganov, Vasilii, 115–16
Kosygin, Aleksei, 228
Koussevitzky, Serge: "Beethoven Celebration" of, 138; Beethoven concerts led by, 152–53, 167, 230; Boston Symphony and Berkshire Music Festival, 135, 138–39; career of, 135–36; caricature of, *135f*; in concert at Lunacharskii's quarters, 160; death of, 140; defiance of ban against German music by, 138, 143n27; emigration of, 138; marriage of, 135; orchestra of, 136; and Tolstoy, 107, 121n43; Volga River tours of, 136–38, *137f*; works commissioned and championed by, 139
Koussevitzky Music Foundation, 139
Kozlova, Leonid and Valentina, 235
Krasnaia zvezda (Red Star) on Beethoven's Ninth, 184
Krein, David, 151
Kreisler, Fritz, 160
Kremer, Gidon, 232
Kremlev, Iulii, 228
Kriukov, Aleksandr, 2
Kriukov, Nikolai, 2, 3
Krupskaia, Nadezhda, 151, 152, 175n10
Krylov, Ivan, 56–57; "The Musicians," 55; "The Quartet," 55, *56f*; "The Village Band," 55
Krylova, Sarra, 149
Kuper, Emil, 167, 183, 186
Kuznetsov, Konstantin, 166–67

Landowska, Wanda, *102f*, 103
Lang, Peter, 70
Large Symphony Orchestra, 188, 189, 197
Lasvrent'eva, P. N., 54
Lavrov, Petr, 109
Lenin, Vladimir: on the *Appassionata*, 191; attempted assassination of, *148f*, 153; birthday celebration for, 150–51; cult of personality around, 169; and *Fidelio*, 187; gymnastic exercise set to honor, 183–84; illness and death of, 154, 175n16; inconsistent attitudes toward music of, 154; love for Beethoven, 147–48, 150, 151–53, 155, 174n7, 175n11, 175n13, 189; *Materialism and Empirio-Criticism*, 157; musical and cultural background of, 149–50; and radio, 188; slogan honoring, 172; and Stalin, 180
Leningrad Affair of 1949–50, 209
Leningrad/Petrograd, programming of Beethoven in, 167, 186–87. *See also* Nine Hundred Days
Leningrad Radio Symphony Orchestra (LRSO), 193, 197, 213n35
Leningrad State Institute of Theater, Music, and Film, 228
Leningrad/St. Petersburg State Academic Philharmonia, 186–87, 193, 232, 234

Lenin Mausoleum, 181, 183, *185f*, 210, 210n1
Lenz, Wilhelm F. von: A.N. Serov's critique of, 75–76; on Glinka's response to the Ninth Symphony, 65; on Krylov, 56–57; and Liszt, 36–37; on Mikhail Viel'gorskii, 32, 36, 42
Lermontov, Mikhail: *A Hero of Our Time*, 53; musical allusions in writings of, 52–54; in Odoevskii's salon, 61; *Princess Ligovskaia*, 53; *The Strange Man*, 53; *Vadim*, 53; in the Viel'gorskii salon, 29
Levin, Semen, 229
Lichnovsky, Karl, 11
Linen Mill, 158, 176n26
Lipiński, Karol, 35
Liszt, Franz: on Anton Rubinshtein, 113; caricature of, *37f*; Koussevitzky's programming of, 136; Ninth Symphony conducted by, 79, 90n96; performances of Beethoven piano sonatas, 36, 57; personal characteristics of, 50n71; in Russian Musical Society concerts, 130; Russian tours of, 35, 37–39, 50n68; Shevyrev on, 67; in the Viel'gorskii salon, 29, 36
Lopukhov, Fedor, *Velichie mirozdaniia (The Grandeur of the Universe)*, *182f*, 183, 211n8
LRSO. *See* Leningrad Radio Symphony Orchestra (LRSO)
Lunacharskaia, Nataliia Aleksandrovna, 160, 161
Lunacharskii, Anatolii Vasil'evich, xiii; articles on Beethoven by, 231; background and career of, 155–57; and Beethoven centenary celebration events, 168, 171; on Beethoven's music, 163–64, 165; and cultural experiences in Paris, 159–60; as culture tsar (Commissar of Enlightenment), xiii, 154, 157; death of, 157, 161; depiction of Beethoven by, 161–63; differences with Lenin, 157; education policies of, 158; essay on, 229; experience of transcendence by, 173–74; following resignation as Commissar, 160–61; on Lenin's lack of support for music, 154; on Lenin's singing, 149; passion for music, 158; poetry recitations of, 159; portrait of, *156f*; private concerts at home of, 160
Lunacharskii, Anatolii Vasil'evich, writings of: "Music, a Dithyramb to Dionysos," 159; *Nocturne for Solo Violin*, 160; *Religion and Socialism*, 157; "The Harp," 159; "The Violinist," 159; *V mire muzyki (In the World of Music)*, 161
Lunin, Mikhail, 2, 3
L'vov, Aleksei, 17, 35–36, *35f*, 38
L'vov, Leonid, 39
L'vov Quartet, 35–36, *35f*

Ma, Yo-Yo, 43, 44
Mahler, Gustav, 90n99
Maingardt, Adolph, 19
Makarova, Nataliia, 235
Malevich, Kasimir, 157
Mal'ko, Nikolai, 171, 186
Mandel'shtam, Osip, 136, 203
Mariia Fedorovna (Empress), 32
Mariia Nikolaevna (Grand Duchess), 38
Marx, A. B., 82–83
Marxism, 155
Matus, Ksenia, 198
Maurer, Ludwig, 38
Maurer, Vsevolod, 35, *35f*
Meichik, Aleksandra, 160
Meingardt, Adolph, 32
Memorial International, 246, 248, 249n5
Mendelssohn, Felix: Dostoevsky and, 96; musical devices of, 77; Rubinshtein and, 126; in Russian Musical Society concerts, 130; Second Cello Sonata, op. 58, 43; *Songs without Words*, 5
Menuhin, Hephzibah, 234
Menuhin, Yehudi, 232, 234
Mersmann, Hans, 83
Messiaen, Olivier, *Turangalîla-Symphonie*, 139
Meyerhold, Vsevolod, 157, 211n8
Miaskovskii, Nikolai, 116, 160, 231
Mikhailovskii, Nikolai, 109
Milstein, Nathan, 161
Mir Iskusstva (World of Art) movement, 116
Missa solemnis in D, op. 123: A. N. Serov on, 76; Beethoven on, 48n38; Beethoven's writing of, 24–25, 100; centenary performances of, 133, 171; Golitsyn and, 21; Koussevitzky-led performances of, 138, 139, 167; Mavrinsky performances of, 234; premiere of, 16, 21, 24, 25–27; publication and autograph copies of, 25; Stalin era

performances of, 187, 212n17; transcription of, 73; Val'ter on, 117
Moore, Douglas, *The Ballad of Baby Doe*, 139
Moscow, concerts of Beethoven's music in, 15–16, 133–34, 186
Moscow Association of Rhythmists, 183
Moscow Conservatory, 61, 125, 131
Moscow State Central (Glinka) Museum of Musical Culture, 230
Mozart, Wolfgang Amadeus: Beethoven compared to, 2, 26, 56, 62; Dostoevsky's love for music of, 96; Herzen on, 69–70; L'vov quartet and, 36; in musical training, 20, 58; Piano Concerto no. 23 in A, K. 488, 239; political aloofness of, 117; in Russian Musical Society concerts, 130; sheet music and, 15; symphonies of, 81; Tchaikovsky on, 84; Turgenev's favorite work of, 94; Ulybyshev's study of, 74, 75
Mravinsky, Evgenii, *233f*, 234
music: and cults in politics, 169; effects of listening to, 1, 7n3; instrumental music's power, 81, 90n102; as the language of revolution, 165; as muse and as text, xi; music making as seditious act, 1; professionalism in music making, 125, 126–32; Russian intelligentsia's lack of interest in, 109, 122n70; struggle and equilibrium in, 163–64; universality of, 231; Westernizers on, 69
music criticism: on Beethoven and his late style, 72–73, 74, 76–77; and boundaries between instrumental and vocal music, 79–81, 90n99; development of Russian Beethoven criticism, 110; freedom from politics, 231; ideological analyses of Beethoven in, 111–18; Lunacharskii on Beethoven's music, 163–64; political interpretations of Beethoven in, 84, 93, 172; Serov as Beethoven authority in, 73–74; Serov's critiques of Ulybyshev and Lenz, 75–76; Stalin-era scholarship on Beethoven, 190–93. *See also* Lenz, Wilhelm F. von; Odoevskii, Aleksandr; Serov, Aleksandr Nikolaevich
Mussorgsky, Modest: *Boris Godunov*, 217–18; *Pictures at an Exhibition*, 139; Stalin and, 181
Muzyka i teatr (Music and Theater), 73
Mylac, Michael, 248
Naiman, Anatoly, 205
Narkompros. *See* Commissariat of Enlightenment (Narkompros)
Naryshkin, Mikhail, 3, 5
Nazi Germany, 192–95, 201
Neizvestny, Ernst, 217
Nekrasov, Nikolai, 29
Nelson, Amy, *Music for the Revolution*, xii
Neuhaus, Heinrich: on Beethoven's Piano Sonata no. 31 in A-flat, op. 110, 205–6; in Fishman's collection of essays, 231; performances by, 233; as piano teacher, 236, 237, 238; and Zinaida Eremeeva, 224
Neuhaus, Stanislav, 227
New Symphony Concert Union, 136
Nicholas I, 68
Nicholas II, 126
Nikolaeva, Tatiana, 237
Nine Hundred Days: casualties during, 200–201; concerts during, 193, 195–96, *196–97f*, 213n35; German encirclement of Leningrad, 193; Kamenskii's performance for dying woman during, 198–200; Leningrad's resistance to the Germans, 193–94; music in psychological warfare of, 198, 200; and new interpretations of Beethoven's Ninth, 195; radio broadcasts of music during, 193, *194f*, 195, 200; and Shostakovich's Seventh Symphony, 196–98
Nobel Prizes, 223, 226
Noshchokina, Vera, 59
Novitskaia, Mariia, 53
Novitskii, Pavel, "Beethoven and the USSR," 168
Nureyev, Rudolph, 235
N. V. Stankevich Circle, 67–68, 69

Ode to Joy: A. N. Serov on, 80, 82–83; David Strauss on, 79–80; Koussevitzky and, 139; Lenin's response to, 152; Lunacharskii's restoration of *joy* in, 164; Pasternak's work compared to, 226; republican ideals expressed in, 116, 118; Soviet era performances of, 168; and the Stalin Constitution, 154, 181, 183, 184, 211n7; substitution of *freedom* (*Freiheit*) for *joy* (*Freude*), xii–xiii, 111–13, 114, 123n82, 177n39; at Tolstoy's centenary celebration, 103; Val'ter on, 117
Odoevskii, Aleksandr, 3, 5, 6, 70

Odoevskii, Vladimir Fedorovich: on Beethoven, 60–61, 64–65; "Beethoven's Last Quartet," 58, 62–64; on Berlioz, 41; on interest in the Philharmonia, 18; Lermontov and, 53; on Liszt, 50n68; on Mikhail Viel'gorskii, 42; portrait of, *61f*; and Pushkin, 59, 60; and the Russian Musical Society, 128; "Saturdays" salon of, 56, 61, 93–94, 96, 102; on spiritual dimension of Beethoven's music, 62; Tolstoy and, 102; on the Viel'gorskii salon, 33–34
Ogarev, Nikolai, 7n3, 68, 69, 70, 71; "Beethoven's Heroic Symphony," 70
Ogden, John, 233
Ogiński, Michal, 18
Oistrakh, David, 181, 232, 234
operas, Russia's first, 41
"Operation Barbarossa," 192–95
Orlov, Georgii, 228
Otechestvennye zapiski on Beethoven's ballet, 22
Oznobishin, Dmitrii, 58

Panov, Valerii, 235
Parfionov, Mikhail, 198
Pasternak, Aleksandr, 224
Pasternak, Boris, 222–27, *223f*; *Doctor Zhivago*, 223, 225–27; "Sounds of Beethoven in the Streets," 224; *Themes and Variations* collection, 224, 242n17; "The Poems of Yuri Zhivago," 225–26, 242nn17–19
Pasternak, Leonid, 222–23
Pasternak, Roza Kaufman, 223
Pasternak, Zinaida Eremeeva, 224
Pears, Peter, 235
Perm'-36 museum: about, 246, *247f*, 248n1; performance of *Fidelio* at, 246–48
Persimfans orchestra, 186
Peter the Great, 17, 66, 67, 158
Petrograd/Leningrad State Philharmonic Orchestra, 167–68, 171
Petrovskii, Dmitrii, "Betkhoven," 224
Petrovskii Zavod (prison), 1, 3, 4–5, *4f*
Piano Concerto no. 5 in E-flat (*Emperor*), op. 73: Al'shvang on, 190; in Beethoven celebrations, 134, 170, 171; early Soviet era performances of, 168; Koussevitzky-led performances of, 137; Liszt's performances of, 35, 38–39, 127; LRSO performances of, 195; Russian Musical Society performances of, 129; Yudina's recordings of, 245n61
Piano Sonata no. 8 in C minor (*Pathétique*), op. 13: Aksakov's hearing of, 67; A. N. Serov's orchestration of, 73; character of, 242n17; Lenin and, 150, 151–52, 155; popularity of, 78; Tolstoy and, 101, 104
Piano Sonata no. 14 in C-Sharp minor (*Moonlight*), op. 27, no. 2: character of, 242n17; essay on, 230; Lenz's recommendation of, 36; Liszt performance of, 38; performance during the siege of Leningrad, 200; poem referring to, 205; popularity of, 78; Tolstoy and, 104; Turgenev and, 94
Piano Sonata no. 23 in F minor (*Appassionata*), op. 57: Clara Schumann performance of, 40; depiction on stamp of, 228; essay on, 230; Lenin and, 147–48, 151–52, 191; Lenz's recommendation of, 36; at the Moscow Conservatory, 131; popularity of, 78; Tolstoy and, 104; Turgenev and, 95
Piatakov, Grigorii, 174n7
Piatigorsky, Gregor, 161
Pike, Lionel, 83
Pisarev, Dmitrii, 109
Pisemskii, Aleksei, 29
Piskarevskoe Memorial Cemetery, 200–201
Plekhanov, Georgi, 155
Pletnev, Mikhail, 233
Pletnev, Petr, 56
Podgorny, Nikolai, 228
Polevoi, Nikolai, 54
political regimes, control of music and musicians by, xi, 248. *See also* Stalin, Joseph
Pollini, Maurizio, 233
Popova, Tat'iana, 192
Pratsch, Johann Gottfried, 13
Pravda: accusations against Khrushchev by, 216; on joining of the national anthem and Beethoven's Ninth, 184; on lack of interest in opera, 187
Preobrazhenskaia, Sofia, 195
Priashnikova, Margarita, 229
Prokofiev, Sergei, 160, 209, 231; Symphonies no. 2 and no. 4, 139; Violin Concerto no. 1, 139

Proletarii (The Proletarian), 155
Proudhon, Pierre, 71
Pushkin, Aleksandr: Golitsyn and, 18, 21; interest in Beethoven, 86n25; Lenin's familiarity with, 149; and the Linen Mill, 158, 176n26; Mikhail Viel'gorskii's relationship with, 42; *Mozart and Salieri*, 59; music and, 58–60, 86n27; in Odoevskii's salon, 61; "The Black Shawl," 60, 86n31; in the Viel'gorski salon, 29
Putin, Vladimir, 246, 249n5

Q'azbegi', Aleksandre, "The Patricide," 180

Raaben, Lev, 228
Rabinovich, Aleksandr, 231
Rachmaninov, Sergei, 186, 239
radio broadcasting: Large Symphony Orchestra's Beethoven cycle, 189–90; musical programming in, 188–89; of music during the Nine Hundred Days, 193, *194f*; as people's conservatory, 188, 190; of Shostakovich to the front lines, 198; ubiquity of, 188
Radio Leningrad, 195, 198, 200
Radziwiłł, Antoni, 18, 21
Ragozina, Galina, 235
Raku, Marina, xiii, 166, 192, 211n8
Rastrelli, Bartolomeo, 18
Ravel, Maurice, 139
Razumovskii, Andrei, 11–13, *12f*, 14. *See also* Beethoven, Ludwig van—string quartets
reception history, xi–xii, 23; society and, xi–xii
Reger, Max, Variations and Fugue on a Theme of Beethoven for two pianos, op. 86, 239
Reichel, Adolph, 71
Repin, Ilia, 106
Reshetovskaia, Nataliia, 221, 242n10
Réti, Rudolph, 83, 91n115
Richter, Sviatoslav, 181, 227, 228, 233, 237–39
Ries, Ferdinand, 14
Rimsky-Korsakov, Nikolai, 84, 136
Rischin, Ruth, 104
Rode, Pierre, 19
Rolland, Romain, 108
Romanovskii, Gavriil, 160, 175n11
Romberg, Bernhard, 19, 32, 34, 47n30
Rostropovich, Mstislav, 181, 234
Roussel, Albert, Symphony no. 3, 139
Rozen, Andrei, 3, 5, 8n6
Rozen, Egor, 41
Rubinshtein, Anton: "About Music in Russia," 130; on Beethoven and freedom, 111–12; as Beethoven champion, 113; characterization of *Arioso dolente* of op. 110, 206; *Dmitrii Donskoi*, 127; as free artist, 131, 240; Piano Concerto in G minor, op. 45, 129; portrait of, *112f*; recital by, 94; and recognition of musicians' artistry, 126–27; and the Russian Musical Society, 128, 129, 130; in the Viel'gorskii salon, 29; work to establish conservatory, 130
Rubinshtein, Nikolai, 29, 61, 102, 131, *131f*
Rubinstein, Artur, 233
Rudolph (Archduke), 24–25
Russia: Beethoven's status in post-Soviet Russia, xiii; civil war in, 153; conservatories in, 130, 132, 157–58 (*See also* Moscow Conservatory; St. Petersburg Conservatory); de-Stalinization campaign, 210n1; flourishing of culture in, 126, 132; modernization of, 125; political criticism through music, 140; revolt of December 14, 1825, 1, 5, 6; Russian national pride, 169; Russian Revolution, 72, 117; war and downfall of the monarchy, 125–26; Westernizer-Slavophile controversy in, 66–67
Russian folk songs, 13–14, 45n5, 45n7, 59, 101, 217, 228
Russian Musical Society: A. N. Serov's honor from, 73–74; Anton Rubinshtein and, 126; Beethoven works in concerts of, 129–30, 131–32; branches established for, 131; chamber music series of, 141n6; concerts of branches of, 131–32, 133; founding of, 43, 125, 127, 128–29; mission and first concerts of, 129–30; Odoevskii and, 61; and performances of Beethoven, xii; and the Russian piano school, 240
Russian Music Publishing House, 135–36
Russian Social Democratic Labor Party (RSDLP), 155
Russian writers: Dostoevsky, 96–100; Drabkina, 152–53, 218–19, *219f*; Gogol, 29, 36, 42, 57–58, 61, 94; Griboedov, 42, 54–55,

Russian writers (*Cont.*)
85nn8–10; Krylov, 55–57, *56f*; Lermontov, 52–54, 61; Pasternak, 222–27, *223f*; Solzhenitsyn, 220–22, *220f*, 226, 242n10, 242n13; Turgenev, 58, 93–95, 109–10, 149. *See also* Akhmatova, Anna; Pushkin, Aleksandr; Tolstoy, Lev
Russia's Beethoven reception history: analysis of, xii; the Decembrists in, 1–6, 7n2, 7nn4–5, 8n6, 8n9; early concert programming of Beethoven's works, 15–18; in Fishman's study, 230–31; importance of Lunacharskii in, 161, 166; increase in programming of Beethoven, 134; linkage of Beethoven with revolutionary struggle, 66, 70, 93, 110–11, 118, 140, 154; literature of the Stalin era and, 190–92; performances in the post-Stalin era, 232–33; the piano in, 236; professionalization of Russian musical life, 126; revolutionary intelligentsia in, 109–10; Russians in Vienna, 11–15; significance of St. Petersburg in, 241; Westernizers and, 66, 67–72. *See also* concerts; conservatories; cult of Beethoven; Golitsyn, Nikolai; Koussevitzky, Serge; Lunacharskii, Anatolii Vasil'evich; music criticism; *Ode to Joy*; Rubinshtein, Anton; Russian Musical Society; Russian writers; Shostakovich, Dmitrii; Soviet era; St. Petersburg Philharmonic Society (Philharmonia); Viel'gorskii salon; specific musical works
Ryleev, Kondratii, 3

salons: in Naryshkin's home, 21; Odoevskii's "Saturday" salons, 56, 61, 93–94, 96, 102; Sollogub salon, 96; in St. Petersburg, 56. *See also* Viel'gorskii salon
Saltykov, Grigorii, 16
Saltykov-Shchedrin, Mikhail, 227
Samarin, Iurii, 67
Samsud, Samuil, 197
Sargeant, Lynn, 132
Schenker, Heinrich, 83
Schiller, Friedrich, 111. See also *Ode to Joy*
Schindler, Anton, 22, 74
Schnabel, Artur, 171
Schneiderhan, Wolfgang, 232
Schnittke, Alfred, 234
Schoenberg, Arnold, 24
Schumann, Clara, 29, 36, 39–40
Schumann, Robert: on the Kapella, 17; Piano Sonata no. 1 in F-sharp minor, op. 11, 221; in Russian Musical Society concerts, 130; Russian tours of, 36, 39, 40; Symphony no. 1 in B-flat (*Spring*), op. 38, 40; in the Viel'gorskii salon, 29, 36
Schuppanzigh Quartet, 13, 21, 44n4
Schwarz, Boris, 237; *Music and Musical Life in Soviet Russia*, xii
Scriabin, Aleksandr, 136, 173, 223; *Poem of Ecstasy*, 186
Semenov, I. I., 34, 49n62
Sendich, Munir, 224
Serebriakova, Galina, 152
Serov, Aleksandr Nikolaevich: as Beethoven authority, 18, 73–74; on Beethoven's Ninth Symphony, 77–79, 80–83, 90n101, 90n106, 110–11; on the *Eroica* symphony, 240–41; introduction to Beethoven's music, 38; legacy of, 83–85; on Lenz, 75–76; on the notion of a music conservatory, 130; on the *Ode to Joy*, 80–81, 82, 90n109, 91n110; portrait of, *72f*; and shift in Beethoven criticism, 76–77, 84, 110–11; transcriptions by, 73, 89n73; on Ulybyshev, 75
Serov, Eduard, 234
Serov, Nikolai Ivanovich, 73
Serov, Valentin, *56f*
Serova, Anna Karlovna (née Gablits), 73
Serova, Valentina Semenovna, 73
Service, Robert, 174n7
Seyfried, Ignaz, 13, 22
Shaverdian, Aleksandr, 187
Shchedrin, Rodion, 234
Shchepin-Rostovskii, Dmitrii, 2
Shevyrev, Stepan, 67
Shimkov, Ivan, 3
Shor, David, 117, 150–51
Shostakovich, Dmitrii: Beethoven anniversary address by, 228; charges of "formalism" against, 209; poem dedicated to, 203; premieres of symphonies of, 234; Richter's performances of, 239; on story of Stalin and Yudina, 240; wartime broadcasts of music of, 193, 200

Shostakovich, Dmitrii, works by: Cello Concerto no. 1, 234; Festive Overture, 234; *Lady Macbeth of the Mtsensk District*, 181; *Song of the Forest*, 234; Symphony no. 5, 225; Symphony no. 7 in C (*Leningrad*), op. 60, 196–97; Twenty-Four Preludes and Fugues, op. 87, 237; Violin Concerto no. 1, 234
Shterenberg, David, 157, 160
Shub, David, 174n7
Slavophiles and classical music, 66–67
Smirnova-Rosset, Aleksandra, 58
Sobinov, Leonid, 160
socialism, Beethoven and, 116
Society of Music Lovers, 21
Sokhor, Arnol'd, 228
Sollertinskii, Ivan, 231
Sollogub, Vladimir, 61
Solomon, Maynard, 83
Solzhenitsyn, Aleksandr, 220–22, *220f*, 242n10, 242n13; *Cancer Ward*, 221, 226; *The First Circle*, 221, 226; *The Gulag Archipelago*, 221; *One Day in the Life of Ivan Denisovich*, 220–21; *The Red Wheel*, 221
Solzhenitsyn, Ignat, 222, 233, 242nn12–13
Soviet era: Beethoven as icon of, 154, 165, 167, 168–69, 170; Beethoven as weapon of propaganda in, xiii, 84, 108, 147, 165–66; Beethoven scholarship in later period of, 91n126; calls for freedom during, 164; Cold War, start of, 201; extramusical programming of Beethoven's music, 183–84, 211n8; "god-building" in, 176n21; mixing of "high" and "low" music in, 184, 211n10; noted pianists in, 236–40. *See also* concerts during the Soviet era; cult of Beethoven; Lenin, Vladimir; Lunacharskii, Anatolii Vasil'evich; Nine Hundred Days; radio broadcasting; Stalin, Joseph
Soviet musicology, 166, 231
Stalin, Joseph: as arbiter of artistic expression, 158, 181, 208–9; and building socialism, 165; and the Cold War, 201–2; death and entombment of, 181, 209, 210, 210n1; emergence as dictator, 180; at Lenin's birthday party, 150–51; and Lunacharskii, 157; objection to Western modernism, 208–9, 210n2; overview of Russia under rule of, 180–81; personality cult developed by, 169; purges of, 154, 209; revolution of, xiii, 158, 180, 208–9; use of Beethoven to serve the state, 179; views on Beethoven, 181–82, 192; and Yudina, 239–40
Stalin Constitution, 154, 183, 184
Stalin Prizes, 181, 210n4
Stasov, Dmitrii, 128
Stasov, Vladimir, 36, 38, 41, 84, 111, 123n79
State Academic Theater of Opera and Ballet, 167
State Philharmonia, 186
State Philharmonic Orchestra of Petrograd, 138
Stein, August Ludwig, 162
St. Petersburg: concerts of Beethoven's music in, 15, 16, 17–18; Koussevitzky-led Beethoven concerts in, 138; premiere of Ninth Symphony in, 77–78, 90n90; significance in Russian Beethoven reception, 241
St. Petersburg Conservatory: Anton Rubinshtein and, 126; birth of idea for, 127; charter for, 130; founding of, 43, 61, 125, 128; location of, 141n9; opening of, 130–31
St. Petersburg Philharmonic Society (Philharmonia): Beethoven centenary celebration, 133; expertise of, 16; founding and popularity of, 17–18, 31; Golitsyn and, 21; performance of the Ninth Symphony by, 77–78, 90n90; performances by, 16–17; performances of Beethoven by, 16, 18, 38, 65, 142n13; promotion of Beethoven's music by, 240. See also *Missa solemnis* in D, op. 123
Stradivari, Antonio, instruments of, 6, 43–44, 51n91
Stradivarius Quartet, 151, 160, 167, 187
Strauss, David Friedrich, 79–80, 81, 90n95
Strauss, Richard, *Death and Transfiguration*, op. 24, 161
Stravinsky, Igor, 24, 234; *Apollon musgète* ballet music, 234; *Petrushka*, 160; *The Rite of Spring*, 160; *Symphony of Psalms*, 139
Stray Dog (*Brodiachaia sobaka*) cabaret, 29–30, 203
Stroganov, G. A., 15
Stuckenschmidt, Hans-Heinz, 240

Stuttgart Ballet, 235
Sverdlov, Iakov, 218
Svetlanov, Evgenii, 228
Sviridov, Georgii, 234
Svistunov, Petr, 2, 3, 5, 7n2, 7n4
Symphonic Orchestra of the USSR, 184, 186, 228
Symphony no. 1 in C, op. 21, 96, 171, 186
Symphony no. 2 in D, op. 36, 33, 96
Symphony no. 3 in E-flat (*Eroica*), op. 55: in all-Beethoven concerts, 152, 167; Al'shvang on, 191; and Beethoven as a revolutionary, 110; Borodin on, 84; at the Fateevka estate, 33; Funeral March of, 114, 134, 168, 171, 175n16, 183, *185f*, 190; humor in, 162; Koussevitzky's programming of, 136; military-revolutionary rhythms in, 172; Odoevskii on, 64, 70; Philharmonia performance of, 240–41; political interpretation of, 117–18; popularity of, 125, 129, 133, 134, 168; premiere of, 20; radio listener guide to, 190; in Russian Musical Society concerts, 132; socialist ideas in, 192; Stalin era performances of, 186, 187; struggle against tyranny in, 114, 190; on themes in, 22, 228, 230; transcriptions of, 171
Symphony no. 4 in B-flat, op. 60: choreography to, 183; at the Fateevka estate, 33; Koussevitzky-led performances of, 167; LRSO performances of, 195; Russian Musical Society performances of, 129, 132; transcriptions of, 171; in the Viel'gorskii salon, 34
Symphony no. 5 in C minor, op. 67: Al'shvang on, 191; broadcasts during the Nine Hundred Days, 195; in centenary celebrations, 134, 171; character of, 110, 114; dedication of, 14; essays on, 230; at the Fateevka estate, 33; Griboedov and, 54; Koussevitzky-led performances of, 136, 137, 167; Lunacharskii on, 172; manuscript of, *99f*; political interpretation of, 117–18, 192; popularity of, 125, 129, 133, 134, 168; in Russian Musical Society concerts, 132; Stalin era performances of, 186, 187; struggle against tyranny in, 190; themes in, 64–65, 100
Symphony no. 6 in F (*Pastoral*), op. 68: A. N. Serov on, 76; Bakunin and, 71, 118n1; dedication of, 14; at the Fateevka estate, 33; Koussevitzky's programming of, 136, 137; Mikhail Viel'gorskii at rehearsal of, 32; in Russian Musical Society concerts, 132; transcriptions of, 38, 171
Symphony no. 7 in A, op. 92: character of, 78, 172; at the Fateevka estate, 33; Koussevitzky-led performances of, 136; Pasternak and, 225; Russian Musical Society performances of, 132; Russian premiere of, 90n93; Soviet era performances of, 171; in the Viel'gorskii salon, 34
Symphony no. 8 in F, op. 93, 78, 90n93, 129, 132, 162
Symphony no. 9 in D minor (*Choral*), op. 125: in all-Beethoven concerts, 167; A. N. Serov on, 77–79, 80, 81–83, 90n101; Bakunin's response to, 71; and Beethoven as the Shakespeare of the masses, 110; and Beethoven's last public concert, 25; broadcasts during the Nine Hundred Days, 195, *196f*; Bulich on, 114; celebratory concerts of, 170, 184, 211n7, 228; compared to Tchaikovsky's Sixth (*Pathétique*), 116; dedication of, 14; Dostoevsky's allusion to, 98; essays on, 230; and formalism, 215n61; Gogol and, 94; humor in, 163; as inaugural concert of Berkshire Music Festival, 139; led by Koussevitzky, 167; Lenin's response to, 152; milestone performance in St. Petersburg, 65–66; Odoevskii on, 65; performance photos of, 230; Philharmonia performances of, 40; popularity of, 125, 129–30, 133, 134, 168; premieres of, 34, 49n64, 61, 90n90; on the radio, 188; republican ideals expressed in, 117; Russian folksong in, 14, 45n7; Russian Musical Society performances of, 129, 132; Stalin era performances of, 186, 187; Stasov on, 111; "The Poems of Yuri Zhivago" (Pasternak) compared to, 226; Tolstoy on, 101; victory through struggle in, 190, 192; in *War and Peace*, 104–5; writing of, 21. See also *Ode to Joy*
Szigeti, Josef, 160, 171
Szymanowska-Wolowska, Maria, 18

Taneev, Sergei, 136, 186
Taruskin, Richard, 66

Tatlin, Vladimir, 157
Taubert, Wilhelm, 31
Taubman, William, 217
Tchaikovsky, Petr: encounter with Tolstoy, 104; Koussevitzky's programming of, 136; Lunacharskii's description of, 165; Piano Trio in A minor, 151; radio programming of, 189; in Russian Musical Society concerts, 130; Stalin and, 181; views on Beethoven, 84; on Wagner, 121n48; wartime broadcasts of music by, 193
Terras, Victor, 98
Thompson, Damian, 236
Thun-Hohenstein, Maria Elisabeth von, 11
Timushev, O., *Mavzolei*, 183–84
Tiutchev, Aleksei, 2, 7n2
Tkachev, Petr, 109
Tolstoy, Lev: Beethoven and, 100, 101, 103–5, 120n38; character of writings of, 100; essay on, 203; on gaiety in Moscow, 16; Gorky's praise for, 150, 151; greatness of, 111; Lenin's familiarity with, 149; on music, 122n65; musical knowledge of, 101–3, 121n43; musical tastes of, 103; music's effect on, 105–8, *106f*; rewriting tendency of, 120n30; with Wanda Landowska, *102f*
Tolstoy, Lev, writings of: "Albert," 101; *Anna Karenina*, 105; *Boyhood*, 104; *Childhood*, 104; *Family Happiness*, 104; *Ressurrection*, 105; "The Kreutzer Sonata," 101, 106, 108, 121n59, 166; *War and Peace*, 49n58, 104–5; *What Is Art?*, 101, 103, 108, 120n34, 121n46; *Youth*, 104
Tolstoy, Sergei Nikolaevich, 107
Tovey, Donald, 83
Trotsky, Leon, 150, 153, 156
Troyat, Henri, 105, 119n15
Trubetskoi, V. S., 15
Turgenev, Ivan, 58, 93–95, 109, 149; *Fathers and Children*, 110
Turgeneva, Ol'ga Aleksandrovna, 94

Ulianov, Aleksandr, 150
Ulianov, Dmitrii, 149
Ulianov, Ilia Nikolaevich, 149
Ulianova, Mariia Aleksandrovna (née Blank), 149
Ulybyshev, Aleksandr D., 74, 75, 103
Unger, Heinz, 186
Union of Soviet Writers, 207, 208, 221, 226
Urhan, Chrétien, 79
Ustvol'skaia, Galina, 234, 244n47
US-USSR cultural exchange agreement, 234

Vadkovskii, Fedor, 3, 5, 6, 7n2, 8n12
Vainkop, Iulian, 191
Val'ter, Victor, "The Ideological Content of Beethoven's Music," 116–17
Veksler, Klimentii, 228
Verdi, Giuseppi, 29
Viardot, Louis, 94
Viazemskii, Petr, 54
Viel'gorskii, Iurii Mikhailovich, 31–32, 48n55
Viel'gorskii, Matvei: cello of, 43–44; death of, 43; in L'vov Quartet, *35f*; musical training of, 31, 32; musicianship of, 2, 19, 35; performances of Beethoven by, 2, 35, 36; portrait of, *30f*; and professionalization of music in Russia, 127–28; summary of accomplishments of, 43
Viel'gorskii, Mikhail Iur'evich: death and burial of, 42–43; death of son, 36; freeing of artists by, 49n62; Glinka on, 42; government positions of, 32, 34; as impresario, 36; and Liszt's performance of the *Emperor* Concerto, 38–39; marriages and exile of, 32; musical training of, 31–32; portraits of, *30f*, *35f*; Pushkin and, 58–59; and Russia's introduction to Beethoven, 11, 15; scholarship of, 42; the Schumanns on, 39; on Slavophiles, 68; symphony of, 34; *Tsigan (The Gypsy)*, 42; understanding of Beethoven, 51n85; and the *Wielhorsky Sketchbook*, 230
Viel'gorskii, M. M., 15
Viel'gorskii salon: Beethoven works featured in, 31, 33, 34–35; Berlioz at, 40–41; description of evening in, 27, 29; Dostoevsky at, 96; in Fateevka, 33; Glinka at, 41–42; Gogol at, 57; in Lermentov story, 52–53; Liszt at, 36–39, *37f*, 127; L'vov quartet at, 35–36; opening of, 33; prestige and influence of, 16, 29, 36; private music making at, 33–34; Pushkin at, 58; the Schumanns at, 39–40; sketch of, *28f*; Turgenev at, 93–94
Vienna and Russian interest in Beethoven, 11

Vieuxtemps, Henri, 34, 35, 36
Vil'de, Gustav, 35, *35f*, 36
Violin Concerto in D, op. 61: centenary concerts of, 170, 171; Koussevitzky-led performances of, 136, 138, 167; post-Stalin era concerts of, 232; premiere of, 20; Stalin era concerts of, 186
Volkonskaia, Mariia, 1, 3, *4f*, 5, 7n1, 7n5
Volkonskaia, Sergei, *4f*
Volkonskaia, Zinaida, 15
Volkonskii, Andrei, 227
Volkov, Sergei, 36, 211n7
Volkov, Solomon, 221–22
Voyager 1 and 2 space probes, 100, 120n32
Vpered (Forward), 155

Wagner, Richard: on Beethoven, 81, 110; Dostoevsky's dislike of, 96; Koussevitzky's programming of, 136; Lenin and, 174n7; Odoevskii and, 62; in Russian Musical Society concerts, 130; Russians' dislike for, 121n48; Serov and, 90n106; Tolstoy's dislike of, 103; at the Viel'gorskii salon, 29
Walker, Jonathan, 186; *Music and Soviet Power, 1917–1392*, xii
Walter, Bruno, 160
Weber, Carl Maria von: *Der Freischütz*, 3, 34; "Russian Song with Variations," 3
Westernizers, 66, 67–72
Wielhorsky Sketchbook, 51n85, 230
Wilson, A. N., 105–6
World War II, Beethoven as solace in, 193, 195

Yarmolinsky, Avrahm, 58
Yeltsin, Boris, 246
Yudina, Maria, 227, 233, *238f*, 239–40, 245n61

Zaslavskii, David, "Muddle Instead of Music," 181
Zasulich, Vera, 155
Zavalishin, Dmitrii, 3, 54
Zeuner, Karl, 21
Zhdanov, Andrei, 207, 209
Zhdanovshchina, 208–9
Zhukovskii, Vasilii, 18, 29, 33, 41, 61, 65
Zoshchenko, Mikhail, 208

FREDERICK W. SKINNER is Professor Emeritus of History at the University of Montana. After acquiring expertise in the field of reception history, he developed a new research agenda that allowed him to combine his knowledge of Russian history with his passion for Beethoven's music.